DUTIES ACROSS BORDERS

DUTIES ACROSS BORDERS

Advancing Human Rights in Transnational Business

Edited by
Bård A. Andreassen
Võ Khánh Vinh

intersentia

Cambridge – Antwerp – Portland

Intersentia Ltd
Sheraton House | Castle Park
Cambridge | CB3 0AX | United Kingdom
Tel.: +44 1223 370 170 | Fax: +44 1223 370 169
Email: mail@intersentia.co.uk
www.intersentia.com | www.intersentia.co.uk

Distribution for the UK and Ireland:
NBN International
Airport Business Centre, 10 Thornbury Road
Plymouth, PL6 7PP
United Kingdom
Tel: +44 1752 202 301 | Fax: +44 1752 202 331
Email: orders@nbninternational.com

Distribution for Europe and all other countries:
Intersentia Publishing nv
Groenstraat 31
2640 Mortsel
Belgium
Tel.: +32 3 680 15 50 | Fax: +32 3 658 71 21
Email: mail@intersentia.be

Distribution for the USA and Canada:
International Specialized Book Services
920 NE 58th Ave Suite 300
Portland, OR 97213
USA
Tel.: +1 800 944 6190 (toll free) | Fax: +1 503 280 8832
Email: info@isbs.com

Duties Across Borders

Cover image: © Kari Johanne Nordheim, Verdighet

ISBN 978-1-78068-376-8
D/2016/7849/16
NUR 828

British Library Cataloguing in Publication Data. A catalogue record for this book is available from the British Library.

PREFACE

Human rights performance is, in many ways, intertwined with large processes of globalisation. One feature of these processes, which has come to the attention of the human rights community over the last two decades, is the impact that multinational business enterprises may have on human rights around the globe. This volume argues that international businesses and the legislation that govern their behaviour represent a new frontier on the struggle for human rights. This frontier has borne witness to many victims, but there are also glimpses of hope and opportunities for expanding the respect and protection of human rights in the corporate sector at local, national, and global levels.

The volume aims to analyse key legal and social issues surrounding the advancement of human rights. The chapters evolve from an international conference organised on 27–28 June 2013 in Hanoi, hosted by the Vietnam Academy of Social Sciences (VASS) with its co-organising partner the Norwegian Centre for Human Rights (NCHR) at the University of Oslo. The conference gathered scholars and practitioners from different regions of the world and from different academic disciplines.

We are very grateful for the support of the Vietnam Program at the NCHR and the generous financial support of the Norwegian Ministry of Foreign Affairs. VASS has provided the project with strong support throughout, and we have benefitted greatly from fruitful research collaborations between our two institutions over the last seven years. At VASS, we are particularly indebted to the Vice Director of the International Cooperation Department, Tuyet Ahn Luu, for her logistical and overall support. At the NCHR we have indeed benefitted from the editorial assistance of Natasha Telson, and appreciate the keen support of Gisle Kvanvig and Mau Don Thi Nguyen of the Vietnam Programme. Finally, we would like to thank Tom Scheirs at Intersentia for his avid interest in driving the project forward.

Bård A. Andreassen and Võ Khánh Vinh
Oslo/Hanoi, October 2015

CONTENTS

Chapter 3.
Ensuring the Protection of the Environment from Serious Damage.
Towards a Model of Shared Responsibility between International
Corporations and the States Concerned?

Chapter 4.
The Business Case for Taking Human Rights Obligations Seriously

Chapter 5. ✗
Corporate Accountability in the Field of Human Rights. On Soft Law
Standards and the Use of Extraterritorial Measures

Chapter 6.
The Viability of the Maastricht Principles in Advancing Socio-Economic
Rights in Developing Countries

PART II. CONTEXTUAL ISSUES

Chapter 7.
The Next Generation of 'Fair Trade'. A Human Rights Framework
for Combating Corporate Corruption in Global Supply Chains

LIST OF AUTHORS

Bård A. Andreassen is Professor at the Norwegian Centre for Human Rights, Law Faculty, University of Oslo. He received his Dr. Polit. degree (political science) at the University of Oslo, and a Diploma of International and Comparative Law of Human Rights from the International Institute of Human Rights, Strasbourg. Andreassen has published on human rights analysis of poverty, power, human rights based approaches to development, business responsibilities, social and economic rights, as well as on governance, democratic change and ethno-politics in African contexts. His most recent books are *Development as a Human Right. Legal, Political and Economic Dimensions*, 2nd revised edition (Intersentia, 2010) edited with Stephen P. Marks, and *Human Rights, Power and Civic Action. Comparative analyses of struggles for rights in developing societies* (Routledge, 2013) edited with Gordon Grawford. He is Editor-in-Chief of the *Nordic Journal of Human Rights* (Routledge).

Võ Khánh Vinh is Vice President of the Vietnam Academy of Social Sciences (VASS), and Chancellor and Professor at the Academy of Social Sciences (GASS). He got his PhD in Law in 1993 at the Institute of State and Law, Vietnam Academy of Social Sciences. His research and teaching areas focus on theories of state and law, criminal justice, human rights and civil society. He is the author, editor and chief-editor of many publications, among them the most recent are, all in Vietnamese: *Sociology of Law: Fundamental Issues* (People's Police Publishing House, 2011); *Mechanism for human rights protection* (Social Sciences Publishing House, 2011); *Conflict and social consensus* (Social Sciences Publishing House 2013); *Overview of 1992 Constitution implementation: Theoretical and urgent practical issues* (Social Sciences Publishing House, 2013).

AUTHORS

Itai Apter is a PhD student at the Law Faculty, Haifa University (Israel). His publications include 'The New International Frontier – the Legal Profession and the Challenges of New 'International Law' in the New Member State', Croatian Yearbook of European Law and Policy (2014), and 'International Rights of Older Persons: What Differences Would a New Convention Make to the Lives of Older People', co-authored with Isreal Doron in the Marquette Elder's Advisor Journal (2010).

Güler Aras is a Professor of Finance and Accounting at Yildiz Technical University in Istanbul, Turkey, and Founding Director of Finance, Corporate Governance and Sustainability. She is also a Visiting Professor at Georgetown University McDonough School of Business. Professor Aras is the editor of Gower Book Series, *Finance, Governance and Sustainability: Challenges to Theory and Practice* and the editor of Gower book series *Corporate Social Responsibility*; she has also served as an editor of *Social Responsibility Journal*. She has published more than 20 books and has contributed over 250 articles in academic, business and professional journals. Her most recent co-authored books are `The Durable Corporation: Strategies for Sustainable Development` (Gower, 2010) `Governance and Social Responsibility: International Perspectives` (Palgrave McMillan, 2012). Professor Aras's latest book `Sustainable Markets for Sustainable Business: A Global Perspective for Business and Financial Markets` was published by Gower at 2015.

Surya Deva is an Associate Professor at the School of Law of City University of Hong Kong. His primary research interests lie in Business and Human Rights, Corporate Social Responsibility, Indo-Chinese Constitutional Law, International Human Rights, and Sustainable Development. He has published extensively in these areas. Surya's books include *Socio-Economic Rights in Emerging Free Markets: Comparative Insights from India and China* (editor) (Routledge, forthcoming in 2015); *Human Rights Obligations of Business: Beyond the Corporate Responsibility to Respect?* (co-edited with David Bilchitz) (Cambridge University Press, 2013); *Confronting Capital Punishment in Asia: Human Rights, Politics, Public Opinion and Practices* (co-edited with Roger Hood) (Oxford University Press, 2013); and *Regulating Corporate Human Rights Violations: Humanizing Business* (Routledge, 2012). Surya has also prepared two major reports on *Access to Justice: Human Rights Abuses Involving Corporations* (concerning India and China) for the International Commission of Jurists (ICJ), Geneva. He is one of the founding Editors-in-Chief of the *Business and Human Rights Journal* (CUP), and sits on the Editorial Board of the *Netherlands Quarterly of Human Rights* and the *Vienna Journal on International Constitutional Law*.

Ebenezer Durojaye is an Associate Professor of Law and Head of the Socioeconomic Rights Project at the Community Law Centre, University of the Western Cape in South Africa. His research interests include focusing on human rights issues raised by the access to HIV/AIDS treatment, intersection between gender inequality and HIV/AIDS response in Africa, as well as women's health and adolescents' sexual and reproductive rights in Africa. Among his latest publications is the book titled 'Strengthening the protection of sexual and reproductive health through human rights in the African region' (Pretoria University Law Press, 2014) edited together with Charles Ngwena.

Nukila Evanty earned her Master's of Law degree from the University of Groningen in the Netherlands. She serves as a visiting lecturer at faculty of law University of Mahendradatta Bali. She is a research associate at the Center for Strategic and International Studies and a senior researcher for the National Coalition for the Elimination of Commercial Sexual Exploitation of Children. Ms. Evanty's research interest focuses on human rights and social justice. She has published two international books; 'Indonesia Human Rights and the International Human Rights Regime' in 2010 and 'the Application of the Doctrine of Command Responsibility in International Law, Prosecuting the Leaders' in 2011.

Stéphanie Gervais holds an MA in international affairs from Carleton University, Canada, and is a PhD candidate in Anthropology with a specialisation in Political Economy. Her early research focused on international investment agreements and human rights, with a special attention on the intersection of both legal systems in the mining sector of Latin America. Her latest areas of interest have concentrated on the organisation strategies of indigenous communities resisting extractive operations on their land.

Hana Ivanhoe has a Juris Doctor degree from Berkeley Law, University of California, where she has been a lecturer in the Advanced Degree Program. She is currently the North American Advocacy Manager for Fairfood International. She is also the Policy and Engagement Manager at the Aquaya Institute, a global non-profit organisation which works to achieve universal access to safe water in the developing world. Having worked on human rights issues and matters of trade and development from both the public and private sector perspectives, her key areas of research interest include transparency, business and human rights and corporate social responsibility.

Matthew Mullen, PhD, is a lecturer at the Institute of Human Rights and Peace Studies, Mahidol University, Thailand. He has published on oppression and resistance, transitional justice, structural and cultural violence, international human rights law, corporate accountability, the human right to play and Burma/Myanmar.

Nguyễn Hong Nga holds a Master's degree in human rights from the University of Oslo, Norway. She is currently working as a researcher for the Institute of World Economics and Politics, a member of Vietnam Academy of Social Sciences. Her major is human rights, human security and related issues including climate change, food, energy and water security, especially human rights in business. She both authored and edited her most recent publication, titled 'Regional and Social Impacts of Industrial Zones in Vietnam'.

Nguyễn Thị Thanh Hải holds an LLM in Human Rights Law from the University of Hong Kong and a PhD in Law from Sydney University, Australia. She is currently a lecturer at the Vietnamese Institute for Human Rights of the Ho Chi Minh National Academy of Politics. Her areas of interest include international human rights law, human rights and globalisation, human rights and corporate responsibility, human rights and gender equality including issues on violence against women, as well as human rights and HIV/AIDS.

Ramute Remezaite is currently is a PhD candidate at the School of Law at Middlesex University and a Legal Consultant at the European Human Rights Advocacy Centre in UK. She litigates cases before the European Court of Human Rights and other international tribunals and advices human rights lawyers in the former Soviet Union states. Her key areas of research include implementation and compliance with judgments of the European Court of Human Rights, civil and political rights, extractive industries and their compliance with human rights law.

Humberto Cantú Rivera is an Associate Researcher and PhD Candidate at the Research Centre on Human Rights and Humanitarian Law (CRDH) of Université Panthéon-Assas Paris II, in France. He has been a Visiting Professional at the Office of the High Commissioner for Human Rights, and a Scholar of The Hague Academy of International Law. He published the first edited book in Spanish with contributions from acting UN human rights mandate holders and the High Commissioner for Human Rights: 'El futuro es hoy: Construyendo una agenda de derechos humanos' (Monterrey, CEDHNL/UANL, 2014).

Miho Taka received her PhD degree in international relations and sociology from Coventry University in, England, where she's currently a senior lecturer at the Centre for Trust, Peace and Social Relations (CTPSR). Dr Miho has various living and working experiences from Japan, England, Sweden and Rwanda. After working as the Country Director of an NGO in Rwanda for four years, she became interested in the relationship between natural resources and violent conflict in sub-Saharan Africa. Her research interests also include natural resource management, global governance, business and human rights, corporate social responsibility and peace-building. She has published several papers, and is a reviewer for several international academic journals in the area of corporate governance.

Gentian Zyberi is Associate Professor at the Norwegian Centre for Human Rights, University of Oslo, Norway. Over the last eleven years he has worked in the field of international law for different universities in the Netherlands, the US, China and Albania. His international legal practice includes working for the defence before the International Criminal Tribunal for the former Yugoslavia (ICTY) and coordinating the work of the Albanian legal team in the *Kosovo* case before the

International Court of Justice (ICJ). His current research focuses on issues related to transitional justice, responsibility to protect, and the protection of community interests under international law.

LIST OF FIGURES AND TABLES

INTRODUCTION

Business' Duties Across Borders: The New Human Rights Frontier

Bård A. ANDREASSEN and Võ Khánh Vinh

1. INTRODUCTION

Modern human rights are dynamic. Through their interpretation, and reinterpretation in new situations and contexts, human rights adapt to new challenges and societal risks to basic human interests. This volume addresses how this insight can be demonstrated through the expanding field of human rights studies in business entities. It presents and examines experiences of the new regulatory turns of commercial actors, and discusses recent developments in human rights standard-setting and advocacy.

Human rights have long been understood as being state-centric: The basic model of human right claims that the individual is the rights-holder and the state (i.e. by all state organs and actors) the duty-bearer. This remains the basic model of human rights, but it is increasingly being modified and developed in a world of rapid change in terms of a relative decline in state authority and the rise of a polycentric world with comparably more powerful non-state actors. Alluding to these changes, Alston argues that there is a need for a re-imagining of 'the nature of the human rights regime in order to take adequate account of the fundamental changes' that have occurred globally in recent decades.[1] The present volume takes account of this insight, and situational human rights theory acknowledges that as part of contemporary globalisation, some types of non-state actors – notably business enterprises – are rapidly gaining influence and power that the human rights regime can no longer neglect.

Legal development – including human rights law – is generally reactive. It responds to new societal experiences that provoke a quest for regulation,

---

[1] P. Alston, 'The "Not-a-Cat" Syndrome: Can the International Human Rights Regime Accommodate Non-State Actors?' in P. Alston (ed.), *Non-State Actors and Human Right* (Oxford: Oxford University Press, 2005), p. 4.

restriction, and control. This is indeed what has happened in the field of human rights and business. Accidents and events that uproar ethical consciousness and public morals, outright violations of workers rights, and communities suffering from ruthless environmental exploitation are all types of experiences that have triggered demands for rights protection. Albeit slowly, attempts to define more precisely the human rights duties of commercial actors have been in process in response to experiences of economic globalisation. Accelerating rapidly with the neo-liberal economic policies introduced in the 1980s, globalisation has been structured by three interrelated processes: First, the growth of international economic, cultural, and normative interaction, ignited by the end of the Cold War, the economic reforms initiated in China under Deng Xiaoping, the invention of the World Wide Web, and a cascade of information technology innovations. The second stage was marked by a rapid spread of cultural norms and practices of consumerism. And thirdly, there has been a process of diffusing cosmopolitan moral and legal norms, where universal human rights have been but one point of reference for legal development, institutional reforms and more recently regulation of commercial market actors. The latter is, indeed, what interests us here: the current extrapolation of human rights duties of commercial actors as transnational norms.

The new regulatory turn of businesses through the mechanism of human rights must be understood and interpreted in this global socio-political context. Human rights dynamism is reflexive to these changes in global co-existence, interaction, and exchange, where the powers of transnational business entities trigger demands for polycentric regulations of business behaviour.

An early move in this direction was the development of corporate social responsibility (CSR), which expanded gradually in western capitalist economies from the 1950s; although CSR had roots dating back to the 1920s, when some argued that corporations should be seen as 'business services to society'.[2] According to Frederick, CSR in the 1950s mainly referred to three ideas: public managers as public trustees; balancing competing claims to corporate resources (share-holders vs. other stakeholders); and philanthropic services to society.[3]

Over the next decades until the 2000s, there were several shifts in the conceptual structuring and application of CSR by businesses. These shifts reflected changes in the normative foundation of corporate governance. In general, we observe a gradual development towards more responsiveness to stakeholders, as a means of keeping with businesses' legitimacy in society. Frederick characterises the 1950s and 1960s as a phase of 'corporate social responsiveness' with enterprises demonstrating some responsibilities to society by charity work and philanthropy. Yet gradually, stakeholders began raising expectations about the functioning and

---

[2]   R.C. Moura-Leite and R.C. Padgett, 'Historical Background of Social Corporate Responsibility' (2011) 7(4) *Social Responsibility Journal* 259.

[3]   W.C. Frederick, *Corporations, Be Good! The Story of Corporate Social Responsibility* (Indianapolis, IN: Dogear Publishing, 2006).

governance dimensions of companies' behaviour. From the 1970s onwards, there was a growing attention to the conduct of doing business in the dominant market economies, with a focus on the effects and consequences of business behaviour on society. Donaldson emphasised that an inherent 'social contract' between businesses and society was emerging and became an ideological justification for CSR.[4] In the 1980s, the conception that CSR was 'good for business' and could improve profits was slowly gaining traction. Focus shifted towards a broader conception of CSR where ethical concerns where combined with institutionally responsive practices internally within companies, e.g. by the establishment of corporate assemblies with worker representation. Reflecting the public political discourse of the time, a focus on the external environmental impact of conducting business emerged.

By the 1990s, the notion of CSR was widely accepted in global markets, with the exception, perhaps, of several rapidly emerging market economies, China being the main case. According to Moura-Leite and Padgett,[5] by the mid-1990s 'the global capabilities of the internet and related technologies improved the power of institutions to create new pressure on companies to foster greater CSR'. CSR was now gradually becoming a financial asset by a restructuring of the reputational space of companies. Increasingly, public reputation was not just determined by, for instance, the qualities if products and services, standard of technical innovation and design, etc.; rather, these economic reputational dimensions were challenged by public perceptions of governance and ethical behaviour, concerns for workplace conditions, environmental awareness, and financial (non-corrupt) performance. For many international companies CSR became part of the business model to improve public relations, and in the early 2000s, CSR demands broadened to include demands for awareness of environmental sustainability, stakeholder communication, and public transparency in the conduct of business.[6] By this time, CSR also began to surface in China. One decade into the new Millennium, Lee concluded, with cautious optimism, that the development of CSR in China was complete. CSR was 'ushered' into China in the late 1990s and was gaining some ground under the control and guardianship of the state. Yet, while it was gaining some ground on environmental issues, this hardly included human rights concerns.[7]

This brings us to the relationship between CSR and the contemporary 'human rights and business' discourse. In the 1990s, human rights began to surface in debates on CSR. It was a new topic. The OECD Guidelines on Multi-lateral Enterprises of 1976 had not referred to human rights, and neither did the revised

---

[4]   T. Donaldson, *Corporations and Morality* (Prentice Hall, Englewood Cliff, NJ, 1982).
[5]   R.C. Moura-Leite and R.C. Padgett, 'Historical Background of Social Corporate Responsibility' (2011) 7(4) *Social Responsibility Journal* 534.
[6]   M.P. Lee, 'A review of theories of social resposibilies: its evolutionary path and the road ahead' (2008) 10 *International Journal of Management Reviews* 297–311.
[7]   *Ibid.*, p. 99.

versions of 1979, 1984 and 1991. However, when the Guidelines were revised again in 2000, reference was made, albeit in general terms, to the UN Universal Declaration of Human Rights, and more specifically to the need for respecting human rights in companies' operations. According to paragraph 2 of the General Policies of the OECD Guidelines (2000), enterprises should '[r]espect the human rights of those affected by their activities consistent with the host government's international obligations and commitments'. Another important international instrument paving the way for a rights approach to business responsibility was the ILO Tripartite Declaration Concerning Multinational Enterprises and Social Policy Reform of 1977. The aim of the Declaration was 'to encourage the positive contributions which multinational enterprise can make to economic and social progress and to minimize and resolve the difficulties to which their various operations may give rise'. Similar to the OECD Guidelines, the ILO Declaration is voluntary in nature. Yet these documents were the cornerstones of international CSR discourses and policies in the 1990s, and indeed laid the foundation for the developments in the first decade of the 2000s.

A major breakthrough in human rights attention to the conduct of business came in 1997 when the Sub-Commission on the Promotion and Protection of Human Rights set up a Working Group on the Working Methods and Activities of Transnational Corporations.[8] In its first session in 1999, the Working Group asked David Weissbrodt, one of the Working Group members, to prepare a code of conduct for the human rights principles for business enterprises. A first draft of a code was discussed at the Working Group's August 2000 session and revised drafts were discussed at the Sub-commission's sessions in 2001 and 2002.[9] A draft was adopted by the Sub-Commission in August 2003 (resolution 2003/16), entitled the Draft Norms on the Responsibilities of Transnational Corporations and Other Business Enterprises with Regard to Human Rights (usually referred to as the Draft Norms)).[10]

In section A, *General Principles*, the Draft Norms hold that '[w]ithin their respective spheres of activity and influence, transnational corporations and other business enterprises have the obligation to promote, secure the fulfilment of, respect, ensure respect of, and protect human rights recognized in international as well as national law'. These and other formulations, for instance, that found in section H paragraph 18 stating that '[i]n connection with determining damages, and in all other respects, these Norms shall be enforced by national courts and/or international tribunals if appropriate', go far in ascribing legal

---

[8] Before 1999, the Sub-Commission on the Promotion and Protection of Human Rights was known as the Sub-Commission on Prevention of Discrimination and Protection of Minorities. It was dissolved by the Human Rights Council, and met for the last time in August 2006. It was followed by a new expert body set up by the Council; the Human Rights Council Advisory Committee, which held its first meeting in August 2008.

[9] E/CN.4/Sub.2/2002/WG.2/WP.1/Add.1.

[10] E/CN.4/Sub.2/2003/12 (2003), www1.umn.edu/humanrts/introduction05-01-02final.html.

obligations to businesses, although they were designed as voluntary standards. Hence, confusion and discontent about the meaning, scope and binding nature of the Draft Norms soon occurred, and they were met with stiff critiques and resistance. The Human Rights Commission, to which the Sub-Commission reported, suggested to its superior UN body, the Economic and Social Council to '[a]ffirm that (the document containing the Draft Norms) has not been requested by the Commission and, as a draft proposal has no legal standing, that the Sub-Commission should not perform any monitoring function in this regard'.[11] The Commission, however, did not put the issue to a close. Instead it asked the High Commissioner for Human Rights to compile a report identifying how to strengthen standards on businesses human rights responsibilities, while taking the Norms into account. In April 2005, the Commission created a position as a Special Representative on the issue of human rights and transitional corporations 'and other business enterprises'.[12] In July 2005, UN General Secretary appointed Harvard Professor John Ruggie as Special Representative.

2. HUMAN RIGHTS AND REGULATION THEORY

This gradually evolving nexus between human rights norms and moral assessment of business behaviour reflects the underlying idea of modern human rights. Theoretically, human rights are instrumental in guiding purposeful action, and represent evaluative norms and criteria for individual and social behaviour. Hence, in modern societies, human rights are social mechanism for protecting against or governing significant social risks in society – or, as Ulrich Beck puts it, risks stemming from industrialisation and globalisation, that is, risks of modernisation.[13] Henry Shue referred to human rights risks as societal 'standards threats' that endangered basic human interests, decent living and a normal healthy life.[14] Increasingly, with expanding globalisation, market agents – in particular powerful transnational corporations – are 'producing' or perhaps more rightly, causing such standard threats, specifically by dictating poor working conditions, polluting local environments, depriving rural people of their land in search for natural resources, and in many other ways.

A standard reference and most deadly industrial disaster in modern history is the massive leak of methyl isconate gas at the Union Carbide's pesticide plant in Bhopal in India on 3 December 1984. It stands out as 'shocking experience' of human atrocities stemming from modern business. The Bhopal case represented

---

[11]   Commission of Human Rights Decision 2004/116, adopted on 20 April 2004.
[12]   Commission on Human Rights Resolution 2005/59, adopted on April 2005.
[13]   U. Beck, *Risikogesellschaft auf dem Weg in eine andere Moderne* (Frankfurt am Main: Suhrkamp Verlag, 1986), p. 30.
[14]   H. Shue, *Basic Rights. Subsistence, Affluence, and US Foreign Policy* (Princeton: University Press, 1980), p. 17.

a watershed in the growing global awareness of negative human impacts on transnational business. Thousands of people in nearby informal settlements died instantly from the leak and tens of thousands became riddled with diseases and disabilities related to the disaster in the years to follow: 'Campaigners put the death toll as high as 25,000 and say the horrific effects of the gas continue to this day'.[15] A quarter of a century later, surviving victims have still not been granted proper assistance and remedy, in spite of numerous lawsuits both inside and outside of India. Fifty per cent of the shares in the Union Carbide plant in India (Union Carbide India Ltd) were owned by Union Carbide in the United States of America, and the rest of shares divided between the Indian state and local Indian shareholders. Shortly after the disaster, a group of US lawyers filed more than 145 lawsuits against the parent company, Union Carbide, in US courts.[16] The Indian state also made numerous lawsuits. However, the Federal High Court of New York, the body handling the cases, dismissed them and argued that US courts amounted to *forum non conveniens*. The cases, the Court held, should be brought before India's own domestic courts. The parent company (based in the US) could not be taken to an Indian court, and hence, its complicity as a majority shareholder was not held liable. The Indian judiciary, however, proved to be highly ineffective in handling cases brought to court, and only in 2010 were eight of the responsible managers of UCIL convicted for being responsible for 'death by negligence' and sentenced to light prison terms and symbolic fines.[17]

The Bhopal case aptly demonstrates the 'standard threats' to which Shue refers. It also shows how a lack of appropriate protection mechanisms renders people powerless and without effective rights safeguards. The case evinces a lack of 'social guarantees' (in this case an effective judiciary, which left people vulnerable to risk and traumatic harm). According to Shue, '[c]redible threats can be reduced only by the actual establishment of social arrangements that will bring assistance to those confronted by forces that they themselves cannot handle'.[18] To be protected from such harms, people need firm institutional protection, 'not protection against any imaginable threat, but defences against predictable remedial threats.[19] It is exactly this function as *institutional mechanisms of protection against standard threats* that is the essence of human rights in practice.

It is important to note that this feature of human rights is adopted by the new business and human rights agenda: to expand the field of social and legal guarantees to protect people from social and human harm that follows from business behaviour. According to Ruggie, '[i]ndeed, history teaches us that markets pose the greatest risks – to society and business itself – when their

---

[15]   See news.bbc.co.uk/2/hi/south_asia/8725140.stm (2010).

[16]   J.G. Ruggie, *Just Business. Multinational Corporation and Human Rights* (New York: W.W. Norton, 2013), p. 7.

[17]   *Ibid.*

[18]   H. Shue, *supra* n. 14, p. 26.

[19]   *Ibid.*, p. 33.

scope and power far exceed the reach of the institutional underpinnings that allow them to function smoothly and ensure their political sustainability'.[20] In studying this issue, much of current research is rooted in the discipline of regulation. The business and human rights field is a new regulatory space[21] that provides justification, legitimacy and human rights based mechanisms for risk management, that is, mechanisms 'to reduce undesirable effects through appropriate modification of the causes, or less desirable, mitigation of the consequences'.[22] A human rights approach implies that we address how human rights are rules of regulation that structure the relationship between businesses and between business, governments, and other stakeholders.

While we recognise that human rights standards have not yet penetrated the normative foundation of business, we see trends toward greater attention, knowledge, and concern for human rights among domestic and international business actors. The assumption that human rights provides both ethical motivations and practical incentives for businesses to take rights seriously is not overtly naïve; human rights are part of a regulatory turn.

This implies that there is a case for both rational and normative institutional perspectives in studies of human rights responsibilities of business behaviour. From a rational business perspective, a company will pursue its legitimate goal of profit maximisation. It adapts to demands of the market. These demands may stem from new norms in the market (competitors invent new ways of operating that are giving competitive success), or they may stem from new state regulations. Hence, demands of the market change over time; the market is not a given, and external regulatory requirements and rules by states or international institutions are continuously influencing domestic and international economic relations. The regulatory space is in constant flux. Human rights and environmentally friendly demands are among the latest regulatory standards that have been introduced. When businesses adopt these standards, their effects turn in the regulatory space. It is, however, paradoxical that this development arises at a time when the neo-liberal economic policies for three decades sought the deregulation of the state and the private sector. One may wonder if the pendulum is beginning its return swing.

---

[20] A/HRC/8/5 (7 April 2008), 'Protect, Respect and Remedy: a Framework for Business and Human Rights', Report of the Special Representative of the Secretary-General on the Issue of Human Rights and Transnational Corporations and other Business Enterprises.

[21] L. Hancher and M. Moran (eds.), *Capitalism, Culture and Economic Regulation* (Oxford: Oxford University Press, 1989).

[22] O. Renn, 'Three Deacdes of Risk Research: Accomplishment and New Challenges' (1998) *Journal of Risk Research* 1, 49–70.

3.   HUMAN RIGHTS LAW AND BUSINESS: CONCEPTS, PRINCIPLES AND CHALLENGES

As noted above, the recent formulation of human rights regulation was spearheaded by the work of the then UN Special Rapporteur on Human Rights and Business, John Ruggie. The 'Ruggie process' restructured and reinterpreted existing human rights standards to make them applicable to market actors, reshaping the regulatory space, and by implication, the competitive environments of businesses.

Ruggie attempted to apply what he refers to as 'principled pragmatism' to his work. Through two mandate periods spanning from 2005–2011, he produced a series of documents through a process of consultation with numerous stakeholders worldwide, and developed a Framework (the 2008 report) and Guiding Principles on human rights and business (the 2011 report). Ruggie's basic approach is institutional combined with legal perspectives. He attributes the 'root cause' of the quandary of human rights and business to governance gaps created by contemporary globalisation 'between the scope and impact of economic forces and actors, and the capacity of societies to manage their adverse consequences. These governance gaps provide the permissive environment for wrongful acts by companies of all kinds without adequate sanctioning or reparation'.[23] Typically, the worst cases of business-related human rights harms occur in countries where governance challenges are greatest – they take place disproportionately in low income countries; and countries with weak rule of law systems, large corruption problems; countries with high levels of internal conflict; and in states with pockets of stateless territories.[24]

By the 1990s, it had become widely recognised that the power of multinational corporations had expanded beyond the reach of effective public governance, and increasingly implied opportunities for companies to commit wrongful acts without sanction or redress. The framework and principles for the conduct of business that were developed, aimed at governing such prevailing governance gaps by regulating and reforming the conduct of both business and governments in a nexus of complementarity between public accountability and private actors' responsibilities.

Ruggie critiqued the Draft Norms for their 'exaggerated legal claims and conceptual ambiguities […] engulfed by (their) own doctrinal excesses'.[25] Rather, Ruggie sought to develop an authoritative source of policy guidance for governments, businesses and civil society actors by 'establishing a common

---

[23]   A/HRC/8/5, *supra* n. 20, p. 3.
[24]   *Ibid.*, p. 6.
[25]   J.G. Ruggie, *supra* n. 16, p. 54.

global platform for action, on which cumulative progress can be built, step-by-step, without foreclosing any other promising longer-term developments'.[26]

The framework – which is referred to in several chapters in this volume, was based on three pillars, and a conceptual architecture for identifying the respective roles of government and business in protecting and respecting human rights, and for their separate and shared responsibility for remedial efforts when human rights harms are committed. Pillar I refers to the state's duty to protect against abuses by third parties (in this context, business enterprises) through appropriate policies, regulation, and adjudication. Pillar II refers to corporate responsibility to respect human rights, which implies duties to avoid infringing on people's human rights, and take action against adverse impact if it occurs. The third pillar refers to responsibilities to remedy and compensate and to provide legal and or non-legal remedies in cases of human rights abuses. Within this three-pillar framework – which does not imply new norms and human rights standards, but a new space for application of existing standards and treaty-based rights – Ruggie identified a set of 31 principles with a number of sub-provisions, specifying the responsibilities of companies and duties of states.

Since the adoption of the Framework and the Guiding Principles, international and national efforts towards their implementation have been made. When the UN Human Rights Council adopted the UNGP in June 2011, it also established an Interregional Working Group on the issue of Human Rights and Transnational Corporations and other Business Entities to oversee and contribute to the implementation of the GPs by the UN.[27] The Working Group was mandated to promote the dissemination of the Principles, identify and learn from good practices, support national capacity-building, develop dialogue with government and other stakeholders, and make recommendations about the implementation of the GPs at national, regional, and international levels.[28] The mandate of the Working Group was renewed in 2014 by the UN Human Rights Council In the renewal Resolution, the Working Group was tasked with, in particular, advancing the development of national action plans for the implementation of the Guiding Principles. In Geneva an annual Global Forum on Business and Human Rights has been held annually from 2012 to promote support and raise debates and dialogue among businesses, governments, non-governmental organisations and human rights academics.

A fundamental feature of the Guiding Principles is that they do not invent new law and new standards; they rest on the existing system of human rights law,

---

[26]   A/HRC/17/31 (21 March 2011), 'Report of the Special Representative of the Secretary-General on the Issue of Human Rights and Transnational Corporations and other Business Enterprises'; J.G. Ruggie, *Guiding Principles on Business and Human Rights: Implementing the United Nations 'Protect, Respect and Remedy' Framework*, p. 7.

[27]   J.G. Ruggie, *supra* n. 16, p. xxi.

[28]   S. Dhanarajan and C.M. O'Brien, 'Human Rights and Businesses. 14th Informal ASEM Seminar on Human Right', Background Paper to the Asia-Europe Meeting in Hanoi, 18–20 November 2014, p. 11.

institutions, and mechanisms. The main obligation of human rights protection and enforcement remains with the state. At the same time, the GPs strengthen the notion that businesses as non-state actors and *organs of society* (Preamble of the Universal Declaration of Human Rights) have responsibilities to respect and not harm human rights norms. This re-orientation of human rights norms has been under way for some time.[29] Its break-through came, as Dhanarajan and O'Brien state, 'at a time when this was essential to ensure their continuing relevance as a narrative responsive to people's lived experience of indignity and injustice'.[30] Yet controversy remains as to whether the best way of making business respect human right is through a legal approach by developing a binding treaty, or a system based on voluntariness, which also entails institutional and cultural changes through awareness, monitoring, and public discourses.

The UNGP represent a middle ground between these approaches. They stress that companies have responsibilities to respect human rights and the 'do no harm' principle. At the same time, the UNGP put emphasis on efforts to be made to develop new business behaviour through *due diligence*, institutional and cultural changes inside business entities, and across business sectors. This duty of companies to respect human rights is, at the same time, nested in the state's duty to protect. A policy response to this duty is the development of the new mechanism on national action plans for business and human rights, encouraged by the UN Working Group.

Disputes on the best strategic paths towards respect for human rights – regulating transnational corporations through an international treaty instrument vs. a more pragmatic position that sees national law and voluntary initiatives as predominant strategies to advance business responsibilities for human rights – continue unabated in spite of the growing impact and dissemination of the UNGPs since their adoption. The issue was made evident in June 2014 when the Human Rights Council passed two resolutions on human rights and business.[31]

The first resolution adopted by a sharply divided vote (20 in favour, 14 against and 13 abstentions) decided to establish an intergovernmental working group with the mandate to elaborate on a legally binding treaty 'to regulate, in international human rights law, the activities of transnational corporations and other business enterprises'.[32] A majority of the Council's members did not vote for the resolution, and most of the home countries of transnational enterprises (the US, EU, South Korea and Japan) voted against, while China supported the resolution with significant conditionality. Quite remarkably, in defining the target of a future treaty, the resolution decides that it should address 'transnational corporations

---

[29]   P. Alston, *supra* n. 1; B.A. Andreassen, 'Development and the Human Rights Responsibilities of Non-State Actors' in B.A. Andreassen and S.P. Marks (eds.), *Development as a Human Right. Legal, Political and Economic Dimensions* (Antwerp: Intersentia, 2010).

[30]   S. Dhanarajan and C.M. O'Brien, *supra* n. 28, p. 12.

[31]   A/HRC/26/L.22/Rev.1, p. 1 f.

[32]   *Ibid.*

and other business entities', but then adds in a footnote that 'other business entities' denotes all business enterprises that have a transnational character in their operational activities and does not apply to local businesses registered in terms of domestic law'. This is certainly highly contentious, and implies, as illustrated, that the language of the proposed treaty would have covered international brands purchasing garments from the factories housed in the Rana Plaza Building in Dhaka in Bangladesh, which collapsed on 24 April 2013 with a death toll of 1,129, and more than 2,500 people injured. Yet it would not cover the local factory owners.[33] Critics of the legalisation of the issue thus argue that in view of past history of the making of human rights treaties, it is highly unlikely that a treaty will emerge and garner wide support in the near future. This certainly begs the question: what shall be done to do 'between now and then'?[34] One straightforward answer is to implement as effectively as possible the UNGPs. However, the danger is that a long-lasting process of drafting a new treaty will significantly undermine efforts to implement the Guiding Principles. This would represent a setback in the effort to advance the human rights and business agenda.

The second resolution reflected the view of the opponents of a treaty and was proposed by a group of states supportive of the continued implementation of the UNGPs. This resolution was adopted unanimously, without a vote, by the Human Rights Council and expresses strong support to the continued implementation of the UNGPs, including development of national action plans for the implementation of the Guidelines, and the role of the Working Group in developing national guidelines for judicial and non-judicial remedial mechanisms for victims of violations. The resolution also called for prolonging the mandate of the Working Group by three years. In fact, the resolution may play an important role in the process ahead: 'In the short run, the consultations it calls for on "the full range of legal options and practical measures to improve access to remedy" led by the Office of the High Commissioner and involving all stakeholder groups, will contribute practical information, insights, and guidance as the treaty negotiations get under way'.[35]

The quest for making businesses responsible for human rights in their operations can hardly be pursued by one regulatory strategy; rather, it calls for composite measures that complement each other. Experiences from the Draft Norms in the early 2000s indicate that this was not a constructive path and should not be repeated. The question whether a legal approach will give better results in terms of businesses' increased awareness, implementation, and enforcement of human rights norms without hard-law regulation is hypothetical and not possible to answer *ex ante*. One issue is the uncertain path towards a treaty and the challenge of having it ratified and implemented by the most central home

---

[33]   J.G. Ruggie, 'The Past as Prologue? A Moment of Truth for UN Business and Human Rights Treaty' (2014) 8 *IHBR Commentary* 1.

[34]   *Ibid.*

[35]   *Ibid.*, p. 6.

states of TNCs. Equally important is the question of how the key actors, that is, the transnational companies and other businesses enterprises, including host country subsidiary suppliers, will respond to different strategic paths. Creating more just business requires that respecting rights is integral to *doing* business. It requires changing conceptions of business as 'organs of society', and institutional and cultural changes in the operation and functions of companies. It requires institutional internalisation of human rights norms. A comparable experience has been made in terms of companies' responsibilities for environmental change in the Sustainability Company Project.[36] The aim of this research and innovation project, which started in 2010, was to examine how environmental concerns could be better integrated into decision-making and operations of companies. By doing this, the project aimed to contribute to sustainable development.[37] This, however, clearly requires mixed strategies. According to the project outline, '[t]aking companies' substantial contributions to climate change as a given fact, companies have to be addressed more effectively when designing strategies to mitigate climate change. A fundamental assumption is that traditional external regulation of companies, e.g. through environmental law, is not sufficient. Our hypothesis, confirmed through research, is that environmental sustainability in the operation of companies cannot be effectively achieved unless the objective is properly integrated into company law and thereby into the internal workings of the company'.[38]

This experience from the field of environmental law reflects limitations of international legal regulation, and emphasises the importance of a mixed strategies that combine national legal regulation (of company law) with changes in company cultures and institutional reforms. It also points to the sectorial dimension of competitive markets. Companies compete within market sectors, and make cost–benefit analyses of the commercial and normative strategies they pursue. Regulations should reflect sectorial approaches that make human rights integral to cost–benefit calculations and as part of building and retaining commitment among business actors. Sectorial approaches in the implementation of the Guiding Principles may help construct and institutionalise intra-sectorial commitment, enhancing the intra-sectorial regulatory spaces. As Deva writes in Chapter 1, respecting human rights should give companies a competitive advantage (enhancing their benefit). They should at the same time serve to manage company risks and help ensure that companies do not negatively impact on human rights as this will undermine their reputation and consequently

---

[36]   This is an international research project at the Department of Private Law, University of Oslo, see: www.jus.uio.no/ifp/english/research/projects/sustainable-companies/ (accessed 1 June 2015).

[37]   www.jus.uio.no/ifp/english/research/projects/sustainable-companies/project-description/ (accessed 2 July 2015).

[38]   *Ibid.* See also: B. Sjåfjell and B. Richardson (eds.), *Company Law and Sustainability – Legal Barriers and Opportunities* (Cambridge: Cambridge University Press, 2015).

their market position (or what Ruggie referred to in his 2008 report as *social expectations*). However, the challenge of the cost–benefit approach to business and human rights is, as Deva rightly points out, marred with the reverse calculus where business may chose a fee or a reputational loss if the expenses of paying fees, or loss in reputational capital, is commercially smaller than the profits of harmful human rights practices. This clearly accounts for invoking legal approaches to ensure respect for human right, primarily by improving national legislation and enforcement. Whether an international treaty will give added force to ensuring rights commitment is, as noted, hypothetical, at best. The argument here is that international law – in case of a new binding treaty on business and human rights – requires domestic jurisprudence as the predominant layer of law, and domestic means of implementation and enforcement. For an international treaty to be effective, recurring gaps of various types of governance need to be managed. This concerns the structure and governance of the legal and policy domains. These are in other words effective norms and practices of national and international law and jurisdictions that are capable of regulating multinational companies in both host and home state's jurisprudence, and legitimate, regulatory political institutions to ensure judicial independence. It also concern the support and advocacy for rights and responsibilities across border by civil society, including independent and effective media as a sphere of civic governance; and it certainly concerns corporate governance – how human rights principles are adopted and internalised by multinational companies and other business enterprises. The main human rights problem of today is not a lack of human rights norms, but the failure of states to *implement* existing binding human rights instruments. A new legal treaty – on state regulation of business behaviour – requires that these norms be internalised in the culture, conduct, and behaviour of multinational and other enterprises. At the same time, the work with a possible treaty should not distract from the implementation of the Guiding Principles which have gained astonishing support over the last four years.

In the first chapter of this volume Surya Deva takes a clear-cut position on the issue of making well-defined legal obligations for businesses. Human rights are not negotiable, he argues, and should not be treated as means to and end but as needs in themselves. There is a tendency to address human rights as 'good for business' as long as it is good for a financial bottom line. While Deva acknowledges that this 'business case' for human rights may have positive impacts on many companies' decisions and behaviour, he warns against making this the main justification for developing human rights duties for business actors. He is also critical of the consensus-building approach that Ruggie employed because it prevented a more 'robust' legal framework to evolve. With the adoption of Resolution 26/9 of the Human Rights Council, it is now time for the open-ended intergovernmental working group to design a treaty and treaty system. While Deva acknowledges that states (or at least those states where most MNCs are domiciled) may not yet be ready to make the move towards a more robust legal regulatory regime, he argues that the current system must be more victim-focused and not just address the 'impact' of business on human rights. In this effort, the role of civil society is essential as a watchdog in monitoring commercial non-state actors. In his analysis, there is need for multiple (and integrated) approaches to make businesses accountable for human right abuses, and a treaty is but one of the approaches he devises.

Itai Apter advances this critique to the current efforts to drive business accountability (Chapter 2). Apter acknowledges that there has been much progress in nurturing an emerging global governance of standards for business behaviour, with a number of new tools that may help bring about remedies for victims and prevent abuses by commercial entities. Soft-law efforts to impose corporate liability for human rights abuse, including universal litigation and international guidelines, are constantly expanding. Yet she takes a critical look at whether existing remedies are effective or rather counterproductive placebos. She asks whether states should instead be encouraged to act domestically rather than through international agreements. She supports integrated, yet multiple strategies for holding companies accountable. There is, historically, no single strategy that has proven successful in its entirety. Yet, there is a need for both political and soft and hard-law solutions to advance accountability and nurture engagement of home regimes in ensuring foreign corporate compliance. Apter identifies strengths and weaknesses of the UN and OECD guidelines, arguing that these can, in certain contexts, contradict victims' best interests. At the same time, she argues that political, inter-state dialogue and solutions may facilitate the imposition of liability and provide remedy, even if they may circumvent legal resolutions and accountability.

One of the most egregious fields of company harm to communities and citizens is environmental damage. The prime example, referred to by several authors of this volume is the oil pollution caused by oil exploration by Shell in the Ogani delta in Nigeria in the 1990s. There are numerous other cases on soil degradation and damage in Latin America, for instance in Ecuador (by Chevron) and Peru, often with catastrophic results for indigenous people living in affected areas. Gentian Zyberi addresses conceptual issues of responsibilities for serious environmental damage caused by commercial enterprises and suggests a model for shared responsibilities between company, host state and home state (Chapter 3). He acknowledges that the distinction between civil liability and state responsibility is proving increasingly difficult to draw with precision, and the nature of the company (whether it is private, state owned, or mixed ownership) influences assessments of responsibilities according to international law. The model of shared responsibility that he suggests resonates with the current debates about the UN Guiding Principles. The host state, Zyberi argues, is responsible for establishing suitable national legal framework to protect against environmental harm caused by companies. At the same time, the home state may have responsibilities for adjudicating disputes. Zyberi argues that only strict legal regulation can prevent companies to make a decision that entails high-level risks for environmental hazard.

While Deva argues that 'the business case for human rights' should not be a major justification for businesses to take human rights seriously, Güler Aras (Chapter 4) assumes that we cannot ignore that there are indeed good business reasons for ethical concerns and social corporate behaviour. Ethical corporate behaviour may have different instrumental justifications and normative and institutional grounding. Interestingly, there seems to be a trend in which companies see less risk in investing in markets with a transparent policy on corporate social responsibility. Aras also refers to consumer awareness that influence corporate behaviour and quotes data from Europe and the US that indicate significant positive shifts in business attention to ethical issues. Less recognised, but equally important, is the impact that CSR behaviour may have on companies' success in employee recruitment, retention and productivity. Although we do not have strong comparative empirical evidence to draw on, ethical concerns seems to emerge as a factor prospective employees take into consideration when choosing which company to work for. Ethical choice of the employee is merged with instrumental concerns of companies to attract good employees in order to save costs of recruitment and reduce turnover rates. Reflecting on debates around the UN Guiding Principles, she supports the position that ethical and corporate responsible behaviour provide a social 'licence to operate', which again is commercially important. It is, at the same time, not just a matter of internal ethical functioning of benevolent principles but, equally importantly, these principles must be seen and perceived by the larger society to have the intended positive effects on businesses.

A main controversy of the business and human rights discourse is the functionality of human rights law in restricting and sanctioning harmful corporate behaviour beyond state borders. A much-debated strategy, still legally unsettled as a doctrine of international law, is the use of extraterritorial adjudication in the pursuit of justice. In terms of foreign cubed cases, the famous *Kiobel* case, referred to by several authors of this volume, was not at all successful in using US courts. Yet, as Humberto Cantú Rivera points out (in Chapter 5), there might be a more promising trend in other countries than the US for holding parent companies responsible in their home jurisdiction for their subsidiaries abroad (so-called 'forum-shopping'). Equally important, perhaps, are efforts to give soft-law a semi-binding character through state practice and case law. An important issue discussed by Rivera is whether the UN Guiding Principles may, in certain instances, receive such powers by the *hardening* of soft law.

The question of extraterritorial human rights obligations is increasingly being addressed in the human rights discourse. The so-called Maastricht Principles adopted by legal scholars in September 2011 is often referred to as the clearest and most comprehensive interpretation of the principle. The Principles continue to inspire the application of extra-territorial reasoning and argumentation, e.g. by the UN Committee on Economic, Social and Cultural Rights.[39] Ebenezer Durojaye argues that the principle of extraterritorial obligations provides potentially important support for holding MNCs responsible for human rights behaviour across and beyond borders. He discusses the Maastricht Principles in detail and addresses how their application may advance states duty to enforce business enterprises' accountability for human rights harms, but also the inherent weaknesses of the principles. Similar to Deva and Rivera, he advocates for hard law human rights instruments at the international level to complement the soft law nature of the Maastricht Principles.

The second section of the volume addresses a series of contextual issues. Can human rights provide guidance for better corporate governance designed to prevent corruption? Who are the main proponents of legal advancement and social activism for changing business practices? How can we address business *sectors*, and learn about their functioning in competitive environments and the scope conditions for heightening the normative and legal human rights thresholds of regulation? And how can we measure the effects of the 'human rights policies' that businesses adopt? In Chapter 7, Hana Ivanhoe argues that it remains contested whether corruption in itself represents a violation of human rights, even if it has significant adverse effects on people's enjoyment of fundamental rights. She addresses corruption in supply chain contexts where the MNC is involved in corrupt practices by bribing for contracts and other favours. This, she argues, is potentially in conflict with the right to self-determination, a view increasingly voiced in the international human rights discourse. We need, however, more empirical evidence to map out the threat that corruption poses to individual human rights; but while we search and systematise such evidence and establish causal relationships, Ivanhoe suggests developing a framework for addressing corruption as a human rights violation. The essential conceptual bricks for such a framework can be extracted and constructed from the doctrine of due diligence, which is inherent in the UN Guiding Principles, notably the duty of businesses to respect human rights, and experiences drawn from e.g. the US Foreign Corrupt Practices Act.

Hence, one important means of raising company awareness about possible human rights harms of their operators, and potentially prevent harms from occurring, is due diligence analysis. The UNGPs refer to due diligence as a method of indicating expected outcomes. Miho Taka (Chapter 8) examines the development and application of due diligence in the extractive industries, taking the Democratic Republic of Congo (the DRC) as a case study. The DRC is not just one of the most important producers of essential minerals for technical industries worldwide, it is also a country with serious internal conflicts in the production zones of extractive mineral. How can standards of due diligence

---

[39] See for instance the Concluding Observation on the Second Periodic Report of China of 23 May 2014, *cf.* E/C.12/CHN/CO/2.

be effectively introduced in such economic and social contexts? Taka offers a detailed discussion of due diligence standards developed by the extractive industry, refers to some important practices of standards, and discusses, most importantly, the many challenges, obstacles and dilemmas to effective human rights due diligence that exist in the DRC. There are serious problems of tracing supply chains responsibilities, and serious governance and security obstacles. An important feature of mining in high-value minerals in the DRC is that it is carried out by artisanal miners which largely have illegal and informal status. Taka addresses some significant dilemmas (and the unintended negative consequences) the application of due diligence standards may lead to in such socio-economic contexts, where the voices of local stakeholders are not taken into account. Human rights due diligence should take this dimension of inclusiveness very seriously in contexts of 'conflict minerals' exploration.

Another important institutional condition for business compliance with human rights standards is explicit corporate commitment to these standards. The UNGPs (Principles 15 and 16) refer to this condition as a demand for formulating corporate human rights policies, as a matter of self-regulation. Yet, critics argue that such voluntary policies easily can become a 'smoke-screen' covering lack of real action in spite of official declarations. Matthew Mullen in Chapter 9 asks what a corporate human rights policy entails, and addresses the need for developing appropriate indicators for human rights policy implementation and monitoring. Based on empirical studies of corporate human rights policy formulation, Mullen suggests a framework for assessing corporate human rights policies, which draws on the human rights based approach model often referred to in the development and human rights discourse. Corporate human rights policies need to be result-oriented, draw on international human rights standards, be inclusive and provide spaces for stakeholder impact, and be transparent and accountable. Corporations need to assume a role as a duty-bearer to respect rights, and he argues that there is a process towards making human rights mandatory due to increasing public interest and demand.

In the final section of this volume, we present three chapters to illustrate how the duty of states to protect against human rights violations by corporate business is undertaken in fields of particular concern. The state duty to protect is global, but particularly acute in emerging transitional economies. Vietnam is a pertinent case, and Ngueyn Thi Than Hai's study explores the role of Vietnamese state institutions in protecting against harmful corporate behaviour (Chapter 10). She argues that this has to be addressed in the context of the governance structures of the country. The chapter reviews relevant legislation and judicial practices and examines state capacity and 'political will' to address CSR and human rights issues consistently. It is typical that CSR is interpreted quite narrowly, without appropriate reflection of human rights standards in policies and institutional set up. At the same time, she finds signs that the new international discourse on human rights and business is taking root in Vietnam. More recently, it has become topic in research, higher education teaching, and is being referred to in the media. Still, a comprehensive state approach to the obligation of public institutions to protect against harmful corporate behaviour is needed.

The second issue concerns the impact that *international investment agreements* may have on the state's capacity to protect from business human rights harms. When countries enter into such agreements, do they to retain enough *policy space* to enable the enforcement of human rights? Investment agreements usually do not explicitly refer to and even less protect human rights. According to the 'regulatory chill theory', a home government who has entered into an investment agreement will freeze its intended human rights policies if those contradict the interests of foreign investors who operate under the agreement. The state does so in order to keep its obligations under the agreement and to avoid expensive litigations and compensation claims from concerned companies. Stéphanie Gervais tests this hypothesis in Chapter 11 by empirically analysing two cases from Latin America (El Salvador and Ecuador). Gervais finds that the two cases partly contradict the regulatory chill hypothesis which provides some scope for optimism. While the legal cases analysed were not fully concluded at the time of writing, the process thus far gives enough evidence to suggest a number of important recommendations about creating a space that may ensure state compliance with its human rights obligations and, at the same time, enable it to enter international investment agreements. Among the recommendations, investment tribunals could create human rights complaint mechanisms in addition to investors' claim mechanisms; include references to workers and communities affected by investments; integrate anti-corruption clause and make explicit reference to the UNGP. Gervais also concludes that experiences from Latin America indicate that governments indeed may object to investment agreements when the effects are detrimental to human rights and environmental concerns.

A significant feature of contemporary globalisation is the establishment of Free Trade Zones (FTZ). Since the first FTZ was established in Ireland in 1959, the number of FTZs and the related Export-processing Zones (EPZs) and Industrial Zones (IZs) has grown immensely. These zones are designed to attract capital by different forms of rule exemptions, not least in rules and regulations about working standards and by temporary tax releases or immunities. The growth of economic and industrial zones has been particularly significant in rapidly emerging transitional economies, and they often have serious human rights problems in terms of working conditions and labour rights and related civil rights of access to information. Again, Vietnam is examined as an example of a transitional economy; the country has combined about 100 IZs and EPZs. In Chapter 12, Nguyen Nga Hong discusses how civil society organisations (CSOs) have developed different strategies for supporting the rights of worker and environmental rights in IZs in Vietnam. She analyses three CSOs who have employed strategies of cooperation, networking, and confrontation to advance workers rights and enhance CSR based on human rights principles. The work of CSOs, however, relies on the political environment. Political institutions often restrict the freedom of CSOs and the independence of trade unions, which undermine the effectiveness of civic action and trade union mobilisation.

Finally do state-owned enterprises' special nature of ownership infer a legitimate demand for stronger regulatory mechanisms? Indeed, many MNCs in the world are mixed by private and state ownership, often with a state as a majority shareowner. Does state ownership entail some sort of state human rights duty beyond the duty to respect, as advised by the UNGP, and hence, imply a request for wider regulation of partially or wholly state owned companies? This is a topical issue, not least in extractive industries, e.g. the oil sector. Ramute Remezaite (Chapter 13) addresses this issue through an analysis of the Azerbaijani state-owned company SOCAR. Although she does not reach at a conclusive legal position, she argue, with reference to the UNGP that state ownership entails added duties of the state to ensure that state-owned companies do not violate human rights. At the same time, she contends that the political environment effectively impacts on the human rights conduct of the state-owned enterprise. She further refers to the authoritarian rule of Azerbaijan, lack of judicial independence and restriction on civil society, factors which do not bode well for regulating SOCAR.

4. CONCLUSION

In spite of significant advances in soft law over recent years, there is still no consensus that corporations should have obligations under international law. What is quite evident is that the work of the UN Special Representative on Business and Human Rights brought in a dynamism in this field of business respect for human rights which was long overdue. The gradualist approach chosen by Ruggie should be commended, although his work was not the end game. In fact, it has opened up for much broader processes of strategic complementarity, that is, further advances in this field need to expand along different lines: voluntary and mandatory, cultural and institutional, economic and political. This is in fact a strategic approach which resembles the integrative framework of corporate regulation proposed by Deva.[40] Of late, much attention has been put on the quest for an internationally binding treaty. This quest is likely to be in the construction phase for a long time, important as it is; yet it should not divert attention from other strategies and issues, in *the indeterminate meantime.* The UNGP discourse has brought a momentum which should not be lost; it has been quite successful, not least, in bringing in companies in the process of gradual attitudinal and behavioural change. This might sound utopian and naïve, but it is not. There is clear evidence that it is possible to advance human rights awareness and concerns

---

[40]   S. Deva, *Regulating Corporate Human Rights Violations. Humanizing Business* (London: Routledge, 2012).

also among business actors. The growth of the Global Compact and other reporting initiatives does, at least, indicate that some change is taking place. We need more knowledge, however, to establish how international voluntary human rights initiatives may lead to business behavioural changes. What is clear is that interest of businesses themselves, achieved by persuasion, conviction based on knowledge or by 'the power of the market' – reputational concerns (or most likely a mix of these factors), have entailed communicative impulses that are required for better human rights respect and compliance by companies. It is essential, moreover, that compliance and respect for human rights does not just concern MNCs but also 'any other business enterprise' – small, medium-sized or large, national as well as transnational. In this exclusion of national companies lies a serious weakness in the ongoing work with a possible new treaty.

Over time, real changes need to be reflected in a variety of legislative measures and regulations. A new and important field of law and regulation is bilateral and multilateral trade agreements; equally important are reforms of domestic company law and regulations. The logic of human rights law requires domestic legal adaptation and compliance, and that states are willing and able to uphold their human rights obligations. State willingness and capacity for human rights compliance is the Achilles heel of human rights law. Hence, business respect for and compliance with human rights norms and law relies on governance reforms and political commitment. But in the case of business and human rights, governance reforms must take place at two levels: corporate governance and state governance. The governance capacity and reforms of states must permeate practices of commercial actors. It is not very likely that this will happen over night, but it is a necessary condition for human rights change in the business and human rights field to take place. The regulatory turn, therefore, requires a nexus of political and economic-institutional processes of change. Law, including a stronger human rights legal framework is an important factor, but conditional on other changes in culture, political commitment, and the normative structuring of markets. Market-sectorial approaches of regulation and reform may help to retain the interest and commitments of commercial actors as long as regulation is conceived as contributing to a fair level playing field of respective sectorial markets.

This collection of conceptual and empirical studies aims to highlight advances, dilemmas and significant policy and economic issues that need further studies and research to advance this new frontier of human rights theory and practice.

PART I
CONCEPTUAL DEVELOPMENTS

CHAPTER 1

BUSINESS AND HUMAN RIGHTS, OR THE BUSINESS OF HUMAN RIGHTS

Critical Reflections on Emerging Themes

Surya DEVA

'Business and human rights'[1] is a vast field touching upon almost anything that one could think of – from footballs to free trade, pollution to prostitution, torture to terror, oil spills to outsourcing, child labour to climate change, sweatshops to surveillance, extraterritoriality to employment, investment to Internet censorship, due diligence to discrimination, corruption to conflict minerals, and poverty to privacy. As it will be a herculean task for me to cover such a wide canvass in one chapter, I aim to reflect only on selected emerging themes in this area. This chapter will focus on the following four themes: the business case for human rights; the work of Professor John Ruggie as the UN Secretary General's Special Representative on the issue of human rights and transnational corporations (SRSG); behaviour of spineless states in regulating corporate conduct impinging upon human rights; and the US Supreme Court judgment in the *Kiobel* case.[2]

However, rather than dealing with them as a laundry list, I wish to weave an argument around these themes. In short, the argument is that most of the key players in the domain of business and human rights have not taken human rights seriously. Taking human rights seriously should have entailed imposing legally binding human rights obligations on all business enterprises and putting in place an enforcement mechanism to ensure adherence to these rights by private actors. Instead of working to achieve these goals, the key players have often employed the human rights discourse to serve other interests. I will call this exercise of treating

---

[1]   My interest in this area was triggered in early 2000 when I joined the National Law Institute University located in Bhopal, a city which symbolises corporate impunity for human rights abuses. The first major article that I published in this area was in 2003. S. Deva, 'Human Rights Violations by Multinational Corporations and International Law: Where from Here?' (2003) 19 *Connecticut Journal of International Law* 1–57.

[2]   *Esther Kiobel v. Royal Dutch Petroleum Co.*, 133 S. Ct. 1659 (2013).

human rights not an end in itself but only means to attain certain other objectives as the 'business of human rights', because whether (and to what extent) human rights are to be respected depends primarily on the potential impact of doing so on maximising profits or serving other interests.

Who are the key players in the area of business and human rights that I am referring to here? The key players are multinational corporations (MNCs) and their representative organisations, states, courts, international institutions, non-governmental organisations (NGOs), trade unions, media organisations, consumers, investors, lawyers and of course scholars. Several of these players are linked to the four themes taken up in this chapter. The first theme – the business case for human rights – engages not only companies but also drivers behind the business case such as consumers, investors, the media, and NGOs. The SRSG's work allows insight into the role of scholars and the politics at the UN level, while the last two themes relate to different organs of the state (including the judiciary). By a critical review of these themes and the involved players from a diverse spectrum, this chapter will shed some light on how human rights have become merely the means to achieve certain ends of the players participating in the business and human rights game.

Before proceeding further, let me make a caveat. For the sake of convenience as well as linkages, the term 'human rights' in this chapter is used in a broad sense so as to include within its fold human rights, labour rights and environmental rights.

1. THE BUSINESS CASE FOR HUMAN RIGHTS

Why should companies have human rights obligations? I think we need to deal with this normative question in a convincing manner for a number of reasons. For one, business entities should know why respecting human rights should be their business. But more importantly, our answer to this question will have a bearing – as I will try to show later – not only on the nature and extent of corporate human rights obligations but also on the enforcement of such obligations.[3]

One very popular response to the 'why' question is that there is a business case for human rights. In other words, companies should respect human rights for the 'bottom line' reasons. There are two broad strands of this rationale,[4] both of which are underpinned by the cost–benefit analysis. The first one is that if a company takes on board human rights, it should have a competitive advantage over its competitors in the market. The competitive advantage may result because

---

[3]   See S. Deva, *Regulating Corporate Human Rights Violations: Humanizing Business* (London: Routledge, 2012), p. 10

[4]   Zadek divides the business case into four interrelated categories: defence (pain alleviation); traditional (cost–benefit); strategic; and new economy (learning, innovation and risk management). S. Zadek, *The Civil Corporation* (London: Earthscan, 2001), pp. 65–68.

of the goodwill generated amongst stakeholders on account of observing human rights. It is suggested that the resultant goodwill is likely to enhance sales, invite more customers, help in attracting as well as retaining better quality employees, and push the share prices up.

The second strand of the business case is that companies should treat compliance with human rights as a risk management strategy. Ignoring human rights norms while taking business decisions might result in loss of profit, project delays, costly legal battles, boycott by consumers and investors, and the media backlash.

Apart from scholars, research centres, international institutions and companies,[5] Professor John Ruggie, the then SRSG, has championed the business case for human rights. It is worth recalling that that the SRSG in his 2008 report had noted that 'the broader scope of the responsibility to respect is defined by *social expectations* – as part of what is sometimes called a company's social licence to operate'.[6] If companies did not discharge their responsibility to respect human rights, this can subject them to '*the courts of public opinion* – comprising employees, communities, consumers, civil society, as well as investors'.[7]

The terminology of 'social expectations' and 'the courts of public opinion', which Ruggie did use in subsequent reports as well, leaves no doubt that there is a business case for respecting human rights. At a conference held in Jakarta in June 2013, Ruggie reiterated this assertion: it was suggested that while observing human rights may not necessarily enhance business profits, violating them could certainly be costly.[8]

It is fair to say that there may be a business case for observing human rights norms, as several past cases studies show. However, I very much doubt if there is a universal or unqualified business case for human rights in all situations for all types of companies operating in all sectors. For example, what could be a business case for tobacco companies, or for those companies which have no public image to protect? In fact, had there been such a clear business case, we might not be

---

5   See e.g. Global Compact Network Ukraine, 'Business Case for the Human Rights Principles', available at: www.globalcompact.org.ua/EN/businesscase/humanrights (accessed 20 June 2013); S. Greathead, 'The Multinational and the "New Stakeholder": Examining the Business Case for Human Rights' (2002) 35 *Vanderbilt Journal of Transnational Law* 719–729; J.A. Newberg, 'Corporate Codes of Ethics, Mandatory Disclosure, and the Market for Ethical Conduct' (2005) 29 *Vermont Law Review* 253; S. Williams, 'How Principles Benefit the Bottom Line: The Experience of the Co-operative Bank' in M.K. Addo (ed.), *Human Rights Standards and the Responsibility of Transnational Corporations* (The Hague: Kluwer Law International, 1999), p. 63.

6   Human Rights Council, 'Protect, Respect and Remedy: A Framework for Business and Human Rights: Report of the Special Representative of the Secretary General on the issue of Human Rights and Transnational Corporations and Other Business Enterprises', A/HRC/8/5 (7 April 2008), para. 54 (emphasis added).

7   *Ibid.* (emphasis added).

8   'Human Rights Violations Can be Costly for Business', *The Jakarta Post* (14 June 2013), available at: www.thejakartapost.com/news/2013/06/14/human-rights-violations-can-be-costly-business.html (accessed 17 June 2013).

having so much discussions, debates and regulatory initiatives concerning the human rights obligations of corporations.

I will offer three main objections to the business case for human rights. First of all, a necessary corollary implicit in the business case is that companies can ignore human rights if doing so does not affect their bottom line, either positively or negatively. Human rights in such a scenario become the subject-matter of a 'cost–benefit' analysis by companies. So, if an MNC saves millions of dollars by outsourcing its manufacturing to a country where labour rights violations are way of life, it can take the risk of suffering any *potential* and *temporary* bad publicity. Similarly, if the cost of polluting a river in terms of a potential fine in future is less than the benefits in terms of significant savings on operational expenses, then the company could opt to continue polluting the river. In other words, 'it is also possible to make a business case for violating human rights'.[9] Such a case is very clear, for example, for companies involved in the business of tobacco, drug trafficking, sex tourism, and killer drones.

Second, the business case for human rights gives the impression of a 'win-win' situation for both companies and society. While this may be the case in certain situations, conflicts between business interests and the interests of corporate stakeholders are inevitable in some other circumstances because these two sets of interests might not converge all the times. Jim Baker, the Coordinator of Council of Global Unions (CGU), rightly reminds us of this:

> One problem with the business case, of 'doing well by doing good', is that it assumes that by seeking the best return as part of a 'triple bottom line' approach, one would naturally respect human rights. At best, that risks confounding the sustainability of the enterprise with the sustainability of society or with sustainable development.[10]

Third, as I have argued elsewhere,[11] the business case is based on four interconnected assumptions which might not come true in all cases. These assumptions are:

(1) that corporation X adopts policies and takes actions consistent with human rights norms whereas its competing corporation Y does not;
(2) that stakeholders such as consumers, investors, employees, the media and NGOs are *aware* of the fact that X is contributing to human rights realisation but not Y;

---

9   J. Baker, 'The "Business Case" for Corporate Responsibility', available at: www.ohchr.org/Documents/Issues/Business/ForumSession1/SubmissionsStatements/CouncilGlobalUnions.pdf (accessed 20 June 2013).
10   *Ibid.*
11   S. Deva, 'Sustainable Good Governance and Corporations: An Analysis of Asymmetries' (2006) 18 *Georgetown International Environmental Law Review* 707, 741–747.

(3) that stakeholders *value* human rights and therefore would be *willing*, as well as *able*, to punish Y and/or reward X for their respective stands *vis-à-vis* human rights issues; and

(4) that the reward and punishment meted out by stakeholders would result in a positive or adverse effect on market share for and goodwill towards X and Y, respectively, thus giving a competitive advantage to the former.

All these four assumptions – which I label as 'goodwill-nomics' – might not always materialise. For example, consumers or investors do not always know which particular company is actually involved in human rights violations. Is it Apple, Foxconn or the relatively unknown suppliers engaged by Foxconn who are responsible for labour rights abuses in factories in China? Alternatively, corporate stakeholders might find the cost of supporting pro-human rights companies too expansive. We know that footballs and carpets made by employing child labourers sell for much cheaper. It is also well known that human beings often have a short memory and consequently 'naming and shaming' or boycotts often have temporary effect.

In short, my claim is very simple. The business case for human rights makes human rights a negotiable and flexible variable which companies could employ (or not employ) as appropriate to further their economic interests. I find this problematic because human rights ought to be a pre-condition of doing business irrespective of the effect of doing so on the bottom line and/or good will of companies.

Furthermore, since the business case for human rights is neither universal nor unqualified, it cannot be a sound basis to ground human rights obligations for *all* types of business entities. Grounding corporate human rights obligations on the business case is also problematic because it adversely affects not only the nature and extent of corporate human rights obligations but also on the enforcement of such obligations. Let me quickly give a few examples to illustrate this. Asking why companies should have human rights obligations essentially concerns the role and place of companies in society. If we construe that role narrowly, the scope and nature of their obligations has to be narrow too. Similarly, if respecting human rights is in the interests of companies as well, then one can safely assume that they would internalise human rights as rational actors – thus making the implementation and enforcement of corporate human rights obligations by external agencies a somewhat less important objective.

2. HAZARDS IN THE SRSG'S WORK

Let me now turn to another aspect that I will use to support the overarching argument about the business of human rights. It is the work done, and the progress made, by Professor Ruggie over the six years as the SRSG (from 2005 to 2011). In the area of business and human rights, the work done by the SRSG is perhaps the most influential so far at the UN level. The Guiding Principles on Business and Human Rights (GPs)[12] and the concept of 'due diligence' have become almost universal currencies in this area within a short period. The GPs have been incorporated into the 2011 update of the OECD Guidelines[13] and the ISO 26000 Guidance on Social Responsibility.[14] The European Commission has issued detailed guides for companies operating in the following three sectors: employment and recruitment, information and communication technologies, and oil and gas,[15] and a few states have developed National Action Plans (NAPs) to implement the GPs.[16] MNCs have also started embedding GPs into their codes of conduct.[17] Last but not least, the International Bar Association has issued draft guidelines for bar associations and lawyers to implement the GPs.[18]

However, rather than being blindfolded by these positive embracement of the GPs, I wish to highlight certain hazards for human rights lurking in the SRSG's work. I pick three examples that lend support to the business of human rights argument developed in this chapter.[19]

My first example relates to the amount of emphasis he placed on consensus-building and the manner in which the so-called consensus was built. The SRSG had noted at the outset that his underlying mandate was to break 'the stalemated

---

[12]   Human Rights Council, 'Guiding Principles on Business and Human Rights: Implementing the United Nations "Protect, Respect and Remedy" Framework', A/HRC/17/31 (21 March 2011).

[13]   OECD Guidelines for Multinational Enterprises: Recommendations for Responsible Business Conduct in a Global Context (25 May 2011), available at: www.oecd.org/data oecd/43/29/48004323.pdf (accessed 10 June 2011).

[14]   International Organization for Standardization, 'ISO 26000 – Social Responsibility', available at: www.iso.org/iso/home/standards/management-standards/iso26000.htm/ (accessed 20 September 2012).

[15]   European Commission, 'European Commission Publishes Human Rights Guidance for 3 Business Sectors', available at: http://ec.europa.eu/enterprise/newsroom/cf/itemdetail.cfm?item_id=6711&lang=en&title=European%2DCommission%2Dpublishes%2Dhuman%2Drig hts%2Dguidance%2Dfor%2D3%2Dbusiness%2Dsectors (accessed 20 June 2013).

[16]   'National Action Plans', available at: http://business-humanrights.org/en/un-guiding-prin ciples/implementation-tools-examples/implementation-by-governments/by-type-of-initiative/national-action-plans (accessed 27 January 2015).

[17]   See e.g. Hitachi Group Human Rights Policy, available at: www.hitachi.com.hk/eng/pdf/top/hitachi_human_rights.pdf (accessed 23 June 2013). See also 'Implementation by Companies', available at: http://business-humanrights.org/en/un-guiding-principles/implementation-tools -examples/implementation-by-companies/general (accessed 27 January 2015).

[18]   International Bar Association, 'The IBA's Business and Human Rights Working Group publishes draft guidance for bar associations and lawyers', available at: www.ibanet.org/Article/Detail.aspx?ArticleUid=67452738-0438-4AD3-88AB-0D1B2C4323AF (accessed 27 January 2015).

[19]   Here I draw on the following book chapter: S. Deva, 'Treating Human Rights Lightly: A Critique of the Consensus Rhetoric and the Language Employed by the Guiding Principles' in S. Deva and D. Bilchitz (eds.), *Human Rights Obligations of Business: Beyond the Corporate Responsibility to Respect?* (Cambridge: Cambridge University Press, 2013), pp. 78–104

debate' over the UN Human Rights Norms and build a consensus.[20] The SRSG has, therefore, taken a special pride in being able to forge a consensus on business and human rights in the form of the GPs.[21] The success of the SRSG's mandate as well as the GPs is also being measured by the consensus barometer. There are historical reasons for this orientation: the GPs have achieved what the previous UN initiatives in this area – namely, the UN Code of Conduct on Transnational Corporations and the UN Human Rights Norms – could not accomplish.

The obsessive focus on achieving the consensus meant that an arguably more important objective of putting in place a robust framework to make companies accountable for human rights violations took a back seat. It was not a coincidence that consensus was built around largely settled or uncontroversial issues. For example, who will dispute that the state duty to protect human rights includes ensuring that private actors within their territory or jurisdiction do not infringe human rights. Similarly, not many companies at this point of time are likely to challenge publicly the assertion that they have a *'responsibility to respect'* human rights.

However, the SRSG hardly made any efforts to reach an agreement on contentious issues. Nor did the GPs contain broad policy recommendations in relation to such issues. For instance, the GPs do not directly address the question of a parent company's liability for human rights abuses by its subsidiaries or make concrete recommendations to states as to what they should do to overcome obstacles in access to justice. Ruggie's rationale behind such omissions might be that 'recommendations addressed to business have to find resonance there or they will be resisted or ignored.'[22] In other words, reaching the consensus essentially meant proposing what was acceptable to MNCs.

My second example concerns the principle – that is, 'principled pragmatism' – that guided the SRSG's work. Principled pragmatism is defined as 'an unflinching commitment to the principle of strengthening the promotion and protection of human rights as it relates to business, coupled with a pragmatic attachment to what works best in creating change where it matters most – in the daily lives

---

[20]   SRSG for Business and Human Rights, 'Opening Statement to United Nations Human Rights Council', 25 September 2006, available at: http://198.170.85.29/Ruggie-statement-to-UN-Human-Rights-Council-25-Sep-2006.pdf (accessed 20 September 2012).

[21]   Out of numerous self-praising instances, see the following observation: the HRC 'in an unprecedented step, endorsed unanimously [the GPs] in June 2011. [...] I enjoyed strong support within all stakeholder groups, including the business community.' J. Ruggie, 'Kiobel and Corporate Social Responsibility: An Issues Brief', 4 September 2012, p. 3, available at: www.business-humanrights.org/media/documents/ruggie-kiobel-and-corp-social-resonsibility-sep-2012.pdf (accessed 20 September 2012).

[22]   'At the end of the day, the instruments that we proposed as part of the Guiding Principles – for example human rights due diligence as a method for companies to identify and address what their adverse human rights impacts might be – have to make sense inside of a company. Otherwise, it is not going to get done.' J. Ruggie, 'Business and Human Rights: Together at Last? A Conversation with John Ruggie' (2011) 35 *Fletcher Forum of World Affairs* 117, 121.

of people.'[23] It seems that it is the pragmatism that dominated the principle of strengthening the protection of human rights. Adoption of a pragmatic approach allowed the SRSG to win the support of companies and states which were (and continue to be) opposed to putting in place a legally binding international instrument.

Achieving a consensus in the form of unanimous endorsement of the GPs at the UN level was not a small achievement. Nevertheless, one should not ignore the price of this pragmatism-induced consensus in achieving the goal of humanising business. Pragmatism is not unknown to the human rights discourse. The progressive realisation of human rights under the International Covenant on Economic, Social and Cultural Rights (ICESCR) is a case in point.[24] Since it is pragmatic to concede that the full realisation of socio-economic rights requires a certain level of resources and capacity that some states might not currently have, it makes sense to realise core rights in the short term, whilst allowing all socio-economic rights to be realised fully in the longer term. However, this pragmatism under the ICESCR is different in nature: it is visible only during the process of realising human rights. When it comes to setting aspirational norms, human rights ought to be principled. In contrast, by introducing pragmatism at the stage of setting human rights norms applicable to business, the SRSG has set the threshold of corporate human rights obligations at a very low level.

The third and final example that I wish to pick relates to the language employed by the SRSG. In order to effectively communicate with companies and bring them on board, it might have been expedient to use the language and terminology that is commonly adopted by business people.[25] However, the use of alternative language to describe human rights obligations of companies might undermine the goal of promoting human rights.[26] Let me offer some examples here. All human rights obligations of companies under the GPs – without any exception – are formulated as part of the 'responsibility to respect'. While the term 'responsibility' may mean liability in certain contexts,[27] the GPs consciously use it to denote the non-legal duties of companies.[28] However, companies do have legally binding obligations in relation to certain egregious human rights violations such

---

[23]   Commission on Human Rights, 'Interim Report of the Special Representative of the Secretary General on the issue of Human Rights and Transnational Corporations and Other Business Enterprises', E/CN.4/2006/97 (22 February 2006), para. 81.

[24]   International Covenant on Economic, Social and Cultural Rights, 993 UNTS 3, Art. 2.

[25]   See J. Ames, 'Taking Responsibility' (2011) 111 *European Lawyer* 15, 16.

[26]   See e.g. C. Ochoa, 'Advancing the Language of Human Rights in a Global Economic Order: An Analysis of a Discourse' (2003) 23 *Boston College Third World Law Journal* 57.

[27]   B.A. Garner (ed.), *Black's Law Dictionary*, 9th edn. (St. Paul, MN: West Thompson Reuters, 2009), p. 1427; International Law Commission, *Draft Articles on Responsibility of States for Internationally Wrongful Acts* (2001), Supplement No. 10 (A/56/10), ch. IV.E.1.

[28]   See L.C. Backer, 'From Institutional Misalignments to Socially Sustainable Governance: The Guiding Principles for the Implementation of the United Nations "Protect, Respect and Remedy" and the Construction of Inter-systemic Global Governance' (2012) 25(1) *Pacific McGeorge Global Business & Development Law Journal* 69, 124.

as torture, genocide and slavery. In such a scenario, the 'responsibility to respect' formulation does not reflect accurately even the existing international law.

It is trite to say that companies can violate human rights. 'Violation' of a (human) right implies that an entity breached its duties in relation to bearers of rights. However, the GPs do not at all use the term 'violation' in relation to companies. The terms employed by the GPs are either 'impact' or 'risk'.[29] This seemingly deliberate attempt to replace the *violation typology* with the *impact typology* again has the potential to undermine human rights. Unlike violation, 'impact' is a neutral term and even qualifying it with the word 'adverse' cannot reflect adequately perspectives of victims whose rights are violated by companies.

The use of 'due diligence' to judge whether a company has discharged its corporate responsibility to respect human rights or not provides another example of how human rights could be undermined by a casual import of certain concepts. Principle 17 of the GPs sums up what companies should do:

> In order to identify, prevent, mitigate and account for how they address their adverse human rights impacts, business enterprises should carry out human rights due diligence. The process should include assessing actual and potential human rights impacts, integrating and acting upon the findings, tracking responses, and communicating how impacts are addressed.

Due diligence is a process well known to companies, as they routinely conduct such investigations in commercial contexts to assess, pre-empt and manage risks.[30] There are, however, key differences between due diligence in a commercial context and in a human rights context[31] and, in view of these differences, a blind importation of the due diligence idea might undermine human rights. Whereas a due diligence investigation in commercial contexts focuses on protecting interests of the company in question (self-interest), the human rights discourse is not about safeguarding the rights of companies. The focus of a human rights due diligence is rather on protecting the rights of people (interests of external parties).

Moreover, the interests protected by resort to due diligence in commercial deals (money or corporate reputation) is quite different in nature from what is at stake in human rights cases (the right to life and various liberties). It is often not possible to recoup fully the sufferings experienced by victims of corporate human rights abuses. Different considerations should then apply in weighing the

---

[29]   One can though notice the use of 'infringing' in Principle 11 and 'abuses' in Principle 23.

[30]   See T. Lambooy, *Corporate Social Responsibility: Legal and Semi-Legal Frameworks Supporting CSR* (The Netherlands: Kluwer, 2010), pp. 279–92; B. Demeyere, 'Sovereign Wealth Funds and (Un)ethical Investment' in G. Nystuen, A. Follesdal and O. Mestad (eds.), *Human Rights, Corporate Complicity and Disinvestment* (Cambridge: Cambridge University Press, 2011), pp. 183, 211–213.

[31]   S. Deva, 'Guiding Principles on Business and Human Rights: Implications for Companies' (2012) 9(2) *European Company Law* 101, 107.

costs and benefits of undertaking, for instance, mining in an indigenous area than when considering whether to acquire another company.

It is true that due diligence under international (human rights) law serves a useful purpose to determine the obligation of states *vis-à-vis* non-state actors, that is, the conduct of third parties.[32] However, the GPs propose to apply – without any clear differentiation – the due diligence process to one's own human rights violative conduct, where responsibility should be discharged only by achievement of the outcome (that is, the realisation of human rights) rather than by merely following a process to achieve the said outcome. Due diligence is only a process and it may or may not achieve the desired outcome – that is, non-violation of human rights – in all cases.

3. SPINELESS STATES

This chapter will now deal with the role played by states in regulating MNCs in such a way that their activities do not infringe upon human rights. By giving several examples, I will try to show that states have generally been over-reluctant in preventing and redressing human rights violations by companies, especially MNCs.

Despite tremendous growth in MNCs' power and clout, states still enjoy and exert tremendous amount of power in both domestic and international arenas. Nevertheless, when it comes to confronting MNCs and putting in place a robust regulatory framework, a great majority of states do not show the required political will to act. Why is this so? One of the reasons may be that states do not really take human rights seriously. In addition, they seem to consider the privatisation of human rights as a challenge to their sovereignty and authority – both as a guardian and violator of human rights.

Since most of the states are relying on investment-driven development, they tend to give priority to economic development at the cost of realising human rights. Rather than conceiving human rights as an integral part of the development process, the primary focus often is on creating investment-friendly environment, especially if there is a race to the bottom to attract foreign investment.

Out of several potential examples, the 2005 memorandum of understanding (MoU) signed between POSCO, a South Korean company, and the government of Orissa, an Indian state, to build an integrated steel plant with an investment of US $12 billion is a case in point.[33] Under the MoU, the Orissa government

---

[32] B. Demeyere, *supra* n. 30, pp. 214–16; R.B. Barnidge Jr., 'The Due Diligence Principle under International Law' (2006) 8 *International Community Law Review* 81, 91–121; A. Cassese, *International Law*, 2nd edn. (Oxford: Oxford University Press, 2005), p. 250.

[33] 'Memorandum of Understanding between the Government of Orissa and M/s POSCO for Establishment of an Integrated Steel Plant at Paradeep' (22 June 2005), available at: www. orissa.gov.in/posco/POSCO-MoU.htm (accessed 3 June 2013) (POSCO MoU).

agreed not only to acquire and transfer to the company all the land required for the project,[34] but also undertook to take care of providing raw materials, security, electricity and water needed for the project.[35] Moreover, the state government had agreed to '*use its best efforts to procure the grant of all environmental approvals and forest clearances from the Central Government within the minimum possible time* for the Project'.[36] While the state government promised all this to POSCO, it paid scant respect to the rights of the local tribal community in drafting the MoU or how the government functioned. For instance, it sought the approval of the central government to divert about 1,253 hectares of forest land for the project,[37] as no tribal people or traditional forest dwellers resided in the said forest area[38] – a claim that has been contested by the civil society.[39]

In addition to establishing investment partnerships with companies, states are also outsourcing public functions to the private sector on the name of efficiency. What is especially problematic in this regard is that the commitment of the private sector is not secured to respect human rights and/or the conduct of such actors is not monitored. This 'hands off' approach in practice may mean that victims of human rights abuses cannot seek an effective remedy against either the government or the private actors.

In recent times, bilateral investment treaties (BITs) have grown at a phenomenal rate. One direct effect of BITs is the creation of rights for non-signatory third parties (that is, companies). Companies can assert these rights directly against states to protect their commercial interests, thus giving them somewhat parity with states under international law. However, BITs do not create direct obligations for companies in relation to human rights, even though they may empower state parties to take appropriate measures to protect human rights.[40] BITs thus add to the existing asymmetry in relation to the rights and obligations of companies under international law.

In a globalised and interconnected world, extraterritorial regulatory measures are becoming critical for states to fulfil their obligations under national as well

---

34   *Ibid.*, para 5.
35   *Ibid.*, paras. 7, 9 and 17.
36   *Ibid.*, para. 11 (emphasis added).
37   Ministry of Environment and Forests (MoEF), 'POSCO: Final Order and Other Relevant Documents' (31 January 2011), p. 1, available at: http://moef.nic.in/downloads/public-information/Posco31012011.pdf (accessed 3 February 2011).
38   MoEF, 'POSCO: Final Order', para. 6.
39   See Fact Finding Report on Human Rights and Environmental Violations of the POSCO Project in Orissa, India (Brief Report), p. 1, available at: http://material.ahrchk.net/india/AHRC-PRL-028-2010-01.pdf (accessed 8 September 2012); 'Holding their Ground against POSCO', *India Together* (11 July 2010), available at: www.samachar.com/Holding-their-ground-against-POSCO-khss6nbdeic.html (accessed 3 February 2013).
40   See, for example, Canadian Model BIT (2004), Art. 11; US Model BIT (2012), Arts. 12 and 13; IISD Model International Agreement on Investment for Sustainable Development (2005), Arts. 20 and 21. See also R. Moloo and J. Jacinto, 'Environmental and Health Regulation: Assessing Liability under Investment Treaties' (2011) 29 *Berkeley Journal of International Law* 1.

as international law.[41] The same could be said about regulating the activities of MNCs. While extraterritorial regulation is not popular amidst states vigorously safeguarding their sovereignty, this is a defensible tool under well-established principles of international law.[42] In fact, I will argue that extraterritorial regulation could partly remedy the mismatch that currently exists between old territory-based regulatory tools and modern corporate human rights violations that are not limited by artificial state boundaries. States have relied on the universality principle in relation to certain *jus cogens* wrongs such as slavery, genocide, piracy and torture. In addition, there is an expanding list of common concerns such as drug trafficking, bribery, terrorism, and child sex trafficking in which states have resorted to extraterritorial regulation. So, if states are reluctant to regulate extraterritorially the human rights violative activities of MNCs, it cannot be due to lack of legal competence.

States have not merely shown hesitation in enacting extraterritorial laws to regulate MNCs; they have also resisted potential creative application of extraterritoriality by courts. It is worth recalling that the US government along with the governments of the UK, Australia and Switzerland had filed *amici curiae* briefs before the US Supreme Court in *Sosa*[43] to oppose the wholesale use of the Alien Tort Statute (ATS) for redressing overseas human rights violations by US-based MNCs.[44] More recently, several states again filed *amici curiae* briefs[45] before the Supreme Court in *Kiobel v. Royal Dutch Petroleum Co.*[46] One major thrust of these two sets of briefs has been to resist extraterritorial use of the ATS to hold companies accountable for their behaviour outside the US territory.

It may not out of place to mention here that when the UN Human Rights Council in June 2014 adopted a resolution tabled by Ecuador and South Africa 'to establish an open-ended intergovernmental working group with the mandate to elaborate an international legally binding instrument on Transnational Corporations and Other Business Enterprises with respect to human rights',[47] several states (including those where most of the MNCs are based) voted against

---

[41] See, for example, the Maastricht Principles on Extraterritorial Obligations of States in the Area of Economic, Social and Cultural Rights (issued on 28 September 2011).

[42] S. Deva, 'Acting Extraterritorially to Tame Multinational Corporations for Human Rights Violations: Who Should Bell the Cat?' (2004) 5 *Melbourne Journal of International Law* 37; S. Deva, 'Corporate Human Rights Violations: A Case for Extraterritorial Regulation' in C. Luetge (ed.), *Handbook of the Philosophical Foundations of Business Ethics* (New York: Springer, 2012), p. 1077.

[43] *Jose Francisco Sosa v. Humberto Alvarez-Machain* 124 S. Ct. 2739 (2004).

[44] S. Joseph, *Corporations and Transnational Human Rights Litigation* (Oxford: Hart Publishing, 2004), p. 55–60.

[45] See ScotusBlog, 'Kiobel v. Royal Dutch Petroleum', available at: www.scotusblog.com/case-files/cases/kiobel-v-royal-dutch-petroleum/ (accessed 23 June 2013).

[46] *Esther Kiobel v. Royal Dutch Petroleum Co.*, 133 S. Ct. 1659 (2013).

[47] Business and Human Rights Resource Centre, 'Binding Treaty', available at: http://business-humanrights.org/en/binding-treaty (accessed 28 January 2015).

the resolution.[48] It raises the question: if states are really supportive of the GPs and do concede that companies have human rights responsibilities, why should they hesitate to turn these soft responsibilities into legally binding obligations?

4.   KIOBEL'S ENCOUNTER WITH AN INCONVENIENT TRUTH

The final example that I offer in support of the argument about the growing business of human rights is the US Supreme Court judgment in the *Kiobel* case.[49] Before looking at this decision, let us review how the matter came before the Supreme Court. The September 2010 judgment of the US Court of Appeals for the Second Circuit in *Esther Kiobel v. Royal Dutch Petroleum Co.*[50] had created a twist in the much celebrated use of the ATS to hold MNCs accountable for human rights abuses. In the instant case, the plaintiff alleged that Dutch, British, and Nigerian corporations engaged in oil exploration and production aided and abetted the Nigerian government in committing human rights abuses in violation of the law of nations.[51]

Justice Cabranes, writing the majority judgment, considered the question whether corporations could be sued under the ATS to be an open and unresolved one.[52] The majority went on to answer the question in the negative. It reasoned that companies cannot be sued under the ATS because 'imposing liability on corporations for violations of customary international law has not attained a discernible, much less universal, acceptance among nations of the world in their relations *inter se*' and that '[n]o corporation has ever been subject to *any* form of liability (whether civil, criminal, or otherwise) under the customary international law of human rights.'[53]

On the other hand, Justice Leval – who concurred with the majority on dismissal of the complaint but disagreed with the reasoning of the majority – noted that the 'majority opinion deals a substantial blow to international law

---

[48] The votes were 20 in favour (Algeria, Benin, Burkina Faso, China, Congo, Côte d'Ivoire, Cuba, Ethiopia, India, Indonesia, Kazakhstan, Kenya, Morocco, Namibia, Pakistan, Philippines, Russia, South Africa, Venezuela, Vietnam), 14 against (Austria, Czech Republic, Estonia, France, Germany, Ireland, Italy, Japan, Montenegro, South Korea, Romania, the Former Yugoslavia, UK, USA) and 13 abstentions (Argentina, Botswana, Brazil, Chile, Costa Rica, Gabon, Kuwait, Maldives, Mexico, Peru, Saudi Arabia, Sierra Leone, UAE). Business and Human Rights Resource Centre, 'UN Human Rights Council 26th Session (Geneva, 10–27 Jun 2014)', available at: http://business-humanrights.org/en/binding-treaty/un-human-rights-council-sessions (accessed 28 January 2015).

[49] *Esther Kiobel v. Royal Dutch Petroleum Co.*, 133 S. Ct. 1659 (2013).

[50] *Kiobel v. Royal Dutch Petroleum Co.*, 621 F. 3d 111 (2nd Cir. 2010).

[51] *Ibid.*, p. 117.

[52] *Ibid.*

[53] *Ibid.*, pp. 145, 148 (emphasis in original).

and its undertaking to protect fundamental human rights.'[54] He highlighted the pitfalls of the majority judgment as follows:

> The new rule offers to unscrupulous businesses advantages of incorporation never before dreamed of. So long as they incorporate […], businesses will now be free to trade in or exploit slaves, employ mercenary armies to do dirty work for despots, perform genocides or operate torture prisons for a despot's political opponents, or engage in piracy – all without civil liability to victims.[55]

Justice Leval found fault in the reasoning of the majority by pointing out that the 'fact that international tribunals do not impose *criminal punishment* on corporations in no way supports the inference that corporations are outside the scope of international law and therefore can incur no *civil compensatory liability* to victims when they engage in conduct prohibited by the norms of international law.'[56] In his view, since international law leaves it to individual states to determine if civil liability should be imposed on companies for violation of its norms and the US has enacted the ATS to impose civil liability, companies can be held liable under it.[57]

When the case reached before the US Supreme Court on appeal,[58] the only question before the court was whether companies could be sued under the ATS. After the oral arguments, however, the Court extended the scope of inquiry to also examine whether and under what circumstances the ATS allows courts to recognise a cause of action for violations of the law of nations occurring within the territory of a state other than the US.

After hearing oral arguments again, on 17 April 2013, the Supreme Court held that the presumption against extraterritoriality applies to claims under the ATS and that this presumption is not rebutted by the text, history or purposes of the ATS.[59] The Court further noted that 'even where the claims touch and concern the territory of the United States, they must do so with sufficient force to displace the presumption against extraterritorial application.'[60] Mere presence of a company in the US will not suffice.[61]

It is significant, however, that the Court decided not to answer the original question. It rather bypassed the said question by noting the following: 'The question here is not whether petitioners have stated a proper claim under the ATS, but whether a claim may reach conduct occurring in the territory of

---

54   *Ibid.*, p. 149.
55   *Ibid.*, p. 150.
56   *Ibid.*, p. 152 (emphasis in original).
57   *Ibid.*, pp. 152–153.
58   *Kiobel v. Royal Dutch Petroleum*, Docket No. 10–1491.
59   *Esther Kiobel v. Royal Dutch Petroleum Co.*, 133 S. Ct. 1659 (2013).
60   Opinion of Chief Justice Roberts. *Ibid.*, p. 1669.
61   *Ibid.*, p. 1669.

a foreign sovereign.'[62] I argue that this judicial prioritisation of legal issues was driven by a desire to avoid facing an inconvenient truth: that companies do not enjoy a complete immunity from liability for commuting human rights violations in breach of the law of nations. It was an inconvenient truth, because holding so would have meant that cases against almost all MNCs could continue before the US courts – an outcome that the corporate lobby did not wish to have.

The Supreme Court could have held that companies could be sued under the ATS, but subject to satisfying certain procedural requirements such as exhaustion of local remedies. But instead of taking this route, the Court significantly curtailed the scope of the ATS on territorial grounds.

Chief Justice Roberts reasoned that the fact the ATS covers actions by aliens does not imply an extraterritorial reach, because the covered wrongs could occur both within and outside the US.[63] Out of the three principal offences against the law of nations – that is, violation of safe conducts, infringement of the rights of ambassadors, and piracy – only piracy could take place outside the territorial boundaries of the US, but Chief Justice Roberts noted that dealing with pirates carries 'less direct foreign policy consequences'.[64] This reasoning again shows the Court's unwillingness to accept extraterritorial reach of the ATS when two plausible interpretations are possible about its scope.[65]

The Supreme Court relied on foreign policy and potential international discord justifications to limit the ATS's scope to wrongs with significant connection to the US territory.[66] But one wonders the extent to which these factors pose real hardship to extraterritoriality. After all, the US has been a leader in adopting extraterritorial measures in several other areas of law.

By way of passing, it is worth noting that when Ruggie filed an *amicus brief* in *Kiobel* to clarify that Shell had misquoted one of his reports to argue that companies cannot be sued under the ATS,[67] he did not take sides with any party. While there may be pragmatic reasons to maintain this diplomatic neutrality, one may ask whether this is consistent with an unflinching commitment to promoting human rights.

---

[62]   *Ibid.*, p. 1664.

[63]   *Ibid.*, p. 1665.

[64]   *Ibid.*, pp. 1666–1667.

[65]   As a contrast, see the opinion of Justice Breyer, who did not read the ATS as limited by the presumption against extraterritoriality, *ibid.*, pp. 1670–1677.

[66]   Opinion of Chief Justice Roberts, *ibid.*, pp. 1664–1665.

[67]   'Brief *Amici Curiae* of Former UN Special Representative for Business and Human Rights, Professor John Ruggie; Professor Philip Alston; and The Global Justice Clinic at NYU School of Law in Support of Neither Party' (12 June 2012), available at: www.americanbar.org/content/dam/aba/publications/supreme_court_preview/briefs/10-1491_neutralamcufmrunspecialrepetal.authcheckdam.pdf (accessed 2 January 2013).

5. CONCLUSION

Business and human rights is not an entirely new area: it has merely become more prominent and popular in recent years. As someone who has followed developments in this area closely since the beginning of the twenty-first century, I have been troubled by the fact that many key players in the realm of business and human rights do not really take their commitment to promoting human rights seriously. Rather they employ human rights to fulfil some other interests. Such a scenario can be described more appropriately as the 'business of human rights', rather than 'business and human rights'.

Taking a walk on the human rights road is a costly business. Doing so would necessarily entail making sacrifices and trade-offs. Is the world community ready and willing to take such a walk? This chapter has tried to show that this may not be the case yet, as most of the companies and states are still often taking only symbolic or superficial steps. NGOs definitely offer some hope in resisting the new world order in which the official guardians of human rights (states) work hand-in-hand with violators of human rights (private actors). Despite the leverage provided to NGOs by the Internet in developing global partnerships and presence, they face challenges in securing adequate funds to run their campaigns.

At least two normative shifts are needed to accomplish the goal of humanising business in coming years. First, the business and human rights discourse must become *victim-centred* both in theory and practice. The usefulness of all current (or the proposed) regulatory initiatives, for instance, must be tested on the touchstone of offering effective access to justice to the victims of corporate human rights violations. Second, as states alone will not be able to make companies accountable for a number of reasons, the role of NGOs as non-state actors should be *institutionalised* as human rights watchdogs in monitoring the conduct of another set of non-state actors (companies).

CHAPTER 2
CORPORATE LIABILITY FOR HUMAN RIGHTS

Effective Remedies or Ineffective Placebos?

Itai APTER

1. INTRODUCTION

Traditionally it was thought that imposing liability on corporations, including for violating human rights is not legally justified, as unlike natural persons, they lack the requisite *mens rea* (mental state) to intentionally cause harm.[1] With the exception of the Nuremberg Trials post-World War II prosecutions involving German companies,[2] the common perception was that while corporations could be subject to litigation in the business context for breach of contract or torts, they cannot be criminally liable for violation of rights, whether directly, or in the more common situation, by aiding and abetting governments. However – and this is equally true in the legal-political sphere – traditions change.

The main facilitator of the change in past decades is the emergence of global governance focused on human security.[3] In our discussion, four main effects are very relevant. The rise of global corporations and their involvement in the development of international law, as well as their exposure to it; the creation of intergovernmental global institutions and norms responsible for monitoring

---

[1]   E. Engle, 'Exterritorial Corporate Criminal Liability: A Remedy for Human Rights Violations?' (2006) 20 *St. John's Journal of Legal Commentary* 287, 289.

[2]   Even in these proceedings the goal was not to impose criminal liability, in itself, on the corporations themselves but only to ascertain whether executives can be subject to criminal proceedings. D. Cassel, 'Corporate Aiding and Abetting of Human Rights Violations: Confusion in the Courts' (2008) 6 *North Western University Journal of International Human Rights* 304.

[3]   Global governance is a term describing the effects of globalisation on law and international law and the change of focus from the state to other actors on the domestic and international fields. For a discussion for its relevancy for human security see L. Axworthy, 'Human Security and Global Governance: Putting People First' (2001) 19 *Global Governance* 22–23.

human rights; the increase in non-governmental organisations (NGOs) involved in the protection of global human rights and the creation of universal human rights norms.[4] All these developments combined serve as the basis for modern attempts to promote corporate responsibility, or, to use the legal term, corporate liability for preserving human rights, alongside development of enforcement mechanisms.

Efforts to impose corporate liability for human rights abuse, including universal litigation and international guidelines, are constantly increasing. The question is whether these are remedies or ineffective placebos,[5] and whether states should instead be encouraged to act domestically or through international agreements.

The latter has merit, acknowledging that regimes involved in alleged corporate abuse include what are considered transformative regimes like Vietnam, Burma, China and Papua New Guinea.[6] Recognising the need for overall solutions and to prevent obstacles to development, engagement of local regimes in ensuring foreign corporate compliance coupled with steps by the corporations' home states can be preferable and effective. This idea is embodied in the understanding that no matter how hard those who support the imposition of corporate liability try to frame the issue in legal terms ultimately the discussion is very political, requiring policy judgments.[7]

Our discussion includes a critical analysis of litigation against corporations in the US and non-US forums, and the UN and OECD Guidelines, arguing that these contradict victims' best interests and states' interests.

Based on this analysis the paper will present an alternative way forward to the way often posited by the legal scholarship in this field. The main idea is that while litigation and law have some benefits in certain situations, ultimately when viewing the picture as a whole, political inter-state solutions and domestic

---

[4] For elaboration on the global governance model versus past models of international law and politics see A. Cavnar, *The Foreign Office Model Versus the Global Governance Model: An Introduction* (New York University Institute for International Law and Justice, 2008), available at: http://iilj.org/courses/documents/GlobalGovernancePaper.pdf (accessed 27 April 2013).

[5] The Oxford Dictionary defines 'placebo' as 'a measure designed merely to humor or placate someone', and for our purposes, an ineffective measure with only symbolic, even if important, value.

[6] Examples include: allegations against multinational companies abuse of workers in Vietnam with cooperation of the government A. Nazeer, *Corporate Globalization & human rights abuses in the sweatshops of Pakistan, Indonesia & Vietnam* (2011), available at: www.sacw.net/IMG/pdf/Corporate_Globalization___Child_Labour.pdf (accessed 27 April 2012); allegations against an international company for receiving assistance from the government of Burma for the construction of a pipeline (*Doe v. Unocal*, suit submitted in California District Court, 1997); allegations against companies cooperating with the Papua New Guinea regime in relation to mining (*Sarei v. Rio Tinto*, suit submitted in California District Court, 2000); and allegations relating to companies assisting the Chinese government for internet surveillance related issues (*Doe I v. Cisco Systems*, suit submitted in California District Court, 2011).

[7] A. Martin, 'Corporate liability for violations of international human rights: law, international custom or politics?' (2012) 21 *Minnesota Journal of International Law Online* 116.

mechanisms can facilitate imposition of liability and preventing abuse. Substantial political and corporate will is needed to advance these kinds of solutions, but it could hopefully one day become the norm making the need for development of legal mechanisms superfluous, and avoid their inherent danger of being political abused and risk a state of corporate backlash.

The main argument is that pursuing this path will often be a much better instrument to achieve true remedies for victims and promote structural changes, yet still fraud with some uncertainty and problems. Throughout the analysis particular attention has been given to examples and cases from Asian countries, including Vietnam.

2.   LITIGATION AND GUIDELINES – A CRITICAL ANALYSIS

Today the main avenues for internationally enforcing or promoting corporate responsibility for human rights include litigation and guidelines by international inter-governmental organisations.

Litigation is considered a leading mechanism for enforcement against corporations with US-based NGOs leading the way, and US judicial forums allowing suits against corporations for alleged violations. Before beginning our review we must remember two key points: litigation is usually unsuccessful,[8] apart from very exceptional settlements,[9] and history demonstrates that victims have usually received compensation not through litigation but rather through a political process.[10]

---

[8]   M.D. Goldhaber, 'Corporate Human Rights Litigation in Non-U.S. Courts: A Comparative Scorecard' (2013) 3 *University of Callifornia Irvine Law Review* 127. According to data, updated to 2012, only 13 out of 180 have ended with settlement, with almost all other cases still pending or dismissed (with very few verdicts in favour of plaintiffs).

[9]   Examples include settlement in a case against a company which was alleged to cooperate with the government of Burma (*Unocal*), and a case against Shell (a global oil company) in relation to events in Nigeria (later discussed in section 3 of this chapter). C. Ryngaert, 'Finding Remedies for Historical Injustices: Dealing with Organizations and Corporations', Working Paper No. 38, January 2010, Leuven Center for Global Governance Studies. Ryngaert argues that the compensation provided by banks and insurance companies to victims of Nazi actions can also be viewed as settlements in ATS type cases, but these cases concern very exceptional circumstances they involve existing bank accounts and insurance policies and so are less relevant to the issues usually discussed in the context of routing ATS corporate litigation. It is also important to note, as will be elaborated upon further, that in order to facilitate the compensation schemes in relation to Nazi era claims agreements between governments were required.

[10]   The leading example is the payment of more than 89 billion dollars by Germany to Jewish victims of Nazi atrocities, based on legal bilateral frameworks between Germany and relevant governments. M. Eddy, 'For 60th Year, Germany Honors Duty to Pay Holocaust Victims', *New York Times*, 17 November 2012.

2.1. US LITIGATION AGAINST CORPORATIONS

Origins of litigation for allegations of corporate abuse in US courts can be traced to the 1789 Alien Tort Statute (ATS) thought to allow plaintiffs, of US or non-US residency or citizenship to sue corporations for actions perpetrated outside the US.[11] While the idea of using ATS is only few decades old, approximately 180 such suits have since been filed.[12]

Right at the outset, we note the very important and relatively recent development in *Kiobel*, where the US Supreme Court clarified, in 2013, that as a general rule the ATS applies only if there is a sufficient connection between the claims and alleged violations and the US.[13] This precedent arose many questions, particularly what should, or would, be considered sufficient connection.

One possibility is that a corporation is registered in the US, and the other is the existence of a US subsidiary. Today, these possibilities are unclear; recently a US Court of appeals ruled that for the ATS to apply it does not suffice that a corporations be registered in the US but there must be a link between the acts abroad and US operations, [14] and the US Supreme Court, also somewhat recently, did not address the subsidiary question despite expectations.[15]

These developments, notwithstanding the fact that litigation against corporations is still an option in the US, albeit an increasingly limited one,[16] leading to the question of whether such litigation facilitates remedies, and even if that is the rare case, at what price.

The ATS scenario is usually simple and the legal questions, putting aside the now crucial question of the sufficient connection, not complicated. The process begins when a victims group sues in a US federal court for alleged violations occurring outside the US. Such was the case in the *Vietnam Association for Victims of Agent Orange* case, where Vietnamese victims of chemical weapons used by

---

[11] A.O. Skyes, 'Corporate Liability for Extraterritorial Torts Under the Alien Tort Statute and Beyond: An Economic Analysis' (2012) 100 *The Georgetown Law Journal* 2161, 2166–2167.

[12] M.D. Goldhaber, *supra* n. 8, p. 129.

[13] *Kiobel v. Royal Dutch*, 569 U. S. ____ (2013), p. 14.

[14] *Cardona v. Chiquita*, No. 12–14898, U.S. Court of Appeals for the Eleventh Circuit, p. 10, 24 July 2014.

[15] *Daimler v. Bauman*, 571 U. S. ____ (2013), 14 January 2014. The court instead created criteria for defining when a corporation would be considered a US subsidiary for a foreign company for the purposes of jurisdiction but did not answer the question of whether if a corporation be determined as a subsidiary will that be sufficient for an ATS claim to survive if the acts took place abroad.

[16] M. Lederman, 'Kiobel Insta-Symposium: What Remains of the ATS?', *Opinio Juris*, 19 April 2013, available at: http://opiniojuris.org/2013/04/18/kiobel-insta-symposium-what-remains-of-the-ats (accessed 7 May 2013). See also the analysis of the dissenting opinion, by Judge Martin in the Chiquita case; a prior conflicting decision by the Court of Appeals for the Fourth Circuit, *Shimari v. Caci*, 30 June 2014, and the arguments for using state, rather than federal, courts for ATS type claims as elaborated in R.P. Alford, 'Human Rights After Kiobel: Choice of Law and the Rise of Transnational Tort Litigation' (2014) 63 *Emory Law Journal* 1089.

the US during the Vietnam War sued the weapons' manufacturer.[17] The court then discusses whether the alleged violations meet ATS standards,[18] laid down by *Sosa*,[19] i.e. violation of any well-defined universally accepted international law rule,[20] and proceeds to decide the case. In *Victims of Agent Orange* both the district and appeal courts determined that the alleged claims do not meet the *Sosa* level.[21]

This result reflects many ATS decisions.[22] Supposedly these outcomes might lead us to conclude that making ATS litigation more effective necessitates relaxing the standards to determine that a direct corporate act, or aiding and abetting (like the *Presbyterian Church of Sudan* case,[23] where it was alleged that an energy company assisted the government with genocide), violates universally accepted international law norms.[24] This approach aligns itself with those viewing courts as an appropriate forum to address legitimate victims' expectations.[25] It could also enhance the civil society's capacity to enforce international criminal law, on the argument that enforcement is not solely for states or intergovernmental bodies.[26]

Legalistically this might be true, even the latter global governance type argument, but ATS corporate litigation also includes political questions.[27] While political elements should not prevent victims from seeking redress, in ATS litigation such elements could determinately affect all involved, including victims.

---

17   *Vietnam Association for Victims of Agent Orange v. Doe Chemical* 373 F. Supp. 2d 7, *18; 2005 U.S. Dist. LEXIS 3644.

18   *Vietnam Association for Victims of Agent Orange v. Doe Chemical,* 373 F. Supp. 2d 7, *18; 2005 U.S. Dist. LEXIS 3644, p. 17. The court would discuss if the claims correspond with the requirements of the ATS even when government defence contractors are the defendants.

19   *Sosa v. Alvarez-Machain,* 124 S. Ct. 2739 (2004).

20   *Sosa v. Alvarez-Machain,* 124 S. Ct. 2739 (2004). The court defined ATS based claims as available when the international norms in question are specific, universal and obligatory at a minimum.

21   *Vietnam Association for Victims of Agent Orange v. Doe Chemical,* 373 F. Supp. 2d 7, *18; 2005 U.S. Dist. LEXIS 364, p. 17; 90 United States Court of Appeals for the Second Circuit, Docket No. 05-1760-cv, *In re 'Agent Orange' Product Liability Litigation,* 22 February 2008, p. 26.

22   M.D. Goldhaber, *supra* n. 8, pp. 137–149.

23   *Presbyterian Church of Sudan v. Talisman Energy, Inc.,* 582 F.3d 244, 259 (2d Cir. 2009).

24   One example is the suggestion to frame aiding and abetting for corporations as direct complicity for abuse, by arguing that corporations are libel through instigation, joint cooperation endeavours, procurement and conspiracy. T.F. Massarani, 'Four Counts of Corporate Complicity: Alternative Forms of Accomplice Liability Under the Alien Tort Claims Act' (2006) 38 *New York University Journal of International Law and Politics* 46.

25   C. Ryngaert, 'Finding Remedies for Historical Injustices: Dealing with Organizations and Corporations', Working Paper No. 38, January 2010, Leuven Center for Global Governance Studies, p. 19.

26   L. Malone, 'Enforcing International Criminal Law Violation with Civil Remedies: The U.S. Alien Tort Claims Act', in C. Bassiouni (ed.), *International Criminal Law – International Enforcement,* 3rd ed. (Leiden: Brill Publisher, 2008), p. 421.

27   As the US Supreme Court Justice Antonio Scalia noted deciding ATS claims 'directly into confrontation with the political branches'. *Sosa v. Alvarez-Machain* 542 U.S. 692, 748 (2004).

The ATS square includes four main corners and interests which should be considered when analysing ATS litigation. The four are: victims (plaintiffs); corporations (defendants); the forum state government; and the government where the corporation is registered (home state). In the US this is especially relevant as the US system allows interested parties to file positions to the courts (amicus briefs),[28] and the courts routinely ask the US government to submit statements of interests (SOI) on US foreign policy. The government can play an adjudicative role, recommending to the court what its decisions should be, provide factual information, for example a diplomat's accreditation, or present its interpretation of a statute relevant to foreign policy.[29]

When considering the ATS square it is vital to acknowledge the fifth element, the government of the state where events took place, apparent in in the analysis of each of the four corners. For our purposes we do not include the 'local' state in the ATS square, because its interests are linked to the political situation in each case, and as ATS cases demonstrate the local government's position can be forever changing due to political transitions.[30]

Aiming to illustrate different political implications, one illustrative south east Asia example is *Sarei*, where residents of an island in Papua New Guinea (PNG) sued mining companies (hereinafter: Rio Tinto) in a California federal court alleging their involvement in abuses by the PNG government.[31] There were many legal questions, but the most interesting are the acts and consequences of the ATS square corners.

Under this frame we briefly examine the different elements.

2.1.1. Victims

In *Rio Tinto*, victims have only sued in California and not in PNG courts. Victims also did not show they attempted suit in UK and Australia, the home states,[32] even tough defendants did not object to such litigation.[33] Apart from cases involving US companies this kind of choice is typical of ATS cases due to the benefits the US

---

[28] For an elaboration on the effect of Amicus Briefs on the US Supreme Court decision making process see P.M. Collins, *Friends of the Supreme Court: Interest Groups and Judicial Decision Making* (New York: Oxford University Press, 2008).

[29] P.B. Rutledge, 'Samantar and Executive Power' (2011) 44(1) *Vanderbilt Journal of Transnational Law* 893.

[30] In the *Sarei* case (to be elaborated upon further), the Papua New Guinea government first requested the US State Department to prevent a suit filed against Rio Tinto, in relation to events in the country, from progressing and after a few years, probably due to a change in government, asked the State Department to allow the suit to move forward. 'Wikileaks expose US & PNG position on Bougainville case against Rio Tinto', *Minds and Communities*, 12 September 2011, available at: www.minesandcommunities.org/article.php?a=11164 (accessed 14 May 2013).

[31] *Sarei v. Rio Tinto*, PLC 671 F.3d 736 (9th Cir. 2011).

[32] E. Sheargold, 'Advocating for Local Exhaustion: The Amicus Brief Submitted on Behalf of the U.K. and Australian Governments in Sarei v. Rio Tinto' (2012) 37 *Columbia Journal of Environmental Law*, Field Reports Archive.

[33] *Sarei v. Rio Tinto*, 221 F. Supp. 2d 1116, 1176 (C.D. Cal. 2002).

legal system provides for mass tort litigation,[34] and also because many US NGOs represent victims and are most comfortable in US courts.[35] Some also argue that US tort lawyers recognise ATS litigation as lucrative as the monetary amount demanded is substantial and they work on contingency.[36]

Acknowledging that *Rio Tinto*, like many other cases but not all, was not settled, the consequences are similar to other ATS litigation. Not only did the compensation not occur as the case was dismissed due to *Kiobel*,[37] but there are other possible effects: it will now be challenging to sue elsewhere;[38] the proceedings forced the US government to take a position against the victims;[39] and defendant companies have invested resources in litigation. Concerning the latter, the likelihood of willingness of Rio Tinto to compensate has probably greatly diminished.

Applying a cross-sectional perspective, in some exceptional circumstances, like *Sarei* and *Vietnam Association*, the local governments do not oppose the litigation.[40] This could imply, although it is hard to tell the relevancy for the cited examples, that the local government is using the litigation to avoid engaging with the corporations or with the governments of the home states even if compensation based on such engagement is more likely.

A final additional important element, broadly defining victims as citizens of developing countries, is that such litigation inherently reduces global corporate activity as corporations face increasing risk and cost of litigation resulting in fewer investments and less development and progress.[41]

---

[34]   Brief of the Governments of the United Kingdom of Great Britain and Northern Ireland and the Commonwealth of Australia as Amici Curiae in Support of the Defendants-Appellees/Cross-Appellants, *Sarei v. Rio Tinto*, No. 02–56256, 2011 WL 5041927 (9th Cir. Oct. 25, 2011), 2009 WL 8174961, p. 9–11. As cited in E. Sheargold, *supra* n. 32.

[35]   For elaboration on the role of civil society organisations in this context see L. Malone, 'Enforcing International Criminal Law Violation with Civil Remedies: The U.S. Alien Tort Claims Act' in C. Bassiouni (ed.), *International Crminal Law – International Enforcement*, 3rd edn. (Leiden: Brill Publisher, 2008), p. 412.

[36]   See L. Malone, 'Enforcing International Criminal Law Violation with Civil Remedies: The U.S. Alien Tort Claims Act', *International Society for the Reform of Criminal Law*, 2008, p. 30, available at: www.isrcl.org/Papers/2008/Malone.pdf (accessed 14 May 2013).

[37]   *Sarei v. Rio Tinto*, PLC, 722 F.3d 1109, 28 June 2013.

[38]   Courts in other forums are very likely to look at the US Supreme Court analysis on the issue, as reflecting the principle that there should be a strong connection between the forum state (where litigation is attempted) and the acts (including in cases where the suit is filed in the corporation home state).

[39]   See the Amicus Brief submitted by the US government in support of Rio Tinto to the Ninth Circuit Courts of Appeals, 28 September 2006, available at: www.state.gov/documents/organization/98376.pdf (accessed 23 August 2014).

[40]   In the *Agent Orange* case Vietnamese government officials reportedly supported the US litigation. M.F. Martin, 'Vietnamese Victims of Agent Orange and U.S.-Vietnam Relations', *CRS Reports for Congress, Congressional Research Service*, 29 August 2012, p. 30.

[41]   B. Reinsch, 'The Alien Tort Statute's impact on the business community', *World Commerce Review*, June 2012, p. 28, 29.

2.1.2. Global Corporations

The interests of defendant corporations are adversely affected by ATS litigation. The first real question is the legitimacy of such interests. Without doubt, corporations must be libel for abuse, whether directly or by knowingly assisting governments engaged in mass operations resulting in widespread criminal death and injury. This has been recognised by the Nuremberg WWII trials declaring corporations criminally responsible for Nazi atrocities (without convicting them).[42] There could be questions about what in corporate activity should be considered a war crime, but the general understanding is that if an act is defined as a war crime even corporations are liable.

The second question is more complex. Even if corporations are liable, should it be the role of a US court to adjudicate foreign corporations' activity?[43]

Framing the dilemmas this way, it is legitimate, even if controversial, to argue that corporations like Rio Tinto have a valid interest in being protected from a US court's decision if they have non, or minimal, US connections contrary to the far more legitimacy of being subject to an international tribunal such as Nuremberg,[44] or an Australian court for alleged abuse in PNG.

Returning to an earlier discussion, as more and more ATS litigation ensues, although this would possibly not be the case in light of *Kiobel*, so will the risk of operating in developing countries grow and corporations will refrain from doing so due to potential exposure to litigation.

2.1.3. Forum Government

In some ATS corporate cases the US government plays a role in the litigation, and even if it does not, its silence has significance. Using *Rio Tinto* as an example, we can arguably assume that the US government was pressured not only, as expected, by the PNG government,[45] but also by each of the other three ATS square corners,

---

[42] N. Gotzman, 'Legal Personality of the Corporation and International Criminal Law: Globalisation, Corporate Human Rights Abuses and the Rome Statute' (2008) 1(1) *Queensland Law Student Review* 49–50.

[43] Brief of the Governments of the United Kingdom of Great Britain and Northern Ireland and the Commonwealth of Australia as Amici Curiae in Support of the Defendants-Appellees/Cross-Appellants, *Sarei v. Rio Tinto*, No. 02–56256, 2011 WL 5041927 (9th Cir. Oct. 25, 2011), 2009 WL 8174961, p. 29.

[44] The Nuremberg tribunals were set up by the US, the United Kingdom, France and the USSR as parties to the London Agreement, *Trials of War Criminals Before the Nuremberg Military Tribunals*, p. XI–XII (1946–1949).

[45] Initially, the PNG government has objected to the litigation but later changes its positions. 'Wikileaks expose US & PNG position on Bougainville case against Rio Tinto', *Minds and Communities*, 12 September 2011, available at: www.minesandcommunities.org/article.php?a=11164 (accessed 14 May 2013).

NGOs representing victims, Australia and the UK,[46] and the corporations themselves to act according to their interests.

It could be that the US government had much criticism towards PNG for its actions, misgivings about the Chinese in relation to the internet surveillance and censorship ATS cases (*Zheng v. Yahoo! Inc.; Doe I v. Cisco Systems, Inc.*),[47]and objections to Burmese (Myanmar) policy in *Unocal*, relating to pipeline construction.[48] However, the US government would probably have preferred to choose when and how to react and not be compelled to do by the litigation. While in *Rio Tinto* the US argued before the court that ATS does not apply to foreign governments' treatment of local citizens,[49] its silence in other cases has significance when courts come to render ATS decisions.[50]

Exploring human rights related international litigation, which in the US does not only include litigation against corporations, but also against foreign sovereigns and current and former foreign officials, illustrates that the US government does not always wish to refrain from making a policy decision in such litigation. For example in cases submitted against foreign officials alleging human rights violations, the US government asked, and the US Supreme Court agreed, to continue to submit its positions on immunity from civil litigation.[51] Arguably, the reason could be that the US sees the decision on submission of the SOI, usually supporting dismissal, as a political tool to motivate states to act one way or another. However, even in such cases, the US seems to prefer that the case be dismissed on other procedural issues, rather than be required to submit an SOI or being asked by the court to do so.[52] This notwithstanding, the US government has in the past urged courts not to use international criminal law to impose civil liability on corporations, due to foreign policy reasons,[53] or national security, including litigation concerning alleged corporate abuse in Indonesia.[54]

---

[46]   As is presumed to have been the case in light of the briefs submitted by the governments to the court. Brief of the Governments of the United Kingdom of Great Britain and Northern Ireland and the Commonwealth of Australia as Amici Curiae in Support of the Defendants-Appellees/ Cross-Appellants, *Sarei v. Rio Tinto*, No. 02–56256, 2011 WL 5041927 (9th Cir. Oct. 25, 2011), 2009 WL 8174961.

[47]   *Zheng v. Yahoo! Inc.* No. C-08-1068 MMC, 2009 WL 4430297 (N.D. Cal. Dec. 2, 2009); *Doe I v. Cisco Sys., Inc.* Demand for Jury Trial and Class Action Complaint, No. CV 11–02449 PSG, 2011 WL 1338057 (N.D. Cal. May 19, 2011).

[48]   *Doe v. Unocal*, suit submitted in California District Court, 1997.

[49]   Amicus Brief submitted by the US government in support of Rio Tinto to the Ninth Circuit Courts of Appeals, 28 September 2006, available at: www.state.gov/documents/ organization/98376.pdf, p. 10.

[50]   In such cases, the courts are independent to make decisions concerning foreign policy, such as immunity of foreign officials, independently. *Yousuf v. Samantar*, No. 11–1479, 4th Cir. (2012).

[51]   *Yousuf v. Samantar*, No. 11–1479, 4th Cir. (2012).

[52]   H. Koh, 'Foreign Official Immunity After Samantar: A United States Government Perspective' (2011) 44 *Vanderbilt Journal of Transnational Law* 1141, 1160.

[53]   US Amicus Brief, *Kiobel v. Royal Dutch*, No. 10–1491, US Supreme Court (submitted June 2012).

[54]   Letter from William H. Taft, Legal Advisor, Dept. of State to Judge Louis F. Oberdorfer, US District Court for D.C. 1 (Jul. 29, 2002), available at: http://ccrjustice.org/files/Doe%20v.%20

These kinds of arguments, not in the context of foreign officials' litigation, demonstrates that the forum state's interests can be disserved by allowing ATS corporate litigation.

Looking at the issue from a human rights perspective, bearing in mind the low success rate of ATS litigation, the conclusion does not necessarily have to be detrimental to the victim's rights. On the contrary, if ATS corporate litigation will be ultimately foreclosed,[55] the political pressure on the US to encourage compensation will increase.

2.1.4. Corporations' Home States

The fourth ATS square component are the home states. In the modern era, major corporations are integral to the political arena where they are based. Considering that such corporations employ thousands and substantially contribute to the home state economy, it is unsurprising that when they US litigation for alleged abuse corporations turn to their government for help.

These arguments explain why home states object to US universal civil jurisdiction over corporations. The question, like when discussing other ATS Square components, is whether such objections are legitimate. As the states themselves claim they are 'committed to the international rule of law, including the promotion of, and protection against violations of human rights'.[56] Building upon previous analysis, the argument is similar here. States can act according to these principles even without supporting US extraterritorial jurisdiction. This idea is supported by both legal and political reasoning.

The legal argument is that exercise of jurisdiction as applied by some US courts violates international law.[57] First, application of universal jurisdiction on a non-territorial basis for civil suits, with no effects on the forum state, is not based on international law or representative of state practice or customary international law.[58] Second, allowing ATS litigation encourages plaintiffs to conduct illegitimate forum shopping, circumventing legal frameworks in other states, including the

---

Exxon%20-%20US%20SOI%20July%202002.pdf (accessed 25 May 2013). The lawsuit was filed in relation to a suit against Exxon-Mobile.

[55]   Center for Justice and Accountability Press Release, *Kiobel v. Shell: Supreme Court Limits Courts' Ability to Hear Claims of Human Rights Abuses Committed Abroad – Courthouse Doors Remain Open to Cases with a Sufficient Link to the United States*, 27 April 2013, available at: http://cja.org/downloads/Kiobel%20Joint%20Press%20Release.4.17.13_1.pdf (accessed 25 May 2013).

[56]   Brief of the Governments of the United Kingdom of Great Britain and Northern Ireland and the Commonwealth of Australia, *Sarei v. Rio Tinto*, p. 1 (2011).

[57]   Brief of the Governments of the United Kingdom of Great Britain and Northern Ireland and the Commonwealth of Australia, *Sarei v. Rio Tinto*, p. 12 (2011).

[58]   Case Concerning the Arrest Warrant of 11 April 2000 (*Democratic Republic of the Congo v. Belgium*), separate opinion Higgins, Koijmans and Buergenthal, para. 48 (2002).

local and home states.[59] Litigation in home states can also bring compensation, including substantial settlement, and is in no way prohibitive to the success of litigation in the human rights context.[60] Third, it is inherently problematic for foreign defendants to conduct a defence in US courts, as well as for courts, and juries, to decide about foreign events.[61] US courts' ATS decision-making when only foreign plaintiffs and defendants are concerned shows lack of comity to the courts of both the local and home states.[62] Finally, home states argue that international law requires that before a forum court can hear a civil claim local remedies must be exhausted, and that there is no practice to the contrary in the context of civil tort claims for human rights abuse.[63]

The legal arguments above seem convincing, but could be controversial, and have sparked ongoing scholarly and judicial debate, likely to be intensified in *Kiobel*'s wake. However, and less controversial, is the political argument, mainly that when it comes to judging policies of a foreign state, whether the local or home state, courts cannot play a global policing role.[64] While some argue that universal criminal jurisdiction, under which courts are essentially allowed to indict foreign war criminals, proves otherwise,[65] such an argument ignores the political difference between universal criminal jurisdiction and civil jurisdiction. The difference lies in that when one state considers pursuing criminal proceedings against a foreign official, the official's home state can request to avoid them. In case of refusal then this is a legitimate political decision. In the universal civil jurisdiction realm, the foreign states involved can, and probably do, approach the forum state's government, but in a world of separation of powers and judicial independence, the forum state can only recommend dismissal and courts can choose whether to accept the recommendation.[66]

To conclude, looking at the different ATS square components – victims, corporations, forum states, and home states – reveals that, arguably, in cases when

---

[59]   Brief of the Governments of the United Kingdom of Great Britain and Northern Ireland and the Commonwealth of Australia, *Sarei v. Rio Tinto*, pp. 10–11 (2011).

[60]   For an analysis of litigation in the corporation home state in this context see R. Meeran, 'Tort Litigation against Multinational Corporations for Violation of Human Rights: An Overview of the Position Outside the United States' (2011) 3(1) *City University of Hong Kong Law Review* 1.

[61]   Brief of the Governments of the United Kingdom of Great Britain and Northern Ireland and the Commonwealth of Australia, *Sarei v. Rio Tinto*, pp. 11–12 (2011).

[62]   Brief of the Governments of the United Kingdom of Great Britain and Northern Ireland and the Commonwealth of Australia, *Sarei v. Rio Tinto*, pp. 10–12 (2011).

[63]   R. Waugh, 'Exhaustion of Remedies and the Alien Tort Statute' (2010) 28 *Berkeley Journal of International Law* 555, 569.

[64]   For an argument supporting such a role for US supreme courts in regards to corporations see J.A. Kirshner, 'Why is the U.S. Abdicating the Policing of Multinational Corporations to Europe?: Extraterritoriality, Sovereignty, and the Alien Tort Statute' (2012) 30 *Berkeley Journal of International Law* 259.

[65]   The Restatement (Third) of the Foreign Relations Law of the United States § 404 comment b.

[66]   Courts can, in some cases, disregard the position of the US government, including in ATS corporate cases and have done so, including in a case involving allegations against corporate activity in Indonesia. B. Stephens, 'Judicial Deference and the Unreasonable Views of the Bush Administration' (2008) 33 *Brooklyn Journal of International Law* 773, 794–780.

there are no settlements, ATS corporate litigation does not optimally correspond with any of their interests. Admittedly, litigation is a remedy with injurious results to defendants, and if they were the only ones hurt, then it would be more difficult to object to ATS litigation, but as this is not the case and such litigation seems to be more a placebo, then alternatives must be explored. One alternative might be similar litigation in non-US courts, but as will be elaborated, not only are there no solutions to the problems posed by the ATS square analysis but there is also no developed state practice of allowing mass tort claims for human rights abuse.

2.2. LITIGATION AGAINST CORPORATIONS IN NON-US COURTS

Litigation concerning allegations of human rights abuse, or violations of international law, in non-US courts usually does not involve the application of universal civil jurisdiction, virtually unknown outside the US.[67] While this was the way that ICJ justices perceived the situation, some still argue that universal civil jurisdiction exists. In 2007, for example, Amnesty International reported that countries like China and Burma apply universal civil jurisdiction.[68] However, as the report itself clarifies, such application follows a criminal conviction,[69] which would mean that the forum state need to first indict the corporation for human rights abuse, an almost non-existent practice. Such practice would be inherently problematic as it will again necessitate one state conducting criminal investigations into the affairs of the other.

Lacking universal civil jurisdiction, examples of non-US litigation include two distinct types. The first is home state litigation. Examples include direct injury cases, based on conventional tort litigation and causes, mainly negligence and breach of duty of care.[70] One example is an Australian suit filed by PNG residents against an Australian corporation for mining related damage.[71] Other examples include cases in EU courts, mainly for environmental-related damages in Africa and South America.[72] While such litigation sometimes succeeds, and there seem to have been relatively more cases of settlement than in ATS litigation, the need

---

[67] Case Concerning the Arrest Warrant of 11 April 2000 (*Democratic Republic of the Congo v. Belgium*), separate opinion Higgins, Koijmans and Buergenthal, para. 48 (2002).

[68] 'The Scope of Universal Jurisdiction', *Amnesty International,* July 2007, available at: www. amnesty.org/en/library/asset/IOR53/008/2007/en/641d0955-d37d-11dd-a329-2f46302a8cc6/ ior530082007en.pdf (accessed 26 May 2013).

[69] 'The Scope of Universal Jurisdiction', *Amnesty International,* July 2007, p. 7 (China), p. 8 (Burma).

[70] R. Meeran, *supra* n. 60.

[71] *Dagi v BHP* [1997] 1 VR 428. The case was settled and compensation granted to the victims with the involvement of the PNG government. G. Banks and C. Ballard (eds.), *The Ok Tedi Settlements: Issues, Outcomes and Implications* (Asia Pacific, 1997).

[72] R. Meeran, *supra* n. 60.

to establish direct links between the corporations and the damage and the lack of aiding and abetting provisions pose difficulties.

The second type of suits is more similar to ATS corporate litigation. In Canada, for example, Canadian corporations have been sued for alleged international law violations abroad. While some cases are ongoing such as a lawsuit filed by residents of Guatemala alleging direct involvement of a Canadian corporation in killings and rape incidents,[73] most Canadian cases failed for procedural reasons, mainly *forum non conveniens*,[74] according to which a cases should be heard where it is most convenient to litigate. There are those who argue that now Canadian courts can be open for such litigation, based on forum of necessity claims, when there is no local remedy,[75] but that has yet to be proven in practice.

A similar example of unclear case law also arises in Dutch experiences. In the Dutch context, a suit against *Royal Dutch Shell* in Netherlands failed to impose liability on a Dutch parent company for alleged environmental damage caused in Nigeria, although liability was imposed on the Nigerian subsidiary.[76] As in the common law examples, other than in the US, the claim was based on direct tort liability.

Concluding this section, we learn that while under certain circumstances litigation against corporation for abuse can succeed, the argument that it does not correspond with the interests of all stakeholders involved has some merit, acknowledging that litigation is always costly, even if victims themselves usually do not bear the cost, and inherently very time consuming. Considering that there are ways to compensate victims and at the same time preserve the interests of the other three corners of the ATS square (corporations, forum states and home states), as well as the interests of the local state, these avenues should be explored and the next two sections focus on two prominent examples, beginning with the OECD Guidelines for Multinational Corporations.

2.3. OECD GUIDELINES FOR MULTINATIONAL CORPORATIONS

The OECD (Organization for Economic Corporation and Development) is an intergovernmental organisation, with 34 member states, set up in 1961 to encourage development following WWII. The organisation's original intent was to create a cooperative economic framework to facilitate growth and development.[77]

---

[73] *Choc v. HudBay Minerals*; *Chub v. HudBay Minerals*; *Caal v. HudBay Minerals*, available at: www.chocversushudbay.com (accessed 26 May 2013).
[74] M.D. Goldhaber, *supra* n. 8, pp. 127, 135–136.
[75] *Ibid.*
[76] *Akpan v. Royal Dutch Shell Plc*, No. 337050/HA ZA 09-1580 (District Court of The Hague, Jan. 30, 2013). As cited in M.D. Goldhaber, *supra* n. 8, p. 134.
[77] 'OECD History', available at: www.oecd.org/about/history (accessed 26 May 2013).

The past decades have seen a shift in the OECD's mission and *modus vivendi* as member states realised that global actions of corporations from member states (mostly leading world economies) particularly in the developing world, can have potentially disastrous effects on growth. Against this background, the OECD shifted some of its focus to the private sector, concentrating first on international bribery,[78] and recently on corporate responsibility for human rights abuse as reflected by the OECD Guidelines.[79]

The OECD Guidelines are recommendations to the private sector in adhering countries, 34 OECD member states and additional states.[80] The recommendations are non-binding and subject to domestic laws,[81] but adhering states are expected to follow them. In 2011, the OECD adopted a new and updated human rights chapter, reflecting principles set by the United Nations and mainly the 'Protect, Respect and Remedy' Framework.[82] The Guidelines incorporate six basic principles, including direct responsibility for human rights abuse, avoiding contribution to violations, preventing abuse, respecting human rights, conducting due diligence in respect to contractors behaviour and remedying injuries.[83]

These principles are broad and lack specificity, as can be expected from any international drafting exercise,[84] but arguably they provide a good comprehensive framework for addressing violations. Like US and non-US litigation, they do seem at first a viable solution, negating the problem of privatisation of foreign policy and illegitimacy, as the Guidelines reflect the outcome of a deliberative process undertaken by OECD members with the involvement of private sector representatives.[85] However, remembering that we are seeking an effective solution for corporate abuse, with maximum chances of compensation and minimal injury to stakeholders, it is questionable whether these Guidelines are practical,

---

[78]   OECD Bribery in International Business Transactions, available at: www.oecd.org/corruption/ anti-bribery (accessed 26 May 2013).

[79]   OECD Guidelines for Multinational Enterprises, available at: www.oecd.org/daf/inv/mne/ (accessed 26 May 2013).

[80]   OECD Guidelines for Multinational Enterprises, available at: www.oecd.org/daf/inv/mne/ oecdguidelinesformultinationalenterprises.htm (accessed 26 May 2013).

[81]   'Commentary on the OECD Guidelines for Multinational Enterprices', *Guidelines for Multinational Enterprices: Recommendations for Responsible Business Conduct in a Global Context*, 25 May 2011, p. 17.

[82]   OECD Guidelines, p. 31.

[83]   OECD Guidelines, pp. 31–34.

[84]   See for example, in reference to peace agreements, but also true for the OECD Guidelines, Bell's definition of constructive ambiguity as '[t]he ambiguity is constructive because it enables parties to reach agreement. This is the language of "symbolic capture" aimed to articulate a compromise in terms that can mean different things to different people'. C. Bell, *On The Law of Peace, Peace Agreements and the Lex of Pacifactoria* (New York: Oxford University Press, 2008).

[85]   For a discussion of the extensive deliberation process leading up to the adoption of the rules, see B. Huerta Maglar, K. Nowrot and W. Yuan, 'The 2011 Update of the OECD Guidelines for Multinational Enterprices: Balanced Outcome or an Opportunity Missed', Martin Luther University Halle-Wittenberg, June 2011, available at: http://telc.jura.uni-halle.de/sites/default/ files/BeitraegeTWR/Heft112_0.pdf (accessed 28 May 2013).

acknowledging that the updated human rights chapter was only relatively recently adopted, and whether they best serve the interests of all involved.

Following in the footsteps of the litigation analysis, the main primary issue when it comes to reviewing the mechanisms is the likelihood of remedy. In the OECD Guidelines the organ responsible for enforcing its provisions are the states themselves, through their NCPs (government National Contact Points).[86] Briefly, the process is that a complaint against a corporation registered and operating in the NCP's jurisdiction is submitted, and the NCP decides how to proceed, including by contacting the NCP in the local state and corporations involved.[87] Examples include a complaint submitted to the Belgium NCP, concerning damages allegedly resulting from a dam, where the NCP met with the parties involved and tried unsuccessfully to mediate an agreed solution;[88] and a case alleging labour rights violations in Indonesia, where the German NCP conducted meetings between the parties leading to some remedial steps by the corporation.[89] Sometimes the NCP sends experts to examine the complaint in the local state. Such was the case with the complaint submitted to the Norway NCP regarding the establishment of a factory in the Philippines by a Norwegian corporation. The case was concluded by an NCP statement recommending the corporation on how to comply with the Guidelines.[90]

The main problem is that even following the 2011 update, NCPs have not been provided with powers to sanction offenders, even if the relevant corporation declared adherence. According to several studies, including those focusing on human rights-related complaints, although mainly pre-2011, the NCP process does not lead to monetary remedies. The only consequence is usually naming and shaming of those found guilty in violation without taking remedial steps.[91]

This outcome is not wholly insignificant, as a recent report about Unilever operations in Vietnam[92] has highlighted, but it does not provide direct remedy. Here too, as for litigation, suggestions to enhance the mechanism by expanding

---

[86]   OECD Guidelines, p. 68.
[87]   The NCPs are usually placed within government ministries responsible for international trade and foreign relations. For an updated list see: www.oecd.org/daf/inv/mne/NCPContactDetails. pdf (accessed 28 May 2013).
[88]   *Proyecto Gato v. Tractebel*, OECD Watch, available at: http://oecdwatch.org/cases/Case_35 (accessed 15 May 2013).
[89]   *CCC v. Adidas*, OECD Watch, available at: http://oecdwatch.org/cases/Case_27 (accessed 15 May 2013).
[90]   *Framtiden i våre hender vs Intex Resources*, available at: http://oecdwatch.org/cases/Case_164 (accessed 15 May 2013).
[91]   B. Linder, K. Lukas and A. Steinkellner, 'The Right to Remedy: Extrajudicial Complaint Mechanisms for Resolving Conflicts of Interest between Business Actors and Those Affected by their Operations', Ludwig Boltzmann Institute of Human Rights, Vienna, April 2013, p. 16.
[92]   According to the report, steps were taken by Unilever (a major multinational consumer goods manufacturer) to reform operations in a factory in Vietnam following several complaints according to the OECD Guidelines in relation to the company's activities in India and Pakistan. See R. Wilshaw, L. Unger, D. Quynh Chi and P. Thu Thuy, 'Labour Rights in Unilever's Supply Chain – From Compliance to Good Practice – An Oxfam Study into Labout Issues in Unilever's Vietnam Operations and Supply Chains', Oxfam, January 2013, p. 86–88.

the option for sanctions were made, including one suggestion to provide NCPs with power to sanction offenders or to obligate states to withhold government subsidies and aid from them.[93] While this could be a possible solution, pursuing it will undoubtedly have implications to stakeholders' interests. Returning to the ATS square, if such steps are taken, corporations would hesitate to declare adherence; home states are likely to be less willing to accept complaints to the NCPs to avoid having to impose sanctions; and consequently victims will lose a venue for submitting complaints. Even if all this does not occur, and sanctions will be imposed by the NCP, this could potentially lead to the closing of operations in the local state, also a risk to be considered. This argument is circular, but it reflects potential realities.

Another proposal is to obligate states to be subject to NCP peer review, where two member or adhering states would review a third,[94] today a voluntary undertaking,[95] as the OECD routinely utilises peer review. [96] The problem here is again that states are likely to object, as it will be an unprecedented use of a complete peer review mechanism in the human rights context.[97] Inherently a decision to sanction a corporation operating in another country, especially when the complaints concern corporations providing services to foreign governments, is adjudication, albeit by the executive authority, of the foreign state's policy. One recent example is the complaint by NGOs to the UK and German NCPs against corporations allegedly supplying spyware software to the Bahrain government.[98]

Assuming that despite these problems, enforcement mechanisms would work, the use of the Guidelines is still problematic.

First, even today, when the Guidelines lack enforcement mechanisms, and this will be even more true if they have such powers, adhering states can, and some argue that this is the reality, see them as an alternative to enacting legislation to

---

The report is available at: www.oxfam.org/sites/www.oxfam.org/files/rr-unilever-supply-chain-labor-rights-vietnam-310113-en.pdf (accessed 8 June 2013).

[93] E. Oshionebo, 'The OECD Guidelines for Multinational Enterprises as Mechanisms for Sustainable Development of Natural Resources: Real Solutions or Window Dressing?' 17(2) *Lewis & Clark Law Review* 545, 587.

[94] B. Linder, K. Lukas and A. Steinkellner, *supra* n. 91, p. 26.

[95] OECD MNE Guidelines website: www.oecd.org/daf/inv/mne/ncps.htm (accessed 1 June 2013).

[96] See for example the OECD Convention on Combatting Bribery of Foreign Public Officials in International Business Transactions. OECD Working Group on Bribery website: www.oecd.org/corruption/countrymonitoringoftheoecdanti-briberyconvention.htm (accessed 1 June 2013).

[97] In 2006, a 'partial' version of peer review concerning human rights was adopted by the UN Human Rights Council concerning human rights compliance, according to which states do not conduct reviews on other states but are subject to questions from other states on implementation of human rights treaties. For elaboration see: 'A Practical Guide to the United Nations' Universal Periodic Review (UPR)', Human Rights Project at the Urban Justice Center, January 2010, available at: www.hrpujc.org/documents/UPRtoolkit.pdf (accessed 1 June 2013).

[98] Our OECD complaint against Gamma International and Trovicor, February 2013, available at: www.privacyinternational.org/blog/our-oecd-complaint-against-gamma-international-and-trovicor (accessed 7 June 2013).

---

regulate exterritorial corporate conduct.[99] Creating the Guidelines themselves, as a declaratory tool and not a treaty, allows governments to not to have enacted obligatory statutory provision on the one hand, and presenting commitment in support of observance of human rights by corporation on the other,[100] and this without taking necessary steps to deal with the phenomenon.

Second, and here lies an important similarity to the consequences of ATS and non-US corporate litigation, we again face the political issue. In some cases complaints to the NCPs, even before the updated human rights chapter, do not relate to direct violations by corporations but to the operation of a corporation in the context of a political situation. In this type of complaint both the corporation and the NCP state where the complaint has been filed are in a problematic situation.

In 2008 a German NGO complained against Volkswagen for promoting the Olympic Games in China, alleging that by doing so the corporation supported human rights violations.[101] The German NCP dismissed the case on procedural grounds, but the associated problems are obvious: by approaching the NCP, the NGO has compelled the German government to make a policy decision on the Chinese situation, with any decision reflecting on the bilateral relationship. For Volkswagen, we can assume, the complaint was disturbing as the only way to prevent it would have been for the corporation to assess China's policies and to make a politically based decision, as no specific human rights breach was alleged. A similar analysis can be made of a complaint to the Norwegian NCP concerning activities of a Norwegian corporation in Western Sahara, which included references to the domestic political situation in a conflict area under dispute for many years (even if the Norwegian NCP has accepted the case).[102]

The analysis of the OECD Guidelines and the examples as well as the fact that in many instances there have been no remedial steps or compensation,[103] reveals that even if the Guidelines would be made more effective by including enforcement mechanism, problems will remain. Briefly exploring the interest of stakeholders, we realise that this mechanism too, like litigation, cannot, inherently, serve as a true remedy. Acknowledging that in some aspects the Guidelines are better suited to the international legal political framework than litigation, as the

---

[99]   I. Cisar, 'OECD Multinational Enterprises Guidelines: Moving from Voluntary Code to the "Hard" Obligations', *COFOLA 2011: the Conference Proceedings*, 1st edn. (Brno: Masaryk University, 2011).

[100]   Some argue that this commitment has a great value, see for example H. Keller, 'Corporate Codes of Conduct and their Implementation: The Question of Legitimacy' in R. Wolfrum and V. Röben (eds.), *Legitimacy in International Law* (Berlin: Springer, 2008), pp. 219, 231.

[101]   *Gesellschaft für bedrohte Völker v. Volkswagen*, OECD Watch, available at: http://oecdwatch. org/cases/Case_185, (accessed 15 May 2013).

[102]   'Initial Assessment: Norwegian Support Committee for Western Sahara vs. Sjovik AS (Sjovik Africa and Sjovik Morocco)', *OECD NCP Norway*, available at: www.oecd.org/daf/inv/ mne/49867514.pdf. (accessed 15 May 2013).

[103]   B. Linder, K. Lukas and A. Steinkellner, *supra* n. 91, pp. 25–26. See also Appendix 2: OECD Guidelines – Specific Instances (5/2001–6/2011) describing the outcomes of complaints to the NCPs.

guidelines are subject to domestic law in the NCP state,[104] it could still be argued that unfortunately they are a placebo, rather than a remedy, even if sometimes a very good placebo serving as a simple platform for making complaints.

One major source for the development of the human rights chapter of the OECD Guidelines are the 2011 United Nations Guiding Principles on Business and Human Rights, and the analysis now explores their capacity to pose an alternative to the mechanisms discussed so far.

3. UNITED NATIONS GUIDING PRINCIPLES ON BUSINESS AND HUMAN RIGHTS

In March 2011, following extensive work, John Ruggie, UN Special Representative on Business and Human Rights submitted the UN Guiding Principles (hereinafter: the Principles) to the UN Human Rights Council. The 31 principles aim at interpreting existing international law for implementation by states, corporations and international organisations.[105] The Principles include vague and principled provisions alongside instructions on how to ensure that corporations prevent human rights abuse in domestic and foreign operations, and at the same time create mechanism to ensure remedies through judicial and non-judicial venues. Ruggie describes the Principles as including three basic tenets: 'protect, by the state, respect, by the corporation and remedy, to be accessed by victims'.[106]

The Principles were endorsed in 2011 and a Working Group was set up for an initial three year duration to explore means and ways to promote implementation.[107] Unlike litigation and the OECD Guidelines, the Principles are a recent instrument and it is difficult to know whether they would be successful. Bearing this in mind, it is still helpful to explore the Principles' implications aiming to understand future directions.

The main criticism directed at the Principles, similar to the arguments concerning the OECD Guidelines, relates to the lack of embodied review or enforcement.[108] The Principles in themselves do not refer to consequences

---

[104]   'Commentary on the OECD Guidelines for Multinational Enterprises', OECD Guidelines, p. 17 (2011).

[105]   J. Ruggie, 'Report of the Special Representative of the Secretary- General on the issue of human rights and transnational corporations and other business enterprises', A/HRC/17/31, 21 March 2013.

[106]   Micheal Connor, 'Business and Human Rights: Interview with John Ruggie', *Buisness and Ethics: The Magazine of Corporate Responsibility*, 30 October 2011, available at:http://business-ethics.com/2011/10/30/8127-un-principles-on-business-and-human-rights-interview-with-john-ruggie (accessed 7 June 2013).

[107]   Operative paragraph 6, Res. 17/4 Human rights and transnational corporations and other business enterprises, A/HRC/RES/17/4, 6 July 2011.

[108]   'The U.N. Guiding Principles on Business and Human Rights Analysis and Implementation', Kenan Institute for Ethics at Duke University, 2012, p. 8. See also Chapter 1 of this volume by Surya Deva.

of breach, by either states or corporations. They also do not include any mechanism for individual complaints against corporations, which according to one commentator was considered during the drafting of the resolution on the Working Group.[109] In this context many ideas for providing the Principles with binding force have been suggested, such as setting up the Principles as a treaty,[110] and linking the Principles to other existing U.N. human rights monitoring mechanisms.[111] An additional suggestion could be to require countries to recognise expansive judicial remedies, including universal civil jurisdiction, returning to the litigation analysis.

The ideas greatly vary, but they all call for stricter and more obligatory norms. Admittedly, any step would make the Principles more effective. However, as was clear regarding the OECD Guidelines, any additional enforcement component in the Principles will be a step further from the international consensus they reflect.[112] If the result of enhancing the rules is likely to be that fewer states and fewer corporations adhere, the Principles' actual relevance and effectiveness will diminish. This will be true even if the goal is not necessarily to provide specific remedies but to serve as a platform for commitment to corporate human rights compliance.

Complementing the criticism on a lack of an enforcement mechanism, some also argue that the drafters choose to reflect minimum standards of human rights compliance rather than aiming to achieve higher ones.[113] Other than the obvious consequence, i.e. that corporations would fail to observe elevated standards, there is also the risk that corporations would declare adherence and use this as a shield from any grievances against them. One example is the declaration by a Canadian corporation to the UN Human Rights Commissioner in which it urges her to not accept as true allegations against it in relation to its PNG activities, arguing that the corporation adheres to the Principles and that if the Commissioner acts upon the allegations, this could deter other corporations from adhering to the Principles.[114]

---

[109]   C. Marquez Carrasco, 'The United Nations Mandate on Business and Human Rights: Future Lines of Action', *Revista de Estudios Jurídicos* No. 12/2012 (Segunda Época) ISSN 1576–124X. Universidad de Jaén (Spain), p. 17.

[110]   For a discussion of this idea and the consensus required see P. Simons, 'International law's invisible hand and the future of corporate accountability for violations of human rights' (2012) 3(1) *Journal of Human Rights and the Environment* 5, 41–42.

[111]   'The U.N. Guiding Principles on Business and Human Rights Analysis and Implementation', Kenan Institute for Ethics at Duke University, 2012, p. 9.

[112]   J. Ruggie, *supra* n. 105, p. 5.

[113]   R.C. Blitt, 'Beyond Ruggie's Guiding Principles on Business and Human Rights: Charting an Embracive Approach to Corporate Human Rights Compliance' (2012) 48 *Texas International Law Journal* 34, 47.

[114]   Barrick Gold Letter, 22 March 2013, available at: www.business-humanrights.org/media/documents/company_responses/barrick-letter-to-un-high-commissioner-re-porgera-22-mar-2013.pdf (accessed 18 May 2013).

The Principles and associated mechanism are relatively recent but there are already several developments providing insight to future practice, although things can change. One such development is the conduct of the Working Group,[115] comprised of five international independent experts. While calls for an expanded mandate for the Working Group have been rejected by the Human Rights Council member states,[116] its initial activities indicate a different practice. In its report on the first country visit to Mongolia, issued in April 2013, the Working Group made expansive conclusions and recommendations to conduct an extensive overhaul to the legal system, alongside many additional references to the need of a structural change to promote corporate human rights compliance.[117] Additional recommendations were made to corporations, but these were vaguer, although still extensive.[118] Somewhat similar patterns emerged from the Working Group's US visit, as the concluding statement to the visit included a relatively lengthy list of issues for concern.[119] To some extent, these indications of methodology are positive signs for future use and implementation of the Principles. However, the reality of such far-reaching recommendations is that they are not likely to be considered as binding by relevant stakeholders, rendering the effectiveness of the Working Group and the Principles far from optimal. This notion is not unique, reflecting a general problem for recommendations by independent experts in the human rights arena.[120]

Like litigation and the OECD Guidelines, we see that while the Principles have potential to provide remedy to corporate abuse and are a very progressive and positive development, they still have placebo characteristics, even acknowledging

---

[115] 'A Call for Action to Better Protect the Rights of Those Affected by Business-Related Human Rights Abuses', Amnesty International, 14 June 2011, available at: www.amnesty.org/ar/library/asset/IOR40/009/2011/en/0ba488bd-8ba2-4b59-8d1f-eb75ad9f3b84/ior400092011en.pdf (accessed 18 May 2013).

[116] 'A Call for Action to Better Protect the Rights of Those Affected by Business-Related Human Rights Abuses Amnesty International', Amnesty International, 14 June 2011, available at: www.amnesty.org/ar/library/asset/IOR40/009/2011/en/0ba488bd-8ba2-4b59-8d1f-eb75ad9f3b84/ior400092011en.pdf (accessed 18 May 2013); J.H. Knox, 'The Ruggie Rules: Applying Human Rights Law to Corporations' in R. Mares (ed.), *The UN Guiding Principles on Businesses and Human Rights – Foundations and Implementations* (Leiden: Martinus-Nijhoff Publications, 2012), p. 51, 67.

[117] Human Rights Council, 'Report of the Working Group on the issue of human rights and transnational corporations and other business enterprises, Addendum, Visit to Mongolia', A/HRC/23/32/ADD.1, 2 April 2013, p. 21–24.

[118] *Ibid.*, p. 24.

[119] OHCHR, 'Statement at the end of visit to the United States UN Working Group on Business and Human Rights', Washington DC, 1 May 2013, available at: www.ohchr.org/EN/NewsEvents/Pages/DisplayNews.aspx?NewsID=13284&LangID=E (accessed 7 June 2013).

[120] The United States, for example, considers any recommendations made by human rights treaty expert bodies as non-binding although there is a process enabling relevant authorities to explore the possibility. See T.J. Melish, 'From Paradox to Subsidiarity: The United States and Human Rights Treaty Bodies' (2008) 34 *Yale Journal of International Law* 389, 443.

that the Principles were never meant to be a panacea or a silver bullet,[121] but only a starting point.

At this stage of the analysis the picture seems to be that all the four available tools (US litigation, non-US litigation, OECD Guidelines, UN Guiding Principles) provide doubtful remedies for corporate abuse. However, this does not mean that the picture is confusing. All of these tools relate to each other, as highlighted by the UN Working Group statement following the US visit which discussed both the litigation aspects, including the decision in *Kiobel* not to apply the ATS exterritorially when there is no US connection,[122] and the OECD Guidelines. The question is if they really can work, and the analysis has shown that is usually not been the case so far.

4. POLITICAL INTER-STATE SOLUTIONS – LOOKING INTO THE PAST TO SUGGEST A WAY FORWARD

The problem of mass human rights abuse is unfortunately not something new. History shows us that there have been many instances where innocent civilian victims have been injured and killed as a result of direct and intentional attacks and collateral damage in times of conflict or as a result of mistakes. In attempting to find a suggested model for finding remedy to corporate human rights abuse it is worthwhile to briefly consider existing examples of compensation to individual victims to see in what way we can apply these models to modern situations of corporate human rights abuse. As will be discussed, such application will use as its basis the existing tools analysed so far in the paper, and in the interest of harmonisation the solution should correspond with the spirit of UN Principles as well as with the mechanisms of the OECD Guidelines. We should also bear in mind that our aim should be, at this stage, to find solutions for mass human rights abuse, in the hope that these solution will have a positive effect on the more minor cases. At the same time any solution would have to correspond in the most optimal way with the interests of all stakeholders involved.

Examples for inter-state political solutions and mass compensation schemes are extremely varied. For illustration, these include: payment by the US of $32.5 million to the Chinese government and families of Chinese victims in the accidental bombing of the Chinese Embassy in Belgrade as part of the NATO campaign in the Balkan crisis;[123] the United States' payment for reparations for

---

[121] As Ruggie himself noted, see J. Ruggie, 'The corporate responsibility to respect human rights', *World Petroleum Council: Official Publication*, 2010, p. 32, available at: www.world-petroleum. org/docs/docs/publications/2010yearbook/P30-32_John_Ruggie.pdf (accessed 7 June 2013).

[122] OHCHR, *supra* n. 119.

[123] C. Sui, 'China Unmoved by CIA Sanctions Over Embassy Attack', *Washington Post*, 11 April 2000, at A24.

Iraqi and Afghani civilian casualties (killed by US forces) between the period of 2003–2006, amounting to approximately $30 million;[124] and the payments of approximately $200,000 by the Australian government for Iraqi civilians injured or dead at the hand of Australian forces stationed in Iraq.[125]

Reviewing these examples, the question of their relevance to our discussion comes to mind, as they concern state-to-state events. For one, in almost all of these cases the compensating states did not assume legal responsibility to the damages caused, and if applied to corporations this could be against the spirit of the UN Principles and OECD Guidelines. However, not only do these examples represent a practice which can be adopted for mass human rights violations, but this kind of methodology of political resolution has in fact been also used, although unfortunately to a much lesser extent, in the context of corporations, albeit not in the same circumstances as usually contemplated when we consider modern cases of corporate human rights abuse.

The first example, which is important, even if less directly relevant, is the provision by the US of $63.4 million to Vietnam for projects related to remedying damage resulting from the use of Agent Orange during in the Vietnam war.[126] As was discussed earlier the use of the chemicals was linked to one particular US corporation, so these payments, and future ones, can arguably be viewed as an inter-state mechanism to solve issues related to corporate human rights abuse. Although there seems to be no specific agreement between the states and the compensation, this remains a controversial issue far from any final resolution.[127]

The second example is the agreement, in 2009, of the Shell Corporation to pay $15.5 million in relation to deaths of protestors in against its operations in Nigeria. Although there was no apparent admission of guilt or responsibility, the payment was considered to be one of the largest payments made in recent years by corporations for human rights abuse.[128] Acknowledging that the payment resulted from UK and US litigation against Shell,[129] brining some support for the beneficial use of court proceedings, there seem to be no reason why this payment should not have been made at the first place. According to Shell itself, it is committed to making payment when causing environmental damage at the

---

[124]   J. Ryan, 'Condolence payments to Afghans total millions', *Army Times*, 23 January 2012, available at: www.armytimes.com/article/20120123/NEWS/201230311/Condolence-payments -Afghans-total-millions (accessed 8 June 2013).

[125]   G. Robinson, 'Australia pays $216,000 to injured Iraqis', *Brisbane Times*, 29 February 2008. Some of the recipients of the payments (awarded $7,770 for injuries resulting from rounds of ammunition fired at their vehicle in Baghdad by Australian soldiers) filed a suit in an Australian court, as the Australian government claims it bears no responsibility or liability to the damages. See M. McKena, 'Family Shoy by Diggers Sues Government', *The Australian*, 28 February 2008.

[126]   M.F. Martin, 'Vietnamese Victims of Agent Orange and U.S.-Vietnam Relations', *CRS Report for Congress, Congressional Research Service*, 29 August 2012, p. 8.

[127]   *Ibid.*, pp. 29–30.

[128]   E. Piknigton, 'Shell pays out $15.5m over Saro-Wiwa killing', *The Guardian*, 9 June 2009.

[129]   *Ibid.*

areas of its operation,[130] and this could, and should, be translated to concrete steps when other associated injury occurs.

The third example, which provides an additional crucial element of a model legal framework, are the mechanisms set up to ensure compensation for victims of Nazi era forced labour as well as life insurance policy holders and their survivors.[131] The underlying circumstances of the related events are cases of extreme human rights violations by corporations, but the principles of the solutions are relatively simple. The corporations make payments upon a certain legal structure and those who are entitled to them can make claims accordingly. Once there is will by all parties involved, the legal structures can then be created to facilitate the compensation process.

Today it is undisputed that corporations took part in the activities of the Nazi regime and the Holocaust where more than 6 million people met their death.[132] Additionally, alongside corporations actively taking place in the atrocities, insurance companies failed to pay life or health insurance policies taken out by victims, in many cases due to confiscation of policies and funds by the Nazi regime.[133] In the late 1990s, following attempted litigation in US courts, all of the stakeholders involved, from all of the four corners of the ATS square (victims, corporations, the forum state (the US) and the corporations' home states) as well as the host state (in this case it was the US and some other countries where Holocaust survivors and their relatives reside), got together and created a political mechanism for compensation based on a legal infrastructure.[134]

This framework, concluded in 2000, has been the subject of much scholarly debate,[135] but in the interest of brevity we mention two key elements: the 2000 Joint Statement,[136] and the agreements signed between the US and Germany,

---

[130]   Unsurprisingly, Shell views litigation as an obstacle to speedy compensation. See M. Sunmonu, 'Letter to the Financial Times from SPDC MD Mutiu Sunmonu', March 2012, available at: www.shell.com.ng/environment-society/our-response/mutius-letter.html (accessed 30 August 2014).

[131]   L. Adler, 'California's Holocaust Victim Insurance Relief Act and American Preemption Doctrine' (2003) 4(11) *German Law Journal* 1193, 1195–1196.

[132]   See for example: P. Hayes, 'Profits and Persecution: German Big Business and the Holocaust', United States Holocaust Memorial Museum Center for Advanced Holocaust Studies, J.B. and Maurice C. Shapiro Annual Lecture, 17 February 1998.

[133]   P. Belkin, K.A. Ruane and B. Webel, 'Holocaust-Era Insurance Claims: Background and Proposed Legislation', *Congressional Research Service*, 21 July 2011, pp. 2–4.

[134]   S.D. Murphy, *United States Practice in International Law Volume II: 2002–2004* (New York: Cambridge University Press, 2006), p. 97.

[135]   See for example: M.A. Ratner, 'The Settlement of Nazi-Era Litigation through the Executive and Judicial Branches' (2002) 20 *Berkeley Journal of International Law* 212; L. Adler and P. Zumbansen, 'The Forgetfulness of Noblesse: A Critique of the German Foundation Law Compensating Slave and Forced Laborers of the Third Reich' (2002) 39(1) *Harvard Journal on Legislation* 1; A. Drukin, 'Comment: The German Foundation Agreement: A Nonexclusive Remedy and Forum' (2008) 42 *University of California, Davis Law Review* 567.

[136]   'Joint Statement on occasion of the final plenary meeting concluding international talks on the preparation of the Foundation "Remembrance, Responsibility and the Future"', 17 July 2000, available at: www.state.gov/documents/organization/6530.doc (accessed 18 May 2013).

France and Austria.[137] The most interesting and relevant feature is that the Joint Statement, articulating the basic principle of the provision of compensation to victims, and their relatives, is also signed by the corporations themselves (the Foundation Initiative of German Enterprises) and the legal representatives of the victims.[138]

The legal framework establishing the compensation framework in this case included two main elements. First, the corporations all agreed to transfer substantial funds to a joint compensation fund, which would provide individual compensation according to agreed criteria, in some cases with the active involvement of victims' organisations.[139] Second, the US has declared that in the event of litigation in its courts, it would inform the courts of this arrangement and ask that cases be dismissed, though the courts are not obligated to accede to the request.[140] The technical components of the mechanism were quite complicated (exceptionally to such mechanisms),[141] but this did not prevent the fund from making payments amounting to approximately $10 billion dollars to compensate for Nazi era-related claims.[142]

The underlying circumstances of the Nazi era compensation framework were very unique and unprecedented. However, some elements can be considered as a potential basis for providing a remedy for corporate abuse in the modern context. Exploring the situation in Vietnam, for the purpose of illustration, we see in some

---

[137]   See 'Agreement between the United States of America and Germany, Treaties and Other International Acts Series 13104', Berlin, 17 July 2000, available at: www.state.gov/documents/organization/126984.pdf (accessed 8 June 2013); 'Agreement between the Government of the United States of America and the Government of France Concerning the Payments for Certain Losses Suffered During World War II', 18 January 2001, available at: www.state.gov/documents/organization/28994.pdf (accessed 8 June 2013); 'Executive Agreement between the Government of the United States and the Austrian Federal Government', 24 October 2000, available at: www.state.gov/documents/organization/6537.doc (accessed 8 June 2013).

[138]   'Joint Statement on occasion of the final plenary meeting concluding international talks on the preparation of the Foundation "Remembrance, Responsibility and the Future"', 17 July 2000, available at: www.state.gov/documents/organization/6530.doc (accessed 18 May 2013).

[139]   United States Statement of Interest, *Holocaust Victims v. Magyar, U.S. District Court Illinois*, No. 10-cv-1884 (submitted 18 February 2011), available at: www.docstoc.com/docs/150616901/38-Magyar-Nemzeti-Bank-Statement-of-Interest---US-Department-of (accessed 8 June 2013), pp. 3–7.

[140]   See for example Article 2(1) to the Agreement between the Government of the Federal Republic of Germany and the Government of the United States of America Concerning the Foundation 'Remembrance, Responsibility and the Future, 17 July 2000, available at: www.state.gov/documents/organization/126984.pdf (accessed 8 June 2013).

[141]   The procedural aspects of the mechanism regarding the German companies were established by the German Foundation Agreement, regulating the handling of claims by the International Commission on Holocaust Era Insurance Claims (ICHEIC), an organisation which included representatives of victims. The agreement is available at the ICHEIC website at: www.icheic.org/pdf/agreement-GFA.pdf (accessed 8 June 2013). Similar arrangements were made in regards to companies from Switzerland and Italy.

[142]   United States Statement of Interest, *Holocaust Victims v. Magyar, U.S. District Court Illinois*, No. 10-cv-1884 (submitted 18 February 2011), available at: www.docstoc.com/docs/150616901/38-Magyar-Nemzeti-Bank-Statement-of-Interest---US-Department-of (accessed 8 June 2013), p. 7.

cases allegations concerning human rights abuse are centred on labour conditions in the manufacturing field.[143] Tough political will on all sides will be required, but it is not far-fetched to envision that the home states, where the corporations are based, and the Government of Vietnam enter into agreements about setting up a framework to be used for compensation, while in parallel the corporations and the governments can declare that such an arrangement reflects the settlement of all claims. Such framework can also include a political commitment from all stakeholders to ensure the observance of human rights standards. This suggestion is of course not unique for Vietnam or the manufacturing sector, but can be applied, when appropriate, to any cases of abuse by foreign corporations of rights of domestic workers.

The advantages of this model are not only for the victims who can obtain compensation, but for all other stakeholders involved. Corporations which do not feel like they have been compelled to make compensation, and enjoy some form of protection from future litigation, and governments of both the state where events took place and the home state of the corporations, which have acted upon their own political will and policy, ensuring that the potential of political misuse of allegations of corporate abuse has been avoided.

The fourth example, and a relatively recent one, is the establishment, in November 2013, of the Raza Plaza trust fund to set up a mechanism for compensating families of victims and those injured in the collapse of a building housing garment factories in Dhaka, Bangladesh, due to the poor working conditions of the facility.[144] The fund, which is aimed at facilitating payments for damages resulting from the event, where 1,100 met their death and thousands more were injured, was set up as a joint project with participation of foreign companies receiving supply from the factories, the local Bangladesh Government and the International Labor Organization (playing a coordinating role) provides us yet another model to consider. Unlike the Nazi era claim model here the legal structure is much simpler, facilitating fast payments for those who can demonstrate direct damage or those dependents of deceased victims.[145] Another relatively unique feature is the commitment to abide by the terms of an international Convention, in the form of the ILO Convention No. 121, which regulates employment injury benefits.[146] The process of providing compensation

---

[143]   For some examples see: R. Wilshaw, L. Unger, D. Quynh Chi and P. Thu Thuy, *supra* n. 92; D. Hoang and B. Jones, 'Why do corporate codes of conduct fail? Women workers and clothing supply chains in Vietnam' (2012) 12 *Global Social Policy* 67.

[144]   'Understanding for a Practical Arrangement on Payments to the Victims of the Rana Plaza Accident and their Families and Dependants for their Losses', 20 November 2013, available at: www.ranaplaza-arrangement.org/mou/full-text, (accessed 26 August 2014).

[145]   For elaboration on the claims process, see: www.ranaplaza-arrangement.org/mou/claims (accessed 26 August 2014).

[146]   ILO Convention 121: Employment Injury Benefits Convention, 1964. It is interesting to note that Bangladesh has not ratified this convention, and that it has only been ratified by 24 states: www.ilo.org/dyn/normlex/en/f?p=1000:11300:0::NO:11300:P11300_INSTRUMENT_ID:312266 (accessed 26 August 2014).

is still ongoing, as the available funds stand, as of August 2014, at $17 million, received from a wide array of bodies including corporations which joined the fund after the initial arrangement to establish the fund. At the time of writing, the fund still does not have enough funds to cover all claims and there are relevant corporations which have yet to participate in the scheme,[147] but nonetheless this relatively quick political process (the fund was set up a few months after the disaster took place), encompassing all relevant stakeholders, including NGOs, demonstrates the great potential in this alternative model for compensation by foreign corporations for mass scale damage events.

The fifth example is interesting because unlike the first four it does not relate to *ex post* situations but to an *ex ante* process. Anglogold Ashanti, a global mining company, was engaged in mining operations in the African country of Mali. In order to proceed with mining operations in a certain area it was necessary to resettle villages in the vicinity of the mining area. Presumably in order to ensure that the process was undertaken in the most appropriate way it decided to take a leading and active role in the process, together with the local government, rather then risk violation of the rights of the local population. The programme, which involved resettlement coupled with compensation, in the period of 1996–2000, was based on a mechanism of payments to locals (to the sum of $10,000 for each village) based on evaluation of property determined by the local government, which accompanied the process throughout.[148] While the scheme was not devoid of problems and required constant efforts from all those involved, it does seem to have provided some model structure for corporations to follow,[149] even for the *ex post* cases which are the main focus of the chapter.

Admittedly, the advantages of the proposed mechanisms can also be their disadvantages. First and foremost, lack of political will of any or all of the stakeholders can be a serious obstacle to achieving a consensual agreement. Secondly, it could be argued that any action taken to limit the right to legal remedy in courts, if such limitation is included in the solution mechanisms, violates the legal remedy provisions of the UN Principles.[150] However, despite these disadvantages if we look to litigation, the UN Principles, and the OECD Guidelines, we see that ultimately the inter-state models can be much more conducive to compensation to victims, while at the same time can best correspond with the interests of other stakeholders. Despite this, one major hurdle is the fact that other than in the context of Nazi era claims this model has not been tried and tested. Considering that other mechanisms have yet to fulfil their promise there is

---

[147] C. O'Connor, 'These Retailers Involved In Bangladesh Factory Disaster Have Yet To Compensate Victims', *Forbes*, 26 April 2014.
[148] L. Placker Rubin, 'Using Communication and Consultation to Protect Human Rights During Village Resettlements' in *Embedding Human Rights in Business Practices* (United Nations Global Compact, 2013) p. 102.
[149] *Ibid.*, p. 109.
[150] Guiding Principle 26 (p. 23) in J. Ruggie, *supra* n. 105.

no reason why future research and development of the application of this model to specific situations of corporate human rights abuse will not bring about positive experiences and a true remedy. The model should not be applied independently of the OECD and UN rules, as well as some of the principles resulting from the litigation, but could potentially incorporate them. In any case, the momentum built in the past few years in the field of corporate human rights abuse can greatly facilitate and support the political will of all involved, rendering the chances of success of the new model potentially higher.

5.   CONCLUDING REMARKS

Corporate human rights abuse is hardly a new phenomenon, and the same is true of the perception that corporations can themselves be responsible for causing harm. What is a new and welcome development, due to the emergence of global governance, is that there is an ever-growing focus on creating tools to provide remedy for victims and to prevent future abuse. As the analysis has shown, existing tools have undoubtedly contributed to establishing the recognition that, like states, corporations too must abide by general notions of human rights compliance. These tools have also significantly raised awareness with victims of corporate abuse that they can demand remedy for their injuries. The problem, as the analysis uncovered, is that these tools, framed as a remedy, failed, for the most part, to fulfil their promise, and to some extent can be not only placebos but also 'poison pills' harming the interests of victims and the cause of preventing corporate human rights abuse. While there are suggestions to reform each of the tools discussed, it still seems that ultimately it will be worthwhile to explore new directions.

One such new direction is to use the model of inter-state solutions, including both victims and corporations in the process. It is hardly surprising that such a model has received little focus in scholarly debate on the issue, as scholars, lawyers and activists are, and maybe rightly so, inherently cynical about motivations of governments and corporations and the strong belief is that for obtaining remedy, non-consensual measures must be taken. However, recent developments proved just the opposite as both corporate and government actors have focused on the corporate human rights abuse issue and finding ways to solve it. Like other tools, the inter-state model will not be a panacea, and it might not even be possible for the smaller scale cases, but it does seem that efforts should be made to utilise it in the most widespread and difficult cases. It is always difficult for lawyers to step aside and let politicians, and in our case also corporate officials, do the work, but in this case it just might be that the better way is for the legal experts to provide legal supporting frameworks for country-level political solutions and for legal, non-consensual models to take a step back.

CHAPTER 3

ENSURING THE PROTECTION
OF THE ENVIRONMENT FROM
SERIOUS DAMAGE

Towards a Model of Shared Responsibility
between International Corporations
and the States Concerned?

Gentian ZYBERI*

1. INTRODUCTION

This chapter focuses on the issue of legal responsibility of multinational corporations for serious environmental damage caused by economic activity which represents a heightened risk of causing widespread, long-term and severe harm to the environment, namely oil pollution in the form of large oil spills and nuclear accidents in terms of ensuring nuclear safety and controlling nuclear waste management.[1] The term 'serious environmental damage' is used to denote

---

*   I am grateful to Ole Windahl Pedersen and Christina Voigt for their comments on an earlier draft. Any mistakes are my own. Comments are welcome at gentian.zyberi@gmail.com.

[1]   As John Ruggie has pointed out, the majority of alleged abuses happen in the extracting industry (oil, gas, mining); see J. Ruggie, Interim Report of the Special Representative of the Secretary-General on the issue of human rights and transnational corporations and other business enterprises, UN Doc. E/CN.4/2006/97 of 22 February 2006, no. 25. The oil spilled by damaged tankers, pipelines or offshore oil rigs causes serious damage to the ecosystems it enters, as for example the 1989 Exxon Valdez oil spill and the 2010 Deepwater Horizon oil spill. The environmental damage caused by nuclear power plant disasters is also very severe and long-term, as for example the Chernobyl Nuclear Power Plant disaster of 1986 and the Fukushima Daiichi nuclear disaster of 2011. While the Chernobyl nuclear disaster affected about 20 states, no legal proceedings have been brought before an international court about this considerable transboundary radioactive pollution. For more information on the Chernobyl nuclear disaster visit: http://news.bbc.co.uk/2/shared/spl/hi/guides/456900/456957/html/nn1page1.stm. See also the Chernobyl Forum: 2003–2005 Report, 'Chernobyl's Legacy: Health, Environmental and Socio-economic Impacts and Recommendations to the Governments

a threshold of environmental damage considered 'significant', 'serious', or above 'tolerable levels' in different relevant international instruments.[2] Different terms, as 'international corporations', 'transnational corporations', 'companies', 'business enterprises' and 'multinational enterprises', are used interchangeably in relevant international instruments and literature, as well as in this chapter.[3] Here the term describes companies whose economic activity takes place in two or more states and whose area of activity involves risk of causing serious environmental damage through oil pollution or nuclear contamination.

The environment is under considerable pressure from the economic activity of large and small international corporations, which eventually results in the gradual degradation of the landscape and ecosystems. The International Court of Justice (ICJ) has defined the environment as 'the living space, the quality of life and the very health of human beings, including generations unborn.'[4] It has been aptly noted that most threats to the environment are attributable to the activities of private entities operating on a state's territory.[5] Environmental damage has generally been defined to include four possible elements: (1) fauna, flora, soil, water and climatic factors; (2) material assets (including archaeological and cultural heritage); (3) the landscape and environmental amenity; and (4) the interrelationship between the above factors.[6] The work of the United Nations Compensation Commission (UNCC) has had important implications for the recognition of: (1) 'pure' ecological loss; (2) temporary loss of resource use; (3) loss valuation by modelling; and (4) compensation for irreparable loss.[7] In that sense, the regime of compensation for serious environmental damage has made

---

[ ] of Belarus, the Russian Federation and Ukraine', IAEA, April 2006, IAEA/PI/A.87 Rev.2/ 06–09181, available at: www.iaea.org/Publications/Booklets/Chernobyl/chernobyl.pdf. For more information on the Fukushima nuclear disaster see: www.guardian.co.uk/environment/ fukushima.

[2] See inter alia Article 1(2) of the 1992 Convention on the Protection and Use of Transboundary Watercourses (1992 Transboundary Watercourses Convention); Article 1(d) of the 1992 Convention on the Transboundary Effects of Industrial Accidents (1992 Convention on Industrial Accidents); Article 8(d) of the 1993 Convention on Civil Liability for Damage Resulting from Activities Dangerous to the Environment (1993 Lugano Convention). See also P. Sands and J. Peel, *Principles of International Environmental Law*, 3rd edn. (Cambridge University Press, 2012), pp. 708–711.

[3] For a general overview of the activity of transnational corporations see inter alia United Nations Conference on Trade and Development (UNCTAD), the Universe of the Largest Transnational Corporations (United Nations Publication, 2007), available at: http://unctad.org/en/Docs/ iteiia20072_en.pdf (UNCTAD, the Universe of the Largest Transnational Corporations).

[4] ICJ, *Legality of the Threat or Use of Nuclear Weapons* (Advisory Opinion), ICJ Reports 1996, p. 241, para. 29.

[5] P.N. Okowa, 'Environmental Dispute Settlement: Some Reflections on Recent Developments' in M. Evans (ed.), *Remedies in International Law: The Institutional Dilemma* (Oxford: Hart Publishing, 1998), p. 159.

[6] P. Sands, J. Peel and A. Fabra Aguilar, *Principles of International Environmental Law* (New York: Cambridge University Press, 2012), p. 700 and pp. 13–15.

[7] P.H. Sands, 'Environmental Damage Claims from the 1991 Gulf War: State Responsibility and Community Interests' in U. Fastenrath et al., *From Bilateralism to Community Interest: Essays in Honour of Bruno Simma* (Oxford: Oxford University Press, 2012), pp. 1250–1254.

considerable progress. Notably, environmental damage caused by oil pollution and nuclear accidents, which is the focus of this chapter, triggers a regime of strict liability under international law.

Generally, economic activity takes a considerable toll on the environment, leading to its degradation over time. Occasionally though, environmental damage occurs within a short period of time in the form of an industrial accident caused by human error or technological malfunction, as in the case of the April–July 2010 BP oil spill in the Gulf of Mexico or the Chernobyl nuclear disaster of April 1986. Such serious damage to the environment might also be set in motion by a natural disaster, as in the case of the nuclear plant disaster in Fukushima, Japan, in March 2011. Several inter-related questions arise in these situations, such as what are the legal obligations of transnational corporations with regard to serious environmental damage caused by their economic activity? How does civil liability on the part of these corporations relate to the responsibility of the host state *vis-à-vis* the affected population for ensuring reparations for environmental damage? Does the home state of an international corporation have any residual responsibilities with regard to preventing serious environmental damage in other states or in addressing liability issues in the aftermath of such damage? And, last but not least, what would be a *forum conveniens* to adjudicate environmental disputes between the persons affected by the environmental damage and the corporation concerned? In addressing these inter-related questions, the aim of this chapter is to identify and assess the existing legal framework for dealing with widespread, long-term and severe cases of environmental damage caused by transnational corporations through oil pollution or nuclear contamination.

Cases of serious environmental damage are different also in terms of the *causal nexus* between the activity of the corporation and the resulting damage. The Ogoniland oil pollution is an example of severe environmental harm caused over an extended period of time.[8] This situation has been subject to fairly extensive litigation in Nigeria, the Netherlands and the US. Another similar case is that of Chevron (Texaco) concerning the pollution of the rainforests and rivers in Ecuador and Peru, resulting in environmental damage and damage to the health of individuals.[9] In these cases the corporations concerned could be held responsible for negligence in failing to take appropriate action to prevent

---

[8]   The 2011 Report on 'Environmental Assessment of the Ogoniland' by the United Nations Environment Programme (UNEP) estimates that cleaning up the pollution and catalysing a sustainable recovery of Ogoniland could take 25–30 years, at a cost of over US $1 billion. See United Nations Environment Programme Report, Environmental Assessment of Ogoniland, August 2011, available at www.unep.org/nigeria. See also O. Oluduro, *Oil Exploitation and Human Rights Violations in Nigeria's Oil Producing Communities* (Antwerp: Intersentia, 2014).

[9]   For more information on this protracted legal dispute see www.business-humanrights.org/ Categories/Lawlawsuits/Lawsuitsregulatoryaction/LawsuitsSelectedcases/TexacoChevron lawsuitsreEcuador (*Aguinda v. Chevron Texaco* case). See also the 1. Chevron Corporation and 2. *Texaco Petroleum Company v. The Republic of Ecuador* (PCA Case No. 2007–2); and Chevron Corporation and 2. *Texaco Petroleum Company v. The Republic of Ecuador* (PCA Case No. 2009–23) before the Permanent Court of Arbitration at: www.pca-cpa.org.

environmental damage or to engage in adequate remedial action. The 2010 BP oil spill relates to an industrial accident with grave environmental consequences, which happened during oil exploration in the deep sea.[10] The responsibility of the international corporations involved therein, namely BP and Transocean, would fall under gross negligence, or other liability doctrines. The 2011 Fukushima nuclear disaster was put in motion by a natural disaster, subsequently magnified by the failure of the safety systems of the Fukushima nuclear power plants. These three different scenarios illustrate the fact that while the responsibility of international corporations for serious environmental damage can be based on different theories of liability, it should be guided by the public interest of safeguarding to the maximum extent possible the protection of the environment and ensuring the rights of the persons affected.

Sections 2 and 3 provide an insight into the specific protection regimes concerning oil pollution and nuclear accidents. These sections lay the ground for a detailed discussion of the issue of responsibility for serious environmental damage by addressing respectively the responsibility of international corporations, of host states and of home states under section 4. As Nollkaemper has noted, the responsibility of transnational corporations for activities that cause harm to the environment is a multidimensional problem, as relevant norms are scattered among different levels of regulation: between national and international levels and between public and private spheres of regulation.[11] This discussion will reveal a model of shared responsibility between the international corporation, the host state and the home state. When discussing issues of responsibility for serious environmental damage, it is necessary to pay attention not only to international treaties and legal practice, but also to bilateral investment treaties.[12] Finally, in section 5, the chapter addresses the complexity of attribution of responsibility and adjudication of cases concerning serious environmental damage. Evidently, the *nature* of the international corporation concerned and the *causal nexus* between its activity and the resulting damage are relevant factors when it comes to the attribution of conduct and responsibility.

---

[10]   For the 2010 Deepwater Horizon oil spill, also known as the BP oil spill, see inter alia: www. whitehouse.gov/deepwater-bp-oil-spill, www.deepwaterhorizoneconomicsettlement.com/docs. php and www.restorethegulf.gov/environment.

[11]   A. Nollkaemper, 'Responsibility of Transnational Corporations in International Environmental Law' in G. Winter (ed.), *Multilevel Governance of Global Environmental Change: Perspectives from Science, Sociology and the Law* (New York: Cambridge University Press, 2006), p. 198.

[12]   See inter alia J.E. Viñuales, *Foreign Investment and the Environment in International Law* (New York: Cambridge University Press, 2012), especially pp. 222–252; A. Kulick, *Global Public Interest in International Investment Law* (New York: Cambridge University Press, 2012), pp. 225–268; R. Diepeveen, Y. Levashova and T. Lambooy, 'Bridging the Gap between International Investment Law and the Environment', Conference Report (2014) 30(78) *Utrecht Journal of International and European Law* 145–160; I. Dekker et al. (eds.), *Bridging the Gap between International Investment Law and the Environment* (The Hague: Eleven Legal Publishing, 2015).

2. ADDRESSING ENVIRONMENTAL DAMAGE FROM NUCLEAR ACCIDENTS

There are a number of specific international instruments regulating liability for environmental damage from nuclear disasters. The 1961 Paris Convention and the 1963 Vienna Convention regulate issues of nuclear civil liability for nuclear damage.[13] Under Article 3 of the 1961 Paris Convention, the operator of a nuclear installation is liable for damage to or loss of life of any person, and damage to or loss of property which is caused by a nuclear incident in such installation or involving nuclear substances coming from such installation. This convention vests jurisdiction with the courts of the country where the nuclear incident has occurred and prohibits discrimination in the application of the law based upon nationality, domicile, or residence. Article 11 of the Paris Convention provides that the nature, form and extent of the compensation, as well as the equitable distribution thereof, is governed by national law.

The 1963 Vienna Convention provides a definition of 'nuclear damage' as

(a) loss of life, any personal injury or any loss of, or damage to, property which arises out of or results from the radioactive properties or a combination of radioactive properties with toxic, explosive or other hazardous properties of nuclear fuel or radioactive products or waste in, or of nuclear material coming from, originating in, or sent to, a nuclear installation;

(b) any other loss or damage so arising or resulting if and to the extent that the law of the competent court so provides; and

(c) if the law of the installation state so provides, loss of life, any personal injury or any loss of, or damage to, property which arises out of or results from other ionising radiation emitted by any other source of radiation inside a nuclear installation.[14]

The Vienna Convention excludes liability of an operator for nuclear damage in two circumstances, namely for nuclear damage caused by a nuclear incident directly due to an act of armed conflict, hostilities, civil war or insurrection or for nuclear damage due to a grave natural disaster of an exceptional character.[15]

---

[13]   Paris Convention on Third Party Liability in the Field of Nuclear Energy (Convention on Third Party Liability in the Field of Nuclear Energy of 29 July 1960, as amended by the Additional Protocol of 28th January 1964 and by the Protocol of 16 November 1982) – with regard to ratifications see www.oecd-nea.org/law/paris-convention-ratification.html (16 States party); Vienna Convention on Civil Liability for Nuclear Damage (1963) – with regard to ratifications see www.iaea.org/Publications/Documents/Conventions/liability_status.pdf (38 States party). For a discussion of the problems with the regime of nuclear damage liability see inter alia D.E.J. Currie, 'The Problems and Gaps in the Nuclear Liability Conventions and an Analysis of how an Actual Claim Would Be Brought under the Current Existing Treaty Regime in the Event of a Nuclear Accident' (2008) 35(1) *Denver Journal of International Law & Policy* 85–127.
[14]   Article I(1)(k), Vienna Convention on Civil Liability for Nuclear Damage (1963).
[15]   Article IV(3), Vienna Convention on Civil Liability for Nuclear Damage (1963).

An important legal aspect of both the Paris and the Vienna Convention is the fact that the operator of a nuclear facility is held liable on the basis of strict liability, that is irrespective of fault concerning the damage caused.

3. ADDRESSING ENVIRONMENTAL DAMAGE FROM OIL POLLUTION

There are a number of conventions concerning oil pollution from ships.[16] An important mechanism is the International Oil Pollution Compensation Funds (IOPC Funds), whose principal role is to pay compensation to those who have suffered oil pollution damage in a Member State who cannot obtain full compensation for the pollution damage from the ship-owner under the relevant Civil Liability Convention.[17] Claimants may be individuals, partnerships, companies, private organisations or public bodies, including States or local authorities. The IOPC Funds appoint experts to monitor clean-up operations, to investigate the technical merits of claims and to make an independent assessment of the losses.

An oil pollution incident can generally give rise to claims for five types of damage:

(a) property damage;
(b) costs of clean-up operations at sea and on shore;
(c) economic losses by fishermen or those engaged in mariculture;
(d) economic losses in the tourism sector;
(e) costs for reinstatement of the environment.[18]

The liability of the owner of the polluting vessel is strict, which means that the owner will be liable irrespective of fault.[19] The ship-owner is exempt from liability where the pollution damage results from an act of war or a natural disaster or is

---

[16] International Convention on Civil Liability for Oil Pollution Damage (1969) and Additional Protocol of 1976; Convention on the Establishment of an International Fund for Compensation for Oil Pollution Damage (1971); Tanker Owners Voluntary Agreement on Liability for Oil Pollution (TOVALOP, 1969); Offshore Pollution Liability Agreement (1974). For a detailed discussion of the international liability and compensation regime for oil pollution from tankers see UNCTAD, 'Liability and Compensation for Ship-Source Oil Pollution: An Overview of the International Legal Framework for Oil Pollution Damage from Tankers', 2012, available at: http://unctad.org/en/PublicationsLibrary/dtltlb20114_en.pdf.

[17] For more information see www.iopcfunds.org/about-us. Since their establishment, the IOPC Funds have been involved in 145 incidents of varying sizes all over the world.

[18] See www.iopcfunds.org/compensation as well as www.itopf.com/spill-compensation. For a detailed discussion see H. Wang, *Civil Liability for Marine Oil Pollution Damage: A Comparative and Economic Study of the International, US and Chinese Compensation Regime* (Alphen aan den Rijn: Kluwer Law International, 2011).

[19] Liability and Compensation for Ship-Source Oil Pollution, p. 15, para. 45.

wholly caused by the intentional act of a third party or the negligence of public authorities in maintaining lights or navigational aids.[20] Under the 1974 Offshore Pollution Liability Agreement (OPOL), operating companies agree to accept strict liability for pollution damage and the cost of remedial measures with only certain exceptions, up to a maximum of US $250 million per incident.[21] These instruments are based on a regime of strict liability for serious environmental damage.

4. ENSURING RESPONSIBILITY FOR SERIOUS ENVIRONMENTAL DAMAGE

Does serious damage give rise to *civil liability* on the part of the relevant transnational corporation or to *state responsibility*? While that question is better answered on a case-by-case basis, Sands and Peel have pointed out that the distinction between state responsibility and civil liability is becoming increasingly difficult to draw, as treaties and other international acts have established an obligation for the state to provide public funds where an operator cannot meet certain costs of environmental damage.[22] The *ownership* of international corporations is another important factor to take into account when discussing issues of responsibility for serious environmental damage. Thus, corporations can be divided into three categories, namely *state owned*, *mixed capital* corporations where the state holds a stake, and *private* corporations. The nature of the corporation is relevant when discussing issues of shared responsibility between a corporation, the host state and the home state.

Having discussed the specific regimes of liability for environmental damage from nuclear disasters and oil pollution, the following three subsections address in more detail issues of responsibility of transnational corporations of host states and of home states respectively. The fourth subsection shall discuss environmental protection as a matter of shared responsibility among the concerned international corporation, the host state and the home state.

4.1. THE RESPONSIBILITY OF TRANSNATIONAL CORPORATIONS

Multinational corporations have to comply with different legal frameworks, depending on the domestic laws and international legal obligations applicable in the state where they exercise their economic activity. In that sense they are

---

[20] Liability and Compensation for Ship-Source Oil Pollution, p. 15, para. 47.
[21] Clause IV, Remedial Measures and Pollution Damage – Reimbursement and Compensation of Claims therefor, Offshore Pollution Liability Agreement (1974), available at: www.opol.org.uk/agreement.htm.
[22] P. Sands and J. Peel, *supra* n. 2, p. 701.

'used' to operating in a fragmented domestic legal framework, which might provide for civil liability, as well as for criminal liability for environmental damage. Besides the regime of civil liability, companies could be held criminally accountable, if they are complicit in committing serious international crimes, such as war crimes or crimes against humanity.[23] At an international level, the International Criminal Court (ICC) can prosecute individuals for widespread, long-term and severe damage to the natural environment caused during an international armed conflict.[24] While the jurisdiction of this international court does not include prosecuting legal persons, as transnational corporations, and the threshold of environmental damage is quite high, international humanitarian law (IHL) prohibits causing widespread, long-term and severe damage to the natural environment.[25] While this legal obligation is primarily addressed to the states party to an armed conflict, corporations could also incur responsibility in domestic jurisdictions.

The law of international responsibility for transnational corporations is much less developed than that for states and international organisations.[26] However, Principle 1 of the 2003 UN Norms, which reflects customary international law, provides that states continue to have primary responsibility to ensure respect for human rights, whereas companies only have responsibilities 'within their respective spheres of activity and influence'. The issue of international responsibility for environmental damage is somewhat complicated by specific

---

[23] Case law in this regard is limited. For a recent case see that against Amesys in France for being complicit in acts of torture by supplying surveillance equipment to the Gaddafi regime in Libya, available at: www.fidh.org/Amesys-File-The-Investigation-12752 For a more detailed discussion see inter alia D. Cassel, 'Corporate Aiding and Abetting of Human Rights Violations: Confusion in the Courts' (2008) 6(2) *Northwestern Journal of International Human Rights* 304–326; K. Magraw, 'Universally Liable? Corporate-Complicity Liability Under the Principle of Universal Jurisdiction' (2009) 18(2) *Minnesota Journal of International Law* 458–497; F. Jessberger and J. Geneuss (eds.), 'Special Issue Transnational Business and International Criminal Law' (2010) 8(3) *Journal of International Criminal Justice*; D. Stoitchkova, *Towards Corporate Liability in International Criminal Law* (Antwerp: Intersentia, 2010); H. van der Wilt, 'Corporate Criminal Responsibility for International Crimes: Exploring the Possibilities' (2013) 12(1) *Chinese Journal of International Law* 43–77; 'Business and International Crimes', Fafo Institute for Applied International Studies (Oslo, Norway), available at: www.fafo.no/liabilities/commentary.htm.

[24] Article 8(2)(b)(iv), ICC Statute.

[25] Article 35(3) of the Additional Protocol I of 1977 to the Geneva Conventions of 1949 prohibits the employment of 'methods or means of warfare which are intended, or may be expected, to cause widespread, long-term and severe damage to the natural environment'; Article 1 of the Convention of 18 May 1977 on the Prohibition of Military or Any Other Hostile Use of Environmental Modification Techniques (ENMOD Convention) prohibits the use of weapons which have 'widespread, long-lasting or severe effects' on the environment.

[26] See the 2001 International Law Commission Articles on State Responsibility for Internationally Wrongful Acts Yearbook of the International Law Commission, 2011, vol. II, Part Two; and the 2011 Articles on Responsibility of International Organizations for Internationally Wrongful Acts, Yearbook of the International Law Commission, 2011, vol. II, Part Two. For a more detailed discussion see generally J. Crawford, A. Pellet and S. Olleson (eds.), *The Law of International Responsibility* (Oxford: Oxford University Press, 2010), respectively pp. 803–815, pp. 877–887; pp. 1005–1023.

elements applicable in this field, including the fact that there is no general consensus as to the notion of the environment.[27] Moreover, the threshold of environmental damage triggering the responsibility of a corporation remains an open issue, since damage to the environment cannot be completely avoided, as it is inherent in industrial development.[28] Additionally, litigation raises a number of complex legal issues including assessing the damage, proving causation and the unacceptable risk and classifying and identifying the victims who should be compensated.[29] While most environmental disputes call for no more than objective evaluation of facts as to the environmental effects of a proposed activity, there might be conflicting scientific evidence.[30] Such evidence would make the assessment of environmental damage a challenging task for any adjudicatory body.

An important concept with regard to compensation for environmental damage is the 'polluter-pays' principle.[31] According to this principle, the costs for countering the pollution must be paid by the entity responsible for causing it. Principle 16 of the 1992 Rio Declaration provides that '[n]ational authorities should endeavour to promote the internalization of environmental costs and the use of economic instruments, taking into account the approach that the polluter should, in principle, bear the cost of pollution, with due regard to the public interest and without distorting international trade and investment.' Besides the Rio Declaration, the 'polluter-pays' principle is embedded in a number of relevant international law instruments concerning nuclear damage.[32] The preamble of the 1990 Oil Pollution Preparedness Convention and of the 1992 Convention on the

---

27   C. Nègre, 'Responsibility and International Environmental Law' in J. Crawford, A. Pellet, and S. Olleson (eds.), *supra* n. 26, p. 803.

28   C. Nègre, *supra* n. 27, p. 803. The ICJ has stated that 'that the environment is not an abstraction but represents the living space, the quality of life and the very health of human beings, including generations unborn' in *Legality of Threat or Use of Nuclear Weapons* (Advisory Opinion), ICJ Reports 1996, p. 241, para. 29.

29   P.N. Okowa, *supra* n. 5, p. 159.

30   *Ibid.*, p. 169. About conflicting scientific evidence introduced by parties to a dispute see inter alia ICJ, *Case Concerning the Gabčíkovo-Nagymaros Project (Hungary v. Slovakia)*, ICJ Reports 1997, p. 77, para. 140 (*Gabčíkovo-Nagymaros*); and *Case Concerning Pulp Mills on the River Uruguay (Argentina v. Uruguay)*, ICJ Reports 2010, pp. 71–73, paras. 165–168 (*Pulp Mills*).

31   See inter alia N. de Sadeleer, *Environmental Principles: From Political Slogans to Legal Rules* (Oxford: Oxford University Press, 2002), pp. 23–60. See also the OCDE/GD(92)81, 'The Polluter-Pays Principle', OECD Analyses and Recommendations, Environment Directorate, Organisation for Economic Co-Operation and Development, Paris 1992; N. de Sadeleer, 'The Polluter-pays Principle in EU Law – Bold Case Law and Poor Harmonisation', in L. Backer, D.K. Fauchald and C. Voigt (eds.), *Pro Natura: Festskrift til Hans Christian Bugge* (Oslo: Universitetsforlaget, 2012), pp. 405–421; O. Vícha, 'The Polluter-Pays Principle in the OECD Recommendations and its application in the International and EC/EU Law' (2011) 2 *Czech Yearbook of Public and Private International Law* 57–67, available at: www.cyil.eu/contents-cyil-2011.

32   See the Paris Convention on Civil Liability for Nuclear Damage of 1960 and the Vienna Convention on Civil Liability for Nuclear Damage of 1963. See also the 1969 CLC and Article 6(4) of the 1977 Civil Liability for Oil Pollution Convention. See also the 1989 OECD Council Recommendation of the Application of the Polluter-Pays Principle to Accidental Pollution.

Transboundary Effects of Industrial Accidents have described the 'polluter-pays' principle as a general principle of international environmental law.[33] An important aspect of enforcing the polluter-pays principle is that of including a minimum liability limit for pollution incidents in relevant international agreements, followed by relevant insurance schemes and enforcement mechanisms, as the International Oil Pollution Compensation Funds (IOPC Funds).[34] Imposing a minimum liability limit ensures that at least some of the initial costs to counter pollution in case of an incident are covered. In the wake of the BP oil spill disaster, the liability limit was increased from US $120 million to 250 million per incident.[35] As the case of the Offshore Pollution Liability Agreement (OPOL) shows, these compensation figures could be revisited, if need be.

Corporations have used a variety of tactics to attempt to evade their environmental obligations, with bankruptcy being one of the most effective strategies.[36] Nevertheless, a number of recent domestic cases show that although the legal process is rather complex and protracted, it is possible to hold companies responsible for serious environmental damage. A number of cases have been brought against international corporations in the US under the Alien Torts Claim Act.[37] Three recent high-profile cases concerning transnational corporations'

---

[33]   See the 1990 International Convention on Oil Pollution Preparedness, Response and Co-operation (OPRC). A Protocol to the OPRC relating to hazardous and noxious substances (OPRC-HNS Protocol) was adopted in 2000. See also the 1973 International Convention for the Prevention of Pollution from Ships (MARPOL) and its 1978 Protocol adopted specifically because of accidents with oil tankers. See also the 1992 Convention on the Transboundary Effects of Industrial Accidents and the 2003 Protocol on Civil Liability and Compensation for Damage Caused by the Transboundary Effects of Industrial Accidents on Transboundary Waters, available at: www.unece.org/env/civil-liability/welcome.html.

[34]   The amounts of minimum and maximum liability vary from one international agreement to another. Thus, according to Article 7 of the Paris Convention on Civil Liability for Nuclear Damage the minimum liability of the operator in respect of damage caused by a nuclear incident shall be no less than less than 5 million Special Drawing Rights (SDR) to a maximum liability of 15 million Special Drawing Rights, as defined by the International Monetary Fund. Article V of the Vienna Convention on Civil Liability for Nuclear Damage sets the liability of the operator to not less than US $5 million for any one nuclear incident. Clause IV of the Offshore Pollution Liability Agreement (OPOL, as amended on 4 July 2012) provides for an overall maximum of US $250 million per incident. The Article V of the International Convention on Civil Liability for Oil Pollution Damage of 1992 sets the liability limits to compensation at 4 million and 510 thousand SDR as defined by the International Monetary Fund for a ship not exceeding 5,000 units of tonnage up to a maximum of 89 million and 770 thousand SDR.

[35]   'UK liability limits to double after BP spill', *Financial Times*, 15 August 2010. See also J.L. Ramseur, 'Liability and Compensation Issues Raised by the 2010 Gulf Oil Spill', *Congressional Research Service*, March 2011, available at: http://assets.opencrs.com/rpts/R41679_20110311.pdf.

[36]   See inter alia L.T. Kishiyama, 'Countering Corporate Evasion of Environmental Obligations through Bankruptcy' (2003) *Vermont Journal of Environmental Law*, available at: http://vjel.vermontlaw.edu/writing-competition/roscoe-hogan-environmental-law-essay-contest/2003-essays/countering-corporate-evasion-of-environmental-obligations-through-bankruptcy/.

[37]   See inter alia M. Koebele, *Corporate Responsibility under the Alien Tort Statute* (Leiden: Martinus Nijhoff, 2009). These cases include *Bowoto et al. v. Chevron Texaco Corp, John Doe v. Exxon Mobil Corp (US)*, *Presbyterian Church of Sudan v. Talisman Energy Inc. and the Republic*

liability for oil pollution include the *Four Nigerian farmers and the Friends of the Earth v. Shell* in the Netherlands,[38] the *Oil Spill by the Oil Rig 'Deepwater Horizon' in the Gulf of Mexico*,[39] and *Kiobel v. Shell*.[40] Notably, on the basis of applicable Nigerian law, The Hague District Court held that Shell Nigeria violated a duty of care and found it liable for tort of negligence about two oil spills near the village Ikot Ada Udo.

In the case against BP concerning the 2010 oil spill, the first phase of the trial is about BP's share of responsibility, with prosecutors claiming gross negligence on the part of the BP. The second phase of this lengthy trial will determine how many barrels of oil were actually spilled in the Gulf of Mexico, with a US federal government estimate of over 4 million barrels.[41] An interesting legal aspect of this case is also the determination of the shared responsibility between three companies, namely BP, Transocean and Halliburton, where Transocean was the owner and responsible for the maintenance and operations of the Deepwater Horizon oil rig, and Halliburton was responsible for designing and testing the cement to seal the well.[42] The US government and Transocean have reached a settlement whereby Transocean has agreed to pay US $1 billion in civil claims and an additional US $400 million in criminal penalties for violating the US Clean Water Act.[43] These recent cases show that it is possible to bring legal proceedings about serious environmental pollution in other domestic jurisdictions with a functioning and independent judicial system. While one might expect that the

---

     of Sudan (Talisman case), Vietnam Association for Victims of Agent Orange v. Dow Chemical Co., Saleh et al. v. Titan et al. (US), etc. For a list of relevant cases and documents visit: www.asser.nl/default.aspx?site_id=36&level1=15248&level2=&level3=&textid=39895.

[38]   District Court of The Hague (Netherlands), Case No. LJN BY9854, 30 January 2013, available at: www.rechtspraak.nl. For a detailed discussion see inter alia Marie Jose van der Heide at: http://invisiblecollege.weblog.leidenuniv.nl/2013/02/08/%EF%BB%BFunique-case-against-shell-the-first-dutch-foreign-direct-liability-case and Roger Alford at: http://opiniojuris.org/2013/02/05/dutch-court-issues-mixed-ruling-on-shells-liability-for-nigerian-environmental-claim. The Press Release of The Hague Court is available at: www.rechtspraak.nl/Organisatie/Rechtbanken/Den-Haag/Nieuws/Pages/DutchjudgementsonliabilityShell.aspx.

[39]   *In re: Oil Spill by the Oil Rig 'Deepwater Horizon' in the Gulf of Mexico*, 20 April 2010, No. 10-md-02179, in the US District Court, Eastern District of Louisiana. For a discussion of the case see inter alia C. Krauss and B. Meier, 'As Oil Spill Trial Opens, Push for a Deal Continues', *New York Times*, 25 February 2013, available at: www.nytimes.com/2013/02/26/business/energy-environment/bp-trial-opens-with-possible-deal-in-background.html.

[40]   See *Kiobel, individually and on behalf of her late husband Kiobel, et al. v. Royal Dutch Petroleum Co. et al.*, 17 April 2013, available at: www.supremecourt.gov/opinions/12pdf/10-1491_l6gn.pdf. The US Supreme Court decided that the presumption against extraterritoriality applies to claims filed under the Alien Tort Statute (ATS). This finding makes it quite difficult to use US domestic courts to adjudicate these kinds of claims.

[41]   For more information on the ensuing litigation see inter alia D. Gregorio, 'Timeline: BP oil spill, litigation at a glance', 2 July 2015, available at: www.reuters.com.

[42]   For more details see C. Krauss and B. Meier, 'As Oil Spill Trial Opens, Push for a Deal Continues', *New York Times*, 25 February 2013.

[43]   Transocean Ltd, a Swiss-based company, owned the Deepwater Horizon oil drilling rig, which sank after an explosion killed 11 workers and spawned the oil spill over a period of three months, namely April–June 2010.

---

potential effect of such litigation could eventually be that corporations are held to a higher environmental protection standard, in principle the governing law in these disputes is the law of the country where the damage occurred. The Shell and BP cases demonstrate that holding transnational corporations to account for environmental damage remains difficult due to corporate reliance on the principle of separate legal personality and the doctrine of *forum non conveniens*.[44]

4.2. HOST STATE RESPONSIBILITY

This section deals with a number of tools and principles which are closely related with the protection of the environment, including environmental impact assessments, the principle of due diligence and that of providing compensation in case of damage. In the absence of universally binding legal standards or lack of agreement on their scope, domestic law regulates the legal obligations of corporations in the field of environmental protection. The host state is expected to ensure that corporations exercising their activity in its territory abide by domestic laws and applicable international legal obligations on environmental matters. By now the protection of the environment is well established under domestic law, since some 140 constitutions in the world, including the overwhelming proportion of those amended or written since 1970, include a state obligation to protect the environment or a right to a safe, healthy, ecologically balanced (or other adjective) environment.[45] At the same time, however, a number of issues including the threshold of environmental degradation required for a human right violation to occur, the position and duties of non-state actors with respect to human rights and the environment, and the extraterritorial reach of state obligations to protect the environment, remain in need of further clarification.

A state's responsibility to create the conditions for public participation with regard to environmental matters is acknowledged in the 1998 Aarhus Convention which enjoins each state party to guarantee the rights of the public to access to information, to participation in decision-making, and access to justice in environmental matters.[46] While this convention can ensure a certain degree of

---

[44]   For a more detailed discussion on the inadequacy of regulatory initiatives see inter alia S. Deva, *Regulating Corporate Human Rights Violations: Humanizing Business* (Abingdon: Routledge, 2012), pp. 64–119.

[45]   See Rio+20: Joint Report OHCHR and UNEP, 'Human Rights and the Environment', August 2012, p. 6, available at: www.unep.org/environmentalgovernance/Portals/8/JointReport OHCHRandUNEPonHumanRightsandtheEnvironment.pdf. See also the OHCHR Analytical Study 2011, para. 30.

[46]   Convention on Access to Information, Public Participation in Decision-Making and Access to Justice in Environmental Matters (Aarhus Convention), 25 June 1998, available at: www. unece.org/fileadmin/DAM/env/pp/documents/cep43e.pdf. For a detailed discussion of this convention see inter alia M. Pallemaerts, *The Aarhus Convention at Ten: Interactions and Tensions Between Conventional International Law and EU Environmental Law* (Groningen: Europa Law Publishing, 2011).

openness and public participation, taking full advantage of it requires that all stakeholders cooperate timely and efficiently and that the public is fairly well-informed and interested in environmental matters. Even in countries with a fairly well-organised civil society, the possibility of the civil society to influence environmental policies and decisions remains limited, when compared with the influence of international corporations and the business sector more generally.

Primary responsibility for ensuring environmental protection from damage caused by non-state actors, including international corporations, rests with the host state. That means that the three-pronged human rights approach to the scope of state responsibility, namely that of respect, protect, fulfil would apply to its full extent. Evidently, the host state is responsible for creating the necessary legal framework concerning environmental protection and for applying it in practice for activity taking place within its territory. The UN treaty bodies have recognised that responsibility on the part of the state with regard to securing the right to health and the right to water to its population.[47] Generally speaking, serious environmental damage does directly affect two key elements for any state, namely its population and its territory. Environmental protection duties on the part of the host state include creating the necessary conditions for public participation, taking prevention measures, and enforcing the applicable legal framework in case of environmental damage.

A state's responsibility to prevent environmental damage is not limited to its own territory. It is well-established under international law that a state incurs responsibility for cross-border environmental damage. As the ICJ has put it,

> The existence of the general obligation of States to ensure that activities within their jurisdiction and control respect the environment of other States or of areas

---

[47] See Committee on Economic, Social and Cultural Rights (CESCR), General Comment No. 14 (2000), The right to the highest attainable standard of health (Article 12 of the International Covenant on Economic, Social and Cultural Rights), UN Doc. E/C.12/2000/4, 11 August 2000. Paragraph 42 of this General Comment provides: 'While only States are parties to the Covenant and thus ultimately accountable for compliance with it, all members of society – individuals, including health professionals, families, local communities, intergovernmental and non-governmental organizations, civil society organizations, as well as the private *business sector* – have responsibilities regarding the realization of the right to health. State parties should therefore provide an environment which facilitates the discharge of these responsibilities' (emphasis added); see also CESCR, General Comment No. 15 (2002), The right to water (Arts. 11 and 12 of the International Covenant on Economic, Social and Cultural Rights), UN Doc. E/C.12/2002/11, 20 January 2003. Paragraph 23 of this General Comment provides that: 'The obligation to protect requires State parties to prevent third parties from interfering in any way with the enjoyment of the right to water. Third parties include individuals, groups, *corporations* and other entities as well as agents acting under their authority. The obligation includes, inter alia, adopting the necessary and effective legislative and other measures to restrain, for example, third parties from denying equal access to adequate water; and polluting and inequitably extracting from water resources, including natural sources, wells and other water distribution systems' (emphasis added).

beyond national control is now part of the corpus of international law relating to the environment.[48]

That a state is responsible for protecting not only its environment, but also that of others, is clear also from the International Law Commission (ILC) 2001 Articles on Prevention of Transboundary Harm from Hazardous Activities as well as other international instruments.[49] A number of cases which concern state responsibility for cross-border environmental damage have been brought before the ICJ. The European Court of Human Rights has also discussed a number of aspects of state responsibility for environmental damage, especially concerning danger to people's health,[50] and other adverse effects on the environment.[51] These cases could potentially lead to a strengthening of environmental standards and the link between the protection of the environment and human rights.[52]

Ratner speaks about three possible scenarios, namely corporations as government agents, corporations as complicit with governments, and corporations as commanders.[53] The 2001 ILC Articles on State Responsibility lay down the essential conditions for attributing responsibility to a state under international law. While international law adopts an approach which generally avoids attributing responsibility to the state for conduct of corporations or collectives linked to the state by nationality, habitual residence or incorporation, a state cannot escape responsibility by a mere process of internal subdivision into a series of distinct legal entities, including corporations.[54] A state could be held responsible for conduct of non-state actors, including international corporations, for failure to take the necessary measures to prevent serious environmental damage. A stronger case in this regard can be made when transnational corporations are state-owned, since that would imply that the state has sufficient control over them.[55] Depending on the circumstances, there could be joint or separate responsibility on the part of a

---

[48] ICJ, *Legality of the Threat or Use of Nuclear Weapons* (Advisory Opinion), ICJ Reports 1996, pp. 241–242, para. 29.

[49] For more information on the 2001 Draft Articles on Prevention of Transboundary Harm from Hazardous Activities see: http://untreaty.un.org/ilc/texts/instruments/english/commentaries/9_7_2001.pdf. See also Xue Hanqin, *Transboundary Damage in International Law* (Cambridge: Cambridge University Press, 2003).

[50] See inter alia *Lopez Ostra v. Spain* (no. 16798/90); *Guerra and Others v. Italy* (no. 14967/89); *Taşkın and Others v. Turkey* (no. 46117/99); *Fadeyeva v. Russia* (no. 55723/00); *Giacomelli v. Italy* (no. 59909/00).

[51] See inter alia *Tatar v. Romania* (no. 657021/01); *Mangouras v. Spain* (no. 12050/04).

[52] See inter alia O.W. Pedersen, 'European Environmental Human Rights and Environmental Rights: A Long Time Coming?' (2008) 21(1) *Georgetown International Environmental Law Review* 73–111; O.W. Pedersen, 'The Ties that Bind: The Environment, the European Convention on Human Rights and the Rule of Law' (2010) 16(4) *European Public Law* 571–595.

[53] S.R. Ratner, 'Corporations and Human Rights: A Theory of Legal Responsibility' (2001) 111(3) *Yale Law Journal* 499–506.

[54] See 'Attribution of Conduct to a State', *Yearbook of the International Law Commission*, 2001, vol. II, Part Two, respectively pp. 38 and 39, paras. 2 and 7.

[55] Some of the major state-owned transnational petroleum companies are Petronas (Malaysia); Lukoil (Russian Federation); Statoil AsA (Norway); China National Offshore Oil Corp. (China); and Oil & Natural Gas Corp. (India). See the 2007 UNCTAD Report.

state and an international corporation for environmental damage for oil pollution and nuclear accidents.

Most importantly, the host state should ensure that corporations comply with the domestic legal framework concerned with the protection of the environment. Thus, in the *Ogoniland* case the African Commission on Human and Peoples' Rights found that governments have a duty to protect their citizens, not only through appropriate legislation and effective enforcement, but also by protecting them from damaging acts that may be perpetrated by private parties.[56] Similar findings have been made by the Inter-American Court of Human Rights and the European Court of Human Rights. In the *Ogoniland* case the African Commission found the Nigerian government in violation of Article 21 of the African Charter for giving the green light to private actors, and the oil companies in particular, to devastatingly affect the well-being of the Ogonis, despite the government's obligation to protect persons against interferences in the enjoyment of their rights, a practice which falls short of the minimum conduct expected of governments.[57]

Environmental impact assessments emerged internationally after the 1972 Stockholm Conference and are now an established international and domestic legal technique for integrating environmental considerations into socio-economic development and decision-making processes.[58] Environmental impact assessments are an important part of the process of vetting large-scale projects.[59] In that sense, this assessment is an important tool in the hands of the state for controlling the effect of a particular project on the environment before that is implemented by a given corporation. Projects concerning the building of nuclear power plants, as well as those concerning oil exploration, processing and storage clearly fall under the category of activities which could have a potentially adverse impact on the environment and thus would require an environmental impact assessment. Principle 17 of the Rio Declaration requires the undertaking of environmental impact assessments as a national instrument. An interesting recent shift in focus is that from 'environmental impact assessments' to 'strategic environmental assessment'.[60] This mechanism can be seen as an important component of the precautionary principle.

---

[56] See *The Social and Economic Rights Action Center and the Center for Economic and Social Rights v. Nigeria*, Communication 155/96 (30th Ordinary Session held in Banjul, The Gambia, 13–27 October 2001), para. 57 (*Ogoniland* case). For the full text of the decision see www.achpr.org/communications/decision/155.96.

[57] *Ogoniland* case, para. 58.

[58] P. Sands and J. Peel, *supra* n. 2, p. 601.

[59] See inter alia N. Craik, *The International Law of Environmental Impact Assessment: Process, Substance and Integration* (Cambridge: Cambridge University Press, 2008).

[60] Strategic environmental assessment consists of a range of 'analytical and participatory approaches that aim to integrate environmental considerations into policies, plans and programmes and evaluate the inter-linkages with economic and social considerations.' For more information on strategic environmental assessment see inter alia: www.oecd.org/environment/environmentanddevelopment/strategicenvironmentalassessment.htm. See also OECD (2012),

Another important principle with regard to liability for environmental damage is that of 'due diligence'. In a December 2012 report renowned experts have noted that there are, at least, four main regulatory approaches through which States can ensure human rights due diligence activities by business, which include requiring due diligence as a matter of regulatory compliance; providing incentives and benefits to companies, in return for their being able to demonstrate due diligence practice; encouraging due diligence through transparency and disclosure mechanisms; and combining one or more of the above approaches.[61]

Compensation for victims of environmental damage has been central to the early international documents concerning environmental protection.[62] Thus, Principle 22 of the 1972 Stockholm Declaration provides that 'States shall cooperate to develop further the international law regarding liability and compensation for the victims of pollution and other environmental damage caused by activities within the jurisdiction or control of such States to areas beyond their jurisdiction.' In a similar vein, Principle 13 of the 1992 Rio Declaration provides that:

> States shall develop national law regarding liability and compensation for the victims of pollution and other environmental damage. States shall also cooperate in an expeditious and more determined manner to develop further international law regarding liability and compensation for adverse effects of environmental damage caused by activities within their jurisdiction or control to areas beyond their jurisdiction.

The International Oil Pollution Compensation Funds (IOPC Funds) provide financial compensation for oil pollution damage that occurs in its member states, resulting from spills of persistent oil from tankers.[63] The IOPC Funds are financed by contributions paid by entities that receive certain types of oil by sea transport, contributions based on the amount of oil received in the relevant calendar year, and cover expected claims, together with the costs of administering the Funds.[64] Since their establishment, the 1992 Fund and the preceding 1971 Fund have been involved in 145 incidents of varying sizes all over the world. In the great majority of cases, all claims have been settled out of court.[65] This is an interesting example

---

Strategic Environmental Assessment in Development Practice: A Review of Recent Experience, OECD Publishing, available at: http://dx.doi.org/10.1787/9789264166745-en.

[61] See inter alia O. de Schutter, A. Ramasastry, M.B. Taylor and R.C. Thompson, 'Human Rights Due Diligence: The Role of States', December 2012, available at: http://accountabilityround table.org/analysis-and-updates/hrdd.

[62] For a more detailed discussion on compensation see inter alia T. Hardman Reis, *Compensation for Environmental Damages Under International Law: The Role of the International Judge* (Alphen aan den Rijn: Kluwer Law International, 2011).

[63] For more information see: www.iopcfunds.org/about-us.

[64] *Ibid.*

[65] *Ibid.*

of shared responsibility and of a joint mechanism for dealing with environmental damage caused by oil spills.

4.3. HOME STATE RESPONSIBILITY

While the number of international corporations is increasing, most of them are incorporated or have their headquarters in a limited number of states. Thus, according to a 2007 UNCTAD Report the United Kingdom and the Netherlands are the largest host countries for international corporations, whereas Brazil and Mexico are among the top hosts for developing economies. This report notes that five countries, namely the United States, United Kingdom, Japan, France and Germany, accounted for 73 per cent of the top 100 firms, while the EU alone represented 53 per cent of all entries.[66] What obligations, if any, do the home countries have in case these corporations cause severe environmental pollution or are involved in serious human rights violations in other countries? And what is the potential scope of extraterritorial application of domestic legal obligations of the home state for violations committed by international corporations in other countries?

A quick glance at the few cases adjudicated so far before domestic courts seems to indicate that these courts have interpreted the legal obligations of home States or parent companies quite restrictively. Thus, the Dutch court in the *Four Nigerian farmers and the Friends of the Earth v. Shell* held that the parent companies generally have no legal duty to prevent overseas damage to third parties by their subsidiaries.[67] Even if that were true with regard to the duty to prevent, what about the obligation to provide reparations for damages? Would that obligation extend from the subsidiaries to the parent companies? The extraterritorial reach of the domestic jurisdiction of the home state with regard to international corporations for serious damage to the environment in other states remains an area in need of further clarification. In an important recent finding in the *Kiobel* case, the US Supreme Court held that presumption against extraterritoriality applies to claims under the Aliens Tort Statute (ATS) and that there was no indication that the ATS was passed to make the United States a uniquely hospitable forum for the enforcement of international norms.[68] While there is an international trend towards trying to hold multinationals accountable in their home state for serious environmental damage caused by their activity or the activity of their subsidiary companies abroad, the cases tried so far before domestic courts reveal numerous jurisdictional hurdles.

---

[66] UNCTAD, 'The Universe of the Largest Transnational Corporations', p. 4.

[67] *Four Nigerian farmers and the Friends of the Earth v. Shell*, paras. 4.24 and 4.26–4.32.

[68] US Supreme Court, *Kiobel, individually and on behalf of her late husband Kiobel, et al. v. Royal Dutch Petroleum Co. et al.*, 17 April 2013, available at: www.supremecourt.gov/opinions/12pdf/10–1491_l6gn.pdf.

4.4. ENVIRONMENTAL PROTECTION AS A MATTER OF SHARED RESPONSIBILITY AMONG THE CORPORATION, THE HOST STATE AND THE HOME STATE

Deregulation, lack of clear legal standards and of a strong judiciary, as well as the asymmetry in bargaining power between certain corporations and host states, create the possibility for potential abuse, especially when the turnover of some of these corporations is comparable or bigger than the GDP of medium-sized countries.[69] An accountability gap then occurs if host states are either *unable or unwilling* to hold companies to reasonable minimum environmental standards.[70] Moreover, at times the state authorities in conflict or post-conflict areas collude with multinational enterprises against the local people and the environment.[71] If we are to ensure compliance with relevant international law obligations, the enforcement of these norms should be a matter not only for the host state, but also for the home state where the company is incorporated.

A closer look at how the relevant environmental protection mechanisms work, however, reveals that this is a matter of shared responsibility between different stakeholders, including multinational corporations and the relevant state authorities. That shared responsibility starts from the duty of notification of emergency situations.[72] With regard to oil pollution emergencies that duty is present in a number of instruments.[73] The same can be said of nuclear accidents.[74] The 1986 Convention on Early Notification of a Nuclear Accident applies in the event of 'any accident involving facilities or activities of a State party or of persons or legal entities under its jurisdiction and control'. Although Japan notified the International Atomic Energy Agency (IAEA) with regard to the 2011 Fukushima accident, it is questionable whether that can be considered to constitute sufficient notice for neighbouring countries. These international instruments are aimed at ensuring timely exchange of information between the competent national authorities, so as to reduce to the maximum extent possible the effects of environmental damage. States have the necessary channels of communication

---

[69] See UNCTAD, 'The Universe of the Largest Transnational Corporations', 2007.

[70] M.T. Kamminga, 'Corporate Obligations under International Law', paper presented at the 71st Conference of the International Law Association, plenary session on Corporate Social Responsibility and International Law, Berlin, 17 August 2004, p. 4.

[71] See inter alia OECD, 'Multinational Enterprises in Situations of Violent Conflict and Widespread Human Rights Abuses', Working Papers on International Investment No. 2002/1, May 2002, available at: www.oecd.org/countries/myanmar/2757771.pdf. See also J.E. Austin and C.E. Bruch (eds.), *The Environmental Consequences of War Legal, Economic, and Scientific Perspectives* (Cambridge: Cambridge University Press, 2000).

[72] P. Sands and J. Peel, *supra* n. 2, pp. 639–644.

[73] See Article 5(1) of the 1969 Bonn Agreement; Chapter 9, UNEP Regional Seas Conventions; Article 198 of the 1982 UNCLOS.

[74] See IAEA Guidelines on Reportable Events, Integrated Planning and Information Exchange of 1985 (IAEA Doc. INFCIRC/321); See also the 1986 Convention on Early Notification of a Nuclear Accident.

and the duty to share that information, so corporations should make available that information immediately to the relevant state authorities. Failure to comply with the obligation of giving notice about emergency situations triggers state responsibility and, most likely, the responsibility of the concerned corporation.

An example of shared responsibility between states and corporations comes also from the UN Convention on the Law of the Sea which prohibits not only states, but also natural and juridical persons from appropriating parts of the seabed or its minerals.[75] Corporations cannot explore for minerals, including for oil, without obtaining the necessary permissions from a state or from the International Seabed Authority.[76] And in granting these permissions the states also accept responsibility in case the exploration causes damage to the environment. International instruments aimed at the protection of the environment need to acknowledge the important role of corporations and address them directly in terms of responsibilities. That should be a standard approach especially in areas of activity which carries a heightened risk of causing serious damage to the environment as oil spills and nuclear safety and waste management issues. Transnational corporations can be held indirectly accountable via the home state by adapting the *due diligence* test and the *decisive influence* standard to the relationship between home states and these transnational corporations.[77]

Shared state responsibility would play an important role also and especially when environmental pollution happens in areas where no state exercises jurisdiction, such as in the open seas. At the same time, it must be recognised that, potentially, shared responsibility might create also an unnecessary burden for companies when both states, namely the host state and the home state, apply their laws simultaneously, not to speak about possible contradictory administrative or judicial decisions or forum shopping. The forum with higher standards of environmental protection and an independent judiciary would be the preferred forum for adjudicating possible environmental disputes. Obviously, solving problems concerning environmental protection from serious harm cannot be left to domestic legislation alone, at a time when corporations operate in many different states, including weak states. In addition, the extraterritorial application of environmental domestic law carries the risk of creating jurisdictional conflicts, with the potential of adversely affecting inter-state relations. A proposal by De Schutter is to work towards a Convention on Combating Human Rights Violations by Transnational Corporations, which could impose on the home states of TNCs

---

[75]   Art. 137(1) UN Convention on the Law of the Sea (1982) provides: 'No State shall claim or exercise sovereignty or sovereign rights over any part of the Area or its resources, nor shall any State or natural or juridical person appropriate any part thereof. No such claim or exercise of sovereignty or sovereign rights nor such appropriation shall be recognized'.

[76]   See the Regulations and Recommendations adopted by the International Seabed Authority under the 'Mining Code', available at: www.isa.org.jm/mining-code.

[77]   See S. Narula, 'International Financial Institutions, Transnational Corporations, and Duties of States' in M. Langford et al. (eds.), *Global Justice, State Duties: The Extraterritorial Scope of Economic, Social and Cultural Rights in International Law* (Cambridge: Cambridge University Press, 2013), pp. 114–149, 148.

an obligation to adopt parent-based extraterritorial regulation, allowing the home state to exercise extraterritorial jurisdiction where this appears necessary to avoid impunity, or where victims would have no effective remedy before the national courts of the host state.[78]

5. THE COMPLEXITY OF ATTRIBUTION OF RESPONSIBILITY AND ADJUDICATION OF CASES OF SERIOUS ENVIRONMENTAL DAMAGE

John Ruggie has proposed a framework for business and human rights based on a three-pillar structure which includes the state's duty to protect against human rights abuses by third parties, including business; the corporate responsibility to respect human rights; and greater access by victims to effective remedies, both judicial and non-judicial. As individuals, communities, and human rights organisations become more informed and more assertive with regard to environmental issues, environmental dispute settlement is changing and national courts are becoming increasingly more involved. However, as noted above, jurisdictional hurdles and other factors related to access to justice make it rather difficult for individuals to adjudicate their claims and grievances, either in host states or in home states. Evidently, the host and the home state share differentiated responsibilities. The host state has a standing interest in preserving the quality of its environment and primary responsibility in ensuring that actors carrying out economic activities in its territory respect its environment.[79] To that aim the host state must sanction corporations for environmental damage, it must investigate alleged violations, and it must provide for effective remedies to victims.

At the same time, it is evident that the home state or even a third state might also be rather important in ensuring corporate compliance with environmental standards, in view of the process of outsourcing, subcontracting, and offshoring to countries with lower production costs, lower wages, and lower labour and environmental standards.[80] States are not only encouraged, but they have an obligation to regulate the conduct of corporations acting extraterritorially.[81] In the case of private transnational corporations this obligation would be limited

---

[78]   O. de Schutter, 'Sovereignty-plus in the era of interdependence: toward an international convention on combating human rights violations by transnational corporations' in P.H.F. Bekker, R. Dolzer, and M. Waibel (eds.), *Making Transnational Law Work in the Global Economy: Essays in Honour of Detlev Vagts* (Cambridge: Cambridge University Press, 2010), pp. 245–284, 283.

[79]   See inter alia J. Ruggie, 'State responsibilities to regulate and adjudicate corporate activities under the United Nations core human rights treaties: an overview of treaty body commentaries', UN Doc. A/HRC/4/35/add.1 of 13 February 2007.

[80]   A. Heinemann, 'Business Enterprises in Public International Law' in U. Fastenrath et al. (eds.), *From Bilateralism to Community Interest* (Oxford: Oxford University Press, 2011), p. 722.

[81]   Report of the Special Representative of the Secretary-General on the issue of human rights and transnational corporations and other business enterprises, J. Ruggie, 'Protect, Respect and

to ensuring that corporations do not violate *jus cogens* norms, especially that they are not directly responsible or complicit in internationally recognised crimes as genocide, war crimes and crimes against humanity. In the case of state-owned, or where the state exercises effective control over a transnational corporation, that legal obligation potentially extends beyond ensuring non-violation of fundamental human rights. The implementation of suitable environmental standards should be based on the principle of subsidiarity, whereby the state in whose territory the violations occur is competent to handle the complaints and otherwise victims should have the right to seek redress in the home state of the company in question.[82] While this solution seems appealing in terms of avoiding unnecessary overlap, the extent of obligations to protect the environment under international law on the part of third states remains debatable. The fact that a host state might be complicit in environmental damage caused by economic activity does not relieve a corporation from its responsibility to compensate the victims for the damage it has caused. Eventually, this can be seen as a matter of shared responsibility, where the state as well as the corporation concerned has to compensate natural and legal persons affected by the environmental damage caused, based on the rules concerning attribution of conduct. Clearly, there are several complex scenarios which might arise in this regard.

How to overcome difficulties arising when disputes which are inherently multilateral are referred to an adjudicatory structure that is designed to operate in a purely bilateral framework?[83] The community interest in making whole the injured justifies the remedy, while it is the wrongful nature of the conduct that supplies the reason for making the wrongdoer pay.[84] A question which arises in the context of environmental damages is that of the desirability of awarding punitive or exemplary damages to the injured party? An award of punitive or exemplary damages makes the admonitory function of the reparation more important and express than it would be if money judgments were limited to compensatory damages.[85] In turn, this practice could prove useful especially in terms of deterrence and punishment of serious offenders.

The ICJ has dealt with a number of cases, where environmental issues have been either central or incidental to the main legal dispute.[86] Three of these cases

---

[   ] Remedy: a Framework for Business and Human Rights', UN Doc. A/HRC/8/5, 7 April 2008, para. 19.

[82] A. Heinemann, *supra* n. 80, p. 734.

[83] P.N. Okowa, *supra* n. 5, pp. 157–172.

[84] D. Shelton, *Remedies in International Human Rights Law*, 2nd edn. (Oxford: Oxford University Press, 2005), p. 354.

[85] *Ibid.*, p. 354.

[86] *Certain Phosphate Lands in Nauru (Nauru v. Australia)*; *Gabčíkovo-Nagymaros Project (Hungary v. Slovakia)*; *Legality of the Threat or Use of Nuclear Weapons* (advisory opinion); *Nuclear Tests Cases (New Zealand and Australia v. France)*; *Aerial Herbicide Spraying (Ecuador v. Colombia)*; *Pulp Mills on the River Uruguay (Argentina v. Uruguay)*; *Certain Activities Carried out by Nicaragua in the Border Area (Costa Rica v. Nicaragua)*.

relate to nuclear weapons and nuclear tests.[87] Another settlement mechanism concerning the effects of nuclear weapons is the Marshall Islands Nuclear Claims Tribunal.[88] Besides the ICJ, which settles inter-state disputes, another possible forum for litigation of disputes of an environmental character are the special tribunals under Article 27 of the European Energy Treaty.[89] The United Nations Environment Program (UNEP) also keeps a list of arbitrators.[90] The Permanent Court of Arbitration has done considerable work with regard to environmental dispute resolution by adopting its Optional Rules for Arbitration of Disputes Relating to the Environment and/or Natural Resources ('Environmental Rules') in 2001 and its Optional Rules for Conciliation of Disputes Relating to the Environment and/or Natural Resources in 2002.[91] Under Article 287 of the United Nations Convention on the Law of the Sea (UNCLOS) of 1982 disputes relating to the protection of the marine environment may be referred to the special arbitral procedure provided for in Annex VIII.[92] There are hints that issues concerning climate change could be brought before the International Court in the future.[93] UNEP has done considerable work with regard to developing guidelines for tackling environmental damage and in 2010 it adopted the Guidelines for the Development of National Legislation on Access to Information, Public Participation and Access to Justice in Environmental Matters and Guidelines for the Development of Domestic Legislation on Liability, Response Action and Compensation for Damage Caused by Activities Dangerous to the Environment.[94]

---

[87]   Namely *Nuclear Tests Cases (New Zealand and Australia v. France)* and *Legality of the Threat or Use of Nuclear Weapons* (Advisory Opinion). See also the recent cases brought in 2014 by the Marshall Islands against India, Pakistan and the United Kingdom.

[88]   For more information see www.nuclearclaimstribunal.com. In June 1983, a formal Agreement between the Government of the United States and the Government of the Marshall Islands for the Implementation of Section 177 of the Compact of Free Association was entered into (Section 177 Agreement). In that agreement, the US recognised the contributions and sacrifices made by the people of the Marshall Islands in regard to the Nuclear Testing Program and accepted the responsibility for compensation owing to citizens of the Marshall Islands for loss or damage to property and person resulting from that testing.

[89]   For more details see www.encharter.org under 'Dispute Settlement'. The list of investor-state dispute settlement cases compiled by the Energy Charter Secretariat contains 33 cases.

[90]   For more information on UNEP see inter alia: www.unep.org/environmentalgovernance.

[91]   For more information on this topic and the full texts of the Optional Rules see: www.pca-cpa. org/showpage.asp?pag_id=1058.

[92]   UNCLOS, 1833 UNTS 397. See also D. Vidas (ed.), *Protecting the Polar Marine Environment Law and Policy for Pollution Prevention* (Cambridge: Cambridge University Press, 2000).

[93]   Palau seems to have been preparing an initiative to bring the issue of climate change for an advisory opinion by the ICJ. More generally on this issue see M.G. Faure and A. Nollkaemper, 'International Liability as an Instrument to Prevent and Compensate for Climate Change' (2007) 26A *Stanford Journal of International Law* 124–176.

[94]   See United Nations Environment Programme Guidelines for the Development of National Legislation on Access to Information, Public Participation and Access to Justice in Environmental Matters, Annex to Decision SS.XI/5 A (2010); United Nations Environment Programme Guidelines for the Development of Domestic Legislation on Liability, Response Action and Compensation for Damage Caused by Activities Dangerous to the Environment, Annex to Decision SS.XI/5 B (2010).

With regard to remedies it must be added that they also include domestic judicial remedies, as well as non-judicial remedies under the National Contact Points (NCPs) system established under the OECD Guidelines,[95] as well as complaints before human rights institutions and others, including remedies offered by the corporations themselves. The OECD Guidelines for Multinational Enterprises provide for an implementation mechanism through the NCPs, which are to handle grievances. However, this mechanism has been criticised by the UN Special Rapporteur on Business and Human Rights for NCPs proximity to governments, their lack of resources and the absence of precise rules.[96] Besides these shortcomings, the NCP system faces a number of other jurisdictional limitations which affect their role in ensuring compliance with environmental standards.

6. CONCLUDING REMARKS

Wolfgang Friedmann suggested long ago that private corporations are participants in the evolution of modern international law.[97] Participating in the making of international law and carrying out economic activity which could potentially seriously damage the environment entails both rights and obligations. That does not mean that the legal obligations concerning the protection of the environment from serious harm are transferred from the host state or the home State to international corporations, but that certain aspects of environmental protection responsibilities can be seen as shared among them. The host state should ensure that a suitable legal framework is in place to protect the interest of the affected population from serious environmental damage arising from oil pollution or nuclear accidents. Home states could also provide an important forum for adjudicating disputes concerning serious environmental damage caused by international corporations in another state's territory. On their part, international corporations must comply with existing legal framework and in case of serious environmental damage caused by their activity have an obligation to provide compensation for those affected.

Specific areas of economic activity which have a high level of risk for damaging the environment, such as oil pollution and nuclear accidents, necessitate a heightened level of supervision and legal regulation. Voluntary commitments on the part of international corporations in these areas are not sufficient. Strict

---

95   See inter alia J.C. Ochoa Sanchez, 'The Roles and Powers of the OECD National Contact Points Regarding Complaints on an Alleged Breach of the OECD Guidelines for Multinational Enterprises by a Transnational Corporation' (2015) 84(1) *Nordic Journal of International Law* 89–126.

96   See J. Ruggie, 'Protect, Respect and Remedy: A Framework for Business and Human Rights', UN Doc. A/HRC/8/5, 7, 26 (April 2008).

97   W. Friedmann, *The Changing Structure of International Law* (New York: Columbia University Press, 1964), p. 230.

legal regulation is necessary since there are few, if any, incentives for international corporations to follow other rules than those which are legally binding. The protection of the environment from serious damage is a case of shared, but differentiated responsibility, on the part of corporation and the states concerned. Notably, responsibilities for ensuring environmental protection from serious damage lay not only with the state where the corporation exercises its economic activity, that is the host state, but also with the state where the corporation is registered, that is the home state. In the case of international corporations which are state-owned it might be possible to speak about a fusion of responsibilities between the state and the corporation concerned, since depending on the circumstances the corporation could be seen as an organ of the state. In cases of international corporations where the state holds a part of the shares, the responsibility for serious environmental damage is shared. In the case of private international corporations, issues of responsibility are more nuanced and suitable mechanisms should be found so as to ensure the protection of the environment and at the same time that the persons affected are able to get compensation in case of serious damage.

CHAPTER 4

THE BUSINESS CASE FOR TAKING HUMAN RIGHTS OBLIGATIONS SERIOUSLY

Güler ARAS*

1. INTRODUCTION

Corporate behaviour is important for company success both financially and concerning the relationship between corporate and business interests (stakeholders). We cannot define corporate behaviour without an ethical and CSR base in order to refer to that behavioural aspect. Corporate behaviour involves legal rules, ethical codes of conduct and social responsibility principles. In other words corporate behaviour is based on all of these components and involves law, ethics and CSR. It is important to recognise also that this behaviour must be ethical but must also be seen to be ethical – perceptions are very important. Corporate behaviour has effects not only on stakeholders and shareholders but also on the entire economy. When a corporation acts ethically and socially responsibly in its business decisions and strategic planning then that corporation will be more sustainable. As we have seen, socially responsible corporate behaviour is increasingly regarded as essential to the long-term survival of companies.[1]

The chapter examines the business reasons for taking human rights obligations seriously. Human rights norms, bereft of business drivers, are not likely to be taken seriously by companies. It is therefore instructive to examine the sound business reasons for embracing the norms in business operations, both from the

* The writer wishes to thank Dennis Driscoll, former Dean of the Law School at the National University of Ireland (Galway) for a number of helpful contributions to this chapter.

[1] See, for example, the 2014 Nielsen Global Survey on Corporate Social Responsibility to the effect that an increasing number of consumers across 60 countries are willing to pay more for products and services by companies committed to CSR: www.nielsen.com/us/en/press-room/2014/global-consumers-are-willing-to-put-their-money-where-their-heart-is.html. See also, for example, M. Blowfield and A. Murray, *Corporate Responsibility: A Critical Introduction* (Oxford: Oxford University Press, 2008), pp. 130–157; and G. Aras and D. Crowther, *Governance and Social Responsibility: International Perspective* (London: Palgrave McMillian, 2012).

point of view of multinational companies as well as from the point of view of their supply chain partners in developing countries. The chapter analyses the business reasons from the viewpoint of companies themselves as well as that of their entire range of stakeholders: investors, consumers, employees, business partners, suppliers, government, and local communities and other elements of civil society. To take a single example, approximately 1,300 organisations; including asset owners, institutional investors with more than $45 trillion under management have pledged that they will integrate CSR (and therefore human rights) into their investment analysis and decision making[2]. This development represents a kind of financial earthquake although it is not yet understood in corporate boardrooms nor by the management of supply chain companies.

It might be helpful at this point simply to make a brief comment about the broad meaning of corporate social responsibility (CSR). In reality, CSR involves a number of quite distinct issue areas: human rights; labour rights (which are of course human rights too); environmental concerns such as pollution, waste management and climate change (all of which may have substantial impacts on the human population); corporate philanthropy, involving, for instance, donations for education and health care; corporate governance, involving the direction and control of companies in terms of strategy and the monitoring of CSR and other risks; and, finally, the broadest category, itself containing a number of quite distinct issue areas, ethical business practices (such as product safety and corrupt business practices).

All of the above issue areas involve a number of human rights norms whether directly or indirectly. For example, the bribery of civil servants in developing countries represents not simply wrongful, criminal activity but, if substantial, the indirect distortion of economic development and the experiences of health care, educational and other opportunities for deprived populations.[3]

Institutional investors have increasingly come to recognise that pursuing CSR goals in business operations is not simply about ethical behaviour. It is also about the minimisation of economic risks that stems from macro economic conditions such as government regulation, exchange rates, and political stability. To take perhaps the most obvious recent example, the explosion of the BP oil rig in the Gulf of Mexico resulted in the death of 11 workers. It has been claimed that BP was insufficiently attentive to the safety of workers.[4] A federal court in New Orleans is currently considering a negligence claim concerning the oil spill itself, which may have led to the discharge of almost 5 billion barrels

---

[2]   Report on Progress 2014, *Principles for Responsible Investment*, October 2014, available at: http://2xjmlj8428u1a2k5o34l1m71.wpengine.netdna-cdn.com/wp-content/uploads/2014_report_on_progress.pdf.

[3]   See, for instance, in the case of Kenya, M. Wrong, *It's Our Turn to Eat* (New York: Harper Collins Publishers, 2010).

[4]   'Deep Water: The Gulf Oil Disaster and the Future of Offshore Drilling', Report to the President, National Commission on the BP Deepwater Horizon Oil Spill and Offshore Drilling, January 2011.

of oil. A finding of gross negligence on BP's part will lead to a fine of as much as approximately $20 billion. Meanwhile, BP has settled a number of civil and criminal claims for approximately $42 billion.[5] Four years after the accident in 2010, the company's share price is still down by 30% over the pre-oil spill price. The BP oil spill appears to be an outstanding example of how inattentiveness to worker safety can lead to the destruction of shareholder value. There could not be a clearer link between a human rights norm and the business incentive to take CSR seriously.

2. THE BUSINESS DRIVERS FOR CSR

Corporate social responsibility is an important issue in contemporary international debates. In the past twenty years, CSR appears to have become more difficult to escape from, being more relevant to corporations all over the world. Carroll (1979: 500) describes CSR in these terms: 'the social responsibility of business encompasses the economic, legal, ethical, and discretionary expectations that society has of organizations at a given point in time'. After his definition, in 2002 Whetten *et al.* defined CSR as 'societal expectations of corporate behaviour; a behaviour that is alleged by a stakeholder to be expected by society or morally required and is therefore justifiably demanded of a business'. After the first definition, the CSR definition, on the one hand, expanded and covered more corporate behaviour and stakeholder expectation. On the other hand, some broad terms – especially 'society' – have been narrowed to 'stakeholders'. Corporate behaviour toward the stakeholders is becoming a much more important concept in every definition. Corporate behaviour is an important concept because it has to be ethical, legal, and responsible behaviour for organisations, stakeholders and society. This aspect of the corporate behaviour has more benefit for society also and so that is why it is more related with ethics and CSR.[6]

The broadest definition of corporate social responsibility is concerned with what is – or should be – the relationship between the global corporation, governments of countries and individual citizens. More locally the definition is concerned with the relationship between a corporation and the local society in which it resides or operates. Another definition is concerned with the relationship between a corporation and its stakeholders. All of these definitions are pertinent and represent a dimension of the issue.

A parallel debate is taking place in the arena of ethics – should corporations be controlled through increased regulation or has the ethical base of citizenship been lost and in need of replacement before socially responsible behaviour will ensue? However this debate is represented, it seems that it is concerned with

---

5   Further, criminal charges have been filed against six BP workers.
6   See G. Aras and D. Crowther, *supra* n. 1.

some sort of social contract between corporations and stakeholders and society. This social contract implies some form of altruistic behaviour – the converse of selfishness whereas self-interest connotes selfishness. Self-interest is central to the utilitarian perspective championed by such people as Bentham, Locke and J.S. Mill. The latter for example advocated as morally right the pursuit of the greatest happiness for the greatest number. Similarly Adam Smith's free-market economics is predicated in competing self-interest.[7] These influential ideas put the interest of the individual above the interest of the collective. The central tenet of social responsibility however is the social contract between all the stakeholders to society, which is an essential requirement of civil society. This is alternatively described as citizenship but for either term it is important to remember that the social responsibility needs to extend beyond present members of society. Social responsibility also requires a responsibility towards the future and towards future members of society.

Subsumed within this is of course a responsibility towards the environment because of implications for other members of society both now and in the future.[8] Moreover corporate behaviour affects responsible and proper economic and institutional improvement. It will also be also an influence on all society and a common benefit.

For the sake of brevity, the important business drivers militating in favour of good CSR behaviour can be regarded as involving five distinct matters:

- investor relations and access to capital;
- competiveness and market positioning;
- employee recruitment, retention and productivity;
- the minimisation of legal risk; and
- preserving the 'licence to operate'.

The discussion will now turn to each of these distinct matters.

2.1. INVESTOR RELATIONS AND ACCESS TO CAPITAL

One of the most important factors for any company is the relationship between it and its various stakeholders. This is important for the general management of the company and not just for its approach to CSR. Many factors affect these relationships. Stakeholders have rights and interests in a company. The agency relationship and the governance arrangements in particular determine the

---

[7] See G. Aras and D. Crowther, *The Durable Corporation: Strategies for Sustainable Development* (Farnham: Gower Publishing Limited, 2009).

[8] See, for example, A. Cramer and Z. Karabell, *Sustainable Excellence* (New York: Rodale, 2010); C. Laszlo, *The Sustainable Company* (Washington: Island Press, 2005); and G. Aras and D. Crowther, *supra* n. 1.

relationship between the managers of the organisation and its stakeholders but particularly its owners and investors.

Agency theory suggests how to govern a modern corporation with a large number of shareholders whose collective capital is controlled and directed by separate shareholders. Jensen and Meckling's (1976) model on agency costs and ownership structure holds a central role in the corporate governance literature.[9]

However, perhaps the single greatest influence, now and in the immediate future, concerning the business case for taking human rights obligations seriously is the adherence to the UN-supported Principles for Responsible Investment by more than 1,380 investment institutions with approximately $59 trillion under management. They own approximately 20% of the shares of all the stock exchanges in the world. The fact that the Principles for Responsible Investment were introduced only in 2006 and have received such extensive support is simply remarkable.[10]

These institutional investors, such as the Norwegian Pension Fund (approximately $725 billion under investment) and the California Public Employees' Retirement System (CalPERS, $255 billion under investment) are exercising a powerful influence on the minds of the executive management of multinational corporations. The Norwegian Pension Fund, for instance, is the largest single shareholder in Europe, owning a total of 1.78% of all shares on European stock exchanges.

Under the Principles for Responsible Investment, institutions solemnly pledge to integrate CSR considerations into investment analysis and decision making. It might be useful to set out the solemn pledges here:

> As institutional investors, we have a duty to act in the best long-term interest of our beneficiaries. In this fiduciary role, we believe that environmental, social and corporate governance [CSR] issues can affect the performance of investment portfolios [...] Therefore, where consistent with our fiduciary responsibilities, we commit to the following:

---

[9]   G. Aras and O. Kutlu Furtuna, 'Does Governance Efficiency Impact Equity Agency Costs? Evidence from Turkey', *Emerging Markets Finance & Trade Journal (EMFT)* (2015).

[10]   It is also appropriate to mention here, however briefly, the UN Guiding Principles on Business and Human Rights (often referred to as the 'Ruggie Principles'). The Principles have three pillars: the State's duty to protect against human rights abuses, including abuses by companies; the corporate duty to respect human rights; and the State's responsibility to provide access to remedies for abuses. The UN Human Rights Council endorsed the Principles in 2011. Corporate support for the Principles has been disappointingly slow in coming. The Business & Human Rights Resource Centre reported that fewer than 400 companies (out of a total of more than 80,000 multinational companies) had adopted a human rights policy as of December 2013. For an account of the development of the Principles, see J. Ruggie, *Just Business: Multinational Companies and Human Rights* (New York: W.W. Norton & Company, 2013). For a recent account of the status of the Principles, see S. Ariel Aaronson and I. Higham, 'Putting the Blame on Governments: Why Firms and Governments Have Failed to Advance the Guiding Principles on Business and Human Rights', available at: www.gwu.edu/~iiep/assets/docs/papers/2014WP/AaronsonHingham201406.pdf (accessed on 25 October 2014).

1. We will incorporate [CSR] issues into investment analysis and decision-making processes.
2. We will be active owners and incorporate [CSR] issues to our ownership policies and practices.
3. We will seek appropriate disclosure on [CSR] issues by the entities in which we invest.
4. We will promote acceptance and implementation of the Principles within the investment industry.
5. We will work together to enhance our effectiveness in implementing the Principles.
6. We will each report on our activities and progress in implementing Principles.

Adherents to the Principles have been active in seeking cooperation with each other in their common goal of enhancing their investor effectiveness on CSR matters. Roughly 400 PRI signatories have joined in one or more of almost 200 collaborative initiatives.

A single example will have to suffice. A coalition of some 30 PRI signatories, with approximately $3 trillion under management, wrote letters to CEOs of non-communicating Global Compact companies[11] to encourage them to fulfil the minimum reporting requirements for continued active Global Compact membership. As a result of that initiative, 76% of the hitherto non-performing companies regained active Global Compact status. The PRI Secretariat comments that '[t]his is the highest success rate for this engagement to date'.[12] Fundamental to this initiative is the importance of giving accurate, transparent CSR information to the market, as will be discussed below.

The United Nations Global Compact, referred to above, has also to be considered separately in terms of the important business drivers for CSR norms. The Global Compact Principles are a series of 10 principles that companies[13] pledge to honour in their business operations. Although the Global Compact Principles are quite well known in the human rights community, it might nonetheless be useful for the sake of convenience to set out the Global Compact pledges here:

---

[11] Global Compact participating companies are required to communicate with their stakeholders on an annual basis concerning their performance regarding the 10 Global Compact Principles. A non-communicating company is a company that has failed to communicate on progress by the relevant deadline for that company. Participating companies who do not communicate two years in a row are de-listed by the Global Compact Secretariat.

[12] 'Collaborations', *Principles for Responsible Investments*, available at: www.unpri.org/areas-of-work/collaborations/?post_id=3213.

[13] And associated stakeholders. For a recent, succinct account of the operation of the Global Compact, see D. Grayson and J. Nelson, *Corporate Social Responsibility Coalitions: The Past, Present and Future of Alliances for Sustainable Capitalism* (London: Greenleaf Publishing, 2013), pp. 328–346. For critical commentary, see S.P. Sethi and D.H. Schepers, 'United Nations Global Compact: The Promise-Performance Gap' (2014) 112(2) *Journal of Business Ethics* 193–208.

Human Rights

Principle 1: Businesses should support and respect the protection of internationally proclaimed human rights; and

Principle 2: Make sure that they are not complicit in human rights abuses.

Labour

Principle 3: Businesses should uphold the freedom of association and the effective recognition of the right of collective bargaining;

Principle 4: The elimination of all forms of forced and compulsory labour;

Principle 5: The effective abolition of child labour;

Principle 6: The elimination of discrimination in respect of employment and occupation.

Environment

Principle 7: Businesses should support a precautionary approach to environmental challenges;

Principle 8: Undertake initiatives to promote greater environmental responsibility; and

Principle 9: Encourage the development and diffusion of environmentally friendly technologies.

Anti-Corruption

Principle 10: Businesses should work against corruption in all its forms, including bribery and extortion.

The signatories to the Global Compact have established a number of working groups to deal with the various Principles, and, remarkably, the Global Compact Secretariat has sponsored more than 1,000 international dialogues since its establishment in 2000 exploring the implications and implementation of the Principles. Such dialogues have an important value, assuming the good faith of the participating companies, because it cannot be assumed that companies understand the full implications of their Global Compact promises simply because they have made them. As an aid to understanding the implementation of the human rights promises, the Global Compact, in cooperation with the Office of the High Commissioner of Human Rights has published a series of practical guidebooks.[14]

---

[14]   'Embedding Human Rights into Business Practice', Joint Publication of the United Nations Global Compact and Office of the High Commissioner of Human Right, available at: www. ohchr.org/Documents/Publications/Embeddingen.pdf; 'Embedding Human Rights into Business Practice II', Joint Publication of the United Nations Global Compact and Office of the High Commissioner of Human Right, 2007, available at: www.ohchr.org/Documents/ Publications/Embedding_II.pdf; 'Embedding Human Rights into Business Practice III', Joint Publication of the United Nations Global Compact and Office of the High Commissioner of

The next thing to observe is that market interest in CSR information is growing both considerably and rapidly. Researchers at Harvard Business School studied access to Bloomberg CSR data over a six-month period from November 2010–April 2011.[15] During that six-month period, there were approximately 44 million 'hits' seeking CSR information. The researchers observe that:

> [The] data show that the market is very interested in knowing a company's degree of transparency around [CSR] performance and policies [...] Our hypothesis is that [...] the market perceives less risk in investing in more transparent companies because there is less uncertainty about their ability to deliver on expected financial performance. This is due to using effective [CSR] management to capture revenue-generating opportunities, achieve cost savings, and minimise the downside of failures, fines, and lawsuits.[16]

The call for improved CSR performance has also affected stock exchanges. A recent analysis of major stock exchanges revealed that the major exchanges were interested in promoting greater corporate disclosure on CSR issues. The Sustainable Stock Exchanges Initiative[17] surveyed 27 major stock exchanges including the London Stock Exchange, the Tokyo Stock Exchange, the Toronto Stock Exchange, the German Stock Exchange, Nasdaq OMX, and a number of large Emerging Market Stock Exchanges. The survey revealed that interest was developing rapidly concerning CSR disclosure. For example, 57% of the stock exchanges reported that they believed that CSR requirements for listed companies made good business sense, up from 38% only two years previously, as shown by figure 4.1.[18]

Human Right, 2009, available at: www.unglobalcompact.org/docs/issues_doc/human_rights/Resources/EHRBIII.pdf.

[15] R.G. Eccles, M.P. Krzus and G. Serefeim, 'Market Interest in Nonfinancial Information', Harvard Business School Working Paper Series 12–018, 22 September 2011. Eccles and Serefeim are at Harvard Business School; Krzus is in fact a business consultant.

[16] *Ibid.*, p. 7. Further, the writers conclude: 'We predict that as more companies disclose more nonfinancial information, as more knowledge is developed by research and teaching programmes in business schools and as more sophisticated valuation models are developed by investors, *market interest in nonfinancial information will exponentially increase in the future*' (p. 15, emphasis added).

[17] The Sustainable Stock Exchanges Initiative is a joint initiative of the UN Principles for Responsible Investment, the United Nations Conference on Trade and Investment, the UN Environment Programme Finance Initiative, and the Un Global Compact. See: www.SSEinitiative.org.

[18] 'Sustainable Stock Exchanges: A Report on Progress. A Paper Prepared for the Sustainable Stock Exchanges 2012 Global Dialogue', Sustainable Stock Exchanges Initiative, p. 33.

Figure 4.1. CSR requirements for listed companies

How much do you agree or disagree with the following statement?
'Having strong [CSR] disclosure requirements for listed makes good business sense for a stock exchange'

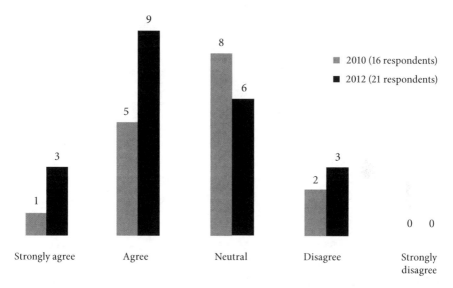

Source: Sustainable Stock Exchanges Initiative, *Sustainable Stock Exchanges: A Report on Progress* (2012).

To take a second example, 76% of the 21 stock exchanges participating in the survey declared that they believed that they had 'a responsibility to encourage greater corporate responsibility of sustainability issues'.[19] It is noticeable that this sense of stock exchanges' own involvement is growing, as table 4.1 below demonstrates.

Table 4.1. Stock exchanges' involvement in CSR

	2010	2012
Stock exchange have a responsibility to encourage greater CSR	63%	76%
Stock exchanges have *no* responsibility concerning CSR	13%	5%

Source: Sustainable Stock Exchanges Initiative, *Sustainable Stock Exchanges: A Report on Progress* (2012).

---

[19]   *Ibid.*, p. 25.

The authors of the Sustainable Stock Exchanges Initiative report argue that:

> [The] strong conviction [that stock exchanges have a responsibility to encourage greater CSR performance] is reflected in advances in
> – including provisions of guidance or encouragement of sustainability disclosure by issuers;
> – the proliferation of sustainability indices; and
> – the transition of voluntary disclosure requirements to a stricter 'comply or explain' basis in some markets.[20]

This brief survey of investor and corporate interest allows us to conclude that many institutional investors have developed a very considerable interest in CSR performance. It is not simply a matter of ethics, although ethics influence some investor thinking. It is also a matter of the minimisation of risk. Corporate behaviour heedless of CSR risks is simply not prudent, nor does it characterise sustainable investment.

2.2. CONSUMERS

It is easy to think that individual customers have little power when faced with the power of large organisation from which goods and services must be purchased. Often there is a tendency to think that if we are not happy with those goods or services, or even with the organisation itself, then our only alternative is to not purchase those goods and services. Thus, we must either purchase alternatives from another supplier or manage without. This is a simplistic view of the relationship between customers and their suppliers as organisations are reluctant to lose customers. In general it costs around six times as much to attract a customer as it does to retain an existing customer, so businesses as a businesses will inevitable try to retain customers as well as attract new ones. This view of the power relationship between individuals and businesses is also somewhat simplistic as customers have exerted significant influences upon businesses.[21] Therefore, we have to consider the ways in which individuals can, and have, influenced organisations through their actions as well as institutions and businesses.

A second important pressure comes from consumers in many industrialised countries and in certain developing countries as well. People in industrialised countries are increasingly interested that companies should behave in a socially responsible way. This has been revealed most graphically in a recent survey commissioned by the European Commission, *How Companies Influence Our Society: Citizens' View*. Considering European Union countries first, an impressive

---

[20] *Ibid.*, p. 5.
[21] See G. Aras and D. Crowther, *supra* n. 1.

79% of those surveyed declared that they were interested in the CSR behaviour of companies operating in their respective countries.[22]

Figure 4.2. How companies influence society

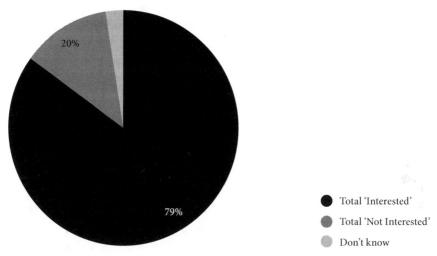

Total 'Interested'

Total 'Not Interested'

Don't know

Source: European Commission, *How Companies Influence Our Society* (2013).

The figure in the United States was even higher: 87% of Americans declared that they were interested in the CSR behaviour of companies operating in the United States. The European Commission also surveyed some large 'emerging markets' and found similarly high levels of interest in CSR in India (77%) and Brazil (73%) but lower levels in Turkey (31%) and China (31%). For the sake of interest, the chart of the 34 countries survey is reproduced in figure 4.3 below.[23]

Ironically enough, companies, especially the famous brands, can simply not afford to ignore consumer interest in their behaviour. To take a contemporary example as this chapter is being written, Facebook and various of its advertisers have encountered trouble with feminist activists concerning Facebook pages that contain hate speech against women. Some of the pages contained names such as 'Violently Raping Your Friend Just for Laughs', and some pages contained graphic images of women being abused.

Activists sent more than 5,000 e-mails to Facebook's advertisers urging them to withdraw their ads from the site. Within days of the start of the campaign, Nissan announced that it was withdrawing from Facebook advertising until it could be assured that its ads would not appear on pages with offensive content. For its part, Facebook acknowledged publicly that 'its systems to identify and

---

[22]   'How Companies Influence Our Society: Citizen's View Report', TNS Political & Social at the request of the European Commission, April 2013, p. 13.

[23]   *Ibid.*, p. 14.

remove hate speech have failed to work as effectively as we would like, particularly around issues of gender-based hate'.[24]

Therefore the relative power of various stakeholder groupings has changed quite radically in recent years. In particular, individuals – as either consumers or customers – have more power and are more willing to use it. This is primarily due to IT and the ability to combine readily with others from different geographical locations around the world. It has taken corporations a long time to realise this and react accordingly.

Figure 4.3. Company CSR interest

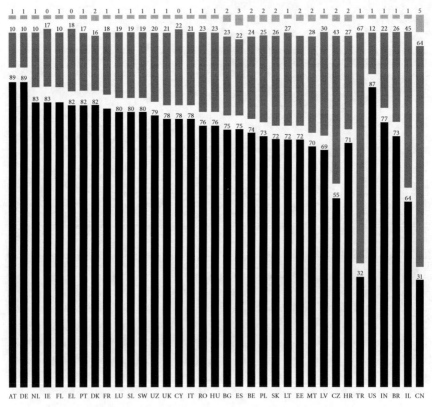

Source: European Commission, *How Companies Influence Our Society* (2013).

---

[24] 'Hate speech drives some advertisers off Facebook', *International Herald Tribune*, 30 May 2013, p. 15. See also 'The lessons from making Facebook take control of its adverts', *Financial Times*, 31 May 2013, p. 7.

Individuals are not necessarily passive in their reaction towards the corporations which supply them with goods and services. Neither do they necessarily behave from selfish motives, as there is ample evidence of altruism and concern for others and for the environment. This, therefore, is a part of the complexity of understanding CSR behaviour. Corporations themselves understand this and act accordingly, and a part of the public relations aspect of corporate behaviour is concerned with understanding and reacting to this aspect of individual behaviour.[25]

2.3. EMPLOYEE RECRUITMENT, RETENTION AND PRODUCTIVITY

Some institutional investors and activists believe that good CSR performance has an impact on employee recruitment, retention and productivity. Added to this is the fact that in many industries worldwide, there is an acknowledged skills shortage – for instance, in accounting, IT, the extractive industries, and engineering. Poor CSR performance therefore has a knock-on effect regarding employment.

An apt example is Shell's difficulties in the mid-1990s concerning two quite different issues: the decision to dump a disused oil storage facility into the North Atlantic; and the trial and subsequent execution of nine Ogoni activists in the Nigerian delta. In spring 1995, Shell decided to dump the disused oil storage facility into the North Atlantic. The NGO Greenpeace objected on environmental grounds and then launched a media campaign that became a major headache for Shell. The media campaign generated a considerable amount of negative publicity in many European countries. In Germany, for instance, Shell's petrol sales fell by 30%. Shell ultimately decided that the reputational damage it was encountering was too severe and the company decided to reverse its decision and *not* to dump the Brent Spar into the sea. Shell towed the oil storage facility to Norway, where it was disassembled. Some months later, in the autumn of 1995, Shell encountered a second difficulty which caused them considerable bad publicity. The Nigerian military government had put on trial nine Ogoni activists who had been protesting about Shell's activities in the Nigerian delta. The activists were tried on murder charges and ultimately sentenced to death. But the trial was regarded as unfair by Amnesty International and some other human rights organisations. Human rights groups urged Shell to intervene with the Nigerian government in order that the men should not be put to death after what was regarded as an unfair trial. The men were subsequently hanged. Human rights groups took the

---

[25]   See G. Aras, 'The Future Perspectives: What We Need for Markets and Business Sustainability' in G. Aras, *Sustainable Markets for Sustainable Business: A Global Perspective for Business and Financial Markets* (Aldershot: Gower, 2015); G. Aras and D. Crowther, *supra* n. 1.

view that Shell had not done enough to intervene with the military government. Once again, Shell found itself involved in a media firestorm of protest.[26]

A year later, Shell's CEO said that the most damaging consequence of the two negative media campaigns was the company's new-found difficulty in recruiting the best science and engineering graduates due to Shell's poor CSR image.

It is believed that a good CSR performance, on the other hand, lends itself to greater success in employee recruitment, retention and productivity. The consulting firm Great Places to Work®, which has specialised in consulting on positive workplace attitudes, puts the matter this way:

> Committed and engaged employees who trust their management perform 20% better and are 87% less likely to leave an organisation, resulting in easier employee and management recruitment, decreased training costs and incalculable value in retained tenure equity. In addition, analysts indicate that the financial performance of publicly-traded companies in our 100 Best Company List consistently outperform major stock indices by 300% and have half the voluntary turnover rates of their competitors.[27]

2.4. THE MINIMISATION OF LEGAL RISK

One thing which is of particular importance for all corporations, and is becoming more important, is the matter of legal risk and the managing of that risk. A stakeholder approach to decision making and managing the organisation is likely to identify more risks and to manage them better. Risk is also closely related to sustainability and we will show that the lack of a full understanding of what is meant by sustainability, and particularly by sustainable development, means that the issue is confused in corporate planning and reporting.[28] Therefore, the identification and management of risk is an important topic for managers at the present time and a great deal of time and effort is being devoted to developing risk management plans. An important point to note, however, is the relationship between corporate governance and the level of risk to which a firm is exposed.

---

[26] See R. Boele, H. Fabig and D. Wheeler, 'Shell, Nigeria and the Ogoni. A study in Unsustainable Development: The story of Shell, Nigeria and the Ogoni People – Environment, Economy, Relationships: Conflict and Prospects for Resolution' (2001) 9 *Sustainable Development* 74–86; 'The Flames of Shell: Oil Nigeria and the Ogoni', *Berkeley Citizen*, available at: www. berkeleycitizen.org/boycott/boycott2.htm; 'Shell's Environmental Devastation in Nigeria', *The Case Against Shell*, available at: http://wiwavshell.org/shell%E2%80%99s-environmental-devastation-in-nigeria/; 'Shell pays out $15.5m over Saro-Wiwa killing', *The Guardian*, 9 June 2009, available at: www.theguardian.com/world/2009/jun/08/nigeria-usa.

[27] 'Identifying Best Places to Work: U.S. and Globally', *Great Place to Work*, available at: www. greatplacetowork.com/best-companies.

[28] See G. Aras and D. Crowther, *supra* n. 7, and G. Aras and B. Yobaş, 'Governance in Capital Market Institutions' in D. Crowther and G. Aras (eds.), *The Governance of Risk: Developments in Corporate Governance and Responsibility Volume 5* (Emerald Group Publishing Limited, 2013), pp. 111–142.

Good governance and socially responsible management reduce corporate risk, including legal risk, and also to protect the companies from taking excessive risk.

CSR principles and initiatives can be delivered and enticed by a broad range of facilitators, including governments, industries and regulatory bodies. They can also be used for the purpose of enhancing the broader notion of corporate governance. Corporate social responsibility involves governments and industries alike encouraging and rewarding moves towards harmonisation of standards and the building of a culture of risk management. Through incentives, it can encourage risk-prevention propriety in business affairs.[29]

Good CSR performance across the range of issue areas – labour issues, human rights issues, environmental issues, corporate governance, and ethical business practices (such as avoiding misleading advertising and avoiding corrupt business payments) – reduce the likelihood of costly litigation, fines and other penalties. The case of the BP oil spill has already been mentioned. To take a second recent example, the pharmaceutical company GlaxoSmithKline was fined $3 billion in July 2012, the heaviest fine in US pharmaceutical history at that time, for the misleading promotion and advertising of three of its drugs.[30] To take a final example, Chevron was successfully sued in Ecuador for $18 billion for claimed environmental damage resulting from oil production operations since the early 1970s.[31]

2.5. THE 'LICENCE TO OPERATE'

The 'licence to operate' refers to the ability of a company to conduct its business operations without special hindrance – in particular, hindrance from government or from local communities neighbouring its business operations. A company with a poor reputation for CSR often faces hindrances to its business plans. The American retailing giant Walmart provides an outstanding example. Well over 100 communities, including the cities of Boston, Chicago, and New York, have frustrated Walmart's expansion plans in the United States due to their sense of Walmart's poor CSR behaviour. Briefly, the claims relate to alleged low wages, poor working conditions, anti-union behaviour, and, finally, the claimed damaging impact of Walmart's presence on local businesses.[32]

---

29 R. Sarre, M. Doig and B. Fiedler, 'Reducing the Risk of Corporate Irresponsibility: The Trend to Corporate Social Responsibility' (2002) 25(3) *Accounting Forum* 300–317.

30 'GlaxoSmithKline to pay $3 billion fine after pleading guilty to healthcare fraud – the biggest in U.S. history', *Mail Online*, 3 July 2012, available at: www.dailymail.co.uk/news/article-2167742/GlaxoSmithKline-pay-3b-fine-pleading-guilty-healthcare-fraud.html. The Japanese pharmaceutical company Takeda has recently been fined $6 billion in the United States for calculatedly hiding cancer risks associated with its blockbuster drug Actos.

31 See Chevron Ecuador Lawsuit, October 2014, available at: www.chevron.com/ecuador/.

32 The 'licence to operate' issue was dramatically depicted in a 2005 documentary about Walmart, 'Wal*Mart: The High Cost of Low Prices'. See also http://makingchangeatwalmart.org/.

Increasingly, a company's wider community of stakeholders may impede the company's plans where the stakeholders take the view, rightly or wrongly, that the company has exhibited poor CSR behaviour. For instance, local communities in countries from Peru to China to South Africa, owing, especially, to claims of environmental degradation and labour abuses, have frustrated multi-billion dollar operations of some of the world's largest mining companies.[33] To take a recent example, the Chilean Government banned mining operations at Barick Gold's $8.5 billion Pascua-Lama gold mine due to the claims of local communities that the mining operations were harming water supplies.[34]

3. CONCLUSIONS

Human rights norms, bereft of business drivers, are not likely to be taken seriously by companies by themselves. It is therefore instructive to examine the sound business reasons for embracing the norms in business operations – both from the point of view of the almost 100,000 multinational companies as well as from the point of view of their supply chain partners in developing countries. The business reasons from the viewpoint of companies themselves as well as that of their entire range of stakeholders: investors, employees, business partners, suppliers, government, NGOs, and local communities and other elements of civil society. The business benefits of good CSR performance are quite diverse, and research evidence now emerging has begun to demonstrate conclusively that the business benefits are real. Corporate behaviour is important for company success both financially and concerning the relationship between corporate and business interests (stakeholders). We cannot define corporate behaviour without an ethical and CSR base in order to refer to that behavioural aspect. Corporate behaviour involves legal rules, ethical codes of conduct and social responsibility principles. In other words corporate behaviour is based on all of these components and involves law, ethics and CSR. It is important to also recognise that this behaviour must be ethical but must also be seen to be ethical – perceptions are very important. Ethical decision-making processes ensure more effective and

---

[33]   See, for instance, mining operations in Peru. Due to protests, the mining industry in Peru decided to cut investment by 33% in 2013, from the projected $6 billion in investment down to $4 billion. Newmont Mining Corporation, to take one example, has been forced to postpone its $5 billion Minas Conga gold mining project because of local protests. Protests and permit delays have forced oil and gas companies to declare force majeure at 23 areas', in 'Peru Protests to Cut 2013 Mine Investment by 33%, Group Says', *Bloomberg*, 6 September 2012, available at: www.bloomberg.com/news/2012-09-05/peru-protests-to-cut-2013-mine-investment-by-33-group-says-1-.html.

[34]   'Chile Bans Operations at Barrick Gold's $8.5 Billion Gold Project', *Energy Business Review*, 27 May 2013, available at: www.bloomberg.com/news/2012-09-05/peru-protests-to-cut-2013-mine-investment-by-33-group-says-1-.html.

productive utilisation of economic resources. Therefore, corporate behaviour has effects not only on stakeholders and shareholders but also on the entire economy.

CSR and ethical behaviour are fundamental to a business and its continuing existence. We also have to consider that business misbehaviour is more costly than good business behaviour.[35]

---

[35] See G. Aras, 'The Future Perspectives: What We Need for Markets and Business', in G. Aras (ed.), *Sustainable Markets for Sustainable Business: A Global Perspective for Business and Financial Markets* (Aldershot: Gower, 2015), p. 26; and G. Aras and O. Kutlu Furtuna, *supra* n. 9.

CHAPTER 5

CORPORATE ACCOUNTABILITY IN THE FIELD OF HUMAN RIGHTS

On Soft Law Standards and the Use of Extraterritorial Measures

Humberto Cantú Rivera*

1. INTRODUCTION

Much has been said and debated over the question of corporate accountability in the field of human rights, particularly in light of recent high-profile cases before domestic courts and the adoption and expansion in the use of the UN Guiding Principles on Business and Human Rights worldwide.[1] This leads us to question

---

* A previous version of this chapter appeared in the 2014 issue of the *Anuario Mexicano de Derecho Internacional*.

[1] Throughout this chapter, we will use the term 'accountability' to refer to the legal responsibility of corporations in the field of human rights. This term is preferred given the use of the term 'responsibility' in the context of business and human rights, which is understood –at least based on the definition used by the UN Guiding Principles on Business and Human Rights and throughout the mandate of John Ruggie – as a moral responsibility without direct legal consequences or implications (i.e. the responsibility to respect human rights) for corporations when they have directly affected or collaborated in a negative human rights impact. For Morgera, the concept of corporate responsibility implies corporate contributions beyond what is required by domestic law, while corporate accountability refers to procedural standards (transparency, reporting and disclosure of information) based on public expectations which may allow for the scrutiny of the performance of a given entity, and thus may allow for its calling into question. In this sense, she considers accountability as a 'way in which public and private actors are considered *answerable* for their decisions and operations, and are expected to explain them when they are asked by stakeholders.' See E. Morgera, *Corporate Accountability in International Environmental Law* (New York: Oxford University Press, 2009), pp. 19, 22–23 (emphasis added). Bernaz shares a similar consideration on the definition of corporate accountability, where she conceives it as a 'concept [that] encompasses the idea that those accountable should be answerable for the consequences of their actions and refers to [both non-legal risks and corporate liability].' *Cf.* N. Bernaz, 'Enhancing Corporate Accountability for Human Rights Violations: Is Extraterritoriality the Magic Potion?' (2013) 117(3) *Journal of*

---

whether certain developments, of both judicial and political nature, can lead to the creation of rules that will be applicable to corporations to at least ensure the respect of human rights, and in some instances, their reparation when they have been infringed.

New perspectives are required to ensure that the law can effectively regulate the phenomena that international reality poses on human rights, since classic approaches on which the foundations of international law are based seem to be insufficient to address them nowadays. From this perspective, two particular topics seem to be especially difficult to tackle: extraterritoriality and the role of soft law.[2] Both topics have been heavily discussed by doctrine and judiciaries in different countries, for their implications at the international level could be profound.

The question of extraterritoriality seems to be particularly important, since sovereignty – the basis of the Westphalian era of international law – is at stake and States have done everything they can to defend their right not to be subject to judicial or other type of intervention in their internal affairs. The *Kiobel* case in the United States Supreme Court highlighted specifically that states must exercise extreme caution when adjudicating claims that do not touch their interests or jurisdiction. However, other domestic tribunals have considered that if certain requirements are met, such as the nationality of the parties or the lack of a reliable judicial recourse at the original forum (and thus the risk of a denial of justice), they could have jurisdiction over a case with few or inexistent links to the forum.

On the other hand, the role of soft law under classic international law has also been given increasing consideration. Even though several states have expressed their opinion that soft law standards are merely guidelines and have no binding force in any sense, some elements in the classic sources of international law could potentially lead to a re-interpretation of this notion. The question that surfaces is whether some recent developments will be enough to trigger a revision of the limits of international law, or if they will just be individual state efforts that will not have any full effect in favour of the promotion and protection of human rights, particularly in the highly complex area of business and human rights.

Under this guise, this chapter will largely focus on whether these two different topics of international law, extraterritoriality and soft law, may tend to move in the same direction and strengthen the cause of human rights in cases in which corporations are involved, specifically when they have negative human rights impacts. Given that they are two different areas of international law, this chapter must be read as a comprehensive approach, basically as developments in

---

    Business Ethics 494. Thus, it is a broader concept that encompasses the regulation of corporate conduct through legal and non-legal means. However, we will focus on the obligation to respond for actions and omissions as a definition of accountability.

2   'We are seeing a gradual hardening of soft law and voluntary practice in the area of human rights, and some moves towards extraterritoriality.' See M. Harding, 'Banking on Human Rights' (2013) 1 *The Business and Human Rights Review* 4.

two fields that may contribute to the protection of human rights from a holistic perspective, and not as an argument that the use of extraterritorial measures and the hardening of soft law are related. In this sense, the chapter will discuss the way that both of these topics can 'collaborate' to develop stronger measures that may lead to a reinforced corporate accountability in the human rights field. The development and clarification of international human rights law in relation to the extraterritorial adjudication and regulation of corporate conduct impacting human rights, particularly through the use of soft law instruments, such as general comments or declarations from authoritative interpreters of the UN Guiding Principles on Business and Human Rights, could be beneficial to reduce the existing gap in the approaches of different states to this issue. In addition, a continuous use and reference to those soft law instruments may potentially contribute to 'harden' their status as general principles or customary rules of international law, providing victims with another interesting tool in their quest for justice and protection from the negative impacts of corporate activity.'

2. THINKING OUTSIDE THE BOUNDARIES: TALKING ABOUT EXTRATERRITORIALITY

Recent discussion has focused largely on the effects that extraterritoriality has, not just in legal affairs but also in politics and international relations. This discussion has at times pointed out that extraterritoriality is at the intersection between public international law and private international law, taking aspects of both to justify efforts to fight against impunity, or on the other hand, to prevent what could be deemed as intervention in internal affairs.

Before delving into the content of this section, we must however define what is understood by extraterritoriality. The question of extraterritoriality is at least a two-faceted notion that includes measures such as regulation on the milder side, and adjudication on the controversial side.[3] In this sense, the phenomenon of extraterritoriality appears when a state acts in relation to conduct that did not take place within its national boundaries. A state may enact legislation that has extraterritorial effects, such as reporting requirements, which does not infringe on the sovereignty of a third state but nevertheless requires certain subjects to comply with domestic measures even when their activities take place abroad;[4] or in some unusual cases, a state may decide to exercise adjudicative jurisdiction

---

[3] Globally, Deva refers to this question as follows: 'Extraterritorial regulation refers to laws enacted, or other regulatory measures taken, by states beyond their territorial boundaries.' Thus, it is related to a wide concept of extraterritorial regulation, which then subdivides into two different species, as described above. See S. Deva, 'Corporate Human Rights Violations: A Case for Extraterritorial Regulation' in C. Luetge (ed.), *Handbook of the Philosophical Foundations of Business Ethics* (New York: Springer, 2013), p. 1078.

[4] '[H]ome state extraterritoriality would mean that a state extends its laws to overseas subsidiaries of (parent) companies incorporated therein.' *Ibid.*

('extraterritorial adjudication') to judicially ascertain a case that did not take place within its borders, which may however infringe upon a third state's sovereignty and create diplomatic or legal tensions.[5]

The following paragraphs will focus on recent examples from the American and Dutch judiciaries that have shown some interesting developments in both theory and practice, and which have dealt to different degrees with the question of extraterritorial adjudication. In the analysis of *Kiobel*, the opinion of the Supreme Court will be briefly analysed under the light of international law practice. On the other hand, the *Friday Akpan* case and the *El-Hajouj* case from the District Court of The Hague will serve as a counterweight to the decision in *Kiobel*, to show the differences in the interpretation of international law by two developed and independent judicial systems.

2.1. SOME COMMENTS REGARDING THE US SUPREME COURT'S *KIOBEL* OPINION

Recent examples of extraterritorial adjudication have shown the extents to which this matter is controversial under international law, not just because of a supposed 'invasion of sovereignty' and 'legal imperialism' but also due to a lack of clarity and certainty of international norms in this field. Indeed, the inexistence of an international legal framework or even specific guidance regarding extraterritorial adjudication raises doubts about what is permissible under international law and the effects that silence has on the possibilities of developing legal standards under national law based on international norms.

This was particularly addressed in the high-profile case of *Kiobel v. Royal Dutch Petroleum*[6] before the United States Supreme Court, which found a profoundly divided and hesitant High Court dealing with the issues of extra-territoriality and applicability of international law (particularly human rights law and international customary norms) to corporations for their involvement or participation in grave human rights violations.[7]

The case was brought under the Alien Tort Claims Act (also known as the Alien Tort Statute), an ambiguous and ancient act of 1789, which sets forth that '[t]he district courts shall have original jurisdiction of any civil action by an alien for a tort only, committed in violation of the law of nations or a treaty of the

---

5   'The exercise of extraterritorial jurisdiction over foreign subsidiaries of companies incorporated in a given state is likely to raise multiple concerns from other states competing to exert jurisdiction on such subsidiaries'. *Ibid.*, p. 1086.

6   *Esther Kiobel et al. v. Royal Dutch Petroleum et al.*, No. 10–1491, Opinion, US Supreme Court, 17 April 2013.

7   While the case law of the United States under the Alien Tort Statute is extensive, we will only make detailed references to the two cases that have been analysed by the Supreme Court, *Sosa* and *Kiobel*, since they have established the basic parameters under which the ATS has been interpreted.

United States.'[8] This statute has been used since the 1980s as a judicial recourse to which victims of human rights violations worldwide have resorted to try to obtain reparation for the damages they have suffered abroad, regardless of the existence of a direct connection between the facts giving rise to the claims and the United States federal courts that would have jurisdiction.[9] To date, no case brought under this act has reached a favourable verdict, although several cases have been settled between the alleged victims and the defendant companies.

The details of the case indicate the alleged aiding and abetting of the Nigerian Government by three corporations of different nationalities (Royal Dutch Petroleum Co., a Dutch company; Shell Transport and Trading Company, plc, a British enterprise; and Shell Petroleum Development Company of Nigeria, Ltd, a Nigerian subsidiary), which helped the government commit different offences under international law against environmental activists who accused the corporations of environmental damage caused by oil pollution in the Niger Delta, such as extrajudicial killings, crimes against humanity, torture and cruel treatment, arbitrary arrest and detention, violations of the rights to life, liberty, security and association, forced exile and property destruction. All these human rights violations were stated by the plaintiffs in their merits brief.

Of the allegations made in their suit, the District Court that heard the case determined that only the allegations of the plaintiffs related to crimes against humanity, torture and cruel treatment and arbitrary arrest and detention, which comply with the criteria set forth by the Supreme Court in its opinion of *Sosa v. Alvarez Machain* regarding definiteness and acceptance among civilised nations, would be examined in interlocutory appeal.

However, the Court of Appeals of the Second Circuit that received the case dismissed the complaint in 2010 on the grounds that customary international law does not recognise corporate liability, based on three considerations: that the scope of liability is determined by customary international law; that the Alien Tort Statute (ATS) requires courts to apply 'specific, universal and obligatory' norms of international law to the scope of defendants' liabilities as recognised under *Sosa*,[10] and that corporate liability is not a universally recognised norm of customary international law. Nevertheless, the Supreme Court granted certiorari in 2011 to consider whether corporations could be liable under the Alien Tort Statute, due to a diverging interpretation in several of the Circuit Courts (with the

---

[8]   28 U.S.C. §. 1350. Originally, it recognised causes of action for offences against ambassadors, for infringement of safe-conducts and for piracy.

[9]   In this sense, cases brought under the Alien Tort Statute have normally involved foreign plaintiffs bringing claims against foreign corporations, for acts that took place outside of the territorial jurisdiction of the United States.

[10]   *José Francisco Sosa v. Humberto Alvarez-Machain et al.*, No. 03–339, Opinion, US Supreme Court, 29 June 2004, in which the Supreme Court established that the ATS would only provide a cause of action for torts that transgressed a norm of international law that is definite and accepted by civilised nations ('specific, universal and obligatory').

Second Circuit denying the existence of corporate liability[11] while the Seventh,[12] Ninth[13] and DC Circuits[14] affirmed it).

After the first round of oral arguments in which the discussion shifted from the initial question that addressed if customary international law recognises corporate liability, to the question if the ATS applies extraterritorially, the Supreme Court ordered the parties to provide supplemental briefing to address whether and under what circumstances the ATS allows courts to recognise a cause of action for violations of the law of nations occurring within the territory of a sovereign state other than the United States, which was then addressed in a second hearing in October 2012.[15] On 17 April 2013, the Supreme Court issued its opinion in *Kiobel*, affirming the decision of the Court of Appeals of the Second Circuit and dismissing the claim on the basis that customary international law does not recognise corporate liability for violation of the law of nations, while vaguely answering its question on what could allow the ATS to grant a cause of action for violations of international law that took place outside of American soil.

The Supreme Court's majority opinion in *Kiobel* focuses largely on the question of extraterritorial adjudication and the original intention of Congress when it enacted the Alien Tort Statute in the First Judiciary Act of 1789. In this sense, Chief Justice Roberts wrote that a presumption against extraterritoriality applies to claims under the Alien Tort Statute, and that nothing in the statute rebuts the presumption. While discussing both points, he relies on a grammatical interpretation of the text which obviously does not make any reference to extraterritorial application of the law,[16] although it does clearly indicate that the

---

[11]   *Esther Kiobel et al. v. Royal Dutch Petroleum et al.*, No. 10–1491, Opinion, US Supreme Court, 17 April 2013.

[12]   *Boimah Flomo et al. v. Firestone Natural Rubber Co., LLC*, No. 10–3674, Judgment, US Court of Appeals for the Seventh Circuit, 11 July 2011.

[13]   *Sarei et al. v. Rio Tinto plc et al.*, No. 02–56256, Judgment, US Court of Appeals for the Ninth Circuit, 25 October 2011.

[14]   *John Doe VIII et al. v. Exxon Mobil Corporation et al.*, No. 09–7125, Judgment, US Court of Appeals for the DC Circuit, 8 July 2011.

[15]   For a detailed reference of the allegations that were discussed during the second hearing in *Kiobel*, see H.F. Cantú Rivera, 'Recent Developments in *Kiobel v. Royal Dutch Petroleum*: An Important Human Rights Forum in Peril?' (2013) 28 *Cuestiones Constitucionales, Revista Mexicana de Derecho Constitucional* 245–250.

[16]   In this sense, the Supreme Court determined in *Morrison v. National Australia Bank Ltd* (2010) that if a statute doesn't clearly indicate that it is intended to have extraterritorial application, it should not be presumed to have any. This same argument was reprised in the *Kiobel* opinion. Some authors, such as Colangelo, have been however hesitant about the decision made by the Supreme Court in *Kiobel*, considering it contradicts not only international and US law, but also its very own precedents: '*Morrison* explained that the presumption against extraterritoriality […] did not operate upon the jurisdictional statute […] and as the *Kiobel* Court openly acknowledged, the ATS is also a 'strictly jurisdictional' statute.' *Cf.* A.J. Colangelo, '*Kiobel*: Muddling the Distinction Between Prescriptive and Adjudicative Jurisdiction' (2013) 28 *Maryland Journal of International Law* 2.

statute was crafted to deal with the situations that involved international law at the time.[17]

However, it is the interpretation of Blackstone's recognition of what constituted a violation of the law of nations in the late 1700s that allows for a discussion on this matter. Piracy was regarded as a violation of the law of nations, and pirates were considered to be fair game (that is, subject to prosecution) wherever found for being a common enemy of all mankind, and where their actions took place in their vessels while sailing the high seas. In this sense, then as well as today, a vessel has the nationality of the flag of the country under which it sails, and thus it constitutes an extension of the territorial jurisdiction of a foreign sovereign; due to this, the adjudication of matters related to piracy unescapably would involve actions that would trespass into a foreign sovereign's jurisdiction, unless it was done only against vessels sailing under the nationality of the country that would bring procedures against it. Nevertheless, this idea seems unlikely, which leads us then to briefly analyse the arguments of the Supreme Court in its *Kiobel* opinion.

Even if the position of the majority is correct in cautioning the use of American law to solve disputes arising somewhere else in the globe, it constitutes an important obstacle to what may be the last hope for victims of corporate human rights abuses.[18] The Supreme Court held that United States law applies and governs domestically, but not globally; nevertheless, in using the Alien Tort Statute the United States would not be applying its laws to regulate conduct occurring within the territory of foreign sovereigns.[19] It has been recognised by the Court itself that the ATS is a jurisdictional statute, therefore only providing jurisdiction and a forum to adjudicate claims in violation of the law of nations that satisfy the requirements set forth in *Sosa*, and not projecting its own laws into foreign soil. This jurisdiction would then constitute a forum to ascertain rights

---

[17] The Supreme Court confirmed this in its *Sosa* precedent and stated that an analogy of what was the law of nations at that time could be equally brought before the judiciary under the Alien Tort Statute today: 'In *Sosa v. Alvarez-Machain*, the Supreme Court held that the ATS allows US courts to recognize federal common law causes of actions 'based on the present-day law of nations [that] rest on a norm of international character accepted by the civilized world and defined with a specificity comparable to the features of the 18th-century paradigms we have recognized.' See W.S. Dodge, 'Corporate Liability Under Customary International Law' (2012) 43 *Georgetown Journal of International Law* 1045.

[18] And this is even more important in light of the important procedural differences that exist between the American civil litigation system and those of other countries, as was pointed out by both the Netherlands and the United Kingdom in their amicus briefs in *Kiobel*. For further details, see *Esther Kiobel et al. v. Royal Dutch Petroleum et al.*, No. 10–1491, Brief of the Governments of the Kingdom of the Netherlands and the United Kingdom of Great Britain and Northern Ireland as *Amici Curiae* in Support of Neither Party (US Supreme Court, 13 June 2012), pp. 27–28. See also J.A. Cabranes, 'Witholding Judgment: Why U.S. Courts Shouldn't Make Foreign Policy' (2015) 94(5) *Foreign Affairs* 125–133.

[19] 'When we talk about extraterritoriality, we think *primarily* about mandates to do or not to do, which are part of substantive law. There is an attempt to project these mandates beyond the physical framework of power connected to state sovereignty, not to the assumption of jurisdiction on the part of its courts.' F.J. Zamora Cabot, 'Kiobel and the Question of Extraterritoriality' (2013) 2 *The Age of Rights* 9.

and duties of confronting parties, both rights and duties deriving directly from international law and not from domestic US law.[20] A conception of *American exceptionalism* is evident in the *interpretation* of international law made by the Court, which at least during the two hearings and the opinion in *Kiobel* seemed to be distant from what international law (and particularly international human rights law) is considered to be and the form that it is largely applied nowadays.

The extraterritoriality question goes way back in time. For example, the Permanent Court of International Justice stated in its well-known judgment in the *S. S. Lotus* case that unless international law specifically prohibited an extraterritorial use of domestic law, states could design and apply its laws outside its boundaries.[21] This permission by what was the highest international tribunal at the time has remained a pillar of international law, which has not been challenged by a judgment in a different sense.[22] Thus it should have been an important asset to the plaintiffs in *Kiobel*, since it redirects the determination of the extraterritorial application of a law to domestic legislation and the legislative body that enacts it, and not to the question of the stance of international law regarding the extraterritorial application of domestic laws.[23]

This argument would nevertheless have been irrelevant to the case due to the recognised adjudicative character that the Alien Tort Statute has. The *Lotus dictum*, on the other hand, was applicable only if the law in question was a substantive law and therefore an exercise of prescriptive jurisdiction, not a procedural act. The presumption of permissibility[24] could have been an interesting

---

[20]   'The fundamental historic development of private international law is based on the diversity of systems of international jurisdiction to adjudicate. Therefore, the *jurisdiction to adjudicate* of the United States, exercised through its courts, does not have to coincide with the criteria of other countries or to cede jurisdiction to those who are supposedly more connected in this or any other matter. The only thing that can be demanded […] is that jurisdiction be *exercised in a reasonable manner* when there is *sufficient nexus* with the State claiming it'. *Ibid.*

[21]   *The Case of the S.S. 'Lotus' (France v. Turkey)*, Judgment, Permanent Court of International Justice, 7 September 1927. See in the same sense N. Bernaz, *supra* n. 1, p. 18, who argues that universal civil jurisdiction is lawful as it is not prohibited by international law; and D. Sloss, 'Kiobel and Extraterritoriality: A Rule Without A Rationale' (2013) 28 *Maryland Journal of International Law* 2, where the author explains the presumption of permissibility under international law.

[22]   Even though it's outside the scope of this chapter, attention should be paid to the ICJ judgment on the *Jurisdictional Immunities* case, passed in early 2012, by which the ICJ determined that immunity applied to civil suits brought by Italian citizens in Italy against Germany, since the latter enjoyed a procedural immunity under international customary law. See *Jurisdictional Immunities of the State (Germany v. Italy)*, Judgment, International Court of Justice, 3 February 2012.

[23]   'International law itself doesn't care about how it is conceptualized or implemented within any given domestic legal system […] that's a matter for a nation's internal law, not international law.' See A. Colangelo, *supra* n. 16, p. 5.

[24]   '[T]he starting point for any jurisdictional analysis is a presumption of permissibility – a presumption that is only overcome by demonstrating that the action is otherwise prohibited by treaty or customary international law.' See D. Stigall, 'International Law and Limitations on the Exercise of Extraterritorial Jurisdiction in U.S. Domestic Law' (2012) 35(2) *Hastings International & Comparative Law Review* 331. This was also the position explained by the

argument based on international law in opposition to the presumption against extraterritoriality that was supported by the Supreme Court.

If international law effectively permits substantive laws with extraterritorial effects, which has been supported by international tribunals for several decades, the choice of the United States Supreme Court not to allow an extraterritorial application of an adjudicative jurisdiction statute would also be a legitimate choice under international law, due to the voluntary and non-mandatory character of the presumption of permissibility. However, it would also undermine the universality of human rights and their protection, which has now left the victims in *Kiobel* without the possibility to seek redress in the forum that corresponds to their place of residence. Thus, the question that remains is what the Supreme Court could have done if it had interpreted the issue at hand from a more neutral perspective based on current global understanding of international law.

An interpretation of the Alien Tort Statute in conformity with current international law would probably observe that at least the core international human rights treaties, customary international law, *jus cogens* norms and general principles of international law constitute accepted norms for the international society.[25] This would normally comply with the standards of what was an accepted practice of international law in the 18th century. In the case at hand, the ratification by 167 countries of the International Covenant on Civil and Political Rights (ICCPR) would clearly demonstrate that it has been almost universally recognised by 'civilised nations' that the norms contained therein are universal values.

Even more, those values are shared by the four countries that are intervening in the dispute: the United States as forum and place of residence of the plaintiffs; The Netherlands and the United Kingdom as the countries where the main defendants are incorporated; and Nigeria as home of the joint venture of both European companies and the country of nationality of the plaintiffs. This fact would provide an even stronger justification as to why at least some of the torts that the plaintiffs alleged in their claim should be recognised as specific, universal and obligatory. The fact that the International Covenant on Civil and Political Rights was ratified by the four aforementioned countries implies a common denominator, perhaps even a rule *inter partes* that would be applicable to all of them. Since all of the claimed rights are included in the Covenant, and

---

Government of Kosovo in its written contribution to the ICJ during the Advisory Proceeding regarding the unilateral declaration of independence of Kosovo. See Written Contribution of the Republic of Kosovo, *Accordance with International Law of the Unilateral Declaration of Independence by the Provisional Institutions of Self-Government of Kosovo*, Advisory Opinion, International Court of Justice, 17 April 2009, p. 138.

[25]   A similar critique was directed to the UN Guiding Principles on Business and Human Rights, precisely on what was considered a 'narrow view' of international law by their author, John Ruggie. See E. Decaux, 'Le projet de l'ONU sur la responsabilité des entreprises transnationales' in I. Daugareilh (ed.), *Responsabilité sociale de l'entreprise transnationale et globalisation de l'économie* (Brussels: Bruylant, 2010), pp. 459–474.

the Member States have the international obligation to guarantee those rights within their territory in accordance with Article 2(1) of the ICCPR, the judicial protection of those rights by the courts of any of the countries would be a *conditio sine qua non.*

Even though the Supreme Court stated in *Sosa* that the ICCPR does not establish a relevant and applicable rule of international law because of its non-self-executing character,[26] this position shows two things. First, it entails the justification of the inapplicability of international law based on domestic considerations and legal systems (particularly a dualist position) despite a formally declared international commitment to the respect of fundamental human rights, which then leads to a lack of fulfilment of its *pacta sunt servanda* obligation. The existing silence under treaty law regarding extraterritorial adjudication leads to a permissible use of jurisdiction to preserve and guarantee the rights of victims of human rights violations. The ratification by the American Congress of the International Covenant on Civil and Political Rights should confirm its adherence and commitment to the respect of international human rights norms, as well as the recognition of this treaty as a source of international law and binding obligations for the United States and for the rest of countries that ratified it.

Second, and on the other hand, a grammatical interpretation of the Alien Tort Statute could lead to the presumption that, if analogously compared to the arguments revolving around piracy made by Justice Breyer in his separate opinion, the law would still provide a cause of action. Most of the focus was centred on the 'law of nations'; however, there was no mention whatsoever in the *Kiobel* opinion regarding the last part of the statute, which clearly states that courts can entertain a civil action by an alien for a tort 'in violation of [...] a treaty of the United States.'

Given that the United States ratified the International Covenant on Civil and Political Rights in 1992, as well as the fact that at least torture and cruel treatment[27] and arbitrary arrest and detention are prohibited by the Covenant,[28] the violation of those treaty rights and not the ambiguous concept that the 'law of nations' has become under the Supreme Court's judicial perception would have provided another justification that should have allowed the civil action to proceed. While the question of the facts taking place within the territory of a

---

[26] 'And, although the Covenant does bind the United States as a matter of international law, the United States ratified the Covenant on the express understanding that it was not self-executing and so did not itself create obligations enforceable in the federal courts.' *José Francisco Sosa v. Humberto Alvarez-Machain et al.*, no. 03–339, Opinion, US Supreme Court, 29 June 2004, p. 41.

[27] This was recognised by the United States in its reservations to the ICCPR, where it stated '(3) That the United States considers itself bound by Article 7 to the extent that "cruel, inhuman or degrading treatment or punishment" means the cruel and unusual treatment or punishment prohibited by the Fifth, Eighth, and/or Fourteenth Amendments to the Constitution of the United States.'

[28] Crimes against humanity, on the other hand, have been dealt with in other international documents, such as the Rome Statute of the International Criminal Court, which the US has only signed but not ratified.

foreign sovereign still remains, at least the part of what constitutes the modern 'law of nations' could be set aside to pursue it from the perspective of the violation of a right contained in an international human rights instrument that is binding for the United States of America, as well as for the other three countries that have a direct interest in the case.

Two more arguments should be shared regarding the decision in *Kiobel*. The first one is related to customary international law, while the second one is in relation to the universality of human rights. These two arguments are important in light of the debate regarding the subjects of international law and the question of extraterritoriality, both of which were given some consideration by the Supreme Court during the two phases of *Kiobel*.

As mentioned by Dodge, 'the norms that are actionable under *Sosa* [...] focus on acts without regard to the identity of the perpetrators.'[29] This normative characteristic is divergent from the classic notion of international human rights law under which the state will clearly and explicitly bear sole primary responsibility for human rights violations taking place within its jurisdiction. However, it must be noted that even though it is the state who will be found responsible for failure to prevent and protect against such type of conducts that are detrimental to human dignity, most international norms dealing with the type of conducts that are actionable in the United States under *Sosa* have nevertheless omitted to establish *who* is capable of committing such human rights violations.[30]

International human rights law, and particularly those conventions and treaties dealing with human rights violations that amount to infringement of customary law or *jus cogens* norms, have also focused on regulating the actions taking place, while leaving the question of the subject who committed the act largely unaddressed. That lack of indication can either be interpreted as an obvious and unnecessary remark in the text of an international treaty, given the already consolidated notion of the state as the only entity capable of violating human rights, or specifically as the intention to not refine the subjectivity question under international law to allow judicial branches (both nationally and internationally) to develop a *corpus juris* in this regard.

The fact that the question of the subject who can violate a norm of international law is unaddressed can play an important role in determining corporate liability for human rights violations. International law does not categorise the actors who can be found liable or non-liable; it merely focuses on the determination of the lawfulness or unlawfulness of an act, regardless of who committed the act.[31]

---

[29] W.S. Dodge, *supra* n. 17, p. 1047.

[30] '[T]he question of corporate liability under customary international law does not depend on finding a norm of customary international law in the abstract, but rather on whether the particular norms at issue reach corporations.' *Ibid.*, p. 1050.

[31] *Ibid.*, p. 1046.

Therefore, the lack of a customary rule of international law determining that corporations enjoy immunity largely tends to indicate that in fact, they do not.[32]

This determination, replicated in the ICJ judgment on the *Jurisdictional Immunities* case, found that the states enjoy a procedural immunity that is entirely different from the existence of responsibility: 'a state that is immune from suit is still capable of violating international law and, despite its immunity, remains responsible for such violations. Corporations generally have no immunity under international law, much less benefit from a trans-substantive rule of non-liability that even states do not enjoy.'[33] Thus, the inexistence of a specific norm denying the determination of liability under international law for non-state actors, paired with the current treaty-law standards that are also silent on the subject to which they are addressed but focused on the lawfulness of a certain action, can largely constitute elements to conclude that a presumption of permissibility to find non-state actors liable for the violation of international law exists.

In relation to extraterritoriality, arguments have been directed to the characteristic of international law as an over-arching, binding framework that is to be applied everywhere and all the time.[34] Even though this notion particularly defends an idealistic position that largely ignores the question of international politics, an argument can be made regarding the universality of human rights, and specifically of non-derogable rights that have been largely recognised and ratified by most countries in the world.

The fact that universally-recognised rights cannot be enforced is a direct attempt against the foundations of international human rights law; thus, future decisions should not just look into the framework and scope of international relations and the question of comity, but into the permanence and strengthening of the universal human rights system, in order to guarantee the development of an internationally coordinated and coherent effort to battle corporate impunity.[35]

Clearer indications and guidelines are needed in relation to the question of extraterritorial adjudication at the international level, especially in the field of human rights. A lack of such a framework will just add to the known fragmentation of international law through which impunity can subsist, and let national efforts dictate the route through which these types of questions can be addressed, under the risk of an even greater polarisation.

---

[32] Although there is also no explicit indication that they can be found liable, thus constituting a normative silence.

[33] W.S. Dodge, *supra* n. 17, p. 1047.

[34] 'International law [...] prescribes conduct-regulatory rules the world over, and thus its application is never really extraterritorial since it covers the globe, particularly with respect to universal jurisdiction violations.' See A. Colangelo, *supra* n. 16, p. 1.

[35] For a holistic approach to the question of corporate accountability for human rights abuses, and particularly for a multi-faceted model to tackle negative human rights impacts by corporations, see generally S. Deva, *Regulating Corporate Human Rights Violations: Humanizing Business* (London: Routledge, 2012).

2.2. EXTRATERRITORIALITY IN THE DUTCH JUDICIAL SYSTEM

Two recent cases, both from the judicial system of the Netherlands, have illustrated a different approach to the question of extraterritoriality, and shown signs, derived directly from private international law, on extraterritorial adjudication of cases that comply with certain requirements.

The first case we will refer to is *Friday Alfred Akpan et al. v. Royal Dutch Shell plc et al.*,[36] brought before the District Court of The Hague. Summarising the facts of the case, it was brought due to the allegations of environmental and personal damages suffered by the plaintiff due to two oil spills occurred in 2006 and 2007 in the Ikot Ada Udo region in Nigeria, which were the result of a lack of diligence from the defendants in the maintenance of its oil-producing operations in the region, which resulted in the loss of his means of livelihood.

After an interesting analysis from the District Court, in which it found that there was a causal link between the violation of a specific duty of care by the Nigerian subsidiary of the Dutch corporate group and the damages suffered by Akpan, and that the Nigerian subsidiary Shell Petroleum Development Company of Nigeria Ltd committed a tort of negligence against the plaintiff for not sufficiently securing an oil-well to prevent the sabotage that was committed in a simple manner prior to the oil spills,[37] the Dutch District Court ordered the Nigerian defendant to pay compensation for the damages suffered by Friday Akpan.

Although it must be noted that the court at The Hague specifically indicated that the case could not be considered a human rights violation committed by the subsidiary company, particularly in light of the passive conduct of the defendant and the lack of a specific action[38] that would implicate a direct transgression of the plaintiff's fundamental rights, this case clearly has implications in the human rights field, particularly in regard to the liability of foreign subsidiaries. This becomes even more relevant after the *Kiobel* ruling in the United States, since ATS cases brought there have usually been filed against (domestic or foreign) parent corporations and their foreign subsidiaries, and the Supreme Court recently decided not to engage in extraterritorial adjudication unless a corporate nationality link is present or the case at hand touches upon American interests with sufficient force.

This exact circumstance was taken into consideration by the Dutch court in its judgment of the *Friday Akpan* case. Since the multinational corporation that was defendant in the case is headquartered in the Netherlands, the District Court determined to exercise an analogy with other cases and international trends:

---

[36]   *Friday Alfred Akpan et al. v. Royal Dutch Shell plc et al.*, Case C/09/337050/ HA ZA 09–1580, Judgment, The Hague District Court, 30 January 2013.

[37]   *Ibid.*, para. 4.45.

[38]   *Ibid.*, para. 4.56.

> [F]or quite some time [...] there has been an international trend to hold parent
> companies of multinationals liable in their own country for the harmful practices
> of foreign (sub-) subsidiaries, in which the foreign (sub-) subsidiary involved was
> also summoned together with the parent company on several occasions.[39]

Although this trend may be considered recent, it would support one of the
arguments that can be inferred from the *Kiobel* opinion: if there is concluding
evidence that there is a close relation between the parent company and the
subsidiary, and that the actions that gave rise to the claim were ordered by the
parent company, or as stated in the *Friday Akpan* judgment, that the parent
company should have known of either a relevant aspect of the facts that originated
the claim or of the unlawfulness of a specific action executed by the subsidiary,
both could be summoned to appear and face trial before the tribunals of the home
State of the multinational.

The Dutch court found, however, that it would be less reasonable that a
duty of care of the parent company existed because the proximity between both
entities was not so relevant as if, for example, both of them operated in the same
country. While relying in the *Chandler v. Cape plc* judgment from the British
judicial system, the court determined that under the circumstances of the case,
it could not be assumed that the parent company would have had more specific
local knowledge of the situation in the foreign country than its subsidiary, which
led to the dismissal of the claims against the parent corporation.

Despite such dismissal, the District Court argued that:

> [T]he forum non conveniens restriction no longer plays any role in today's
> international private law. The District Court is of the opinion that the jurisdiction
> of the Dutch court in the matter against [the foreign subsidiary] based on Section
> 7 DCCP[40] does not cease to exist in the event that the claims against [the parent
> company] were to be dismissed, not even if subsequently, in fact, no connection or
> hardly any connection would remain with Dutch jurisdiction.[41]

The judgment in the *Friday Akpan* case leads to several thoughts regarding
the effects it has on the human rights field. First of all, the judgment was
based on national law, not international law. Even if this type of case could be
a clear indication that only through national law will any degree of corporate
accountability be reached, it also shows that the lack of a binding international

---

[39]   *Ibid.*, para. 4.5.
[40]   Dutch Code of Civil Procedure, Article 7(1). If legal proceedings are to be initiated by a writ
of summons and a Dutch court has jurisdiction with respect to one of the defendants, then
it has jurisdiction as well with respect to the other defendants who are called to the same
proceedings, provided that the rights of action against the different defendants are connected
with each other in such a way that a joint consideration is justified for reasons of efficiency.
[41]   *Friday Alfred Akpan et al. v. Royal Dutch Shell plc et al.*, *supra* n. 36, para. 4.6.

framework has led and will continue to lead to the exploration of national judicial avenues and causes of action, which will most likely lead to the development of a sphere of comparative law in cases dealing with corporate accountability and extraterritorial adjudication, as shown by District Court of The Hague in this case.

Secondly, the ruling by the District Court was based on substantive Nigerian law, as well as on common law from the British system, which was binding before the independence of Nigeria and continues to serve as reference after it. On the other hand, the jurisdiction of the Dutch courts is based on Dutch law, specifically if the nationality of the parent company is Dutch.

What these two characteristics show is that, based on private international law, conflicts of law and comparative law, an effort can be made to hold corporations accountable under national law independently of the place where the actions occurred, and as recognised by the Dutch court itself, may help to reduce the transcendence of the *forum non conveniens* restriction that usually has tried to be applied to this type of cases. Therefore, even foreign-cubed cases could potentially be extraterritorially adjudicated if a minimum link is found that could grant jurisdiction over a foreign judiciary (e.g. the place where the claim is filed).

On the third place, the *Friday Akpan* ruling was based on a reasonable duty of care – a measure of due diligence – and therefore a tort of negligence, and not on a human rights violation. It is clear that cases based on torts have been more successful and more explored than human rights claims, and have been generally resolved in a more favourable manner because the rights disputed are more ascertainable judicially. However, independently of the denomination they are given, it is also clear that this type of judgment, despite being classified as torts, also has human rights implications. [42]

In this sense, exploring human rights through the tort angle may be an interesting solution to pursue and further in the national level the cause of human rights, particularly if corporations are headquartered or incorporated in countries whose national judicial systems have a liberal and global approach to the question of extraterritorial adjudication and the use of private international law.

Another interesting example that emerged recently from the Dutch judicial system, dealing with torture and extraterritorial adjudication, is that of *Ashraf Ahmed El-Hojouj v. Harb Amer Derbal et al. (Libya)*. [43] This case saw the plaintiff, a Bulgarian-Palestinian national, file a claim in the Netherlands for having been illegally detained and tortured by the Libyan regime, which accused him of infecting 393 children with HIV. After having confessed under torture, the plaintiff

---

[42] 'Although by tort claims private parties may seek vindication of private interests, judgments in these cases affirm much wider interests manifested in the norms that the community is prepared to enforce.' *Vid.* D.F. Donovan and A. Roberts, 'The Emerging Recognition of Universal Civil Jurisdiction' (2006) 100 *American Journal of International Law* 154.

[43] *Ashraf Ahmed El-Hojouj v. Harb Amer Derbal et al. (Libyan Officials)*, Case 400882/HA ZA 11–2252, Judgment, The Hague District Court, 21 March 2012.

was condemned to the capital punishment, but later granted pardon and released by the authorities. However, the plaintiff filed a complaint in the Netherlands (which gave him refugee status) for the commission of an international crime by the Libyan regime, despite the default of appearance of the defendants before the tribunal.

The District Court in The Hague that heard the case considered that it had international jurisdiction pursuant to Article 9(c) of the Dutch Code of Civil Procedure, which states that Dutch courts will have jurisdiction if it would be unacceptable to demand from the plaintiff that he submits the case to the judgment of a foreign court. Therefore, it constituted itself as a *forum necessitatis* – a forum by necessity – since denying jurisdiction to the plaintiff would risk an evasion of justice from the defendants.[44] Thus, ascertaining the claim brought by El-Hajouj would possibly implicate that the enforcement of the judgment, given the default of the defendants in the case, would turn into a political issue, while justice would have still been at least declared in favour of the claimant.

This decision by the District Court of The Hague implied therefore an act of universal civil jurisdiction to award reparations to the plaintiff against the Libyan officials involved in his torture (who, since acting as state agents, compromised the international criminal responsibility of the Libyan state), for the commission of a gross violation of human rights that amounted to an international crime. In effect, the non-derogable nature of torture and its recognition as a *jus cogens* norm would support the exercise of universal jurisdiction to defend the interests of the victim and to promote the respect of human rights, founded on the international duty of all states to prohibit and prosecute this type of conducts.

While both cases deal with very different scenarios and cannot be interpreted uniformly, they do suggest two interesting developments. First of all, when a victim is facing a denial of justice based on a question of jurisdiction, a court may act to protect them or award them damages for the atrocities they suffered if it deems that no contravention of international law would take place. Secondly, parent companies and their subsidiaries may be held accountable, even extraterritorially for their careless or reckless behaviour in the conduction of their operations, if a lack of diligence has an important negative effect on the livelihoods and rights of communities that were affected by their activities. The degree of accountability may depend on the level of involvement and knowledge of the situation that they are expected to have.

---

[44]   This figure was suggested by Justice Sotomayor in the second hearing of the *Kiobel* case before the Supreme Court of the United States, who indicated that to avoid a denial of justice, the American courts could become a last-resort forum. See *Esther Kiobel et al. v. Royal Dutch Petroleum et al.*, No. 10–1491, Transcript of Oral Argument, Supreme Court, 1 October 2012, p. 13.

3. ENHANCING THE ROLE OF SOFT LAW: FROM GUIDELINES TO OBLIGATIONS?

Soft law has been much debated in international human rights law, particularly due to the fact that doctrine and human rights activists have tried to give it a more binding nature than what normally would be the case under international law. In this sense, what has been recognised as the paradigm rule containing the sources of international law, Article 38 of the Statute of the International Court of Justice has remained unchanged since its adoption, thus being a helpful tool for powerful states that would prefer to maintain the binding character of international norms to a minimum. Nevertheless, recent developments in several areas in the human rights realm have shown that judicial interpretation and State practice can give soft law norms a semi-binding character, to say the least.[45]

It is this idea which will be the focus of this section. Firstly, a brief analysis will be made of what the classic sources of international law are, which have nevertheless been interpreted in a progressive way by international courts, thus evolving the status of some international human rights declarations through its case law. Secondly, a brief review of the status of soft law under international law will be examined, trying to share some thoughts on the potential development of soft norms, such as the Guiding Principles on Business and Human Rights, into binding rules of customary international law through state practice and case law. The basic elements for the formation of international custom are of particular interest.

3.1. THE CLASSIC SOURCES OF INTERNATIONAL LAW ACCORDING TO THE ICJ STATUTE

According to the Statute of the International Court of Justice, the classic sources of international law are of two kinds: primary and secondary. Within the first group are international conventions and treaties, both multilateral and bilateral; international custom, as evidence of a general practice that has been internationally accepted as law, and general principles of law recognised by civilised nations. The second group, which is specifically contained in Article 38(d) of the Statute, are judicial decisions and doctrine from the most highly qualified publicists, with the exception stated in Article 59 of the Statute, which provides that judicial decisions of the Court only have binding force between the contending parties and in respect to that specific case.

---

[45] In this chapter, we identify the semi-binding character of soft law as the moment when a soft norm starts developing into a formal source of international law, be it through its metamorphosis into a general principle of international law or as a customary norm, thus acquiring a more formal and coercive value than it had when it was just a declarative statement (a soft norm).

While these classic sources remain relevant and have basically not been contested but from a doctrinal standpoint,[46] some of them have been subjected to progressive interpretations by the International Court of Justice itself, as well as by some regional courts dealing with *lex specialis*, such as the Inter-American Court of Human Rights. A few examples will be used to illustrate this assertion.

Between 1969 and 1986, the International Court of Justice modified its assessment on the formation of a rule of customary international law. In 1969, in its judgment of the *North Sea Continental Shelf Cases*, the ICJ reasoned that State practice must reflect the belief that such practice is obligatory based on the existence of a rule of law requiring it.[47] Therefore, the Court determined that it was only through *opinio juris* that state practice could be confirmed, which would be the foundation of custom conceived through the traditional approach.[48]

Nevertheless, in its judgment of the case of *Military and Paramilitary Activities in and Against Nicaragua*,[49] 17 years later, the Court determined that the existence of the rule in the *opinio juris* of states must be confirmed by practice.[50] Thus, the ICJ evolved its assessment on international custom to add a more important value to *opinio juris*, which had been secondary to state practice up to that point.[51]

This evolution in the ICJ assessment on the formation of customary international law has been accompanied by the growth and development of the concept of universality of human rights. In this field, international actors (international tribunals, multilateral organisations and publicists) have had an important role to play in trying to achieve a result that is more favourable to their area of work, and have supported a transition from state practice to diplomatic

---

[46] See generally F.A. Cárdenas Castañeda, 'A Call for Rethinking the Sources of International Law: *Soft Law* and the Other Side of the Coin' (2013) 13 *Anuario Mexicano de Derecho Internacional* 355–403.

[47] *North Sea Continental Shelf Cases (Germany v. Netherlands; Germany v. Denmark)*, Judgment, International Court of Justice, 20 February 1969.

[48] 'The traditional approach to identifying a rule of customary international law is to rely on *opinio juris* to confirm state practice, or even to infer *opinio juris* from state practice [… thus] the traditional approach is to attach more value to what states do (physical acts) than what they say (verbal acts).' M.T. Kamminga, 'Final Report on the Impact of International Human Rights Law on General International Law' in M.T. Kamminga and M. Scheinin (eds.), *The Impact of Human Rights Law on General International Law* (Oxford: Oxford University Press, 2009), p. 7.

[49] *Military and Paramilitary Activities in and Against Nicaragua (Nicaragua v. United States of America)*, Judgment, International Court of Justice, 27 June 1986.

[50] See generally A.A. Cançado Trindade, 'International Law for Humankind: Towards a New Jus Gentium (I)', *Collected Courses*, Vol. 316 (Leiden: Martinus Nijhoff, 2006), particularly Part III, Chapter VI.

[51] '[The ICJ in its Nicaragua judgment gave] the impression that, as long as *opinio juris* is not in doubt, the consistency of state practice, a cherished and arguably primordial element of a customary rule, is not to be the first consideration.' See J. Wouters and C. Ryngaert, 'Impact on the Process of the Formation of Customary International Law' in M.T. Kamminga and M. Scheinin (eds.), *The Impact of Human Rights Law on General International Law* (Oxford: Oxford University Press, 2009), p. 113.

action to prove the existence of an international custom.[52] Even more, '[i]t is often argued [...] that the method of customary law formation in the field of human rights [...] would allow *opinio juris* to play a more important role than state practice.'[53]

This has not just been the result of unequal state practice, but of a different set of values and principles that are required to face the reality of the challenges posed by human rights, which greatly vary from those existing in other fields of international law. Nevertheless, one of the standing paradigms of general international law has been that the key element for the formation and consolidation of international law is, in fact, the existence of a generally consistent state practice relying on the widespread use and application of a certain behaviour or norm.

An important question that surfaces is what degree of application or use of a norm of conduct or behaviour is required to determine the existence of a general international practice. One possible response would be that practice is not only reflected within national boundaries, but also within international action in multilateral fora; in theory, and following a quantitative approach to state action before international organisations, actions carried out by states while participating in diplomatic activities would demonstrate a clear intent on their part (*opinio juris*) as to what they consider to be a common practice, usually within their jurisdictions.[54]

Therefore, this would normally be an important step to the development of customary rules and of general principles of international law, based on the declarations and actions made by the states at the international level, and thus a confirmation of state practice. As well, the interpretation of international or regional courts regarding such state practice at the diplomatic level as reflected in declarations or non-binding resolutions, has in some cases lead to the evolution of those norms to acquire at least a semi-binding character. A case in point is the UN Declaration on the Rights of Indigenous Peoples.[55]

In this sense, international law has also evolved under the wing of regional human rights tribunals. An interesting example is that of the Inter-American

---

[52]   '[W]hen identifying state practice, [human rights treaty bodies and international criminal courts] emphasize what states say rather than what they do.' M.T. Kamminga, *supra* n. 47, pp. 7–8. See also F.M. Mariño Menéndez, *Derecho Internacional Público: Parte General*, 3rd edn. (Madrid: Trotta, 1999), p. 366, who refers to the validity of State practice in multilateral organisations for the formation of international custom.

[53]   J. Wouters and C. Ryngaert, *supra* n. 51, p. 111.

[54]   'However, if verbal state practice in and *vis-à-vis* international fora is taken into account, another picture emerges. Modern positivism allows for the consideration of statements by states in international fora, of the (tacit) acceptance of international tribunals' statutes and judgments, and of the widespread adoption of treaties dealing with the subject matter.' *Ibid.*, p. 125.

[55]   This document, a declaration of principles and rights, has been construed by the Inter-American Court of Human Rights to contain some dispositions that have reached the status of general principles of international law, which are binding on the States that have accepted its jurisdiction, given their recognition as basic prerogatives of the human nature.

Court of Human Rights. Neither the American Convention on Human Rights, nor the Statute of the Inter-American Court of Human Rights or its Rules of Procedure established a taxonomic system of the sources of law under which it would base its rulings. As has been understood, the sources of law applicable to the cases over which it has jurisdiction are those of general international law, contained in Article 38 of the ICJ Statute. However, an exception was established recently through the inter-American case law, specifically in regard to Article 59 of the ICJ Statute, which set forth that the judicial decisions of the Court were only binding *inter partes* and not *erga omnes*.

Nevertheless, in its judgment of the *Radilla Pacheco* case, the Inter-American Court of Human Rights found that the defendant state had the obligation to implement not just what had been decided in the case at hand, but the developments and decisions contained in the case law of the regional court regarding military justice.[56] In this guise, what the Court specifically did was to broaden the legal horizon that imposed obligations on the state, which witnessed an evolution of the effects of the judgment that went from being *inter partes* to become an *erga omnes* obligation applicable to all the state parties in the hemisphere.[57] To the effects of clarifying this position, the corresponding parts of the judgment are transcribed:

> Within this task, the Judiciary shall take into consideration not only the treaty but also the interpretation the Inter-American Court, final interpreter of the American Convention, has made of it.
>
> 340. Therefore, it is necessary that the constitutional and legislative interpretations regarding the material and personal competence criteria of military jurisdiction in Mexico be adjusted to the principles established in the jurisprudence of this Tribunal, which have been reiterated in the present case.[58]

What the Court achieved through this judgment, which it has also done in previous cases, was the determination of the constitution of a general principle of international human rights law, applicable to the states that have agreed to its jurisdiction. Thus, reiterative criteria of international courts and tribunals have in some instances led to the development of both general principles of international law and international customary law, even if these apply only to a specific number of states.

---

[56] *Case of Radilla Pacheco v. Mexico*, Judgment, Inter-American Court of Human Rights, 23 November 2009, paras. 339–340.

[57] The Inter-American Court of Human Rights reached the same conclusion in the *Gelman* case, where it stated that even when some States are not parties to an international procedure, they are obliged to a certain extent by the precedents or case law that has been issued by that regional human rights body. *Case of Gelman v. Uruguay*, Monitoring Compliance with Judgment, Inter-American Court of Human Rights, 20 March 2013, paras. 67, 69.

[58] *Case of Radilla Pacheco v. Mexico*, Judgment, Inter-American Court of Human Rights, 23 November 2009, paras. 339–340 (emphasis added).

What both examples show is that even though the sources of international law contained in the ICJ Statute have basically remained unchanged, new developments and interpretations have added more width to their scope, in some cases with the clear intention of better serving the interests of international justice in the field of human rights. Given that human rights in particular have shown to be a dynamic field of international law, it is necessary to adapt the applicable legal framework to the reality it is facing; in theory, this is at least the teleological use of law, to regulate human conduct to what it should be.

Due to the enormous difficulties to conclude specific and binding hard international law (in the form of treaties), and on the uncertainty of what constitutes principles and customary rules of international law, *soft law* has gained a wider recognition as one of the initial steps to the development of general state practice. In this sense, a few comments will be made below, particularly in relation to the case of corporate accountability for its involvement in human rights abuses.

3.2. A PERMANENT CALL FOR 'RETHINKING' THE SOURCES OF INTERNATIONAL LAW: THE ROLE OF SOFT LAW

In the opinion of Pierre-Marie Dupuy, *soft law* is a paradoxical term for defining an ambiguous phenomenon in the field of international law. First of all, this is because the rule of law is usually considered compulsory, something that soft law lacks. In the second place, it is because its legal effects vary widely depending on the field and situation at hand, which makes them difficult to identify and classify.[59] While it is true that soft law has not been recognised as a formal source of international law, and is even doubted as having any effects other than declaratory, it has been a useful tool to engage states in the discussion and elaboration of declarations and other type of international documents that show the *status quo* of a particular question at that specific moment in time. Therefore, it has been relevant to advance questions that probably would not have enough support to be discussed in a treaty-making process.[60]

The multitude of soft law instruments attest to this reality, and are also a reflection of the decentralised nature of international law, of the lack of an

---

[59]   P.-M. Dupuy, 'Soft Law and the International Law of the Environment' (1991) 12(2) *Michigan Journal of International Law* 420.

[60]   F.A. Cárdenas Castañeda, *supra* n. 46, p. 369: 'soft law […] instruments […] emerged as a response to the legal need faced by the international community. They are the result of reality modeling international law, of international practice modeling the sources!' See also W.M. Reisman, 'The Quest for World Order and Human Dignity in the Twenty-First Century: Constitutive Process and Individual Commitment', *Collected Courses*, Vol. 351 (Leiden: Martinus Nijhoff, 2012), pp. 132–135, where the author discusses the value of soft law as opposed to hard law.

international legislator or even a political-legal international structure resembling that of the nation state. At its current state, the international arena has become an organised chaos in which hard law in the form of treaties, customary rules and general principles of international law are constantly challenged and interacting with each other and with soft law instruments, therefore blurring the thin lines that were used before to distinguish what state practice actually is and what the concept of 'general practice' means. It is therefore useful to share a few comments on the role soft law is currently having in some domains within the human rights field, and how it can be used in the context of business and human rights.

First of all, soft law is already incrusted in international law. It is an important tool used by states in international fora (thus, an international state practice) and a source for interpretation and consideration by at least regional human rights tribunals. In this sense, soft law is an international development that has helped states and other non-state actors face with varying degrees of success the effects that globalisation has had worldwide. The main question related to this is whether soft law instruments can be of any use to develop and impose binding obligations on states and other international actors, in what has been labelled as the hardening of soft law.[61] Considering the current status of international law, the most likely option would be its hardening through the development of either a customary rule or a general principle of international law.[62] For the purposes of this chapter, we will focus on the development of custom.

For soft law to turn into hard law, some of the classic elements of the formation of hard international law must converge, but given the differentiated approach with which declarations and guidelines are treated by states, some of them may be embedded already in their participation for the adoption of the instruments containing such soft dispositions.[63] Clearly, any disposition that would eventually become at least a semi-compulsory obligation must enjoy the pre-requisite of state

---

[61] For references to the hardening of soft law in the business and human rights context, see N. Bernaz, Nadia, *supra* n. 1, p. 15; and S. Deva, 'Multinationals, Human Rights and International Law: How to Deal with the Elephant in the Room', paper presented at the GLOTHRO Workshop on the Direct Human Rights Obligations for Corporations (Slovenia, January 2013), p. 9.

[62] '[W]hat is required for the establishment of human rights obligations *qua* general principles is essentially the same kind of convincing evidence of general acceptance and recognition [...] in order to arrive at customary law.' B. Simma and P. Alston, 'The Sources of Human Rights Law: Custom, *Jus Cogens* and General Principles' (1992) 82 *Australian Yearbook of International Law* 105.

[63] '[UN] resolutions can themselves constitute practice of States, or express the *opinio juris*, so as to be creative of customary law.' H.W.A. Thirlway, *International Customary Law and Codification: An Examination of the Continuing Role of Custom in the Present Period of Codification of International Law* (Leiden: A.W. Sijthoff, 1972), p. 66. See also *Legality of the Threat or Use of Nuclear Weapons*, Advisory Opinion, International Court of Justice, 8 July 1996, para. 70, where it states the following: 'The Court notes that General Assembly resolutions, even if they are not binding, may sometimes have normative value. They can, in certain circumstances, provide evidence important for establishing the existence of a rule or the emergence of an *opinio juris*. [...] Or a series of resolutions may show the gradual evolution of the *opinio juris* required for the establishment of a new rule.'

practice, for without a general use of its content, no possibilities of hardening would exist. On the other hand, the subjective element (*opinio juris*) must also be present for a rule of customary law to develop.[64]

Discussions have been held for a long time in relation to one particular set of circumstances linked to *opinio juris*, particularly within the framework of multilateral organisations such as the UN. In this sense, the question of what unanimous adoption implies for a normative project (especially in non-binding instruments) has had particular relevance: 'if a resolution [...] is adopted by a sufficient majority to be regarded as generally representative [...] then it will probably be impossible to challenge the authority of the rules so stated on the ground that the *opinio juris* is lacking or unproved.'[65] This assertion is particularly relevant if examined in light of the most recent set of rules adopted in the field of corporate responsibility, the UN Guiding Principles on Business and Human Rights.

The Guiding Principles on Business and Human Rights, the result of the six-year mandate of Professor John Ruggie as the Special Representative on the issue of human rights and transnational corporations and other business enterprises, were unanimously adopted and endorsed by the UN Human Rights Council on 6 July 2011.[66] As a soft law development, they would normally only serve as guidelines for states in order to address the negative impacts that corporate activities may have within their national boundaries. However, the fact that they were unanimously adopted could very well also reflect a common concern and belief of states that the guidelines contained in the instrument are a globally accepted minimum for the respect of human rights by corporations. If this holds true, there is a strong case to be made that the unanimity in their adoption was the reflection of *opinio juris*, the subjective element that lies at the heart of customary rules,[67] which could eventually be the foundation for the development of a customary rule of international law.

In addition, a case can be made regarding the diplomatic activity of the states who participated in the adoption of the Guiding Principles, for 'It cannot be denied that when a resolution is formally adopted in so universal an organisation as the United Nations, the resolution is something more than the consistent

---

[64] In relation to this, one author disagrees: 'although the traditional view of customary law is that it contains two constitutive elements, the material and the psychological, in fact the material element of usage is 'purely evidentiary. [... T]here is no need of any usage or practice provided that the *opinio juris* can be clearly established.' A. D'Amato, 'On Consensus' (1970) 8 *Canadian Yearbook of International Law* 111. In the opinion of the author, both *opinio juris* and state practice are interdependent and mutually reinforcing.

[65] H.W.A. Thirlway, *supra* n. 63, p. 66.

[66] Human rights and transnational corporations and other business enterprises, UN Res. A/HRC/RES/17/4 (6 July 2011).

[67] 'If *all* states subscribe to a declaration that a particular formula expresses an existing rule of law, then that is the end of the matter, for what states *believe* to be international law is international law common usage.' A. D'Amato, *supra* n. 64, p. 106.

statements or wishes of the member States'.[68] In this sense, as stated by Wouters and Ryngaert, verbal state practice reflected through their statements in discussion of topics in multilateral organisations usually is an evidence of both state practice and the belief of that particular state regarding the topic discussed, which would fulfil the material (practice) and psychological (*opinio juris*) requirements for the formation of customary international law.[69]

Despite the previous affirmation, which could be debatable, another set of state practices that are external to the United Nations or the Human Rights Council are clear indices that the Guiding Principles are being given consideration as at least a developing rule of international law. This can be shown through the adoption of different plans of action and implementation of the Ruggie Principles throughout the world, as is the case of the European Union and its member countries (with the European's Commission guidance projects on the oil and mining sector, on information and communications technology and on employment and recruitment agencies, as well as the development and implementation of national action plans), or of some countries in the Latin-American region.

In this regard, it is important to keep in mind that state action may refer to the actions of any organs of the state, including for example the work of national human rights institutions, which may help in the implementation, diffusion and growth in the corresponding legal culture of the values contained in the UN resolution.[70] In addition, its use by national courts may reflect state practice,[71] useful for the development of a customary rule regardless of the effects that a series of judicial resolutions may have within the national legal framework.[72] As has been discussed before, reiterative interpretation of soft law by courts (such as the Inter-American Court of Human Rights) has in some instances developed its status, at least regionally, as a compulsory criterion to which states under its jurisdiction are bound.

Therefore, a more consistent global practice could eventually lead to the development of an emerging rule of customary international law, if the *opinio juris* expressed in the Human Rights Council's resolution adopting the Guiding

---

[68] H.W.A. Thirlway, *supra* n. 63, p. 65.

[69] J. Wouters and C. Ryngaert, *supra* n. 51, p. 115.

[70] As is the case, for example, of the Casino Royale recommendation of the Human Rights Commission of the State of Nuevo Leon, Mexico, where it largely relied on the Ruggie Framework to determine the probable responsibility by omission of a corporation in a fire that took place in August 2011 and that killed 52 people. For a more detailed explanation of the case, see H.F. Cantú Rivera, 'Corporations and Compliance with International Human Rights Law: From a "Responsibility to Respect" to Legal Obligations and Enforcement' in J.L. Cernic and T. Van Ho, *Human Rights and Business: Direct Corporate Accountability for Human Rights* (Oisterwijk: Wolf Legal Publishers 2015).

[71] '[J]ust as judicial decisions of international tribunals can clarify certain questions of International Law and also of domestic law, judicial decisions of national tribunals can likewise do so when dwelling upon questions of International Law.' A.A. Cançado Trindade, *supra* n. 50, p. 159.

[72] As would be, for example, the development of legal precedents that could make the Guiding Principles on Business and Human Rights binding under domestic law.

Principles of Business and Human Rights can be construed as the expression of the acceptance by the international community of a set of minimum standards that are expected from both states and corporations in relation to the effects and impacts that the activities of the latter can have in the enjoyment of human rights.

While it is expected that some states may oppose to the interpretation of this resolution as being the expression of a general belief of the international community, and would generally rely on the traditional approach to the formation of customary law requiring state practice primarily and *opinio juris* secondarily, it is true that international and domestic practice usually reflect legal developments that formal methods to ascertain international law may not be able to reach, given the different paces to which reality and law are bound.

4. GENERAL CONCLUSIONS

A few general conclusions can be drawn from the arguments exposed in the preceding paragraphs, particularly regrouped in the two broad fields that were discussed: extraterritoriality and the hardening of soft law.

As regards extraterritoriality, from the opinion given by the Supreme Court in *Kiobel*, it can be inferred that a particularly strict approach will be followed in the next ATS cases that are granted jurisdiction. Thus, a link with American interests or nationality will be required for their courts to have jurisdiction, while foreign-cubed cases seem to have been *prima facie* excluded from their reach. However, the fact that courts in other countries are dealing with cases in which extraterritorial adjudication is taking place will probably switch the focus of victims, who will continue resorting to forum shopping in order to find a jurisdiction that is more prone to analysing the merits of their causes.

Under international human rights law, however, there is a need to develop a non-binding instrument on which states can rely to guide them in the processes involving extraterritorial adjudication. As has been discussed before, a soft law instrument will have a better opportunity to evolve into a binding obligation for states than creating an international treaty on this subject, and would normally have an interesting opportunity to develop standards if several states are adjudicating cases that involve extraterritorial elements. Given that there is already some practice in this field, although scarce, it would appear that an international instrument conceived either through the machinery of the Human Rights Council or the Working Group on the issue of human rights and transnational corporations and other business enterprises could serve to determine international non-binding standards, and therefore offer guidance in one of the most politically and legally difficult topics in human rights.

As regards the hardening of soft law, for soft law to become something more than just mere diplomatic or academic exercises and references with no binding character, frequent practice by the different actors of the international community is required. As has happened with a few examples, for instance the UN Declaration on the Rights of Indigenous Peoples, or with several environmental principles contained in UN Declarations, practice and a general acceptance by states has elevated them to at least the rank of general principles of international law, which could be considered the weakest line in the hard sources of international law. However, continuous usage has the possibility of eventually becoming hard law, either through the traditional approach that emphasises state practice, or as a confirmation of the general *opinio juris* that is more favoured by the human rights approach, thus evolving into a customary rule. Even though some states, usually the most powerful, may be reluctant to accept their characterisation as binding norms, the use and implementation by a growing number of states could eventually pressure those objectors to yield and accept them, in limited circumstances perhaps, as rules that would be considered and perceived as mandatory by the international community.

Even though these types of developments will not be easily achieved, we must bear in mind that this is a basic characteristic of general international law: long processes will be required for the community of states to eventually accept and try to regulate the challenges posed to them by a constantly changing reality.

CHAPTER 6

THE VIABILITY OF
THE MAASTRICHT PRINCIPLES IN
ADVANCING SOCIO-ECONOMIC RIGHTS
IN DEVELOPING COUNTRIES

Ebenezer Durojaye

1. INTRODUCTION

Traditionally, states are regarded as the subject of international law. This position is reinforced under international human rights instruments, where human rights obligations are imposed on states. In most international and regional human rights instruments, the obligation to respect, protect, and fulfil human rights are addressed to states parties to the instruments. This has led to the belief, albeit erroneously, that non-state actors cannot be held accountable for human rights violations. However, in recent times, the activities of multinational companies are beginning to have adverse effects on the enjoyment of human rights across the world, particularly in developing countries. Documented evidence exists of how activities of multinational companies (MNCs) have led to gross human rights violations in developing countries.[1] Such practices range from unfair labour practices, degradation of the environment to complicity in attacks on union leaders or members. These hitherto unnoticed negative activities of multinational companies have been exposed by concerted efforts of activists and civil society groups in developing countries. Notable among these include labour malpractices committed by Nike in Indonesia and other Southeast Asian countries and the complicity of Royal Dutch Shell in the execution of Ken Saro-Wiwa and other human rights activists in Nigeria.[2] More recent campaigns have targeted Coca-Cola for alleged involvement of its bottlers in Colombia in the assassination of trade union leaders.

---

[1] Amnesty International, *Undermining Rights: Forced Evictions and Police Brutality around the Porgera Gold Mine, Papua New Guinea* (London: Amnesty International, 2010).

[2] Amnesty International, *Nigeria: Petroleum, Pollution and Poverty in Niger-Delta Area* (London: Amnesty International, 2009).

Sadly, human rights abuses committed by multinational companies often go un-redressed in many developing countries. This is often due to the fact that most multinational companies have their headquarters somewhere else and host countries are sometimes either unwilling or lack the political will to take up actions against these companies. There is now a growing consensus under international law that multinational companies should be held accountable for the human rights violations they commit. Indeed, over the years different initiatives have been adopted to hold MNC accountable for human rights violations. These include the concept on horizontality of human rights, enactment of national legislation, such as the Alien Tort Claims Act, and more recently the adoption of the Principles on Extraterritoriality of Obligations in the Area of Economic, Social and Cultural Rights, by a group of lawyers and human rights experts at a gathering convened by the Maastricht University in September 2011.

The purpose of this chapter is to examine the effectiveness of these initiatives, paying particular attention to the Principles on Extraterritoriality of Obligations on Socioeconomic Rights. Although not a binding document by any standard, the Maastricht Principles seek to provide a lasting solution to impunity, often exploited by big multi-national companies regarding their activities in many developing countries. Thus, the Principles aim to ensure that home states of companies bear the responsibilities for human rights violations committed outside their territories. This chapter critically analyses the content of the Principles on Extraterritoriality with a view to ascertain its viability of holding non-state actors, particularly multinational companies (MNCs), liable for human rights violations committed outside their headquarters.

2. ARE MNCs SUBJECT TO INTERNATIONAL HUMAN RIGHTS LAW?

In many parts of developing countries, MNCs have continued to play major roles in the economic activities of the people by providing employment opportunities and building the capacity of indigenous people. In addition, MNCs have continued to explore business opportunities and provide the necessary technical support to their host countries. MNCs are involved in various aspects of economic activities including mining, oil exploration, manufacturing and building, and construction activities thereby improving the income of host countries and citizens' overall standard of living. However, while MNCs contribute greatly to annual earnings of host countries, sometimes they are either directly or indirectly involved in human rights violations within the territories of the host states. Such violations include complicity in offences committed by the host state's police and military forces, the use of forced and child labour, suppression of rights to freedom of association and speech, violations of the rights to cultural and religious practice, infringement of rights to property (including intellectual property), and gross infringements of environmental rights.[3] This has raised an important question as to whether human rights obligations can be imposed on MNCs.

Unfortunately, most human rights instruments, beginning with the Universal Declaration on Human Rights to the binding human rights treaties, do not directly impose obligations on MNCs. However, the traditional notion that obligations under international law are imposed solely on states is fast changing as non-state actors can in some circumstances bear obligations under international law. A good example of this is in the area of international criminal law. Recall that during the Nuremberg Tribunal individuals were held accountable for their roles in the grotesque violations of human rights and crimes against humanity committed during the Second World War. This could be described as the turning point in the attempt to impose obligations under international law on non-state actors.

More than ever before, commentators have vehemently argued that, though created for making profits, MNCs are under legal and moral obligations to respect and protect human rights.[4] In recent times, different attempts have been made to ensure that MNCs are directly responsible for human rights violations they commit. Beginning from the mid-1970s, the international community has adopted initiatives towards this end. These include the Sullivan Principles of 1970, the UN Draft Code of Transnational Corporation of 1977, the Organization for Economic Cooperation and Development (OECD) Guidelines for Multinational Enterprises of 1976 (which have been revised on several occasions), and the International Labour Organization Tripartite declaration of principles concerning MNEs of 1977.[5] The OECD Guidelines impose obligations on MNCs to 'respect and protect human rights of those affected by their activities consistent with the host government's international obligations and commitments'.[6]

Today, these Guidelines remain one of the most widely used instruments defining the obligations of multinational enterprises.[7] It has been noted that the

---

[3]   D. Kinley and S. Joseph, 'Multinational Corporations and Human Rights: Questions about their Relationship' (2002) 27 *Alternative Law Journal* 7–11.

[4]   B. Frey, 'The Legal and Ethical Responsibilities of Transnational Corporations in the Protection of International Human Rights' (1997) 6 *Minnesota Journal of Global Trade* 152–188, 153; S. Ratner, 'Corporations and Human Rights: A Theory of Legal Responsibility' (2001) 111 *Yale Law Journal* 443–542, 443.

[5]   S. Katuoka and M. Dailidaitė, 'Responsibility of Transnational Corporations for Human Rights Violations: Deficiencies of International legal Background and solutions offered by National and Regional Legal Tools' (2012) 19 *Jurisprudence* 1301–1316, 1304.

[6]   See OECD Guidelines for Multinational Enterprises, chapter on 'General Policies', para. 2.

[7]   The Guidelines are addressed to the governments of the 30 state parties of the Organisation, but have also been adopted by Argentina, Brazil, Chile and the Slovak Republic. These governments 'recommend to multinational enterprises operating in or from their territories the observance of the Guidelines' (Declaration on international investment and multinational enterprises, 27 June 2000, I.). There is therefore no territorial limitation to the application of the Guidelines. As most multinational enterprises are domiciled in industrialised countries members of the OECD, the Guidelines are practically of almost universal applicability to transnational business enterprises.

Guidelines were adopted as part of the Declaration on International Investment and Multinational Enterprises, which:

> in its other parts sought to facilitate trade among OECD countries in particular by requiring the parties to adopt the principle of national treatment and by seeking to minimize the risk of conflicting requirements being imposed on multinational enterprises, the Guidelines were seen as a means to encourage to opening of foreign economies to foreign direct investment.[8]

They sought to ensure that all states parties would contribute, by the setting of national contact points and their cooperation with the OECD Investment Committee (previously known as the Committee on International Investment and Multinational Enterprises (CIME)), to ensuring a certain level of control on the activities of multinational enterprises incorporated under their jurisdiction, even if this supervision remains purely voluntary and may not lead to the imposition of sanctions.

In addition to the initiatives of the OECD, the International Labour Organisation (ILO) has adopted the Tripartite Declaration of Principles concerning Multinational Enterprises and Social Policy.[9] The preamble of the Declaration explains that it is founded on the belief that:

> the advances made by multinational enterprises in organizing their operations beyond the national framework may lead to abuse of concentrations of economic power and to conflicts with national policy objectives and with the interest of the workers. Furthermore, the preamble explains that the complexity of multinational enterprises and the difficulty of clearly perceiving their diverse structures, operations and policies sometimes give rise to concern either in the home or in the host countries, or in both.

Thus, one of the important aims of the Tripartite Declaration is to 'encourage the positive contribution which multinational enterprises can make to economic and social progress and to minimize and resolve the difficulties to which their various operations may give rise, taking into account the United Nations resolutions advocating the Establishment of a New International Economic Order'.

More importantly and in addition to the existing rights of workers – such as references to the principles of freedom of association[10] and the right to collective

---

[8]   O. De Schutter, *Transnational Corporation and Human Rights: An Introduction. Global Law Working Paper* (Hauser Global Law School New York: University of New York, 2005), p. 13.

[9]   The Tripartite Declaration was adopted by the Governing Body of the International Labour Office at its 204th Session, on 16 November 1977.

[10]   *Ibid.*, para. 41–47.

bargaining,[11] the prohibition of arbitrary dismissals,[12] or the protection of health and safety at work[13] – guaranteed by the different ILO Conventions and recommendations,[14] the Tripartite Declaration places emphasis on the respect for the fundamental rights of workers. In particular, paragraph 8 of the Tripartite Declaration contains a detailed and general provision on respect for human rights:

> All the parties concerned by this Declaration should respect the sovereign rights of States, obey the national laws and regulations, give due consideration to local practices and respect relevant international standards. They should respect the Universal Declaration of Human Rights and the corresponding International Covenants adopted by the General Assembly of the United Nations as well as the Constitution of the International Labour Organization and its principles according to which freedom of expression and association are essential to sustained progress. They should also honour commitments which they have freely entered into, in conformity with the national law and accepted international obligations.

It can be said that the Tripartite Declaration is of moral significance, having been adopted by consensus by the ILO Governing body, which is usually made up of governments, employers, and workers. Be that as it may, the Declaration remains, as such, a non-binding instrument.[15]

In addition to the OECD Guidelines, the UN began the new millennium by exhibiting an interest in making MNCs directly responsible for human rights violations across the world. Initiatives include the Global Compact (2000), the UN Norms on the Responsibilities for Transnational Corporations and Other Business Enterprises with Regard to Human Rights (2003), the Report of the Special Representative of the Secretary General on the issue of human rights and transnational corporations and other business enterprises, and John Ruggie – 'Protect, Respect and Remedy: a Framework for Business and Human Rights' (2008, discussed in detail below). In particular, the UN Draft Code of Conduct on Transnational Corporations was prepared in readiness for adoption in 2003. The Code of Conduct provides, inter alia, that:

---

[11]   *Ibid.*, paras. 48–55.

[12]   *Ibid.*, para. 27.

[13]   *Ibid.*, paras. 36–39.

[14]   See for instance, ILO Declaration on Fundamental Principles and Rights at Work, adopted in June 1998 by the International Labour Conference.

[15]   The Addendum to the Tripartite Declaration of Principles concerning Multinational Enterprises and Social Policy adopted by the Governing Body of the International Labour Office at its 238th Session (Geneva, November 1987) and 264th Session (November 1995) states that: 'In keeping with the voluntary nature of the Declaration all of its provisions, whether derived from ILO Conventions and Recommendations or other sources, are recommendatory, except of course for provisions in Conventions which are binding on the member States which have ratified them'.

Transnational Corporations shall respect human rights and fundamental freedoms in the countries in which they operate. In their social and industrial relations, transnational corporations shall not discriminate on the basis of race, colour, sex, religion, language, social, national and ethnic origin or political or other opinion. Transnational Corporations shall conform to government policies designed to extend equality of opportunity and treatment.

Sadly, however, due to stiff opposition by MNCs and disagreements between developed and developing countries regarding international law and the responsibilities of MNCs, the Draft Code of Conduct failed to be adopted.[16]

It is only recently that the UN, through its special mechanism, attempted to make the link between the activities of corporations and their implications for the enjoyment of human rights. The Ruggie framework, which culminated in a UN Guidelines on Business and Human Rights, remains today the most comprehensive attempt to hold MNCs accountable for human rights violation across the world. The framework hinges on three pillars, namely the state duty to protect against human rights human abuses by third parties including corporations through appropriate laws policies and adjudication; the duty of corporations to respect human rights through due diligence and to avoid infringing the rights of others; and the state duty to ensure greater access to effective remedy (judicial and non-judicial) for victims of human rights violations. The Guidelines propose five priority areas through which states can work to promote corporate respect for human rights and prevent corporate-related abuses. The areas are: (a) striving to achieve greater policy coherence and effectiveness across departments working with business, including safeguarding the state's own ability to protect rights when entering into economic agreements; (b) promoting respect for human rights when states do business with business, whether as owners, investors, insurers, procurers, or simply promoters; (c) fostering corporate cultures respectful of human rights at home and abroad; (d) devising innovative policies to guide companies operating in conflict-affected areas; and (e) examining the cross-cutting issue of extraterritoriality.

In addition, the Guidelines deal with the notion of corporate responsibility to respect and protect human rights. According to the Guidelines, corporations are expected to take due diligence so that human rights abuses will not occur by reason of their activities. Generally, the notion of due diligence is often applied to hold states accountable for their failure to prevent the violations of human rights

---

[16]   W. Spröte, 'Negotiations on a United Nations Code of Conduct on Transnational Corporations' (2005) 33 *German Yearbook of International Law* 331–345; UN Sub-Commission on Prevention of Discrimination and Protection of Minorities 1996; P. Muchlinski, 'Attempts to Extend the Accountability of Transnational Corporations: The Role of UNCTAD' in M.T. Kamminga and S. Zia-Zarifi (eds.), *Liability of Multinational Corporations under International Law* (The Hague: Kluwer International Law, 2000); N. Jägers, *Corporate Human Rights Obligations: in Search of Accountability* (Antwerp: Intersentia, 2002).

by a third party. Thus, in cases of violence against women, the UN Declaration on Violence against Women and the CEDAW Committee in its General Recommendation 19 have both noted that a state could be held accountable for acts of violence perpetrated against women in private should it fail to adopt appropriate laws and policies to prevent this from taking place. It remains to be seen how this principle will be applied to corporations.

The use of the term 'responsibility' rather that 'duty' would seem to suggest that respecting rights is not currently an obligation that international human rights law generally imposes directly on companies, although elements of this may be reflected in domestic laws. This weak language would tend to reinforce the difficulty often encountered by the international community in holding corporations accountable for the execution of human rights violations. Given that the Guidelines on Business and Human Rights are rooted in human rights principles and standards, stronger language could have been more appropriate for this purpose. An alternative argument in this regard would be that the use of the word 'responsibility' instead of 'duty' is a question of nomenclature and does not in any way diminish the obligations of corporations to ensure that their activities conform with human rights standards.

It is important to note here that a business entity's corporate responsibility to respect human rights applies across its business activities and through its relationships with third parties connected with those activities – such as business partners, entities in its value chain, and other non-state actors and state agents. In addition, companies need to consider the country and local contexts for any particular challenges they may pose and how those might shape the human rights impacts of company activities and relationships.

Despite the different attempts to make MNCs directly responsible for human rights violations, little or no success has been achieved. The major setbacks are due to the fact that most of these initiatives lack binding force and can be described as nothing more than hortatory. More importantly, the different initiatives fail to establish a monitoring and accountability mechanism to ensure proper enforcement of the rules. The fact that these different attempts are codified in non-binding documents implies that compliance is voluntary and will depend on good faith on the part of MNCs.

Katuoka and Dailidaitė have argued that the voluntary nature of these initiatives can both be advantageous and disadvantageous:[17] MNCs are more willing to cooperate so as to ensure the success of these initiatives when they are not being compelled. Yet, since MNCs are under no obligation or compulsion to comply with these initiatives, they tend to be complacent in implementing the provisions of the different initiatives.[18] This is perhaps the distinguishing factor

---

[17]   S. Katuoka and M. Dailidaitė, 'Responsibility of Transnational Corporations for Human Rights Violations: Deficiencies of International legal Background and solutions offered by National and Regional Legal Tools' (2012) 19 *Jurisprudence* 1301–1316.

[18]   *Ibid.*

between soft law and treaty. Under international law, once a state has ratified a treaty this serves as a binding declaration to be bound by its provisions, except where the state has entered reservations to specific provisions of the treaty.[19] In addition, to ensure compliance with provisions of human rights treaties, treaty monitoring bodies (TMBs) have been established to monitor states' actions. These bodies issue authoritative General Comments and Recommendations to clarify the comments of human rights treaties. More importantly, TMBs issue concluding observations after considering states parties' reports. These reports are meant to show the steps and measures taken by states to ensure compliance with their treaty obligations. While treaty monitoring bodies cannot compel a state to enforce its concluding observations or recommendations, they sometimes rely on 'naming and shaming' to ensure that states take their concluding observations seriously.

Soft law often refers to declarations and resolutions made by governments at different meetings and fora and clarifications provided by treaty monitoring bodies in the form of general comments, recommendations and concluding observations to states parties. Soft law is not legally binding on states; however, it imposes moral obligations on states and provides a very good source of law under international law. Over the years, several declarations and resolutions have been made at international and regional levels which may impact on the enjoyment of human rights. For instance, during the adoption of the Universal Declaration on Human Rights (UDHR), the international community agreed that the need to uphold human dignity and affirm human rights of every individual, regardless of race, gender and class, is essential to peace and world order. The fact that the UDHR has become a highly influential human rights instrument and has almost attained the status of customary international law testifies to the importance of soft law and its ability to influence states' human rights actions internationally.

The limitations of these initiatives to address the serious challenge of holding MNCs directly responsible for human rights violations bring to the fore once more the weakness of international human rights law in this regard.

3. ATTEMPTS AT THE NATIONAL LEVEL TO MAKE MNCs RESPONSIBLE FOR HUMAN RIGHTS VIOLATIONS

In addition to various initiatives to ensure that MNCs are directly responsible for human rights violations, some attempts have equally been made at the national level towards making MNCs accountable for violations of human rights. It should

---

[19] Ratification is one of the many ways a state can be bound by the provisions of a treaty. For other ways by which a treaty may become binding see Articles 12–17 of the Vienna Laws of Treaties 1969.

be borne in mind that most of the human rights violations perpetrated by MNCs often occur within the territory of the host state. In most cases where the host state is a developing or least developed country it becomes very challenging if not impossible to hold MNCs responsible for such violations. This is particularly true in a situation where the MNC involved plays a crucial role in the economic development of the host state. Due to this challenge, recent developments have shown that some 'home states' are making attempts at regulating the activities of MNCs carried out in other jurisdictions. There are generally two approaches by constitutions with regard to holding non-state actors liable for human rights violations. The traditional approach exemplified by the constitutions of the United States of America and Canada is to not impute human rights obligations on non-state actors. Conversely, more recent constitutions, such as those of South Africa and Ireland, tend to recognise human rights obligations of non-state actors.[20] Although the US Constitution does not impose obligations on non-state actors, recent developments on the interpretation of legislation appear to indicate an attempt to hold non-state actors responsible for human rights violation in certain situations. The most often cited example relates to the Alien Tort Claims Act (ATCA 1789) of the United States. This Act permits people to bring an action extraterritorially in the Federal Court of the US. It provides that '[t]he district courts shall have original jurisdiction of any civil action by an alien for a tort only, committed in violation of the law of nations or a treaty of the United States.'[21] This provision has been interpreted purposively by US courts to mean that they have jurisdiction over enterprises either incorporated in the United States or having a continuous business relationship with the United States, where foreigners are the victims of violations of international law.[22] Regardless of where such violations have taken place, the victims may seek damages from the enterprises concerned, whether they have committed the violations directly or are indirectly complicit in actions committed by state agents.[23] In addition, a Second Circuit Court has noted that the rules of international law are not cast in

---

[20] See D. Chirwa, 'The horizontal application of constitutional rights in a comparative perspective' (2006) 10 *Law, Democracy and Development* 21–48.

[21] 28 U.S.C. §1350.

[22] The US Supreme Court considers that, when confronted with such suits, the US federal courts should 'require any claim based on the present-day law of nations to rest on a norm of international character accepted by the civilized world and defined with a specificity comparable to the features of the 18th-century paradigms [violation of safe conducts, infringement of the rights of ambassadors, and piracy]' which Congress had in mind when adopting the First Judiciary Act 1789 (*Sosa v. Alvarez-Machain*, No. 03–339, slip op. at 30–31 (US Sup. Ct. 2004)).

[23] See in particular *John Doe I v. Unocal Corp.*, 395 F.3d 932, 945–946 (9th Cir. 2002) (complicity of Unocal with human rights abuses committed by the Burmese military); and *Sarowiwa v. Royal Dutch Petroleum Co.*, 2002 WL 319887, *2 (S.D.N.Y. 2002) (complicity of Shell Nigeria and its parent companies Shell UK and Royal Dutch in the human rights abuses committed by the Nigerian police).

stone but change with time. This therefore makes it necessary to invoke the ATCA as a tool for the protection of human rights in Federal Courts in the US.[24]

Under the South African Constitution of 1996, an attempt was made to recognise the horizontal application of human rights. For instance, Section 8(2) of the Constitution states that the provisions of the Bill of Rights bind both natural and juristic persons if, and to the extent that, it is applicable. To further give credence to the horizontal application of human rights obligations in the South African Constitution, Section 9(4) provides that '[n]o person may unlawfully discriminate directly or indirectly against anyone on any grounds listed in the Constitution. In furtherance of this provision, the South African government has enacted the Promotion of Equality and Prevention of Unfair Discrimination Act No. 4 of 2000. This Act specifically provides that 'all persons' have the duty and responsibility to prevent discrimination in the country. These provisions would seem to suggest that non-state actors – including MNCs – could be held accountable for human rights violations in the country. However, the question remains: to what extent can a non-state actor be held liable for human rights violations, especially those concerning socio-economic rights? This is by no means an easy question to answer. In what would seem to be a response to this question, Chirwa reasons as follows:[25]

> The state action paradigm could serve as a useful basis for distinguishing the level of responsibility of non-state actors for socioeconomic right. Specifically speaking, conventionally this standard has been used to determine whether a given private actor should be held liable for human rights violations. Thus, a plaintiff will not succeed in suing a non-state actor unless he/she has established that the conduct of the non-state actor amounted to state action or was linked to the state.

Despite the promising nature of this law and various court cases against MNCs under the ATCA, no decision has been made against any MNC in any of the cases which have come before the courts. This, once more, points to the difficulty in holding MNCs accountable for human rights violations they commit. It also serves as a reminder of the weakness of international human rights in addressing this very important situation. In particular, it reinforces the extraterritorial limitation of national legislation in curbing the negative activities of MNCs. Kinley and Joseph have argued that the court might be more willing to find against MNCs in violations relating to the *jus cogens* norms including rights to be free from slavery, life and freedom from torture than contentious socio-economic rights including the right to health, clean environment and trade union.[26] This realisation acts as a

---

[24]   T.R. Posner, '*Kadic v. Karadzic* 70 F.3d 232' (1996) 90(4) *American Journal of International Law* 661.

[25]   D. Chirwa, 'Non-state actors' responsibilities for socioeconomic rights: The Nature of their Obligations under South African Constitution' (2002) 3(3) *ESR Review*.

[26]   D. Kinley and S. Joseph, *supra* n. 3, pp. 7–11.

further indication of the limitation of using domestic legislation to make MNCs accountable for human rights violations.

De Schutter has identified some of the initiatives that have led to the development of extraterritorial obligation under international law as discussed below.[27]

One of the first attempts at invoking extraterritorial jurisdiction relates to the efforts to combat international crimes. Recent developments within international humanitarian law, such as the Rome Statute and the Convention against Torture, tend to allow for extraterritorial jurisdiction to deal with war crimes or crime against humanity. These initiatives allow a state to investigate and prosecute international crimes even when these crimes are committed outside their national jurisdiction and regardless of whether the perpetrators or victims are nationals of the state concerned. Sometimes these principles are often invoked to apply to natural persons but may also apply to juristic persons.

In addition, attempts to address transnational crimes such as terrorism or human trafficking have given rise to the invocation of the extraterritorial jurisdiction to deal with these crimes. For example, the International Convention for the Suppression of the Financing of Terrorism adopted in 2000 provides in Article 5 that each state party, 'in accordance with its domestic legal principles, shall take the necessary measures to enable a legal entity located in its territory or organized under its laws to be held liable when a person responsible for the management or control of that legal entity has, in that capacity, committed an offence' as defined by the Convention by reference to the existing international treaties on combating terrorism. Moreover, Article 8 obligates state parties to exercise jurisdiction over the offence of financing terrorism whether or not the offence is committed within their territory. Furthermore, Article 7(2)(c) permits states parties to establish jurisdiction to cover the funding of terrorist acts which are directed towards or have resulted in terrorist acts in the territory of or against a national of that state, or against a state or government facility of that state abroad, including diplomatic or consular premises of that state; or which are committed in an attempt to compel that state to do or abstain from doing any act; by a stateless person who has his or her habitual residence in the territory of that state; or on board an aircraft which is operated by the Government of that state.

Another attempt to invoke extraterritorial jurisdiction to control transnational corporations is based on political objectives by exacting pressures on the state where the crime was committed. A good example of this relates to the measures adopted by the United States government targeting persons doing business in Cuba. Consequently, the United States adopted the Cuban Liberty

---

27   O. De Schutter, 'Extraterritorial Jurisdiction as a tool for improving the Human Rights Accountability of Transnational Corporations', *Background Paper to Seminar organized in collaboration with Office of the UN High Commissioner for Human Rights*, Brussels, 3–4 November 2006, available at: http://198.170.85.29/Olivier-de-Schutter-report-for-SRSG-re-extraterritorial-jurisdiction-Dec-2006.pdf (accessed 3 December 2014).

and Democratic Solidarity (Libertad) Act,[28] better known as the Helms-Burton Act in 1996 as part of the campaign to seek international support for sanctions against Cuba. A provision of the Act allows United States nationals who have been expropriated following the 1959 revolution to seek damages against any natural or legal person having 'trafficked' such 'confiscated property'; another provisions permits the Secretary of State to deny visa to anyone found' implicated in the trafficking of confiscated property as well as any 'corporate officer, principal, or shareholder with a controlling interest of an entity which has been involved in the confiscation of property or trafficking in confiscated property, a claim to which is owned by a United States national'.[29]

4. HOW RELEVANT ARE THE MAASTRICHT PRINCIPLES IN ADVANCING SOCIO-ECONOMIC RIGHTS?

In 2011, a group of legal experts convened a meeting in Maastricht, the Netherland and produced a document known as the Principles on Extra-territorial Obligations of States in the Area of Economic, Social and Cultural Rights. This document seeks to address the ever perennial challenge of holding multinational corporations legally accountable for the violations of socio-economic rights that occur outside their countries of registration. The preamble to the Principles provides thus:

> The human rights of individuals, groups and peoples are affected by and dependent on the extraterritorial acts and omissions of States. The advent of economic globalization in particular, has meant that States and other global actors exert considerable influence on the realization of economic, social and cultural rights across the world.

It is further stated in the preamble that the essence of the document is to clarify the extraterritorial nature state obligations to realise economic, social and cultural rights with a view to advancing and giving full effect to the object of the Charter of the United Nations and international human rights. Deva has noted that there are four broad ways of exercising control over the activities of MNCs: unilateral, bilateral, multilateral and international regulations.[30] He notes further that of these four, the unilateral and international regulations would seem to be the most

---

[28] Cuban Liberty and Democratic Solidarity (Libertad) Act of 1996 (Codified in Title 22, Sections 6021–6091 of the US Code) P.L. 104–114. Sect. 302.
[29] *Ibid.*, Sect. 401. See also Sect. 302 of the Act.
[30] S. Deva, 'Acting extraterritorially to tame Multinational Corporations for Human Rights Violations: who should "Bell the Cat"?' (2007) 5 *Melbourne Journal of International Law* 37–65, 37.

feasible.[31] Under the unilateral model – which could either be 'home state' or 'host state' regulation – a state could impose or enforce internationally recognised rights on MNCs.[32] In the case of international regulation, the international community assumes the responsibility to regulate the activities of MNCs in the context of human rights violations. Under international law, the general principle is that the exercise of authority by a state over activities that occur outside its jurisdiction is deemed to impinge the sovereignty of the country where the activities occur.[33] Therefore, regulations of an extraterritoriality nature are often permitted only in exceptional cases.

Although the Maastricht Principles do not specifically provide reasons to justify extraterritoriality of obligations, Devas has identified four crucial points justifying the need for extraterritorial obligations for MNCs.[34] First; extraterritoriality of obligations does not apply to all MNCs, but only to those which have connections with the state concerned. Secondly, given that extraterritorial law seeks to implement international – as opposed to national – policy, it is more likely to be condoned than an extraterritorial domestic law seeking to promote foreign policy. This reasoning would seem to be gaining more attention when one considers that the protection of human rights is no longer a domestic matter. This point was emphasised by the International Court of Justice in the *Advisory Opinion on the Legal Consequences of the Construction of Wall in the Occupied Palestine Territory*.[35] While commenting on the scope of application of the International Covenant on Civil and Political Rights, the Court noted as follows:

> [W]hile the jurisdiction of States is primarily territorial, it may sometimes be exercised outside the national territory. Considering the object and purpose of the International Covenant on Civil and Political Rights, it would seem natural that, even when such is the case, States parties to the Covenant should be bound to comply with its provisions.[36]

This position has been reiterated in the case of *Democratic Republic of the Congo v. Uganda*[37] where the court confirmed that human rights law may extend extraterritorially in respect to core human rights instruments.

---

[31]   *Ibid.*, p. 42.

[32]   *Ibid.*, p. 43.

[33]   J. Cassels, *The Uncertain Promise of Law: Lessons from Bhopal* (Toronto: University of Toronto Press, 1993), p. 273; D. Senz and H. Charlesworth, 'Building Blocks: Australia's Response to Foreign Extraterritorial Legislation' (2001) 2 *Melbourne Journal of International Law* 69–84, 2.

[34]   S. Deva, *supra* n. 30, pp. 37–65.

[35]   *Legal Consequences of the Construction of a Wall in the Occupied Palestinian Territory*, Advisory Opinion 2004 ICJ 136, 9 July 2004.

[36]   *Legal Consequences of the Construction of a Wall in the Occupied Palestinian Territory*, Advisory Opinion 2004 ICJ 136, 9 July 2004.

[37]   *Armed Activities on the Territory of the Congo (DRC v. Uganda)*, 2005 ICJ 26, 19 December 2005.

Thirdly, it can be argued that labelling MNC regulations as extraterritorial is 'misleading' and in fact far less 'extraterritorial' in nature. This is because such regulation affects only the parent corporation incorporated within the territory but operating abroad through its corporate hand.[38] Fourthly, it is now incontestable that the home and host states are both under obligations under international law (and in some cases national law) to respect and protect human rights. This would seem to imply that they must ensure that all entities within their jurisdiction comply with human rights standards.[39]

Principle 3 of the Principles on Extraterritoriality declares that '[a]ll States have obligations to respect, protect and fulfil human rights, including civil, cultural, economic, political and social rights, both within their territories and extraterritorially'. To avoid any confusion on this point, the Principles then proceed by attempting to provide a definition of extraterritorial obligations. According to the Principles, extraterritorial obligations encompass:

a) obligations relating to the acts and omissions of a State, within or beyond its territory, that have effects on the enjoyment of human rights outside of that State's territory; and

b) obligations of a global character that are set out in the Charter of the United Nations and human rights instruments to take action, separately, and jointly through international cooperation, to realize human rights universally.

The implication of Principle 8 is that a state will not only take necessary steps to prevent violations of socio-economic rights within its jurisdiction but will also be obligated to prevent such violations outside of its jurisdiction. In this regard, the Committee on Economic Social and Cultural Rights has noted as follows:

When an external party takes upon itself even partial responsibility for the situation within a country (whether under Chapter VII of the Charter or otherwise), it also unavoidably assumes a responsibility to do all within its power to protect the economic, social, and cultural rights of the affected population.[40]

This is based on the principle affirmed during the Vienna Programme of Action that the protection of human rights is the primary responsibility of all states.[41] In other words, 'while the beneficiaries of human rights obligations are the

---

[38] See for instance, A. Lowenfeld, *International Litigation and the Quest for Reasonableness: Essays in Private International Law* (New York: Oxford University Press, 1996), p. 106.

[39] D. Kinley, 'Human Rights as Legally Binding or Merely Relevant?' in S. Bottomley and D. Kinley (eds.), *Commercial Law and Human Rights* (Aldershot: Ashgate, 2002), pp. 38–42.

[40] General Comment No. 8, 'The relationship between economic sanctions and respect for economic, social and cultural rights', *Committee on Economic Social and Cultural Rights*, E/C.12/1997/8, 12 December 1997.

[41] Vienna Declaration and Programme of Action, Adopted by the World Conference on Human Rights, 25 June 1993, A/CONF 157/24, Part 1 ch. III.

rights-holders who are under a state's authority and control, the legal obligations to ensure the rights in question are owed to the international community as a whole'.[42]

Principle 8(b) echoes provisions in the UN Charter and other human rights instruments, by calling on states to take action, separately or jointly, through international cooperation with a view to preventing human rights violations.[43] This emphasises an important point, namely that the protection of human rights, particularly socio-economic rights, is a joint responsibility of states, regardless of their level of development. Implicit in this provision is that developed countries as much as developing countries are obliged to prevent violation of socio-economic rights across the world. Given that most of the MNCs have headquarters in developed countries, it is imperative for these countries to work with developing countries where most MNCs operate so as to avoid or minimise socio-economic rights violations that may occur as a result of the activities of MNCs. Experience has shown that most developed countries have often been complicit with regard to human rights violations perpetrated by MNCs in developing countries. This certainly betrays the 'separate and joint' obligations of states to prevent human rights violations.

Principle 9(a) and (b) of the Principles explains when extraterritorial obligation may arise. Extraterritorial obligations arise when a state exercises control, power, or authority over people or situations located outside its sovereign territory in a way that could have an impact on the enjoyment of human rights by those people or in such situations. All states are bound by these obligations in respect to human rights. In addition, extraterritorial obligations may arise on the basis of obligations of international cooperation set out in international law. This is more or less a reinstatement of states' commitment under the UN Charter. Under Article 56 of the Charter of 1945, states pledge 'to take joint and separate action in cooperation with the Organization' to achieve the purposes set out in Article 55 of the Charter. Such purposes include: 'universal respect for, and observance of, human rights and fundamental freedoms for all without distinction as to race, sex, language, or religion.[44]

The Maastricht Principles describe situations under which states have an obligation to respect, protect and fulfil socio-economic rights. Such situations include circumstances where: the state exercises full control over the acts or omission of a state may affect the enjoyment of socio-economic rights; or where 'the State, acting separately or jointly, whether through its executive, legislative or

---

[42]   O. De Schutter, A. Eide, A. Khalfan, M. Orellana, M. Salomon and I. Seidermanf, 'Commentary to the Maastricht Principles on Extraterritorial Obligations in the Area of Economic, Social and Cultural Rights' (2012) 34 *Human Rights Quarterly* 1084–1169.

[43]   See particularly, Articles 55 and 56 of the UN Charter, which adopt the phrase 'joint and separate action' compare with Article 2(1) of the International Covenant on Economic, Social and Cultural Rights, which prefers the phrase 'individually and through international cooperation'.

[44]   The Charter of the United Nations was signed on 26 June 1945.

judicial branches, is in a position to exercise decisive influence or to take measures to realize economic, social and cultural rights extraterritorially, in accordance with international law'.[45]

Principle 12 deals with an important aspect of international human rights law. It notes that states may be responsible for the acts or omission of a non-state actor acting under direct instruction or control of the state. This is often referred to as the doctrine of due diligence under international law. The CEDAW Committee in its General Recommendation 19 (1983) on violence against women has noted that acts of violence perpetrated by a private actor can be imputed to the state based on the doctrine of due diligence.[46] Some human rights tribunals have adopted a similar position. For instance, in *SERAC and another v. Nigeria* the African Commission on Human and Peoples' Rights found the Nigerian government to be in violation of various provisions of the African Charter for failing to prevent human rights violations occasioned by the activities of Shell in Ogoniland.[47] This is an important decision which can be invoked to hold a state accountable for human rights violations carried out by a private actor or entity outside the jurisdiction of the state. Indeed, this is the primary aim of Principle 12.

Under the section dealing with the obligations to respect, the Maastricht Principles identify that both direct and indirect actions of states may lead to the violations of socio-economic rights. Therefore, states are enjoined to refrain from taking any action that may directly or indirectly interfere with the enjoyment of socio-economic rights outside their territories.[48] With regard to the obligation to protect, the Maastricht Principles provide that states must regulate the activities of non-state actors so that they do not interfere with the enjoyment of socio-economic rights. These include taking administrative, legislative, investigative, adjudicatory, and other measures. Principle 25 provides that states must take measures to protect socio-economic rights in the following situations;

a) The harm or threat of harm originates or occurs on its territory;
b) Where the non-State actor has the nationality of the State concerned;
c) As regards business enterprises, where the corporation, or its parent or controlling company, has its centre of activity, is registered or domiciled, or has its main place of business or substantial business activities, in the State concerned;
d) Where there is a reasonable link between the State concerned and the conduct it seeks to regulate, including where relevant aspects of a non-State actor's activities are carried out in that State's territory;

---

[45] See Principle 9(c).
[46] CEDAW, General Recommendation 19, 'Violence against Women', adopted August 1983 (CEDAW/C/7), p. 1.
[47] *Social and Economic Rights Action Centre (SERAC) and Another v. Nigeria* (2001) AHRLR 60 (ACHPR 2001).
[48] See Principles 20 and 21.

e) Where any conduct impairing economic, social and cultural rights constitutes a violation of a peremptory norm of international law. Where such a violation also constitutes a crime under international law, States must exercise universal jurisdiction over those bearing responsibility or lawfully transfer them to an appropriate jurisdiction.

Regarding the obligation to fulfil, the Maastricht Principles highlight a number of actions states must take. This includes taking 'deliberate, concrete and targeted steps, separately, and jointly through international cooperation, to create an international enabling environment conducive to the universal fulfilment of economic, social and cultural rights'.[49]

5. LIMITATIONS OF THE PRINCIPLES

There is no doubt that the Principles on Extraterritorial Obligations contain important provisions that can be useful in safeguarding socio-economic rights in developing countries. The challenge, however, is that like most other 'soft law' instruments they are not legally binding. It remains to be seen whether states, particularly those from developed regions, will take them seriously. This is more so when one considers that an initial attempt by the UN to impose obligations on MNCs for human rights violations committed outside their headquarters was met with resistance. The success or otherwise of these Principles will depend largely on the willingness of developed countries and MNCs to abide by their spirit and tenets. It should be noted, however, that similar non-binding documents such as the Limburg Principles on the Implementation of Socioeconomic Rights and the Maastricht Principles have both commanded respect at the international level and are often cited as interpretative guides in clarifying the nature and content of socio-economic rights.

One of the glaring shortcomings of the Maastricht Principles is the failure to establish any accountability mechanism to ensure proper compliance with their provisions. The Maastricht Principles fail to create a body that will monitor compliance with the provisions contained therein. Given that the Maastricht Principles are not legally binding one may understand the reason for not creating a body to monitor its implementation. However, it can be argued that the non-binding nature of the Maastricht Principles does not preclude the establishment of an expert body made up of individuals, civil society organisations and representatives of MNCs from assuming similar responsibilities like that of treaty monitoring bodies. This expert Committee should be charged with the duty of receiving complaints on human rights violations by MNCs, investigating and making findings on such violations. This will ensure that the laudable provisions

---

[49]   See Principle 29.

of the Principles do not become promises merely on paper. Such an expert Committee can be funded through funds raised from private donor agencies. Given that the Maastricht Principles are not a treaty per se, it remains to be seen whether states or even MNCs will be willing to cooperate with the body set up to monitor compliance with Principles.

It can also be argued that the adoption of the concept of foreseeability known in the law of tort to determine state liability with regard to extraterritorial obligations of human rights violation can potentially weaken the efficacy of the Principles. De Schutter *et al.* have commended this approach arguing that it 'constitutes a strong incentive for states to assess the impact of their choices on the enjoyment of economic, social, and cultural rights abroad, because their international responsibility will be assessed on the basis of what their authorities knew or should have known'.[50] However, since violations of human rights have been based on strict liability, the foreseeability approach may give room for home states to raise excuses regarding human rights violations committed by MNCs. In fact the foreseeability approach would seem to contradict the due diligence approach earlier affirmed in the Maastricht Principles.

6. CONCLUSION

For many years MNCs have continued to engage in activities inimical to the enjoyment of human rights, particularly socio-economic rights, in many parts of developing countries. These violations have occurred without redress or remedy due to a number of factors. These include the fact that MNCs are not often regarded as subjects of international law, and in most cases they have their office of registration in another country different from where they operate. Moreover, because of the important roles MNCs play in the economic development of many developing countries, governments of these countries often lack the political will to take drastic actions to regulate the activities of MNCs. Even when developing countries are willing to regulate the activities of the MNCs, it is sometimes difficult to do so given that most MNCs are registered elsewhere. The adoption of the Maastricht Principles on the Extraterritoriality of Obligations on Socioeconomic Rights is no doubt a reinstatement at the international level to ensure that MNCs are held responsible for human rights violations they commit outside their country of incorporation. The Maastricht Principles provide a great opportunity to hold states (including MNCs) accountable for human rights violations committed outside of their jurisdiction.

Despite the potential of the Maastricht Principles to impose extraterritorial obligation on states, the fact that they lack a monitoring body to oversee their

---

[50] O. De Schutter, A. Eide, A. Khalfan, M. Orellana, M. Salomon and I. Seidermanf, *supra* n. 42, pp. 1084–1169.

implementation, coupled with the Principles' non-binding nature, leaves much to be desired. The success or otherwise of these Principles depend largely on good will of states. This falls short of what we should expect, as the promotion and protection of human rights are not a matter of charity but legal responsibilities of states. While the Maastricht Principles can be commended for being the first step towards holding MNCs accountable for human rights violations committed outside their place of registration, it has become imperative that a binding instrument be adopted at the international level to address this very serious challenge.

PART II
CONTEXTUAL ISSUES

CHAPTER 7

THE NEXT GENERATION
OF 'FAIR TRADE'

A Human Rights Framework for
Combating Corporate Corruption
in Global Supply Chains

Hana Ivanhoe

1. INTRODUCTION

From Nike to Coca-Cola to Apple, the emergence of the corporate social
responsibility (CSR) movement has led to the recognition of a duty on the part
of multinational corporations (MNCs) to work to prevent and remedy human
rights violations committed by their foreign subsidiaries and suppliers, regardless
of where in the world the violations occur. The international community must
now strengthen and utilise the momentum of the CSR movement and apply such
a human rights framework to the problem of corruption in global supply chains.

On the heels of more than a decade of calls for the recognition of a human
right to live free of corruption,[1] United States President Barack Obama lent
legitimacy to the concept when he referred to pervasive corruption as a 'violation
of basic human rights' in 2010.[2] In the years preceding and since, a fair amount
has been written about whether such a right exists and if so whether it could be
deemed to bind corporations such that any causes of action arising there from
could be adjudicated in an international or domestic court of law.

---

[1]   See e.g. N. Kofele-Kale, 'The Right to a Corruption-Free Society as an Individual and Collective
        Human Right: Elevating Official Corruption to a Crime under International Law' (2000) 34
        The International Lawyer 149. See also A. Brady Spalding, 'Four Unchartered Corners of
        Anti-Corruption Law: In Search of Remedies to the Sanctioning Effect' (2012) *Wisconsin Law
        Review* 661.
[2]   National Security Strategy, White House (2010), available at: www.whitehouse.gov/sites/
        default/files/rss_viewer/national_security_strategy.pdf.

This chapter accepts the prevailing view that international human rights protections generally do not bind corporations as a matter of hard law (with some notable exceptions). However, it also maintains that there is effectively an indirect, derived right to live in a corruption-free society, resulting from the relationship between corruption and human rights violations, i.e. systemic corruption frequently leads to and may cause violations of human rights. It further maintains that this right applies to corporations under John Ruggie's 'Protect, Respect and Remedy' framework (hereafter the Ruggie Framework or the Framework) and therefore must be incorporated into corporations' CSR policies and internal compliance.[3]

While dispute remains as to whether corruption itself constitutes a human rights violation, it is certainly the prevailing view that systemic corruption entails and precipitates human rights violations. It follows that in order for companies to comply with their duty to respect human rights under the Ruggie Framework, those companies must prevent corruption from occurring within their supply chains. It is not possible to respect human rights without preventing corruption; therefore companies cannot be said to sufficiently respect human rights in their supply chains without making affirmative efforts to prevent corruption therein.

As a result, this chapter argues that, under the Ruggie Framework, the understood relationship between corruption and human rights violations gives rise to a corporate duty to prevent corruption such that the multinational corporations at the consumer end of global supply chains have a heightened duty to ensure those supply chains are free of corruption. In sum, given that corruption leads to violations of fundamental human rights, and corporations have a duty to affirmatively and actively respect fundamental human rights under the Ruggie Framework, corporations have a duty to protect against corruption in their supply chains.

The chapter will first provide a brief overview of the problem of corruption in supply chains with an emphasis on its adverse effects on people's enjoyment of their fundamental human rights. It will then summarise academic support for the contention that corruption leads to human rights violations and therefore should be addressed via a human rights framework. It then argues that under the Ruggie Framework, multinational companies have a duty to prevent corruption in supply chains pursuant to their duty to respect human rights and that, absent a hard law standard and judicial jurisdiction, this duty can be enforced in the court of public opinion via a robust CSR approach that includes non-profit campaigns and media activism.

---

[3]   'Guiding Principles on Business and Human Rights', United Nations Office for the High Commissioner for Human Rights (2011), available at: www.ohchr.org/Documents/Publications/GuidingPrinciplesBusinessHR_EN.pdf.

2. THE RELATIONSHIP BETWEEN CORRUPTION AND HUMAN RIGHTS VIOLATIONS

This section will provide a brief overview of the problem of corruption and the support and justification for viewing the problem through a human rights framework.

2.1. OVERVIEW OF THE PROBLEM: WHAT IS THE IMPACT OF CORRUPTION IN GLOBAL SUPPLY CHAINS?

Transparency International, the global coalition against corruption, defines corruption as 'the abuse of entrusted power for private gain.'[4] For a definition of corruption reflecting the consensus of the international system, one might refer to the UN Convention Against Corruption (hereafter the Convention Against Corruption), but it refrains from defining the term. The definition provided under the US Foreign Corrupt Practices Act (FCPA), widely believed to be one of the predecessors to the Convention Against Corruption, may prove useful for reference. In sum, the relevant (so-called anti-bribery) provisions of the FCPA prohibit US persons and businesses, and certain foreign persons and businesses, from making corrupt payments to foreign officials to obtain or retain business.[5] It should be noted that the FCPA is often considered narrower in scope than the UN Convention Against Corruption in terms of prohibited behaviour.

The United Nations Global Compact (UNGC) view of corruption is also likely informative to the instant analysis and is of significant relevance to the discussion of corporate social responsibility below. The UNGC explicitly recognises a corporate duty to prevent corruption in supply chains in the form of its Principle 10, which states 'businesses should work against corruption in all its forms including extortion and bribery.'[6]

Corruption adversely impacts social and economic development thereby contributing to keeping the world's poorest peoples in a state of perpetual poverty.[7] MNCs have the power to encourage global development through trade

---

[4]   Transparency International, *Frequently Asked Questions on Corruption*, available at: www.transparency.org/whoweare/organisation/faqs_on_corruption#defineCorruption.

[5]   'FCPA: A Resource Guide to the US Foreign Corrupt Practices Act', Criminal Division of the US Department of Justice and the Enforcement Division of the US Securities and Exchange Commission (2012), available at: www.justice.gov/criminal/fraud/fcpa/guide.pdf; see also Foreign Corrupt Practices Act of 1977, *Public Law*, No. 95–213, 91 Stat. 1494 (codified as amended at 15 U.S.C. 78m(b), (d)(1), (g)–(h), 78dd-1 to -3, 78ff (2006).

[6]   UN Global Compact, Principle 10, available at: www.unglobalcompact.org/aboutthegc/thetenprinciples/principle10.html.

[7]   United Nations Global Compact, 'Corporate Sustainability with Integrity: Organizational Change to Collective Action' (2012).

and investment, but are also duty bound to ensure that such trade and investment are pursued ethically at every level of the corporations' supply chains so that they do not become counter-productive to development efforts.

Yet 36 years after the passage of the FCPA, debate still persists as to whether corporate acts of corruption by the subsidiaries and contractors/sub-contractors of MNCs should be regulated and if so, whether developed countries or the international community as a whole should fulfil this regulatory role. Andrew Spalding has argued that developed country anti-bribery legislation has the effect of economic sanctions against developing countries.[8] For the sake of brevity, though, this chapter assumes that anti-corruption regulation (via either domestic law or international legal agreement) is justified and necessary for the advancement of global development and a productive global economy.

The following section provides a snapshot of what corruption in supply chains looks like and seeks to demonstrate how even seemingly minor acts of corruption impact the citizens of corruption-riddled countries.

2.2. CORRUPTION IN SUPPLY CHAINS: SNAPSHOTS OF EMERGING DEVELOPMENTS

The purpose of this paper is not to analyse the various cultural and socio-economic contexts that give rise to societal corruption, but rather to propose a holistic approach for MNCs to combat corruption within their global supply chains, particularly when doing business in societies in which corruption is rampant.

The following discussion provides a brief overview of two prominent examples of allegations of corruption in the global supply chains of MNCs, although time constraints and the confidential nature of ongoing legal investigations and settlements do not permit a thorough examination.

Wal-Mart Stores, Inc., one of the world's largest retailers, is undeniably the highest-profile company currently under public scrutiny for allegations of corruption in its global supply chain. In 2012, the New York Times broke news of reported bribery and cover-ups at a Wal-Mart subsidiary in Mexico.[9] Reports indicate that Wal-Mart's Mexican subsidiary made corrupt payments totalling upward of $24 million in order to obtain the permits necessary to allow it to build and open new stores across Mexico.[10] Although many of the facts of the

---

8   See e.g. A. Brady Spalding, 'Unwitting Sanctions: Understanding Anti-Bribery Legislation as Economic Sanctions Against Emerging Markets' (2010) 62 *Florida Law Review* 351.

9   C. Savage, 'With Wal-Mart Claims, Greater Attention on a Law', *New York Times*, 25 April 2012, available at: www.nytimes.com/2012/04/26/business/global/with-wal-mart-bribery-case-more-attention-on-a-law.html.

10   D. Barstow, 'At Wal-Mart in Mexico, A Bribe Inquiry Silenced', *New York Times*, 21 April 2012, available at: www.nytimes.com/2012/04/22/business/at-wal-mart-in-mexico-a-bribe-inquiry-silenced.html.

case remain unknown as government investigation is still pending, should the allegations prove accurate, it would appear that the Wal-Mart subsidiary's practice of making corrupt payments was persistent and significant.[11]

Paying bribes in exchange for new building permits has troubling potential implications for the country in which those bribes are paid for a number of reasons. First, reports indicate that in one such instance bribes were paid in exchange for Wal-Mart being permitted to build one of its stores on the site of ancient ruins, which would have been prohibited by zoning laws had the Wal-Mart subsidiary executives not allegedly made payments in exchange for having the zoning map redrawn.[12]

Second, construction permits are often required for the protection of health and safety and circumventing such a permitting requirement (or at least removing compliance with that requirement from government oversight and regulation) could potentially present health or safety concerns for Wal-Mart employees and/or customers.

Third, the types of permits allegedly waived in exchange for the illicit payments reportedly made by Wal-Mart officials included in at least one instance environmental permits. As a result, 'Wal-Mart built a vast refrigerated distribution center in an environmentally fragile flood basin north of Mexico City.'

Fourth, bribery of local permitting officials can result in the wrongful dispossession of land by local inhabitants. According to reporting on the issue by the New York times, Wal-Mart executives allegedly paid hundreds of thousands of dollars in bribes to be able to build a store on land used by a local woman to grow alfalfa crops.[13]

Fifth and finally, depending on the specifics of the payments made and the advantages obtained in exchange for those payments, it is also possible that the payment of those bribes enriched certain private individuals at the expense of providing the state needed revenues that could have supported infrastructure development or other social welfare programmes.

In 2011, another major brand-owning company, Diageo plc, one of the world's largest beverage companies and owner of the Guinness, Jose Cuervo and Bailey's brands, settled an FCPA action with the US Securities and Exchange Commission. As part of the settlement, the company agreed to pay more than US $16 million

---

[11]   P.J. Henning, 'Taking Aim at the Foreign Corrupt Practices Act', *New York Times*, 30 April 2012, available at: http://dealbook.nytimes.com/2012/04/30/taking-aim-at-the-foreign-corrupt-practices-act/.

[12]   A. D'Innocenzio, 'Details Emerge in Wal-Mart Bribery Case', *Huffington Post*, 10 January 2013, available at: www.huffingtonpost.com/2013/01/11/details-emerge-on-wal-mart-bribery-case_n_2455981.html.

[13]   D. Barstow and A. Xanic von Bertrab, 'The Bribery Aisle: How Wal-Mart Got Its Way in Mexico', *The New York Times*, 17 December 2012, available at: www.nytimes.com/2012/12/18/business/walmart-bribes-teotihuacan.html?pagewanted=all&module=Search&mabReward=relbias%3Ar%2C%7B%222%22%3A%22RI%3A13%22%7D.

and make significant enhancements to its internal enforcement programme.[14] According to the SEC, Diageo made almost US $3 million in improper payments to government officials in India, Thailand and Korea in exchange for 'lucrative sales and tax benefits.'[15]

Improper payments such as those Diageo is alleged to have made are sometimes issued by companies to avoid paying the taxes they would otherwise owe the governments of developing countries which rely on revenues from foreign trade, including from the collection of such taxes, to fuel development. When regulations in place to ensure the receipt of those revenues by a country's citizenry are effectively sidestepped through corrupt payments, those revenues may not reach the citizenry at large. As a result, when a corporation makes improper payments in order to avoid paying the taxes it owes to a country in which it operates, the people of that country may be deprived of revenue they are rightfully owed under the law.

2.3. ACADEMIC AND EMPIRICAL SUPPORT FOR THE CONCEPT OF CORRUPTION AS A HUMAN RIGHTS VIOLATION

Corruption is also a threat to people's enjoyment of their basic human rights. In addition, the last decade has seen the emergence of a growing consensus around the concept of a human right to live in a society free of corruption. Numerous academics, the United Nations and the President of the United States have directly and indirectly supported this contention.[16] This has contributed to a growing consensus that pervasive corruption is disruptive and counter to the respect and protection of fundamental human rights.

This manifests in a number of ways, some of which are quite vivid. But even outside of the more egregious stories illustrating the intersection of corruption and human rights violations that dominate what little media coverage there is of this topic, seemingly innocuous acts of corruption may also violate human rights protections.

By way of example, corporate corruption can violate the right to food where corrupt payments lead to wrongful distribution of agricultural land that results in loss of livelihood for the people with rightful claims to that land.[17] It can also lead

---

[14] US Securities and Exchange Commission Press Release 2011–158, *SEC Charges Liquor Giant Diageo with FCPA Violations*, February 2011, available at: www.sec.gov/news/press/2011/2011–158.htm.

[15] *Ibid.*

[16] See generally J. Thuo Gathii, 'Defining the Relationship between Human Rights and Corruption' (2009) 31 *University of Pennsylvania Journal of International Law* 125; see also N. Kofele-Kale, *supra* n. 1.

[17] See e.g. J. Bacio-Terracino, *Corruption as a Violation of Human Rights* (2008), International Council on Human Rights Policy (forthcoming).

to the violation of peoples' political rights where corporate interests make illegal payments to politicians to effectively 'buy' votes and decisions on legislation beneficial to them.

The UN has acknowledged the interrelatedness of incidences of corruption and human rights violations. The foreword to the Convention Against Corruption states, 'corruption is an insidious plague that has a wide range of corrosive effects on societies. It undermines democracy and the rule of law [and] leads to violations of human rights.'[18] The UN High Commissioner for Human Rights also recognises the role corruption plays as an obstacle to the realisation of robust human rights protections.[19]

Whether a corrupt act itself constitutes a violation of human rights law is a different (albeit related) question. Many convincingly argue that there is sufficient evidence in state practice and customary international law to support the recognition of a human right to a corruption-free society. This argument is supported by the view that such a right is necessary for the respect of the fundamental rights to life, dignity and equality, as exemplified by the case studies highlighted in the previous section.[20] According to Ndiva Kofele-Kale, '[t]he right to a society free of corruption is inherently a basic human right because life, dignity and other important human values depend on this right. That is, it is a right without which these essential values lose their meaning.'[21]

The right to live in a society free of corruption is said to derive from the right to economic self-determination, specifically the right of a people to exercise sovereignty over their natural resources.[22] This view is supported by human rights activist Dr Kolawole Olaniya, who argues in his most recent book that corruption itself constitutes a human rights violation where it dispossesses people of their natural wealth and resources.[23]

The right is also said to be grounded in common Article 1 of the International Covenant on Civil and Political Rights and the International Covenant on

---

[18]   UN General Assembly, United Nations Convention Against Corruption, 31 October 2003, A/58/422, available at: www.refworld.org/docid/4374b9524.html (accessed 10 June 2013).

[19]   United Nations High Commissioner for Human Rights, Implementation of General Assembly Resolution 60/251 of 15 March 2006 entitled 'Human Rights Council, Note by the High Commissioner for Human Rights transmitting to the Human Rights Council the report of the seminar on anti-corruption measures, good governance an human rights' (Warsaw, Poland, 8–9 November 2006), A/HRC/4/71, 12 February 2007.

[20]   See S. Coquoz, *Corruption and Human Rights: An International and Indonesian Perspective*, presented at the Pusham UII / Norwegian Centre for Human Rights Workshop on Corruption and Human Rights, 15–16 May 2012, in Yogyakarta, Indonesia; see also N. Kofele-Kale, *supra* n. 1.

[21]   N. Kofele-Kale, *supra* n. 1, p. 163.

[22]   *Ibid.*, p. 164.

[23]   K. Olaniyan, *Corruption and Human Rights in Africa* (Oxford: Hart Publishing, 2014).

Economic Social and Cultural Rights.[24] Common Article 1 states that '[a]ll peoples have the right of self-determination. By virtue of that right they [...] freely pursue their economic, social and cultural development.' The Article further specifies that:

> All peoples may, for their own ends, freely dispose of their natural wealth and resources without prejudice to any obligations arising out of international economic co-operation, based upon the principle of mutual benefit, and international law. In no case may a people be deprived of its own means of subsistence.[25]

Although not explicitly invoking Common Article 1, US President Barack Obama lent legitimacy to this concept when he referred to pervasive corruption as a 'violation of basic human rights' with significant practical implications for both the public and private sectors in the 2010 US National Security Strategy.'[26]

As a matter of customary international law, the view of corruption as an international human rights violation is supported by a diverse set of factors: (a) consistent, widespread and representative state practice proscribing and criminalising acts of corruption in foreign jurisdictions (e.g. the US FCPA[27] and the 2010 British Bribery Act,[28] as well as presumably the laws of at least thirty-eight other state parties that ratified or acceded to the Organization for Economic Cooperation and Development (OECD) Convention on Combating Bribery of Foreign Public Officials in International Business Transactions (the OECD Convention) and were therefore required to adopt such law); (b) use of clear and prohibitive language condemning acts of corruption in multilateral and international treaties governing corruption (e.g. the UN Convention Against Corruption[29] and the OECD Convention);[30] (c) state pronouncements condemning corrupt practices through the use of severe and weighty language and claims that corruption threatens democracy, the rule of law and human rights; (d) a general will among states to cooperate for the prevention of acts of corruption

---

[24] See International Covenant on Civil and Political Rights, 993 UNTS 171, 6 ILM 368 (entered into force 23 March 1976); see also International Covenant on Economic, Social and Cultural Rights, 993 UNTS 3, 6 ILM 360 (entered into force 3 January 1976).

[25] Common Article 1, International Covenant on Civil and Political Rights, 993 UNTS 171, 6 ILM 368 (entered into force 23 March 1976); International Covenant on Economic, Social and Cultural Rights, 993 UNTS 3, 6 ILM 360 (entered into force 3 January 1976).

[26] National Security Strategy, White House (2010), available at: www.whitehouse.gov/sites/default/files/rss_viewer/national_security_strategy.pdf.

[27] Foreign Corrupt Practices Act of 1977, Pub. L. No. 95–213, 91 Stat. 1494 (codified as amended at 15 U.S.C. 78m(b), (d)(1), (g)–(h), 78dd-1 to -3, 78ff (2006).

[28] The British Bribery Act of 2010 (c.23).

[29] UN General Assembly, United Nations Convention Against Corruption, 31 October 2003, A/58/422, available at: www.refworld.org/docid/4374b9524.html (accessed 10 June 2013).

[30] Convention on Combating Bribery of Foreign Public Officials in International Business Transactions and related Documents, 17 December 1997, pmbl, available at: www.oecd.org/corruption/oecdantibriberyconvention.htm.

(as demonstrated by the aforementioned international agreements); and (e) as already alluded to above, the growing body of literature recognising corruption as a (direct or indirect) violation of human rights.[31] Ultimately, however, it is not clear that the opinio juris element of customary international law is sufficiently met.

Notably, there is also little empirical data available regarding specific incidences of corruption in the developing world and the effects and ramifications of that corruption on the protection of people's human rights. This empirical analysis is needed and vital to the ability to reach a conclusion as to whether there is in fact an enforceable human right to live in a society free of corruption as a matter of customary international law. The purpose of this chapter, however, is limited to the presentation of a proposed framework for addressing corruption as it relates to human rights violations. Future research and empirical analysis is needed in order to form a final conclusion as to whether there is in fact a human right to live in a society free of corruption as such a right is not as of yet codified in international human rights agreements.

In sum, there appears to be a growing movement in support of the recognition of corruption as a violation of human rights, but at this time it does not appear that such recognition can be found as a matter of international human rights law.[32] For purposes of this discussion, it is sufficient to merely accept the premise that corruption gives rise to and creates an environment conducive to human rights violations.

3. DUTY OF MULTINATIONAL CORPORATIONS TO RESPECT HUMAN RIGHTS IN THEIR SUPPLY CHAINS

Corporations are generally not subject to most international human rights treaties or the jurisdiction of international human rights courts and tribunals (with the exception of corporate complicity in violations of international criminal law).[33] I accept as the current prevailing view that corporations have traditionally not been subject to international human rights law because they are not state

---

[31] N. Kofele-Kale, *supra* n. 1, p. 172.

[32] For more support of the contention that a human right to live in a society free of corruption is becoming increasingly recognised by a growing community of human rights activists and scholars, see D. Kinley, *A New Human Right to Freedom from Corruption*, Sydney Law School Research Paper no. 14/12; see also K. Olaniyan, *supra* n. 23.

[33] Due to the limited scope of this paper, it is not possible to include a discussion of prosecution for corporate violations of international human rights law in US courts under the Alien Tort Statue or before the International Criminal Court. For a thorough evaluation of these issues, see e.g. D. Cassel, 'Corporate Aiding and Abetting of Human Rights Violations: Confusion in the Courts' (2008) 6 *Northwestern Journal of International Human Rights* 304. See also the Rome Statute.

actors and that for this reason they until recently were outside the mainstream of international law.[34] The adoption of the Ruggie Framework and the statements, declarations and debates that preceded it marks a shift in this. This analysis will now address the effectiveness of the application of international human rights standards to corporations *vis-à-vis* this Framework.[35]

3.1. OVERVIEW OF THE PROTECT, RESPECT AND REMEDY FRAMEWORK AND ITS APPLICATION

As discussed in the introduction and first chapter of this book, in June 2011 the UN Human Rights Council endorsed the Guiding Principles on Business and Human Rights: Implementing the United Nations 'Protect, Respect and Remedy' Framework, establishing and re-affirming that states have a duty to protect human rights, corporations have a responsibility to respect human rights and victims of human rights violations have a right to access remedies.[36]

In this way, the Ruggie Framework can notably be distinguished from comparable international attempts at creating standards for business and human rights in that it creates a clearly defined duty beholden upon companies, rather than essentially consisting of a good conduct guide or restatement of existing human rights protections (e.g. freedom of association, the elimination of forced or compulsory labour) and then leaving it to state governments to enforce these protections *vis-à-vis* their corporate constituencies (see e.g. the OECD Guidelines for Multinational Enterprises and the ILO Declaration on Fundamental Principles and Rights at Work).[37]

Admittedly, the Ruggie Framework has been widely criticised since its inception as an insufficient means of enforcing international human rights laws against companies on the one hand, and as UN overreach by business representatives on the other. In the face of this criticism from all sides, it is important to note that the Framework is firmly rooted in existing international norms. The SRSG makes the point that businesses commit to complying with social norms everywhere they operate as consideration for obtaining the social

---

[34] E. Duruigbo, 'Corporate Accountability and Liability for International Human Rights Abuses: Recent Changes and Recurring Challenges' (2008) 6 *Northwestern Journal of International Human Rights* 222.

[35] See J. Ruggie, 'Report of the Special Representative of the Secretary-General on the Issue of Human Rights and Transnational Corporations and Other Business Enterprises', United Nations Human Rights Council, A/HRC/8/5, 7 April 2008.

[36] 'Report of the SRSG: Guiding Principles on Business and Human Rights: Implementing the United Nations 'Protect, Respect and Remedy' Framework', United Nations Human Rights Council, A/HRC/17/31, 21 March 2011; J. Ruggie, *supra* n. 35.

[37] OECD Guidelines for International Enterprises, available at: http://mneguidelines.oecd.org; About the ILO Declaration on Fundamental Principles and Rights at Work, available at: www.ilo.org/declaration/thedeclaration/lang--en/index.htm.

licence to operate in those respective areas.[38] One such norm with which they must comply, and which is now internationally recognised, is the corporate responsibility to respect human rights.[39]

The authority for the respect principle is further found in the statements and behaviour (i.e. practice) of the corporations themselves and rooted in soft law. Companies, therefore, may be considered to be bound by certain requirements even where not enshrined in hard law, because they believe, publicly state and in many instances behave as though they are bound by such requirements. As the SRSG proffered, 'the corporate responsibility to respect is acknowledged by virtually every company and industry CSR initiative, endorsed by the world's largest business associations, affirmed in the Global Compact and its worldwide national networks, and enshrined in such soft law instruments as the ILO Tripartite Declaration and the OECD Guidelines.'[40] Chapter 1 of this book further discusses the common critiques of the Framework in greater detail, but for now it is important to acknowledge the degree to which corporations have accepted and operationalised their duty to respect throughout their global supply chains.

The Framework's requirement that companies respect human rights gives rise to a number of additional requirements by implication, including affirmative duties to prevent the occurrence of human rights violations within their supply chains. Most notably, the corporate responsibility to respect human rights enshrined in the Ruggie Framework requires corporate due diligence for the prevention of human rights violations or, where they have already occurred, the alleviation of their adverse impacts.[41] According to the Framework, this due diligence is defined as 'a process whereby companies not only ensure compliance with national laws but also manage human rights harm with a view to avoiding it.'[42]

Although the word 'corruption' admittedly appears only once in the text of the Ruggie Framework, this due diligence requirement ultimately translates into a corporate duty to adopt and implement certain internal controls, policies and practices necessary for the prevention of human rights harms in the course of that company's global supply chain operations.[43] As a result, given that it is widely accepted that corruption gives rise to and perpetuates human rights violations, companies must prevent corruption in their supply chains as a matter of their affirmative obligation to take proactive measures to ensure their respect of human rights under the Ruggie Framework (e.g. the due diligence requirement).

---

[38]   'Promotion of all human rights, civil, political, economic, social and cultural rights, including the right to development', United Nations Human Rights Council, A/HRC/11/13, 22 April 2009, para. 46.
[39]   *Ibid.*
[40]   *Ibid.*, para. 47.
[41]   *Ibid.*, para. 59.
[42]   J. Ruggie, *supra* n. 35, para. 25.
[43]   *Supra* n. 38, para. 59.

3.2. ROLE OF CSR AND VOLUNTARY STANDARDS IN ADVANCING RESPECT FOR HUMAN RIGHTS

In a few short years the Ruggie Framework has arguably become a widely (albeit not universally) accepted standard for business and human rights. As alluded to above, the movement by business toward increasingly recognising and accepting its responsibility to respect human rights has manifest at the corporate level in a number of different ways. Two of the most common means of operationalising the corporate duty to respect human rights throughout supply chains (including the due diligence and grievance mechanism requirements) are involvement in multi-stakeholder initiatives (MSIs) and the adoption of corporate supplier codes of conduct.

First, beginning in the 1990s with the Nike and Levi Strauss sweatshop scandals and subsequent media blitz, companies began joining and in some cases founding MSIs to address the challenges they were publicly facing. MSIs, best defined as collective initiatives between governments, intergovernmental agencies, the private sector and non-profit organisations,[44] have grown in popularity and significance since they first emerged in the field of business and human rights more than twenty years ago. MSIs are now formed for just about any purpose and fulfil a variety of different roles, ranging from third party certification (e.g. Social Accountability International's SA 8000 certification) to public disclosure schemes (e.g. the Global Reporting Index).[45] Their most basic unifying characteristic is that they include multiple and somewhat diverse stakeholders coming together for collective action. One group of scholars summarised the MSI phenomenon as follows: 'By incorporating all relevant actors in joint processes, MSIs seek to achieve a comprehensive approach to individual and common problems facing each actor and to find appropriate collective solutions.'[46]

Admittedly, MSIs receive founded criticism as ineffective and futile because they are entirely voluntary and can sometimes emphasise collaboration and conversation over concrete commitments.[47] In recent years, however, a trend has emerged by which MSIs now offer clear standards and often audited certification schemes under which companies may commit to sourcing their needed supply of a given commodity that has been grown, processed and traded in accordance with

---

[44]   L. Koechlin and R. Calland, 'Standard Setting as Cutting Edge: An Evidence Based Typology for Multi-Stakeholder Initiatives', in A. Peters et al. (eds.), *Non-state Actors as Standard Setters* (New York: Cambridge University Press, 2000).

[45]   For a comprehensive overview of the different types of MSIs and other CSR institutions within and among companies, see J. Moon, A. Crane and D. Matten, 'Corporations and Citizenship in New Institutions of Global Governance' in C. Crouch and C. Maclean (eds.), *The Responsible Corporation in a Global Economy* (Oxford: Oxford University Press, 2011).

[46]   L. Koechlin and R. Calland, *supra* n. 44, p. 86.

[47]   See e.g. J. Martinsson, 'Multistakeholder Initiatives: Are they Effective?', *The World Bank*, 1 May 2011, available at: http://blogs.worldbank.org/publicsphere/multistakeholder-initiatives -are-they-effective.

that MSI's standards. These companies thereby effectively commit themselves to those standards in a way that can then be both monitored (via audits) and enforced by any number of stakeholders (e.g. the MSI secretariat, NGOs and activists, and industry media).

By way of example, Bonsucro (formerly known as the Better Sugarcane Initiative), an MSI dedicated to making sugarcane production and processing more sustainable, began in 2005 as a dialogue among industry actors, but has since developed concrete standards (including, for example, compliance with ILO labour conventions governing child labour, forced labour, discrimination and freedom of association and the right to collective bargaining). Some of the world's largest food and beverage companies now source or have committed to source part or all of their sugarcane product from producers certified under those standards.[48]

Recent years have also marked the emergence of increasingly rigorous corporate supplier codes of conduct addressing human, labour and environmental rights throughout MNCs' often complex supply chains.[49] Similarly subject to criticism for their voluntary nature, the codes are often beneficially used as a means of outlining a company's human rights responsibilities and binding or at least guiding their subsidiaries and suppliers (sometimes even secondary and tertiary) to comply with the same throughout the company's global supply chain.[50] 'Although [these] codes are not generally legally enforceable, they are backed by the reputation of the company that adopts them, supported by the ever present threat of media exposure.'[51] As will be discussed in the next section, the desire to protect against this reputational risk is a frequently cited source of motivation for voluntary corporate reform.

It should also be noted that some supplier codes are in fact legally enforceable, where those codes are incorporated explicitly or by reference into a company's supplier contracts.[52] Even in those cases, however, the code would only be

---

[48]   See e.g. S. Hills, 'Coca-Cola Snaps up First Bonsucro Certified Sugarcane', *Food Navigator*, 22 June 2011, available at: www.foodnavigator.com/Financial-Industry/Coca-Cola-snaps-up-first-Bonsucro-certified-sugarcane; see also Our Spirit is Clear: Bacardi Limited Corporate Responsibility Report 2012, available at: www.bacardilimited.com/Content/uploads/corporate/responsible/pdf/corp_resp_report_2012.pdf.

[49]   Interestingly to the instant analysis, such codes are largely derived from the codes of ethics that emerged as popular in the 1970s and focused largely on preventing corruption in supply chains. For more on this, see A. Florini, 'Business and Global Governance: The Growing Role of Corporate Codes of Conduct' (2003) 21(2) *The Brookings Review* 4–8.

[50]   J. Nolan, 'With Power Comes Responsibility: Human Rights and Corporate Accountability', University of New South Wales Faculty of Law Research Series, Working Paper 11, February 2010, p. 583.

[51]   *Ibid.*, pp. 589–590.

[52]   M. Azizul Islam and K. McPhail, 'Regulating for Corporate Human Rights Abuses: The Emergence of Corporate Reporting on the ILO's Human Rights Standards within the Global Garment Manufacturing and Retail Industry' (2011) 22 *Critical Perspectives on Accounting* 790–810, 806.

enforceable by the sourcing company against its suppliers as a breach of contract or other related cause of action.

As of 2009, there were already more than 300 industry or sector codes of conduct addressing social, labour, environmental and other related practices and many firms had opted to develop their own company-specific codes.[53] Admittedly, the content of these codes and the standards they invoke (as well as their quality) vary widely. It is however now common for these codes to include direct reference to the ILO and its various legal provisions and principles for the protection and advancement of labour rights.[54] Generally, even where such codes do not explicitly invoke ILO conventions, they often include certain basic fundamental ILO standards (for example, prohibiting child labour).

These codes, however, also serve a purpose beyond merely protecting the rights that are clearly enumerated in their provisions. Proponents of supplier codes of conduct view such codes as a tool for building consensus and garnering support around new societal norms that could ultimately become the basis of mandatory law. Sceptics often dismiss the viability of such codes as tools for governing corporate behaviour on the grounds that they are soft law at best and amount to mere marketing for the companies who abide by and publicise them.[55] The statement that such codes are being adopted for marketing purposes, however, serves to highlight the importance of at least apparent corporate compliance with minimum human rights standards to these companies' marketing campaigns and brand identities.

One study of the global garment manufacturing and retail industry found that the number of companies adopting and reporting on the ILO's workplace human rights standards has substantially increased in the last 15 years.[56] According to Ann Florini, writing for the Brookings Institution, 'almost every self-respecting large corporation [now] has a code of conduct.'[57] Perhaps most significantly, the practice of hiring an independent third party to audit a company's global supply chain against the human rights provisions codified in its supplier code is becoming increasingly common among multinational corporations (particularly those with their origins in the US and Europe, but operating and sourcing from production sites all over the world).[58]

---

[53]   D. Vogel, 'The Private Regulation of Global Corporate Conduct: Achievement and Limitations' (2010) 68(1) *Business & Society* 49, 72.

[54]   See e.g. Apple Supplier Code of Conduct, available at: www.apple.com/supplierresponsibility/ pdf/Apple_Supplier_Code_of_Conduct.pdf; see also PepsiCo Global Supplier Code of Conduct, available at: www.pepsico.com/Download/supplier_code_of_conduct/English.pdf.

[55]   A. Florini, *supra* n. 49.

[56]   M. Azizul Islam and K. McPhail, *supra* n. 52, p. 790.

[57]   A. Florini, *supra* n. 49.

[58]   There has been disturbingly little research completed seeking to quantify the number of relative percentage of companies auditing their supplier codes of conduct. Unfortunately, such research was outside of the scope of this paper. One would also be justified in questioning just how independent such an auditor is given they are effectively on the company payroll. This

NGOs and civil society activists have already begun capitalising on this development by calling on laggard companies to seek and in some cases release the results of third party audits where they have not already.[59] Those NGOs and activists then draw public attention to the results of those audits when they expose violations.

As mentioned, there are valid concerns regarding the effectiveness of MSIs and codes in preventing human rights violations in corporate supply chains. Because they are by nature voluntary and discretionary, they vary by initiative and company; as a result, certain codes and initiatives are more robust than others. Further, in the absence of third party auditing, they lack a monitoring mechanism.

There is, however, increasing support of the view that MSIs and codes are trending toward increased effectiveness and robustness. Leading international CSR consultancy Sustainalytics recently wrote:

> At the corporate level, there has been a notable improvement not only in the number of companies with human rights policies, but also in the quality and scope of these policies, which are increasingly incorporating elements recommended in the Guiding Principles such as human rights due diligence procedures and grievance mechanisms.[60]

While the degree to which corporations are currently being held liable for human rights violations in their supply chain is arguable to say the least, it also seems that corporations are taking measures designed to increase their compliance with human rights standards in greater numbers and perhaps at a greater level of quality than before the adoption of the Ruggie Framework.[61] Should the same framework be applied to corruption and supply chains, it is possible that companies would come to adopt a similar approach of proactively taking measures to prevent acts of corruption in their supply chains above and beyond what is already required of them to ensure compliance with relevant domestic laws.

---

dilemma has proved challenging for NGOs in the field given that they lack sufficient financial resources to fund such audits themselves.

[59]   See e.g. Human Rights Watch, *Bangladesh: Tragedy Shows Urgency of Worker Protections*, 25 April 2003, available at: www.hrw.org/news/2013/04/25/bangladesh-tragedy-shows-urgency-worker-protections (statement issued by Human Rights Watch following the tragic building collapse which caused deaths of hundreds of garment industry workers in Bangladesh).

[60]   I. Griek, 'UN Forum on Human Rights: Assessing the Ruggie Framework', *Sustainalytics Reporter*, Issue No. 13, February 2013.

[61]   For a more in depth discussion of the argument that voluntary private sector regulations of corporate conduct are not a sufficient substitute for state-based regulatory enforcement, see D. Vogel, *supra* n. 53, p. 68.

4. CORPORATE DUTY TO PREVENT CORRUPTION IN THEIR SUPPLY CHAINS AS A MATTER OF THEIR DUTY TO RESPECT HUMAN RIGHTS

By virtue of the derivative nature of the causal relationship between corruption and human rights already discussed, and the recognised duty of companies to take proactive steps to ensure human rights are not violated in their supply chains as a product of their duty to respect, corporations have a duty to prevent corruption in their supply chains.[62]

The recognition by companies of their duty to prevent corruption could have huge potential implications, particularly for the branded, multinational corporations at the consumer end of global supply chains. This would give rise to the creation of a heightened duty whereby those companies must ensure that every aspect and level of their global supply chains are free of corruption. Moreover, under the Ruggie Framework, this would require the development of internal due diligence policies and procedures designed to prevent and ferret out instances of corrupt acts by those companies' subsidiaries and/or suppliers throughout the chains. It could also require creation of a grievance reporting mechanism whereby victims of corporate corruption could report those instances and elicit some sort of ameliorative action from the company in response.

This duty would extend beyond what is already required of companies under the domestic law counterparts of the applicable UN and OECD anticorruption conventions, regardless of the fact that this duty may not be applied or enforced via international human rights courts or tribunals.[63]

Instead, this duty to prevent corruption in global supply chains would be expressed in the supplier codes of conduct and general CSR policies/practices of corporations operating transnationally, to then be enforced against those companies in the courts of public opinion at the hands of media and activists as prosecutor.

As one author explains:

> [H]uman rights practitioners today recognize the responsibilities of multinational companies and other private companies in human rights violations and the notion of corporate social responsibility (CSR) is more and more used to call on businesses to be more sensitive to the needs of all stakeholders impacted by their activities. One of the major promises of linking corruption and human rights is indeed the ability to hold accountable businesses for acts of corruption.[64]

---

[62] 'Promotion of all human rights, civil, political, economic, social and cultural rights, including the right to development', United Nations Human Rights Council, A/HRC/11/13, 22 April 2009, para. 52.

[63] See generally Foreign Corrupt Practices Act of 1977, *Public Law*. No. 95–213, 91 Stat. 1494 (codified as amended at 15 U.S.C. 78m(b), (d)(1), (g)–(h), 78dd-1 to -3, 78ff (2006).

[64] S. Coquoz, *Corruption and Human Rights: An International and Indonesian Perspective*, presented at the Pusham UII / Norwegian Centre for Human Rights Workshop on Corruption and Human Rights, 15–16 May 2012, in Yogyakarta, Indonesia.

I now turn to a comprehensive discussion of the CSR movement and its utility in effectively 'enforcing' the corporate duty to prevent corruption.

5. NON-JUDICIAL ENFORCEMENT OF THIS DUTY UNDER A CSR APPROACH

Recognising that there is a corporate duty to ensure that supply chains are free of corruption as a matter of the corporate duty to respect human rights, I now turn to the issue of how such a duty can be enforced given that there is currently not a satisfactory legal or judicial enforcement mechanism for holding corporations accountable for violations of international human rights. As alluded to above, I propose that the solution may be found within the CSR movement if utilised correctly.

Harvard University's John F. Kennedy School of Government provides a comprehensive definition of CSR whereby CSR encompasses not only what companies do with their profits, but how they earn them, i.e. how they operate:

> [CSR] addresses how companies manage their economic, social, and environmental impacts, as well as their relationships in all key spheres of influence: the workplace, the marketplace, the supply chain, the community, and the public policy realm.[65]

From an economic perspective, CSR can be said to have had the result of pressuring global firms into 'internalizing some of their negative social and environmental externalities and increasing the private provision of some public goods.'[66]

Many critique the CSR movement on the grounds that it is voluntary and lacks a compliance mechanism with independent dispute settlement bodies.[67] This critique, however, is not asking the right threshold question: as David Vogel posits, any accurate assessment of regulation by CSR 'should compare it not to an ideal world of effective global economic governance but to actual policy alternatives.'[68]

To this end, it is worth noting that most CSR provisions are likely more effective than the legally enforceable, codified labour and human rights regulations of many developing countries. These countries frequently sourced from by multinational corporations, often lack transparent, democratic governments and established rule of law and therefore tend not to have sufficient regulations in place for the protection of human and environmental rights.[69] As a result, the pertinent

---

[65]   John F. Kennedy School of Government, *Corporate Social Responsibility Initiative: Defining Social Responsibility*, available at: www.hks.harvard.edu/m-rcbg/CSRI/init_define.html.

[66]   D. Vogel, *supra* n. 53, p. 68.

[67]   See generally R. McCorquodale, 'Corporate Social Responsibility and International Human Rights Law' (2009) 87 *Journal of Business Ethics* 385, 394; See also J. Nolan, *supra* n. 50, p. 589.

[68]   D. Vogel, *supra* n. 53, p. 80.

[69]   *Ibid.*

question is not whether a CSR approach allows enforcement of corporate duties in a court of law, but rather whether there is in place a system and mechanism by which companies publicly bind themselves to certain duties that (in the absence of CSR) they would otherwise have no requirement to discharge.[70]

5.1. EFFICACY OF A CSR APPROACH IN COMBATING CORRUPTION IN GLOBAL CORPORATE SUPPLY CHAINS

A thorough analysis that proves beyond doubt the efficacy of a CSR approach is outside the scope of this chapter, but the following discussion will provide a brief overview of some of the supporting evidence of the effectiveness of CSR in advancing the corporate duty to respect human rights generally and prevent corruption specifically.

First, it is reasonable to conclude that international human rights standards matter to corporations because corporations say that they matter: companies write voluntary internal corporate codes and guidelines outlining these obligations (often directly invoking relevant ILO and UN provisions) and then expend significant resources engaging third parties to audit their supply chains and ensure those codes and guidelines are being complied with. This practice provides some support for the premise that corporations seek to abide by international human rights duties via their corporate social responsibility programmes, even where compliance with such duties is not required of them by law.[71]

Second, although the degree of its effectiveness is debatable, many agree that the CSR movement (including and accompanied by increased activism by advocacy NGOs) has motivated numerous multinational corporations to make at least incremental changes in their policies and practices so as to better prevent human rights and related violations throughout their supply chains.[72]

By way of example, Oxfam International's GROW campaign, which aims to reform the global food system, recently published a report highlighting issues of gender discrimination and inequity in cocoa supply chains and subsequently began publicly campaigning against three of the world's largest buyers of cocoa,

---

[70]   This author also disputes the aforementioned argument on the grounds that it does not account for the role of civil society, campaigning NGOs and the media in taking to companies to task for failing to meet (even voluntary) CSR commitments they have made.

[71]   P. Lund-Thomsen and K. Khalid Nadvi, 'Global Value Chains, Local Collective Action and Corporate Social Responsibility: A Review of Empirical Evidence' (2010) 19 *Business Strategy and the Environment* 1.

[72]   For support of this premise, consider the massive move toward third party auditing and certification in the cocoa industry. Companies headquartered in the US and Europe spend thousands more to ensure traceability of their supply chains to ensure that their supply is not produced in reliance of child labour in West Africa.

Nestle, Mars and Mondelez.[73] Following less than a month of public action on the issue that included a 65,000 signature petition, Nestle and Mars announced commitments in line with Oxfam's demands, including plans to sign onto the UN Women's Empowerment Principles.[74]

The Brookings Institution has noted the power of such organisations to name and shame companies for unethical behaviour observing that these organisations were 'proving adept at shaming or coercing corporations into paying attention to what activists say are the broader social responsibilities of the private sector,' and concluding that those same corporations were in fact capitulating and meeting the demands of these activist campaigns.[75]

To better understand this phenomenon, it is informative to briefly examine companies' various rationales for adopting CSR programmes and voluntarily binding themselves to them. Corporations are (in many jurisdictions, as a matter of legal requirement) first and foremost concerned with their fiduciary duty to maximise profit for their shareholders.[76]

Accordingly, any measures taken must serve this purpose in some form. In line with this, it is possible to deduce that companies decide to make changes in their policies and practices as a matter of CSR for one of the following four reasons: (a) risk mitigation and avoidance (legal and otherwise); (b) preservation of positive brand reputation and identity;[77] (c) insurance of a reliable and continuous supply of goods and services by increasing supply chain transparency and traceability; and (d) attraction and retention of socially conscious employees and investors.[78]

Admittedly, the 'court of public opinion' as a viable non-judicial enforcement mechanism requires a robust and active media and civil society to shed light on instances in which companies fail to abide by their social and environmental commitments. Provided media and civil society continue to play this role, they will continue to direct public attention to companies that fail to respect human rights.[79]

---

[73]   'Oxfam food Company Campaign Delivers Win for Women Cocoa Farmers' *Oxfam International*, 25 March 2012, available at: www.oxfam.org/en/grow/pressroom/pressrelease/2013-03-25/oxfam-food-company-campaign-delivers-win-women-cocoa-farmers).

[74]   *Ibid.*

[75]   A. Florini, *supra* n. 49, p. 5; D. Vogel, *supra* n. 53, p. 76.

[76]   L.E. Strine, Jr., 'Our Continuing Struggle With the Idea That For-Profit Corporations Seek Profit' (2012) 47 *Wake Forest Law Review* 135.

[77]   D. Vogel, *supra* n. 53, p. 71.

[78]   See e.g. Council on Ethics for the Government Pension Fund, Annual reports 2006 and 2007, available at: www.regjeringen.no/en/sub/Styrer-rad-utvalg/ethics_council/annual-reports. html?id=458699, noting the decision of the Norwegian Government pension fund to divest from Wal-Mart for complicity in human rights violations. See also J. Nolan, *supra* n. 50, p. 592.

[79]   'Promotion of all human rights, civil, political, economic, social and cultural rights, including the right to development', United Nations Human Rights Council, A/HRC/11/13, 22 April 2009, para. 47.

Building on these considerations, the failure of companies to meet the baseline responsibility of respecting human rights (and therefore of preventing corruption), will, in the words of the SRSG, subject those companies 'to the courts of public opinion – comprising employees, communities, consumers, civil society, as well as investors,' thereby harming their bottom line: profit.[80]

5.2. WHY IS A CSR APPROACH BENEFICIAL?

As already discussed, scholars have recently begun addressing the question of whether corporations might be held liable under an international legal human rights system for complicity in government corruption.[81] Ultimately, however, these endeavours seem to have largely (albeit reluctantly) produced more or less the same conclusion: international human rights law generally, and the right to live in a society free of corruption specifically, are not enforceable against private sector entities.[82] In the words of one author: 'Ultimately, the state-centered nature of the international human rights system limits the utility of any complicity standard for non-state actors.'[83]

It is also widely accepted that international human rights law currently lacks a mechanism by which victims might seek remedy for wrongs committed against them from liable corporations.[84] In other words, there is no legal or judicial means for enforcement of a company's duty to respect, and therefore no such mechanism for enforcement of their duty to prevent corruption. This unfortunate truth underscores the necessity of the CSR paradigm for the enforcement of human rights protections. Admittedly, the CSR approach lacks a grievance and redress mechanism for victims of corporate human rights abuses.

As already discussed, there are numerous incentives for companies to adopt meaningful CSR programmes. Under the Ruggie Framework and a CSR approach to its implementation, these incentives could also apply with respect to the adoption of anticorruption measures. Some potential examples of such incentives both in terms of benefits of voluntary compliance and risks of failing to adopt such voluntary compliance are provided in the below table compiled by the International Chamber of Commerce (adapted from a joint report of the UNGC, International Chamber of Commerce, TI and the World Economic Forum):

---

[80]   J. Ruggie, *supra* n. 35, para. 54.
[81]   C. Rose, 'The Application of Human Rights Law to Private Sector Complicity in Governmental Corruption' (2011) 24 *Leiden Journal of International Law* 715.
[82]   See e.g. R. McCorquodale, *supra* n. 67, p. 385; see also C. Rose, *supra* n. 81, p. 715.
[83]   C. Rose, *supra* n. 81. For an opposing viewpoint, see e.g. A. Clapham, 'The Human Rights Obligations of Non-State Actors in Conflict Situations' (2006) 88(863) *International Review of the Red Cross*. Unfortunately, a thorough comparative analysis of these articles is beyond the scope of this piece.
[84]   C. Rose, *supra* n. 81, p. 722.

Table 7.1. The business rationale for fighting corruption[85]

Benefits of engaging	Risks of not engaging
– Reduce the cost of doing business – Attract investments from ethically oriented investors – Attract and retain highly principled employees, improving employee morale – Obtain a competitive advantage of becoming the preferred choice of ethically concerned customers/consumers – Qualify for reduced legal sanctions in jurisdictions like the US and Italy	Criminal prosecution, in some jurisdictions both in company and senior management levels which can lead to imprisonment – Exclusion from bidding processes, e.g. for international finance institutions and export credit agencies – 'Casino risk' – no legal remedies if a counterpart does not deliver as agreed and/or keeps increasing the price for doing so – Damage to reputation, brand and share price – Tougher fight for talent when hiring new employees – Regulatory censure – Cost of corrective action and possible fines
– Create a level playing field overcoming the 'prisoner's dilemma' – Improve public trust in business – Influence future laws and regulations	Missed business opportunities in distorted markets – Increased magnitude of corruption – Policy-makers responding by adopting tougher and more rigid laws and regulations – internationally, regionally and nationally

The addition of an international human rights framework and the status of international human rights protection to the existing regime of internal anticorruption compliance could augment the business rationale for fighting corruption. It would add compliance with internal human rights policies and the Ruggie Framework to the benefits of engaging column, and the risk of failing to protect those rights and the threat of subsequent complicity in a potentially public human rights scandal to the risks of not engaging column. These factors in aggregate would increase the likelihood of corporate compliance with such policy.

Adopting a human rights and CSR perspective for addressing issues of corruption in supply chains also invites companies to incorporate key anticorruption standards and provisions into their human rights policies and supplier codes of conduct such that those anticorruption standards could ultimately be audited throughout the companies supply chains in the same manner as the other human rights protections codified in their codes.

Ultimately, therefore, the Ruggie Framework applied via the CSR movement offers a needed alternative for the imposition of human rights (and other ethical) duties on private sector entities, to which they might not otherwise be subject. Because the effectiveness of a CSR approach does not require the trying of a corporation in an international tribunal or court of law, it is possible for CSR to

---

[85]   'Clean Business is Good Business', *International Chamber of Commerce*, 2008, available at: www.unglobalcompact.org/docs/news_events/8.1/clean_business_is_good_business.pdf.

effectively advance the corporate respect of human rights even in the absence of international hard law obligations.

To be clear, I doubt that even the most ardent CSR supporter would argue that this is an optimal approach for enforcing corporate human rights or anticorruption requirements, but until the international community comes up with a legally binding standard and mechanism for adjudication, CSR may offer a viable alternative tactic for holding companies to some degree of account for human rights violations in their supply chains.

5.3. WHY IS A CSR APPROACH TO COMBATING CORRUPTION NEEDED GIVEN THE DOMESTIC ANTI-CORRUPTION LAWS ALREADY IN PLACE?

For the sake of brevity, this section will focus primarily on the US FCPA as arguably the most robust example of domestic anticorruption legislation.

The most obvious critique of the use of domestic laws in combating global corruption is that they are limited to the national legal sphere, rather than international. At first glance this appears to be a valid critique, but taking the FCPA as an example, it must be acknowledged that it has, through its extraterritoriality provisions, global reach. The provisions of the FCPA apply to US persons and businesses (including their foreign subsidiaries), US and foreign public companies listed on US stock exchanges (or those required to file periodic reports with the SEC), and certain foreign persons and businesses acting while in the territory of the US. As a result, foreign business entities and nationals have been charged under the FCPA for the bribery of public officials (in their own countries as well as in foreign countries), even where no material acts have occurred in the United States.[86]

Moreover, the FCPA and other domestic laws like it prohibiting corrupt acts in foreign jurisdictions carry with them threat of significant penalties, including both hefty fines and jail time in some instances.[87] As a result, one could argue that the extraterritorial reach of the FCPA and other domestic laws like it, combined with the concrete penalties it threatens, effectively render the alternative human

---

[86]   D.P. Ashe, 'The Lengthening Anti-Bribery Lasso of the United States: The Recent Extraterritorial Application of the U.S. Foreign Corrupt Practices Act' (2004) 73 *Fordham Law Review* 2897.

[87]   In 2011, the former president of Terra Telecommunications Corp. was sentenced to 15 years in prison for his role in a scheme to pay bribes to Haitian government officials at a state-owned telecommunications company in Haiti. 'Executive Sentenced to 15 Years in Prison for Scheme to Bribe Officials at State-Owned Telecommunications Company in Haiti', Department of Justice, 25 October 2011, available at: www.justice.gov/opa/pr/2011/October/11-crm-1407.html (accessed 18 May 2013). For more information on the largest penalty ever paid for violation of the FCPA, see E. Lichtblau and C. Dougherty, 'Siemens to Pay $1.34 Billion in Fines', *New York Times*, 16 December 2008.

rights/CSR framework proposed here unnecessary. There are, however, a number of reasons why an additional tool for combating corruption is advantageous.

The effective enforcement of domestic laws like the FCPA is too vulnerable to a host of external influences. Again taking the FCPA as example, as long as the most effective regulatory tool for penalising acts of corporate corruption remains a product of US law, it will be subject to political whims and the varying climates of enforcement that characterise each US presidential administration and congress. The 113th United States Congress, the previous Congress in power, for example, reached new heights of political infamy for its refusal to support even the most basic government regulations and agencies. By way of illustration, in 2011 Congressman Louie Gohmert (R-Tex.) called for the abolition of the nonpartisan Congressional Budget Office, responsible for the exceptionally uncontroversial calculation of legislative costs.[88] It is not hard to imagine this Congress turning its attention to dismantling the FCPA, particularly given the impassioned anti-FCPA lobbying efforts of the highly influential and exceedingly well-funded US Chamber of Commerce and a former US attorney general.[89]

The FCPA is also at the whim of prosecutorial discretion. The history of FCPA enforcement is marked by a clear and obvious trend toward settlement over prosecution, even where evidence of wrongdoing is seemingly plentiful. In particular, this tendency toward settlement seems even more pronounced where the prospective defendants are highly influential and exert some sort of direct or indirect pressure on US foreign policy or the global financial system.

Spalding argues that certain FCPA enforcement actions from the last decade demonstrate that foreign policy considerations are being brought to bear on FCPA enforcement by the relevant US regulatory agencies.[90] For example, in 2008, Siemens, the global electronics powerhouse, agreed to pay an $800 million fine for violations of the FCPA, an outcome widely viewed as favourable to the company.[91] Siemens had allegedly paid bribes to government officials in order to win a metro transit contract in Venezuela, a power plan contract in Israel, a contract for the development of high voltage transmission lines in China and a contract for the sale of power stations to Iraq under the UN Oil for Food Program.[92]

Notably, among other benefits, avoiding a bribery conviction meant that Siemens would not be barred from future bidding on US government contracts.[93]

---

[88]   E. Klein, 'Trashing the CBO, and undermining any chance at fiscal responsibility', *Washington Post*, 20 January 2011, available at: www.washingtonpost.com/wp-dyn/content/article/2011/01/20/AR2011012005852.html.

[89]   P.J. Henning, 'Taking Aim at the Foreign Corrupt Practices Act', *New York Times*, 30 April 2012, available at: http://dealbook.nytimes.com/2012/04/30/taking-aim-at-the-foreign-corrupt-practices-act/; S. Rubenfeld, 'Chamber Picks Apart Guidance in Letter, Demands Statutory FCPA Reform', *Corruption Currents, Wall Street Journal*, 19 February 2013.

[90]   A. Brady Spalding, *supra* n. 1, p. 681.

[91]   *Ibid.*, p. 684.

[92]   *U.S. Securities and Exchange Commission v. Siemens Aktiengesellschaft*, Complaint, 12 December 2008 at 2.

[93]   E. Lichtblau and C. Dougherty, *supra* n. 87.

Ensuring that Siemens would be eligible to bid on potential US procurement contracts was such a significant factor in making the decision to seek settlement in lieu of prosecution that the US Department of Justice specifically stated in Siemen's sentencing memorandum that its 'analysis of collateral consequences included the consideration of the risk of debarment and exclusion from government contracts.'[94] Perhaps most concerning, the pressure and influence being exerted on these enforcement decisions and the subsequent tendency toward settlement and abstinence from prosecution is all occurring in secret protected from public review and scrutiny.

A similar dynamic is likely occurring with respect to FCPA defendant companies significant to international financial markets, the 'too big to fail' banks and firms.[95] Although not an FCPA case, the 2012 settlement between HSBC and the US Department of Justice for violations of US sanctions and anti-money laundering laws demonstrates the manner in which US government decisions on whether to prosecute a corporate defendant are often dictated by outside concerns. Then Assistant Attorney General Lenny Breuer admitted as much during the press conference announcing the HSBC settlement when he stated that 'had the US authorities decided to press criminal charges, HSBC would almost certainly have lost its banking licence in the US, the future of the institution would have been under threat and the entire banking system would have been destabilized.'[96] Given the nature of US foreign policy and the global financial system, these dynamics are unlikely to change and as a result FCPA enforcement will remain vulnerable to political whims and external influences.

As touched on in the last section, the CSR model also provides clear avenues for civil society engagement and public pressure around the issue of corruption as a human rights violation not already provided under domestic laws like the FCPA. As one author posits:

> If corruption is perceived as a violation of human rights it will raise awareness among people of the consequences of corruption on individual interests and how detrimental a minor corrupt practice may be for victims and the population generally. This might engage large sectors of the citizenry into strong supporters in fighting corruption.[97]

It would also augment the existing efforts of both human rights and anticorruption based NGOs worldwide.

---

[94]   Department's Sentencing Memorandum at 11, *United States v. Siemens Aktiengesellschaft,* No. 08-CR-367-RJL (D.D.C. Dec. 12, 2008), available at: www.justice.gov/opa/documents/siemens-sentencing-memo.pdf.

[95]   M. Taibbi, 'Gangster Bankers: Too Big to Jail', *Rolling Stone,* 14 February 2013.

[96]   *Ibid.*

[97]   J. Bacio-Terracino, *Corruption as a Violation of Human Rights,* International Council on Human Rights Policy (2008).

Finally, grounding corporate anticorruption compliance in the context of universal human rights provides the benefit of shifting the focus of such compliance. In Spalding's words, 'if the principal focus of FCPA enforcement is protecting against human rights violations, then our emphasis must shift from the corporations to the victims in developing countries.'[98] Consequently, if there is a recognised corporate duty to prevent corruption as an extension of the corporate duty to respect human rights, in order to meet their obligations under this duty, companies would have to ensure not only compliance with relevant domestic legislation (i.e. that their employees and subsidiaries refrain from corrupt acts), but also take some affirmative action for the prevention of other corrupt acts more generally in the jurisdictions in which they are operating, including where such acts are committed by the third party suppliers from which they source.

6. CONCLUSIONS

Acknowledging that companies have a duty to prevent corruption throughout their global supply chains by virtue of their duty to respect and adopting a CSR approach to the same would allow companies to take ownership of their anti-corruption policies and practices and make them a part of their branding, rather than merely a product of legally mandated corporate compliance. It would also provide NGOs and activists an opportunity to advocate to, engage in dialogue with, and potentially campaign against, corporations that fail to sufficiently prevent corruption in their supply chains.

Ultimately, the true potential for change in the way corporations operate internationally presented by this new approach is in the opportunity it presents for additional means of monitoring these companies and ultimately putting pressure on them to operate in a way that is fairer, more ethical and socially just. Under the approach proposed herein, NGOs and civil society organisations could apply the same tactics they now use to bring attention to human rights violations to global corruption such that corporations face name and shame campaigns for instances of corruption in their supply chains. Relevant media sources could highlight corrupt corporate acts and their ramifications in the same manner that they currently feature stories about companies that have infringed on peoples right to associate in a labour union or contaminated a community's water supply.

In short, the approach proposed herein would allow international civil society groups and media to bring the issue of global corruption into the mainstream and increasingly popular human rights discourse, thereby shedding light on the issue and holding companies to task for corrupt acts if not in a court of law, then at least in the court of public opinion.

---

[98]   A. Brady Spalding, *supra* n. 1, p. 675.

CHAPTER 8
A CRITICAL ANALYSIS
OF HUMAN RIGHTS DUE
DILIGENCE FRAMEWORKS
FOR CONFLICT MINERALS

Challenges for the Electronics Industries

Miho TAKA

1. INTRODUCTION

The eastern provinces of the Democratic Republic of Congo (DRC) have been plagued with violent conflict and insecurity since 1996, creating one of the world's worst humanitarian crises. The crisis has claimed more than five million people's lives and caused approximately 2.7 million internally displaced persons (IDPs) as well as around 500,000 Congolese refugees.[1] The country has also been given a label of the 'rape capital of the world' by Margot Wallstrom, the then UN Special Representative on Sexual Violence in Conflict.[2]

The eastern DRC is also endowed with valuable minerals such as tantalum, tin, tungsten and gold that have wide ranging applications, especially in high-tech consumer products such as smart phones and laptop computers. These 'technology minerals' have experienced growing demand since the 1990s and caused large price spikes owing to a sudden increase in the demand followed by recent technological and industrial developments.[3] The violent conflict in the eastern DRC is largely understood to be motivated and sustained by the profits from these mineral resources, supported by the prominent 'resource curse' hypotheses. Le Billon explains that 'control, exploitation, trade, taxation, or

---

[1]   UNHCR, '2015 UNHCR country operations profile – Democratic Republic of the Congo', available at: www.unhcr.org/pages/49e45c366.html (accessed 15 June 2015).
[2]   'UN official calls DR Congo "rape capital of the world"', *BBC News*, 28 April 2010.
[3]   B. Buijs and H. Sievers, 'Critical Thinking about Critical Minerals: Assessing risks related to resource security', Polinares Working Paper no. 33, March 2012.

protection' of 'conflict resources' contribute to armed conflict or benefit from the context of armed conflict.[4]

Numerous studies have been conducted to understand the role of the production and trade of mineral resources in fuelling and sustaining the violent conflict in the eastern DRC. A series of investigations and reports made by the United Nations (UN) Panel of Experts between 2001 and 2003[5] was notable in highlighting the role of business in fuelling the DRC conflict. These reports were the first to publish a list of companies which were involved in the illegal exploitation of natural resources in the DRC. The sphere of influence of the electronics industry in the DRC conflict was also questioned in this regard by a report commissioned by an electronics industry association, the Global e-Sustainability Initiative (GeSI).[6] These investigations were followed by a number of other research initiatives by the UN Group of Experts, the Initiative for Central Africa (INICA), the Department for International Development (DFID) and Resource Consulting Services, to name some.[7] In addition, NGOs such as Global Witness, Make ITfair and the Enough Project have been advocating the cause of the DRC conflict and lobbying governments and electronics companies for action for several years.

At the same time, there has been a growth of the literature on the role of business in conflict since the 1990s, reflecting on the globalised operations and the increasing size of corporations.[8] In order to provide guidance for global companies operating in conflict-affected and/or weak governance areas, several frameworks such as the OECD Risk Awareness Tool for Multinational Enterprises in Weak

---

[4]   P. Le Billon, 'Getting It Done: Instruments of Enforcement', in I. Bannon and P. Collier (eds.), *Natural Resources and Violent Conflict: Options and Actions* (Washington DC: The World Bank, 2003), pp. 215–286, p. 216.

[5]   UN, Final Report of the Panel of Experts on the Illegal Exploitation of Natural Resources and Other Forms of Wealth of the Democratic Republic of the Congo, UN Doc. S/2002/1146, available at: www.srwolf.com/reports/UNCONGO.pdf.

[6]   K. Hayes and R. Burge, *Coltan Mining in the Democratic Republic of Congo: How tantalum-using industries can commit to the reconstruction of the DRC* (Cambridge: Fauna & Flora International, 2003).

[7]   Department for International Development (DFID), 'Trading for Peace: Achieving security and poverty reduction through trade in natural resources in the Great Lakes area', Research Report, October 2007; Initiative for Central Africa (INICA), 'Natural Resources and Trade Flows in the Great Lakes Region', Phase 1 Report, 2007; N. Garrett and H. Mitchell, 'Trading Conflict for Development: Utilising the Trade in Minerals from Eastern DR Congo for Development', April 2009, Resource Consulting Services; UNSC, Final Report of the Group of Experts on the Democratic Republic of the Congo, UN Doc. S/2008/773, 12 December 2008.

[8]   V. Haufler, 'Is There a Role for Business in Conflict Management?' in C.A. Crocker et al. (eds.), *Turbulent Peace: the challenges of managing international conflict* (Washington, DC: United States Institute of Peace, 2003), pp. 659–675.

Governance Zones,[9] the OECD Guidelines for Multinational Enterprises[10] and the Voluntary Principles on Security and Human Rights[11] have been developed.

Furthermore, an emerging scholarship on business and human rights has become widely known when John Ruggie, the then Special Representative of the UN Secretary General, developed a business and human rights framework, which includes corporate responsibility to respect human rights through applying due diligence. Therefore, companies are vulnerable to reputational risk from being associated with any human rights abuses within their supply chain even when they are not operating in the context of armed conflict or weak governance directly; the management of global supply chain has become one of the key strategic management issues for business in recent years.[12]

The aforementioned tantalum, tin, tungsten and gold originated from the eastern DRC are discussed as 'conflict minerals' in this regard; global awareness and concern for the 'conflict minerals' have grown significantly as the demand for these minerals remains strong even in the stagnant global economy. However, the mineral supply chain in the eastern DRC is complex because minerals are mostly extracted by informal, unregulated artisanal mining sector and are largely traded in the informal economy partly due to the weak governance capacity of the DRC state. In this context, various initiatives have been developed in order to address the issue of conflict minerals from the DRC by applying human rights due diligence within mineral supply chain.

This chapter sets out to review the emergence of human rights due diligence frameworks to address conflict minerals in global supply chains and to discuss the implications and challenges for implementing these frameworks. As the development and implementation of these initiatives are still at an early stage at the time of writing, a variety of resources is consulted for the purpose of this chapter, ranging from the relevant literature, reports, press release, news to data collected from fieldwork in Rwanda, conducted in 2009.[13] The chapter is structured in five parts. The following section provides a brief outline of the development of the human rights due diligence concept. The third section provides a synopsis of emerging initiatives that seek to facilitate human rights due diligence in order

---

[9]   OECD, 'OECD Risk Awareness Tool for Multinational Enterprises in Weak Governance Zones' in *Annual Report on the OECD Guidelines for Multinational Enterprises 2006: Conducting Business in Weak Governance Zones,* 1 December 2006, OECD Publishing, doi: 10.1787/mne-2006-4-en.

[10] OECD, 'OECD Guidelines for Multinational Enterprises – 2011 edition', 2011, OECD Publishing, available at: http://dx.doi.org/10.1787/9789264115415-en.

[11] Voluntary Principles on Security + Human Rights, 'The Principles', available at: www.voluntaryprinciples.org/principles/introduction (accessed 16 July 2012).

[12] M. Shtender-Auerbach, 'The Top 5 Socio-Political Business Risks for 2010', 13 January 2010, available at: www.huffingtonpost.com/michael-shtenderauerbach/the-top-5-socio-political_b_421466.html (accessed 23 February 2010).

[13] The fieldwork was conducted in Rwanda by the author as part of PhD research, 'Conflict coltan: Local and international dynamics in the Democratic Republic of Congo', between 2007 and 2011.

to curb the trade in conflict minerals. The fourth section discusses the current debates on these initiatives and the challenges to applying human rights due diligence in the mineral supply chain. The fifth section explores the implications of the initiatives on the mineral supply chain in the DRC, leading to conclusions in the final section.

2. THE CONCEPT OF HUMAN RIGHTS DUE DILIGENCE

Reflecting the considerable expansion of the private sector and transnational economic activity in recent decades, the awareness and discussion of the role of business in conflict and human rights violation have grown since the 1990s, making business and human rights issues a global policy agenda. In response to the growing need for guidance to address business impacts on human rights, John Ruggie was appointed as a Special Representative of the UN Secretary General in 2005 to develop a business and human rights framework. The UN framework was established in 2008 and comprises three core principles of 'the State duty to protect against human rights abuses by third parties, including business, the corporate social responsibility to respect human rights, and the need for more effective access to remedies.'[14] A new set of Guiding Principles for Business and Human Rights,[15] which outlines how to implement the above UN framework to 'Protect, Respect and Remedy', was endorsed by the United Nations Human Rights Council on 16 June 2011.[16] The second principle of the framework states that the corporate responsibility to respect human rights is the 'basic expectation society has of business,' which requires due diligence.[17] The framework defined due diligence as 'a process whereby companies not only ensure compliance with national laws but also manage the risk of human rights harm with a view to avoiding it' and hence strive to 'do no harm.'[18]

The human rights due diligence became a key concept of the international movement for corporate accountability, following the development of the UN business and human rights framework, and provides a cornerstone in efforts

---

[14]　J. Ruggie, 'Protect, Respect and Remedy', Report of the Special Representative of the Secretary-General on the issue of human rights and transnational corporations and other business enterprises, Human Rights Council, UN Doc. A/HRC/8/5, 7 April 2008.

[15]　Human Rights Council, 'Report of the Special Representative of the Secretary-General on the issue of human rights and transnational corporations and other business enterprises, John Ruggie – Guiding Principles on Business and Human Rights: Implementing the United Nations "Protect, Respect and Remedy" Framework', UN Doc. A/HRC/17/31, 21 March 2011.

[16]　United Nations Office at Geneva, 'UN Human Rights Council Endorses New Guiding Principles on Business and Human Rights', News & Media, 16 June 2011, available at: www.unog.ch/unog/website/news_media.nsf/(httpNewsByYear_en)/3D7F902244B36DCEC12578B10056A48F?OpenDocument (accessed 16 July 2012).

[17]　J. Ruggie, supra n. 14, p. 5.

[18]　Ibid., p. 9.

to address conflict minerals in global supply chains. Achieving traceability of minerals is critical in these efforts but is extremely difficult because minerals supply chain 'may span thousands of miles across the globe, involve numerous suppliers, retailers, and consumers, and be underpinned by multinational transportation and telecommunication networks.'[19] The upstream supply chain of minerals in the eastern DRC poses a particular challenge to establish traceability and apply due diligence processes owing to its extensive and complex networks, comprising artisanal mining and informal economy activities.

Despite the complex minerals supply chain in the DRC, performing human rights due diligence became a requirement rather than a recommendation when the Dodd-Frank Wall Street Reform and Consumer Protection Act[20] (hereafter the Dodd-Frank Act), containing a conflict minerals provision in Section 1502, was enacted in the US in July 2010. The Securities and Exchanges Commission (SEC) only finalised the rules of the provision in August 2012, as the rules proposed in 2010 had been criticised for being extremely complex and vague in terms of the scope of the requirements and audit standards.[21] While the SEC rules do not prohibit companies from sourcing conflict minerals, it obliges at least 6,000 publicly traded companies in the US to verify whether their products contain tantalum, tin, tungsten, gold or their derivatives originating from the DRC or its neighbouring countries.[22] If they do, companies must trace the origin of minerals in their products, perform due diligence on their supply chain and publish a Conflict Mineral Report. This process is expected to affect a huge number of suppliers worldwide. While there is a strong resistance to legally binding legislation amongst some US commercial groups such as the US Chamber of Commerce and the National Association of Manufacturers,[23] similar legislation has been considered by Canada and the EU, which will affect even more companies.

The development of the concept of human rights due diligence, therefore, suggests a significant shift in supply chain management in two aspects. Firstly, full traceability of minerals required to apply human rights due diligence extended producer responsibility in the entire supply chain, to the upstream supply chain at the extraction stage of raw materials. Secondly, the development of legislation

---

19   A. Nagurney, *Supply Chain Network Economics: Dynamics of Prices, Flows and Profits* (Cheltenham: Edward Elgar, 2006), p. 3.

20   Securities and Exchange Commission, Dodd-Frank Wall Street Reform and Consumer Protection Act. 2010, available at: www.sec.gov/about/laws/wallstreetreform-cpa.pdf (accessed 20 August 2012).

21   KPMG, 'Conflict Minerals Provision of Dodd-Frank: Immediate implications and long-term opportunities for companies', Report, August 2011, p. 5.

22   Securities and Exchange Commission, 17 CFR PARTS 240 and 249b [Release No. 34–67716; File No. S7–40–10], RIN 3235-AK84, available at: www.sec.gov/rules/final/2012/34-67716.pdf (accessed 6 June 2013).

23   J. Low, 'Dodd-Frank and the Conflict Minerals Rule', *Directors & Boards*, Fourth Quarter 2012, KPMG, pp. 44–45, available at: www.kpmg.com/US/en/IssuesAndInsights/Articles Publications/dodd-frank-series/Documents/dodd-frank-and-conflict-minerals-rule-q4.pdf (accessed 6 June 2013).

such as the Dodd-Frank Act made efforts to supply chain due diligence legally binding, signalling a departure from voluntary supply chain management based on individual and/or collective codes of conduct. This paradigm shift enforced the furtherance of various initiatives for traceability and human rights due diligence in conflict minerals supply chain. The next section reviews most advanced initiatives to address conflict minerals in order to illustrate the current approaches to human rights due diligence and their progress.

3. INITIATIVES TO IMPLEMENT HUMAN RIGHTS DUE DILIGENCE IN MINERAL SUPPLY CHAINS

The growing initiatives to address conflict minerals from the DRC can be categorised broadly into three distinct types, namely guidelines, verification and independent audit of a chain of custody and closed-pipe supply chain. This section examines these three approaches by elaborating some existing initiatives.

Firstly, specific guidelines are created to help companies to source minerals. The most prominent guidelines are the OECD Due Diligence Guidance for Responsible Supply Chains of Minerals from Conflict-Affected and High-Risk Areas[24] (hereafter the OECD Guidance), developed by the Organisation for Economic Co-operation and Development (OECD). The OECD Guidance aims to help companies to purchase minerals without violating human rights or contributing to conflict. It has been developed through a collaborative approach to espouse the complex issues of conflict minerals. The process involved numerous stakeholders such as African and OECD countries, industry, civil society, the UN Group of Experts on the DRC and the Technical Assistance and Training Service for Small-Scale Mining (SASSECOM),[25] the DRC government authority responsible for organising and supervising the artisanal mining sector. The OECD Guidance represents the common position and political commitment of adhering countries since the establishment of the guidance was recommended by the OECD Council in 2011.

The OECD Guidance takes into consideration the complex operating environments in the eastern DRC and has defined due diligence as follows:

> an ongoing proactive and reactive process whereby companies take reasonable steps and make good faith efforts to identify and respond to risks of contributing to conflict and serious abuses in accordance with internationally agreed standards,

---

[24]   OECD, 'OECD Due Diligence Guidance for Responsible Supply Chains of Minerals from Conflict-Affected and High-Risk Areas', Paris, 2011.

[25]   *Service d'Assistance et d'Encadrement du Small Scale Mining* (Technical Assistance and Training Service for Small-Scale Mining).

with a view to promoting progressive improvements to due diligence practices through constructive engagement with suppliers'.[26]

In addition, the OECD developed standards for risk-based due diligence in the conflict mineral supply chain:

- establish strong company management systems;
- identify and assess risks in the supply chain;
- design and implement a strategy to respond to identified risks;
- carry out independent third-party audit; and
- report on supply chain due diligence.[27]

Although the OECD Guidance does not explain how supply chain due diligence can be carried out,[28] with these standards, it is expected to help companies establish a process to exercise due diligence and generate the information for disclosure to comply with the aforementioned Dodd-Frank Act conflict minerals provision.[29]

The OECD Guidance has been widely accepted as an international due diligence standard for conflict minerals. The SEC refers to the OECD Guidance as an acceptable starting point for companies to base their policies for compliance with the Dodd-Frank Act. Similarly, the UN Group of Experts' due diligence guidelines,[30] provided in the UN Group of Experts final report in 2010, support and rely on the OECD Guidance. The DRC government also issued a directive in September 2011 to require all mining and mineral trading companies operating in the country to conduct supply chain due diligence in order to prevent supporting armed groups in the eastern DRC, in line with the OECD Guidance.[31] The directive was incorporated into national law in February 2012. Other initiatives which use the OECD Guidance include: ICGLR Regional Initiative against the Illegal Exploitation of Natural Resources; ITRI Supply Chain Initiative; Conflict-Free Tin Initiative; Solutions for Hope; Conflict-Free Sourcing Initiative (CFSI);

---

[26] OECD, 'A Joint Letter to U.S. Security and Exchange Commission', dated 29 July 2011, p. 4, para. 2, available at: www.sec.gov/comments/s7-40-10/s74010-282.pdf (accessed 16 July 2012).

[27] KPMG, *supra* n. 21, p. 7.

[28] *Ibid.*

[29] OECD, 'Note of Clarification', 29 July 2011, p. 2, para. 4, available at: www.oecd.org/investment/investmentfordevelopment/48889221.pdf (accessed 16 July 2012).

[30] The guidelines is provided in UN Security Council, 'Letter dated 15 November 2010 from the Chair of the Security Council Committee established pursuant to resolution 1533 (2004) concerning the Democratic Republic of the Congo addressed to the President of the Security Council', S/2010/596, 29 November 2010, available at: www.un.org/ga/search/view_doc.asp?symbol=S/2010/596 (accessed 21 May 2012), and adopted in the UN Security Council, Resolution 1952, UN Doc. S/RES/1952 (2010), 29 November 2010, available at: www.un.org/ga/search/view_doc.asp?symbol=S/RES/1952 (accessed 21 May 2012).

[31] 'Congo government enforces law to curb conflict mineral trade', *Global Witness*, 21 May 2012, available at: www.globalwitness.org/library/congo-government-enforces-law-curb-conflict-mineral-trade (accessed 6 June 2013).

World Gold Council's Conflict-Free Gold Standard; London Bullion Market Association's Responsible Gold Program; Dubai Multi-Commodities Center's Responsible Sourcing of Precious Metals; and Responsible Jewellery Council's Chain of Custody Certification.[32]

Secondly, several verification mechanisms, using independent audits, are developed to provide a chain of custody and the origin of minerals, thereby enabling companies to purchase conflict free minerals. Below, four different mechanisms are examined in some detail.

3.1. ICGLR REGIONAL INITIATIVE AGAINST THE ILLEGAL EXPLOITATION OF NATURAL RESOURCES

The International Conference on the Great Lakes Region (ICGLR), a regional body of eleven African country members,[33] signed the Pact on Security, Stability and Development in the Great Lakes Region in 2006, which includes a Protocol on the Fight against the Illegal Exploitation of Natural Resources that outlines a comprehensive approach to put an end to the predatory use of natural resources. The Regional Initiative against the Illegal Exploitation of Natural Resources (RINR) has been established to translate the Protocol into concrete actions. The RINR aims specifically at breaking the link between mineral revenues and rebel financing. The initiative uses six tools to curb the illegal exploitation of natural resources in the Great Lakes region, the most important of which is the Regional Certification Mechanism. The Regional Certification Mechanism provides a regionally harmonised supply chain due diligence framework in the ICGLR member states, including mine site inspections by the national mining authority, chain of custody management, mineral export shipment certification and data management and exchange with the ICGLR Secretariat for the above processes. The ICGLR supports the OECD Guidance and has integrated it into the Regional Certification Mechanism and a Certification Manual on Natural Resources that has been adopted recently.

3.2. CONFLICT-FREE SMELTER

Two electronics industry associations, the Electronic Industry Citizenship Coalition (EICC)[34] and the Global e-Sustainability Initiative (GeSI),[35] view responsible sourcing as a priority for their members and aim to extend their

---

[32]   OECD, 'Implementing the OECD Due Diligence Guidance', n.d., available at: www.oecd.org/daf/inv/mne/implementingtheguidance.htm (accessed 4 June 2013).
[33]   International Conference on the Great Lakes Region, available at: www.icglr.org/.
[34]   Electronic Industry Citizenship Coalition, available at: www.eicc.info/.
[35]   Global e-Sustainability Initiative, available at: www.gesi.org/.

influence beyond their immediate suppliers to improve social and environmental conditions throughout their extensive supply chains. Since 2005, they have been working together through the joint EICC and GeSI Extractive Workgroup and have developed the Conflict Free Smelter (CFS) programme[36] for tin, tantalum, tungsten and gold to enable companies to source conflict-free minerals.

The CFS is a voluntary programme in which an independent third party assesses smelters to determine whether they are able to demonstrate that all the materials they process are from conflict-free sources, based on a business process review and material analysis review. As a result, the CFS is able to provide a list of conflict-free smelters and simplify the due diligence process for companies using tin, tantalum, tungsten and gold in their products as they only need to trace their mineral supply chains to the level of the smelter. Industry participants for the CFS have rapidly increased after the SEC explained that reasonably reliable representations from the mineral processing facility in the supply chain is one way to fulfil the requirement for reasonable enquiry of the country of origin under Section 1502 of the Dodd-Frank Act.[37]

3.3. ITRI TIN SUPPLY CHAIN INITIATIVE

The International Tin Research Institute (ITRI), a tin industry association based in the UK, has been developing a chain of custody and due diligence system, the ITRI Tin Supply Chain Initiative (iTSCi),[38] since 2008. The iTSCi process aims to support upstream companies, from mine to smelter, in adhering to the OECD Guidance at a very practical level though the companies remain responsible for their sourcing practices. It consists of three components, namely, chain of custody data collection to achieve traceability, risk assessment and independent third party audits. The chain of custody data collection involves barcoded mine tag and *négotiant*/processor tag,[39] each with unique reference numbers, added to the bags of minerals. The tagging is accompanied by detailed data collection via purpose designed log books to provide records and data. All members in the upstream supply chain are audited by an iTSCi auditor; smelters will be audited by the aforementioned CFS as the iTSCi chain of custody system provides information required by the CFS. The iTSCi is also expected to assist companies in fulfilling the reporting requirement of the Dodd-Frank Act. While the initiative's first pilot project, which was launched in South Kivu in 2010, had to be suspended following

---

[36] Conflict Free Sourcing Initiative, available at: www.conflictfreesmelter.org/; Electronic Industry Citizenship Coalition Program, available at: www.eicc.info/CFSProgram.shtml.

[37] K.E. Woody, 'Conflict Minerals Legislation: The SEC's new role as diplomatic and humanitarian watchdog' (2012) 81 *Fordham Law Review* 1315–1351.

[38] International Tin Research Institute (ITRI), 'iTSCi Project Overview', available at: www.itri. co.uk/index.php?option=com_zoo&view=item&Itemid=189 (accessed 28 May 2012).

[39] Middleman, who organises purchase of ores from mines/local markets for trading houses.

a six-month mining ban posed by the DRC government in September 2010, it will be restarted in the near future if several conditions are met, such as approval of conflict-free mines and availability of funding and buyers. The initiative has also been implemented in Rwanda and in the DRC's Katanga Province since 2011 with a possibility to expand to the entire Great Lakes region. Furthermore, ITRI has signed a partnership agreement with the ICGLR to set up the aforementioned Regional Certification Mechanism for tin.

3.4. CERTIFIED TRADING CHAINS AND ANALYTICAL FINGERPRINT

The German Federal Institute for Geosciences and Natural Resources (BGR)[40] have been a driving force in the advancement of minerals certification in the Great Lakes region. They started two research projects to provide assurance and the origin of tantalum in 2006. The BGR currently has four ongoing projects, namely the G8 pilot project Certified Trading Chains (CTC) in Mineral Production in Rwanda, the Mineral Certification in the DRC, the Analytical Fingerprint (AFP), and support to the above-mentioned ICGLR RINR.[41] These projects are based on the CTC and AFP that have been developed from the two initial research projects.

The CTC is a means to foster traceability, transparency and responsible production standards in the artisanal and small-scale mining sector, and includes performance monitoring, through third party baseline audits and compliance audits, to provide the base for potential certification at a national level. In Rwanda, it was launched in cooperation with Rwandan Geology and Mines Authority (OGMR) in 2008; in the DRC, it started to support the Ministry of Mines in its effort to strengthen transparency and control in the mining sector through Mineral Certification in 2009, leading to the first issuance of a ICGLR export certificate for the CTC-certified tin mine of Kalimbi.[42] Most CTC standards have been incorporated into the ICGLR Regional Certification Mechanism as progress criteria.

The AFP was initiated in 2006 in order to verify the origin of minerals by mineralogical and geochemical analysis of ore samples and comparison with the AFP database. The BGR has developed methods to track independently the origin

---

[40]   Bundesanstalt für Geowissenschaften und Rohstoffe, available at: www.bgr.bund.de.
[41]   Federal Institute for Geosciences and Natural Resources (BGR), 'Mineral Certification at the BGR', available at: www.bgr.bund.de/EN/Themen/Min_rohstoffe/CTC/Home/CTC_node_en.html;jsessionid=9D214EA0D26CB7B286445EA3D89606E7.1_cid289 (accessed 30 May 2012); BGR, 'Mineral Certification: Certified Trading Chains (CTC) and the Analytical Fingerprint (AFP)', *Newsletter* 01/2012, available at: www.bgr.bund.de/EN/Themen/Min_rohstoffe/CTC/Downloads/newsletter_01_2012.html (accessed 30 May 2012).
[42]   BGR, 'Mineral Certification DR Congo-Roadmap', available at: www.bgr.bund.de/EN/Themen/Min_rohstoffe/CTC/Mineral-Certification-DRC/Roadmap/roadmap_drc_node_en.html (accessed 12 September 2014).

of tantalum ore concentrates produced in Central Africa and has been developing a similar AFP scheme for tin ore concentrates with a plan to expand the scheme to tungsten ore concentrates. As part of support to the ICGLR, the BGR has been helping to establish the AFP to be used in the ICGLR Regional Certification Mechanism as an independent monitoring tool.

Thirdly, the most recent development is an attempt to create closed pipe supply chain to source conflict-free minerals from the DRC to address the *de facto* embargo of minerals from the DRC following the enactment of the Dodd-Frank Act in 2010. The closed pipe supply chain includes a defined set of key producers and traders to supply minerals from a specific mine in the DRC and uses the aforementioned iTSCi traceability process. It corresponds with a suggestion for the third generation responsible supply chain management mechanism 'to create 'CSR risk free sourcing and investment zones' in demarcated territory, inclusive of all suppliers and sub-suppliers in a specific area.'[43] At present, there are two such mechanisms operating in the DRC: the Solutions for Hope Project to source tantalum and the Conflict-Free Tin Initiative for tin.

The Solutions for Hope Project (SfH)[44] was launched in July 2011 by Motorola Solutions Inc.,[45] a leading communications equipment manufacturer and AVX Corporation,[46] a leading tantalum capacitor manufacturer. It is a pilot initiative to secure conflict-free tantalum from the DRC, using a closed pipe supply line, and to promote economic stability of the area. The project is implemented at the Mai Baridi, Kisengo and Luba mines in northern Katanga province, the concessions of the Mining Minerals Resources SPRL (MMR).[47] The MMR contracts with *Coopérative Des Artisanaux Miniers du Congo* (CDMC), a mining cooperative, to manage artisanal miners. The minerals produced from the mines are weighed and logged at the mines as part of the iTSCi traceability process by a local SAESSCAM agent and transported to an MMR depot for export. The AVX Corporation purchases the minerals with the global market price at this point and the F&X Electro-Materials Limited and the Global Advance Metals (GAM), both CFS compliant smelters, process the minerals into tantalum powder and wire for the AVX Corporation. The conflict-free tantalum capacitors manufactured by the AVX Corporation are used by Motorola Solutions Inc., HP, Intel, Nokia, Foxconn and other participants in the project.

The SfH project was verified to be a reliable system by the project evaluation conducted in January 2012 and operates at full scale. It aims to enhance its sustainability and expandability and is open for participation by all

---

43   S.S. Thorsen and S. Jeppesen, 'Changing Course – A study into Responsible Supply Chain Management', Executive Summary, Authored by GLOBAL CSR and Copenhagen Business School for the Danish Ministry of Foreign Affairs, 2011, p. 9.
44   Solutions for Hope, available at: http://solutions-network.org/site-solutionsforhope/.
45   Motorola Solutions, available at: www.motorolasolutions.com/.
46   AVX Corporation, available at: www.avx.com/.
47   Vinmart Group, available at: www.vinmartgroup.com/associates/mmr-sprl.

companies including mining, smelters, component manufacturers and product manufacturers. The project supports the iTSCi, CTC and ICGLR processes so that the materials mined at its sites will be issued with ICGLR certificates. The MMR also participates in the Upstream Pilot Implementation of the OECD Guidance and was audited twice by an independent auditor against the OECD Guidance. The Mai Baridi mine was evaluated for compliance with the CTC and has been designated as a 'Green' site.

The Conflict-Free Tin Initiatives (CFTI)[48] is another pilot programme to source conflict-free tin from the Kalimbi mine in Kalehe, South Kivu province, announced in September 2012 by industry partners convened by the Dutch government. The CFTI aims to promote responsible sourcing and economic development in the DRC. Using a tightly controlled supply chain including confirmed buyers of conflict-free tin from the Kivus, the pilot aims to create demand for conflict-free tin and reverse the *de facto* embargo on the minerals in the DRC posed by the Dodd-Frank Act. The CFTI uses the iTSCi traceability and due diligence system, operated by Pact, an independent NGO, and is structured within the framework of the ICGLR, involving the DRC government and local civil society, in order to facilitate the reform initiatives by the DRC government and the Mines Ministry.[49] It is consistent with the OECD Guidance. The CFTI is currently participated by AIM Metals & Alloys, Alpha, Apple, BlackBerry, Fairphone, HP, ITRI, Malaysia Smelting Corporation Berhad, Motorola Solutions, Nokia, Royal Philips, Tata Steel and Traxys and open for participation by all companies.

The project has been successful in validating the Kalimbi mine as conflict-free by a team consisting officials from the DRC government, the UN, the BGR, iTSCi as well as local business and civil society. It has also seen the production of more than 200 tonnes of tin and seven shipments to the smelter. The CFTI also claims its success in other areas: the number of miners increased from 100 to 1,200; the income of miners increased from US \$2 to US \$4–6 per kilo; and working conditions and the health and safety standards are improved, thereby contributing to the formalisation of the sector.[50] While the Kalimbi mine remained open during the recent security situation in North Kivu,[51] the CFTI recognises that its progress depends on the security situation in South Kivu[52] and has expanded its mining operation to Maniema, next to South Kivu.

---

48   Conflict-Free Tin Initiative, available at: http://solutions-network.org/site-cfti/.
49   Conflict-Free Tin Initiative, 'Conflict-Free Tin Initiative announced', *Press Statement*, 18 September 2012, available at: http://solutions-network.org/site-cfti/files/2012/09/Press-statement-Conflict-Free-Tin-Initiative-Press-Release-18-Sept.pdf (accessed 4 June 2013).
50   Conflict-Free Tin Initiative, available at: http://solutions-network.org/site-cfti/.
51   *Ibid.*
52   Conflict-Free Tin Initiative, *supra* n. 49.

4. CHALLENGES OF APPLYING HUMAN RIGHTS DUE DILIGENCE IN MINERAL SUPPLY CHAINS

The existing literature and frameworks on supply chain management do not offer definitions of boundaries of supply chain responsibility, and defining responsibility remains one of the most challenging issues in Corporate Social Responsibility field.[53] As a result, responsible supply chain management initiatives have advanced mostly on an *ad hoc* basis, but usually require responsibility over first, second or third-tier suppliers, reflecting the Global Compact's call for acting within the sphere of influence. Whilst the issue of conflict minerals extended supply chain management to an entire supply chain and has prompted the various human rights due diligence initiatives reviewed in the preceding section, mechanisms and methodologies to enable responsible supply chain management have yet been developed to serve specific situations that companies and sectors face.[54] Therefore, the development of these initiatives provoked heated discussions amongst industries, policy makers and NGOs alike. Diverse views expressed in the debate partly reflect the rapidly evolving nature of responsible mineral supply chain management, as well as the unknown implications, advantages and drawbacks of a total supply chain responsibility placed on the end-users of materials.

This section discusses the challenges of applying human rights due diligence in mineral supply chain posed by placing a total supply chain responsibility on the end-users of conflict minerals, such as electronics companies, all the way to the distant-tier supply chain participants at the raw materials extraction phase. The challenges are identified at the production stages of consumer goods and raw materials, or downstream supply chain and upstream supply chain levels.

Firstly, at the downstream supply chain level, there is a serious question about the feasibility of achieving traceability of minerals to perform human rights due diligence. The viability of minerals traceability is still not known despite being paramount in supply chain management. Metal supply chains are extensive and complex because of the nature of metal markets and trade, which creates strong barriers to effectively implementing traceability processes.[55] Metals such as tantalum are usually traded through direct long-term contracts between buyers and sellers, and the line-of-sight between the seller and the buyer gets lost, owing to the confidentiality of contracts and the mixing of metals from different sources in the supply chain. When metals are traded in commodity markets, such as the London Metal Exchange and the New York Mercantile Exchange, the metals

---

53   S.B. Young et al., 'Principles for responsible metals supply to electronics' (2010) 6(1) *Social Responsibility Journal* 126–142.

54   *Ibid.*

55   S.B. Young, 'Social and Environmental Responsibility in Metals Supply to the Electronic Industry', GHGm Report, 20 June 2008, available at: www.eiccoalition.org/media/docs/publications/SERMetalsSupplyreport.pdf (accessed 27 January 2010).

are mixed from various sources, and buyers do not see sellers. Furthermore, at the extraction stage in the eastern DRC, as explained in more detail below, minerals are extracted by artisanal miners, often informally in remote areas where infrastructure is poor, and are transported and traded largely within the extensive informal sector, thereby posing a significant challenge to achieving traceability. As an illustration of the challenge, Intel claims to have travelled over 120,000 miles and has visited 30 smelters in pursuant of a conflict-free supply chain since 2009 and had mapped out 92 per cent of the tantalum, tin, tungsten and gold supply lines for its business by the end of 2011.[56]

Notwithstanding the enormous challenge of achieving· traceability of minerals from the DRC, according to an industry insider, it is inevitable that minerals, especially tantalum, will be sourced from the DRC because of the size of reserves, high grades and the ease of mining.[57] One estimate suggests that approximately half of the tantalum being used to manufacture electronics is sourced from a conflict area due to the shortage of the minerals in the conflict-free region.[58] This may also include the tantalum and tungsten mines controlled by the Revolutionary Armed Forces of Colombia (FARC) and other criminal gangs in Colombia.[59] According to another study, 22 per cent of tantalum was produced in Rwanda and DRC in 2009/2010, following mine closures in Australia and Canada in 2009 as a result of the financial crisis.[60] New mines can be hard to develop because of the obstacles to finding investment and the high costs to meet various standards; the supply of critical metals like tantalum and tungsten is expected to be problematic.[61]

According to a survey conducted with companies in the US in April 2013, more than 35 per cent of them have not started compliance planning for the Dodd-Frank Act's conflict provision while only 7.5 per cent responded that they are well-prepared for compliance.[62] As a matter of fact, only about 1,300 companies out of 6,000 listed companies submitted conflict mineral filings to the SEC by the

---

[56] M. Smith, 'Intel Plans Conflict-Free Tantalum Microprocessors', *Tantalum Investing News*, 7 June 2012, available at: http://tantaluminvestingnews.com/2346-intel-plans-conflict-free-microprocessors-tantalum-tin-gold-tungsten.html.

[57] *Ibid.*

[58] *Ibid.*

[59] C. Jamasmie, 'Colombian armed rebels tighten control over gold mining' *Mining*, 13 December 2012, available at: www.mining.com/colombian-armed-rebels-tighten-control-over-gold-mining-99114/ (accessed 4 June 2013).

[60] H. Sievers and L. Tercero, 'European dependence on and concentration tendencies of the material production', POLINARES Working Paper no. 14, March 2012, available at: www.polinares.eu/docs/d2-1/polinares_wp2_chapter2.pdf (accessed 4 June 2013).

[61] B. Sylvester, 'The Conflict over Conflict Metals: Lisa Reisman', *The Gold Report*, 4 June 2013, available at: www.theaureport.com/pub/na/15333 (accessed 5 June 2013).

[62] IHS, 'IHS Survey reveals more than one-third of companies completely unprepared for US Conflict Minerals Rules', Press Release, 18 April 2013, available at: http://press.ihs.com/press-release/design-supply-chain/ihs-survey-reveals-more-one-third-companies-completely-unprepared (accessed 25 April 2013).

first filing deadline of 2 June 2014.[63] Companies may be concerned about the cost of implementation,[64] the confidentiality of supply chain partners, manufacturing processes and contracts[65] and their lack of influence over suppliers.[66] Moreover, according to previous studies, overlapping standards can present a significant obstacle to responsible supply chain management programmes, and duplication should be carefully avoided.[67] For this matter, industry-wide mechanisms can reduce the costs and complexity of compliance for suppliers, as exemplified by the CFS, developed by the EICC and GeSI, and may create a 'critical mass' of industry support.[68] As in the CFS, smelters are considered to be a good control point in minerals traceability to simplify due diligence efforts.[69] In spite of the numerous challenges to comply with due diligence requirements, there are also some potential benefits of conducting supply chain due diligence for end-user companies, such as identification of opportunities for supply chain simplification, rationalisation and cost reduction, improvement in customer brand recognition and implementation of other impending standards and certifications in the area of environment and sustainability.[70] In other words, legislation such as the Dodd-Frank Act may provide companies an opportunity to enhance ethical standards and efficiency.[71]

Secondly, the situation at the upstream supply chain level where minerals are produced in the eastern DRC is more likely to be the key challenge for human rights due diligence efforts. The DRC suffers from weak governance, in particular in the eastern DRC where there is a lack of government control in many areas. This is likely to hinder effective implementation and enforcement of various human rights due diligence frameworks. Africa Progress Panel had observed weak enforcement mechanisms for programmes, such as the iTSCi and the CTC, and attributed the problem to the limited government authority in many of the

---

[63]   PWC, *2014 Conflict minerals filing review*, available at: www.pwc.com/en_US/us/cfodirect/assets/pdf/automotive-conflict-minerals-benchmarking.pdf (accessed 12 September 2014).

[64]   KPMG, *supra* n. 21.

[65]   D. Bannerman, 'One Step Forward for Conflict Minerals, but What Impact on Congo?', *Greenbiz*, 10 August 2010, available at: www.greenbiz.com/blog/2010/08/10/one-step-forward-conflict-minerals-what-impact-congo?page=full (accessed 19 May 2011).

[66]   Informal conversation, Corporate Responsibility Senior Manager of a mobile phone company, at the Conference Board, 'European Council on Corporate Responsibility & Sustainability', British American Tobacco, London, 6 February 2009; S.B. Young et al., *supra* n. 53.

[67]   H.B. Jørgensen et al., 'Strengthening Implementation of Corporate Social Responsibility in Global Supply Chain', Investment Climate Department of the World Bank, October 2003, Washington, DC.

[68]   D.E. Krueger, 'The ethics of global supply chains in China – convergences of east and west' (2008) 79 *Journal of Business Ethics* 113–120.

[69]   IHS, 'IHS Survey reveals more than one-third of companies completely unprepared for US Conflict Minerals Rules', Press Release, 18 April 2013, available at: http://press.ihs.com/press-release/design-supply-chain/ihs-survey-reveals-more-one-third-companies-completely-unprepared (accessed 25 April 2013).

[70]   KPMG, *supra* n. 21.

[71]   Africa Progress Panel, 'Africa Progress Report 2013 – Equity in Extractives: Stewarding Africa's natural resources for all', Geneva, p. 88.

conflict areas and the continuing support of some neighbouring governments to armed groups operating in mining areas.[72] Local stakeholders also raised a strong doubt about the feasibility of traceability mechanisms, based on some practical issues, such as the lack of sensitisation, organisation and capacity of stakeholders at the grassroots level in order to adapt to new requirements, the insufficient capacity and wages for civil servants to be involved in the implementation of these initiatives and the absence of support to artisanal miners and people living around mining areas.[73] There is also a lack of trust in the ability of government agencies to implement the traceability mechanisms without fraud and corruption.[74] Local actors emphasise that the state is impoverished and does not function in many parts of the country, particularly in the eastern provinces,[75] and express their concerns about the selection of mines for due diligence projects where the national army and police, with grave human rights records, are present.[76]

The limited capacity for enforcement within the DRC was already evident in the implementation of the Kimberley Process Certification Scheme (KPCS)[77] in the DRC since 2003. The KPCS is a multi-stakeholder certification process to curb production and trade in diamonds from conflict zones. Although the scheme succeeded in increasing the state revenue to a degree by collecting export taxes on diamonds and licence fees, the implementation in the country appears to have largely failed as smuggling of conflict and illicit diamonds remains widespread in the DRC.[78] According to the reviews of the KPCS implementation in the DRC, there are a number of problems, such as smuggling, undervaluing to evade tax, secrecy and extensive corruption, mainly owing to weak internal controls within the DRC.[79] The weak internal controls is largely attributed to the lack of government control in many areas, causing insecurity in the areas[80] and the difficulty in monitoring pervasive, uncontrolled artisanal mining in the vast

---

[72]   *Ibid.*
[73]   P. Pöyhönen et al., 'Voices from the Inside: Local views on mining reform in Eastern DR Congo', Finnwatch & Swedwatch, Helsinki and Stockholm, October 2010.
[74]   D. Johnson, 'Who's in charge? Putting the Mineral Trade in Eastern DRC under International Control: An Overview', August 2010, Pole Institute, Goma.
[75]   Pole Institute, 'Blood Minerals: The Criminalization of the Mining Industry in Eastern DRC', Goma, August 2010.
[76]   P. Pöyhönen et al., *supra* n. 73.
[77]   The Kimberly Process, available at: www.kimberleyprocess.com/.
[78]   J. Bavier, 'Kimberley Process failing Africa – campaigners', *Reuters*, 18 October 2009, available at: http://af.reuters.com/article/topNews/idAFJOE59H06Q20091018.
[79]   PAC (Partnership Africa Canada) and CENADEP (*Centre National d'Appui au Développement et à la Participation Populaire*), *Diamond Industry Annual Review: Democratic Republic of the Congo 2005* (Ottawa: PAC and Kinshasa: CENADEP); PAC (Partnership Africa Canada), *Diamonds and Human Security Annual Review 2009* (Ottawa: PAC, October 2009).
[80]   J. Burbank, 'The Effect of the Kimberley Process on Governance, Corruption, & Internal Conflict', *The Fund for Peace Globalization & Human Rights Series*, The Fund for Peace Spring, Washington DC, 2006.

country.[81] In addition, the relevant government agencies lack incentives[82] and adequate resources to perform their responsibilities.[83] Without the provision of significant funding and capacity building, these same government agencies cannot be expected to serve efficiently to ensure the effective implementation of human rights due diligence processes.[84]

A wider problem of enforcement within the DRC is also manifested by the temporary suspension from the Extractive Industries Transparency Initiative (EITI), a global transparency framework for extractive industries, on 17 April 2013.[85] While the EITI Board recognised the significant progress made by the DRC towards enhancing transparency and accountability by completing two EITI validations over the past five years since the country's progression to an EITI candidate in 2008, the DRC failed to meet the EITI standard in full disclosure and assurance of the reliability of the figures, resulting in the candidate status suspension on 18 April 2013. The country has only been recognised as a full member of the EITI based on its remedial actions to meet the requirements set out in the EITI Standards.[86]

Nonetheless, the DRC government demonstrated its commitment to mineral supply chain due diligence through the ICGLR and the issuance of a directive in September 2011 to oblige all mining and mineral trading companies to perform supply chain due diligence in line with the OECD Guidance and the UN Security Council Resolution 1952 (2010)[87] which was incorporated into national law in February 2012.[88]

---

[81]   C. Dietrich, 'Hard Currency: The Criminalized Diamond Economy of the Democratic of the Congo and its Neighbours', The Diamond and Human Security Project Occasional Paper no. 4 (Ottawa: Partnership Africa Canada, 2002); Global Witness and PAC (Partnership Africa Canada), *Rich Man, Poor Man – Development Diamonds and Poverty Diamonds: The Potential for Change in the Artisanal Alluvial Diamond Fields of Africa* (Ottawa: PAC, October 2004); PAC and CENADEP, 2005, *supra* n. 79; J. Burbank, *supra* n. 80.

[82]   J. Burbank, *supra* n. 80; R. Perks and K. Vlassenroot, 'From Discourse to Practice: A Sharper Perspective on the Relationship between Minerals and Violence in DR Congo' in J. Cuvelier (ed.), *The complexity of resource governance in a context of state fragility: The case of eastern DRC* (London: International Alert, November 2010), pp. 64–69.

[83]   Email communication, DRC National Coordinator for the ICGLR, 20 March 2010; R. Perks and K. Vlassenroot, *supra* n. 82.

[84]   R. Perks and K. Vlassenroot, *supra* n. 82; D. Verbruggen et al., 'Guide to Current Mining Reform Initiatives in Eastern DRC', April 2011, Antwerp: IPIS (International Peace Information Service), p. 22.

[85]   Extractive Industries Transparency Initiative (EITI), 'Democratic Republic of the Congo temporary "suspended"', *News*, 18 April 2013, available at: http://eiti.org/news/democratic-republic-congo-temporary-suspended (accessed 25 April 2013).

[86]   EITI, 'DR Congo becomes full member of EITI', *EITI News*, 2 July 2014, available at: http://eiti.org/news/dr-congo-becomes-full-member-eiti (accessed 12 September 2014).

[87]   The Government of Democratic Republic of Congo, 'Note Circulaire', 002/CAB.MIN/MINES/01/2011, available at: www.globalwitness.org/sites/default/files/library/Note_Circulaire_OECDguidelines_06092011.pdf (accessed 20 July 2012).

[88]   'Congo government enforces low to curb conflict mineral trade', *Global Witness*, 21 May 2012, available at: www.globalwitness.org/library/congo-government-enforces-law-curb-conflict-mineral-trade (accessed 20 July 2012).

There are also various issues on the ground which hinder the effective implementation of human rights due diligence mechanisms. The biggest impediment is posed by security conditions. This is confirmed by a visit by the Public-Private Alliance for Responsible Minerals Trade (PPA)[89] in February 2012 to assess the situation in the eastern DRC and consider the types and criteria of projects for sourcing conflict-free minerals from the Great Lakes region. The report of the PPA visit[90] underscored that security is a critical prerequisite for developing a pilot conflict-free supply chain. The recent halt of the embryonic iTSCi bag and tag process to certify the origin of tin and gold in North Kivu, following the heavy clashes, which started in April 2012, vividly illustrates the need for security and stability to conduct the tagging process as part of due diligence mechanisms. In contrast to the bag and tag system in North Kivu, the SfH closed pipe supply chain in Katanga Province has so far been considered to be successful largely because of the relative security and existing political will in the province.[91] Political will has also been named as a condition of effective due diligence processes in the aforementioned PPA report. While there seems to be a general shift in attitude towards due diligence processes amongst local traders in the DRC,[92] it is necessary to have the political will and commitment by wider stakeholders through the ownership of the initiatives.[93]

Other issues on the ground which may affect the implementation of due diligence processes include mine ownership, the status of artisanal mining and governance in the DRC. There have been conflicts over mine ownership in the eastern DRC involving government forces, rebel groups and private companies, owing to the duplication and complexities of mine ownership in part derived from three contradicting laws in the DRC, namely the Mining Code, the General Property Law and customary law. The Mining Code[94] explicates that the state possesses all deposits of minerals and can grant mining and exploration rights,[95] which do not entail surface rights. Surface rights are stipulated by the General Property Law, which clarifies that the state has the property of land and can grant

---

[89] The Public-Private Alliance for Responsible Minerals Trade (PPA, www.resolve.org/site-ppa) was launched in 2011 as a joint effort of the US State Department, the US Agency for International Development, NGOs and companies/industry organisations to support supply chain solutions to conflict minerals challenges in the DRC and the Great Lakes region.

[90] M. Loch, J. Celorie, S. Lezhnev, F. Bafilemba and R. Robinson, 'PPA Governance Committee Members Summary Trip Report', 4–8 February 2012, available at: www.resolv.org/site-ppa/files/2011/09/In-region-Trip-Report-Kivu-Leg.pdf (accessed 20 July 2012).

[91] M. Loch, J. Celorie, S. Lezhnev, F. Bafilemba and R. Robinson, *supra* n. 90.

[92] S. Pickles and A. Dunnebacke, 'SEC Delays Risk Undermining Efforts to Curb Congolese Conflict Minerals', *Huff Post World*, 19 April 2012, available at: www.huffingtonpost.com/sophia-pickles/sec-delays-risk-undermini_b_1438364.html (accessed 25 May 2012).

[93] J. Bavier, 'Thaisarco suspends Congo tin ore purchase', *Reuters Africa*, 18 September 2009.

[94] The Government of the Democratic Republic of Congo, LAW No. 007/2002 of 11 July 2002 Relating to the Mining Code, available at: www.unites.uqam.ca/grama/pdf/DRC2002.pdf (accessed 12 November 2009).

[95] *Ibid.*, Article 3.

surface rights to private or public parties.[96] To make the land ownership matter more complex, despite the introduction of the General Property Law in 1973, which has removed the existing customary ownership of land and enabled purchases of individual land rights from the state,[97] the customary land tenure system still exists on the ground.[98] Furthermore, large parts of the eastern DRC are controlled by rebel groups since the emergence of conflict in 1996, and the mine ownership disputes have been further complicated and continue on the ground.[99] However, the Mining Code does not clarify how to solve conflicts over mine ownership, or problems with other contradicting legislation, thereby affecting the security condition in the mining areas.[100] The mine ownership conflict is a very sensitive issue since land is a vital source of livelihood in the densely populated eastern DRC.[101] Hence disputes over land ownership can significantly affect the security and stability of the mine areas and thereby undermine the implementation of due diligence processes.

The above-mentioned Mining Code, together with the Mining Regulations of 2003, provides a clear division between industrial and artisanal mining and is intended to regulate artisanal and small-scale mining and minerals trading.[102] The artisanal mining sector, while being prevalent in developing countries and considered to be an important activity with significant economic impact,

---

[96]   H. André-Dumont and G. Carbonez, 'Democratic Republic of the Congo' in S. Farrell et al. (eds.), *Getting the deal through: Mining 2009* (London: Law Business Research, 2009), pp. 44–48, p. 45.

[97]   C. Huggins et al., 'Conflict in the Great Lakes Region – How is it linked with land and migration?' (2005) 96 *Natural Resource Perspectives*, The Overseas Development Institute (ODI); S.W. Meditz and T. Merrill (eds.), *Zaire: a country study* (Washington, DC: Library of Congress Federal Research Division, 1994).

[98]   The three-tiered Native Authority in Kivu consists of a chief of the locality at the lowest level, the *Chef de Groupement* and the Mwami of the *Collectivité* at the highest level. Only the *Chef de Groupement* and the Mwami of the *Collectivité* have the customary authority in administration and to verify ethnic belonging, issue identity cards, distribute customary land for livelihood and deliver customary justice; however, 'non-indigenous' people generally have only the chief of the locality from amongst their own ranks and are being disadvantaged. For more details, see M. Mamdani, 'Understanding the Crisis in Kivu: Report of the CODESRIA Mission to the Democratic Republic of Congo, September 1997', text of report to be submitted to the General Assembly of the Council for the Development of Social Research in Africa (CODESRIS), Centre for African Studies, University of Cape Town, Dakar, 14–18 December 1998, available at: www.ukzn.ac.za/ccs/files/mamdani.kivu.pdf (accessed 23 June 2010).

[99]   J. Cuvelier (ed.), 'The complexity of resource governance in a context of state fragility: The case of eastern DRC', International Alert Report, November 2010; PPA, *supra* n. 89.

[100]   D. Johnson and A. Tegera, 'Digging deeper: How the DR Congo's mining policy is failing the country', Pole Institute report, December 2005, Goma.

[101]   E. Sosne,'Colonial Peasantization and Contemporary Underdevelopment: A View from a Kivu Village' in G. Gran with G. Hull (eds.), *ZAIRE, the Political Economy of Underdevelopment* (New York: Praeger, 1979), pp. 189–210; F. Van Acker, 'Where did all the land go? Enclosure & social struggle in Kivu (D.R.Congo)' (2005) 32(103) *Review of African Political Economy* 79–98; T. Turner, *The Congo Wars: Conflict, Myth and Reality* (London: Zed Books, 2007).

[102]   For details of the articles provided in the Mining Code and Mining Regulations to regulate artisanal mining activities, see 'PROMINES Study: Artisanal Mining in the Democratic Republic of Congo', Pact, Inc., June 2010.

lacks a universally agreed definition, owing in part to the diversity of activities in the sector.[103] The artisanal mining sector is widely understood as the most rudimentary domain of the mining sector[104] and is mostly carried out informally.[105] The formalisation of this sector, in order to reduce the negative environmental and socio-economic impacts and to enhance the potential economic impact of poverty reduction, has been a focus of various research projects and donor initiatives. However, the lack of understanding of the dynamics of the sector[106] as well as the contradicting economic reform effort,[107] which promotes foreign direct investments in industrial mining, hinder the formulation of effective instruments, with the result that the sector remains largely informal, illegal and hence vulnerable.

In the DRC, the growth of artisanal mining and informal economy activities was triggered by the decline of industrial mining operations and state capacity following the economic crisis the country faced in the 1980s.[108] Consequently, an estimated 90 per cent of minerals are produced by artisanal miners[109] and more than half of natural resource exports from the DRC are not officially recorded, owing to underreported exports for tax evasion and the lack of governance capacity within the state institutions.[110] A study in 2011 confirmed the extent of the informal trade in the DRC by claiming that 80 per cent of gold produced in the DRC is illegally exported.[111]

Without exception, the attempt to formalise the artisanal sector in the DRC seems to be failing. According to the DRC Mining Code, artisanal miners do not have legal mining rights; however Congolese artisanal miners can apply for a one-year Artisanal Exploration Card (*carte de creseur*) from the Provincial Mining Division, after paying fees and attending training, and mine within a designated

---

[103] 'Small scale mining', The World Bank, available at: www.artisanalmining.org/index.cfm?page=page_disp&pid=3305 (accessed 6 November 2009).

[104] G.M. Hilson, 'General Introduction' in G.M. Hilson (ed.), *The Socio-Economic Impacts of Artisanal and Small-Scale Mining in Developing Countries* (London: Taylor & Francis, 2003)

[105] G.M. Hilson, *supra* n. 104.

[106] G.M. Hilson and O. Maponga, 'How has a shortage of census and geological information impeded the regularization of artisanal and small-scale mining?' (2004) 28(1) *Natural Resources Forum* 22–33.

[107] S.M. Banchirigah, 'How have reforms fuelled the expansion of artisanal mining? Evidence from sub-Saharan Africa' (2006) 31 *Resources Policy* 165–171; G.M. Hilson and N. Yakovleva, 'Strained relations: A critical analysis of the mining conflict in Prestea, Ghana' (2007) 26 *Political Geography* 98–119.

[108] L. Zeilig, 'Crisis, resistance and the failed rebellion in the Democratic Republic of Congo' in N. Vidal with P. Chabal (eds.), *Southern Africa: Civil Society, Politics and Donor Strategies – Angola and its neighbours – South Africa, Namibia, Mozambique, Democratic Republic of Congo and Zimbabwe* (Luanda and Lisbon: Media XXI & Firmamento, 2009), pp. 223–238.

[109] World Bank, 'Democratic Republic of Congo: Growth with Governance in the Mining Sector', Report No. 43402-ZR, May 2008, Oil/Gas, Mining and Chemicals Department.

[110] DFID, *supra* n. 7.

[111] ICGLR (International Conference on the Great Lakes Region), 'Newsletter on the ICGLR Regional Initiative in Natural Resources (RINR)', 3rd edn., February 2012, available at: https://icglr.org/IMG/pdf/RINR_NEWSLETTER_EN_3_FEB_2012_2_.pdf (accessed 16 July 2012).

zone for artisanal exploitation. Areas covered by a valid mining title cannot be converted into artisanal mining zones, and artisanal mining zones cannot receive a mining title for industrial mining though the security of tenure is not adequately protected for artisanal mining zones. These provisions appear to be inappropriate as few Artisanal Mining Exploration Cards are issued[112] and designated artisanal mining areas were not created in the Kivu provinces until recently, largely due to the lack of resources and capacity of the relevant authorities, exacerbated by the distance from the capital and the absence of infrastructure.[113] While at least 13 artisanal mining zones have been created in the Kivu provinces recently, it is unlikely that artisanal miners will develop these sites given the fact that necessary information, resources and technical skills to do so are not widely available.[114] In fact, allocating artisanal mining areas on potentially lucrative deposits would contradict the Mining Code, which is drafted by the World Bank, to facilitate economic reform through attracting large mining investments.[115]

Consequently, these inadequate provisions for artisanal mining encourage fraud and leave the artisanal mining sector illegal and unregulated without providing any legal protection for artisanal mining communities.[116] Though the presence of military and security forces in mines is clearly forbidden in the Mining Code, illegal taxation by armed groups and the national army at various road blocks is common[117] which threatens the effectual implementation of the due diligence schemes, such as the iTSCi bag and tag system. While the iTSCi system has been incorporated into other programmes like the SfH and CFTI, the need for the iTSCi to have onsite monitoring reduces its scalability.[118] A study conducted in 2010[119] also pointed out the lack of capacity on the ground to differentiate sources

---

[112]   S. Geenen, 'A dangerous bet: The challenges of formalizing artisanal mining in the Democratic Republic of Congo' (2012) 37(3) *Resource Policy* 322–330; D. Johnson and A. Tegera, *supra* n. 100; PACT, *supra* n. 102.

[113]   S. Geenen, *supra* n. 112; D. Johnson and A. Tegera, *supra* n. 100; B. Radley, 'What needs to be done to improve the working conditions and quality of life for people working at or near the bottom of the mineral supply chain in the Kivus? Part I', *Kivu Mining*, 19 June 2012, available at: http://kivumining.org/2012/06/19/what-needs-to-be-done-to-improve-the-working-condi tions-and-quality-of-life-for-those-working-at-or-near-the-bottom-of-the-mineral-supply-chain-in-the-kivus/ (accessed 25 July 2012).

[114]   PACT, *supra* n. 102, pp. 52–53.

[115]   Personal interview, Artisanal mining expert, Stoke-on-Trent, 25 September 2009.

[116]   N. Garrett, 'The Extractive Industries Transparency Initiatives (EITI) & Artisanal and Small-Scale Mining (ASM): Preliminary Observations from the Democratic Republic of the Congo (DRC)', Draft Report, 22 October 2007, available at: http://eiti.org/files/Garrett_EITI_10_2007. pdf (accessed 22 January 2010).

[117]   'The Hill belongs to Them: The Need for International Action on Congo's Conflict Mineral Trade', Report of the Global Witness Organisation, December 2010, pp. 23–25.

[118]   E. Blackmore and C. Holzman with A. Buxton, 'Scaling up certification in artisanal and small-scale mining: Innovations for inclusivity', *IIED (International Institute of Environment and Development) Linking Worlds Working Paper No. 2*, 2013, p. 13.

[119]   'Tracing a Path Forward: A Study of the Challenges of the Supply Chain for Target Metals Used in Electronics', Report by Resolve, April 2010.

of minerals and to ensure independence from operations which may support warring groups as one of the major challenges to achieve traceability in the DRC.

Moreover and most importantly, artisanal mining communities do not benefit from the trade of their products as the powerful trading houses, linked to the web of vested interests in the DRC and beyond, control the access to international buyers and markets. On the contrary, the communities suffer from environmental damage, socio-economic problems and insecurity.[120] The existing human rights due diligence processes to secure conflict-free minerals appear to be weak without addressing the largely illegal and informal status of artisanal mining in the DRC and 'social upgrading, or the concerns for the livelihoods of artisanal miners in the Congo'.[121]

5. IMPLICATIONS OF THE HUMAN RIGHTS DUE DILIGENCE INITIATIVES

The development of human rights due diligence frameworks, the Dodd-Frank Act in particular, has led to a concern that the requirement for due diligence will result in an embargo on sourcing minerals from the region as an easier option to achieve a conflict-free supply chain. This *de facto* ban on minerals from the DRC and its neighbouring countries is believed to cause unintended and undesirable outcomes on the already very limited livelihood of the local population, who have been suffering from the continuous conflict and insecurity in the area.[122] There are an estimated 200,000 to 300,000 artisanal miners operating on a regular, seasonal or supplementary basis in the Kivu provinces.[123] In fact, a *de facto* embargo on minerals from the eastern DRC was observed after 2010, and many actors in the mining sector have been forced to move to other areas such as Katanga Province in the southeast[124] or to seek illegal parallel markets.[125] While the *de facto* embargo is often attributed to the Dodd-Frank Act,[126] it is not clear to what extent the Dodd-frank Act or other schemes have caused the decrease in the mineral trade from the DRC.

There was an expectation that the minerals that are verified as conflict-free through the verification schemes can fetch better prices and thereby benefit the

---

[120] D. Johnson and A. Tegera, *supra* n. 101.
[121] N.D.S. Sarkar, 'Blood on your mobile phone? Capturing the gains for artisanal miners, poor workers and women', Capturing the Gains Briefing Note 2, February 2011, available at: http://ssrn.com/abstract=1990229 (accessed 4 June 2013).
[122] N. Garrett and H. Mitchell, *supra* n. 7; M. Smith, *supra* n. 56; S.B. Young, *supra* n. 55, p. 136.
[123] PACT, *supra* n. 102.
[124] SOMO, 'Roundtable on Conflict Minerals Legislation: Towards prevention of trade in conflict minerals and promotion of trade in clean minerals from Congo', European Parliament, Brussels, 26 May 2011; 'DRC: The Mineral Curse', Report by the Pole Institute, October 2011, pp. 30–34.
[125] E. Kajemba, 'A Congolese perspective on legislation', in SOMO, *supra* n. 124, pp. 9–10.
[126] SOMO, *supra* n. 124.

artisanal mining community. However, the recent visit to the eastern DRC by the PPA revealed that the tagged minerals receive 'a fair market price' and that untagged minerals are highly discounted because it is illegal to export them.[127] In addition, stockpiles are not considered to be conflict-free if they are not tagged and, therefore, cannot be sold, or will be sold at much lower prices. The vulnerable status of artisanal miners means that the lower prices received for untagged minerals by traders will be passed on to artisanal miners and others at the extraction stage, hence adversely affecting their economic conditions. Moreover, any endeavour to regulate artisanal mining and trade through due diligence, or to change any aspects of the existing systems within the mining sector, will impact on or exclude some vested interests and is, therefore, likely to meet strong resistance. If such tensions are not managed carefully, these reforms could result in provoking or intensifying violence and conflict in the area, rather than reducing the conflict and the predatory exploitation of minerals.[128] Artisanal miners and others at the extraction stage may face even more severe exploitation as a consequence.[129]

Most importantly, even if the challenges to perform due diligence in the area are met, it is not likely that the application of due diligence alone will delink the mineral extraction and trade from the violent conflict in the eastern DRC. This is because warring parties may easily diversify their sources of funding and other industries and companies may continue sourcing from these regions.[130] Furthermore, the dynamics of the mining sector and conflict on the ground[131] are largely neglected in the design of various due diligence schemes. The relationship between the conflict and mineral extraction and trade is much more complex than the prevailing simplistic view on conflict minerals,[132] which forms the basis of the human rights due diligence approach; however, there appears to be a grave limitation in the empirical analysis of the motivations and processes of conflict in the eastern DRC to corroborate such a linear hypothesis. For instance, in contrast to the assumption that it is the profit from minerals which drives and sustains the violent conflict, the military strategy to control mineral-rich areas can be an attempt to deprive the opponent.[133] Armed groups also attempt to control the areas where they conquered.[134] The collaboration between opposing forces at mine sites is often interpreted as evidence of the economic interests of actors, regardless

---

[127] PPA, *supra* n. 89.
[128] PACT, *supra* n. 102, p. 9.
[129] N. Garrett and H. Mitchell, *supra* n. 7; S.B. Young, *supra* n. 55.
[130] N. Garrett and H. Mitchell, *supra* n. 7; S.B. Young, *supra* n. 55.
[131] R. Perks and K. Vlassenroot, *supra* n. 82; M. Taka, 'Coltan mining and the conflict in the eastern Democratic Republic of Congo (DRC)' in M. McIntosh and A. Hunter (eds.), *New Perspectives on Human Security* (Sheffield: Greenleaf Publishing, 2010); M. Taka, 'Conflict Coltan: Local and International Dynamics in the Democratic Republic of Congo', unpublished PhD thesis, 2011.
[132] M. Taka, 2010, *supra* n. 131; M. Taka, 2011, *supra* n. 131.
[133] M. Taka, 2011, *supra* n. 131.
[134] R. Perks and K. Vlassenroot, *supra* n. 82.

of the larger problem of poverty and the informal sector in the DRC.[135] Resource exploitation is not always motivated directly by military strategies or linked to conflict dynamics but serves various incentives in the socio-economic as well as political systems.[136] This is confirmed by interviews with local actors as they did not attribute the conflict in the eastern DRC to the mineral resources in the area but rather pointed out other causes, such as trade disputes, behind different conflicts around mines that they distinguish from one another.[137] The limited understanding of the dynamics and systems of mineral extraction and trade, which are part of the larger informal economy in the eastern DRC and beyond stems from the generalisation of the systems of exploitation and the narrow focus on mineral exploitation, based on the research conducted on a limited number of mine sites.

In addition, the historical context of the armed groups and conflict in the region has not been taken into account in the due diligence movement. The issues of migration, ethnicity, citizenship and land have been intertwined since the colonial period, creating grievances and insecurity, thereby replicating violence and conflict in the region. Without appreciating this long-standing, complex causality of violence and conflict, the efforts to mitigate the conflict through due diligence schemes may produce unintentional impacts on the local conflict dynamics. Moreover, the efforts by the international community to strengthen the state authority in the eastern DRC, where the experience with the state has been negative owing to corruption and state violence, worry local actors in the area.[138] There is a concern that strengthening the state in the area may shift the balance in the conflict and will not reduce conflict because the Congolese state historically distributed wealth to limited individuals, rather than to the general public.[139]

It can be argued that the neglect of the above socio-economic and political issues and the narrow, technical focus within the schemes are as a result of the externally driven nature of the conflict mineral agenda to secure ethically sourced conflict-free raw materials.[140] Moreover, principal actors from the upstream supply chain communities are excluded in the development of the due diligence schemes.[141] However, there is difficulty in consulting with these local stakeholders to gather their voices to help formulate effective policies and measures to improve the conditions on the ground. For example, most artisanal miners in the region are not organised to express their issues and concerns freely and constructively,[142] and where there are some artisanal mining cooperatives, these cooperatives have

---

[135]   M. Taka, 2011, *supra* n. 131.
[136]   R. Perks and K. Vlassenroot, *supra* n. 82.
[137]   M. Taka, 2011, *supra* n. 131.
[138]   P. Pöyhönen et al., *supra* n. 73.
[139]   D. Johnson D, *supra* n. 74.
[140]   *Ibid.*
[141]   *Ibid.*; R. Perks and K. Vlassenroot, *supra* n. 82.
[142]   N. Garrett, 'Observations from the DRC' (2008) 3(1) *African Analyst* 79–97.

different purposes and do not necessarily protect the interests of the miners.[143] There is also a question as to whether they have the capacity and resources to organise themselves so that they can manifest their views to influence the policies and measures that affect them.[144] Moreover, it is not realistic to consult armed groups despite their significant influence on the local conditions, since companies cannot be seen to be engaging with armed groups.

6.   CONCLUSIONS

This chapter reviewed the recent development of the human rights due diligence concept and the challenges and implications of applying the approach to conflict minerals supply chains from the DRC. Human rights due diligence as a process that seeks to 'do no harm,' in addition to complying with national laws, has become an important concept in the business and human rights literature and in the global economy. The increasing demand for critical minerals, which are essential for industries like the electronics industry, combined with the responsible supply chain management imperative, appear to be driving the due diligence mechanisms to source conflict-free minerals.

The initial concern for the *de facto* embargo on minerals from the DRC, which would affect the artisanal mining communities in the eastern DRC, seems to be addressed by the development of closed pipe supply chains such as the SfH and CFTI. While the closed pipe supply chains may offer a responsible supply chain management solution, badly needed by the electronics industry, security situations and the limited capacity of enforcement on the ground may hinder the progress of the programmes. The implementation of the human rights due diligence programmes on the ground requires strengthening the DRC government authority in the area; however, this may not improve the conditions on the ground. The limited focus of the due diligence mechanisms on traceability is not only effective in curbing finance for belligerents or in reducing conflict in the eastern DRC, but it will also not improve the livelihoods of the artisanal mining community and may affect the ongoing conflict in an unexpected way. The human rights due diligence programmes, therefore, need to be combined with broader efforts to improve the artisanal mining sector governance and the local socio-economic conditions.

---

[143]   PACT, *supra* n. 102; M. Taka, 2011, *supra* n. 131.
[144]   N. Garrett N, *supra* n. 142.

CHAPTER 9

THE PURSUIT OF SUBSTANTIVE CORPORATE HUMAN RIGHTS POLICIES

Matthew MULLEN

1.   INTRODUCTION

In order to meet their responsibility to respect human rights, businesses are to create corporate human rights policies (CHRPs). The United Nations' Guiding Principles on Business and Human Rights: Implementing the United Nations 'Protect, Respect and Remedy' Framework (A/HRC/17/31), establishes this much in Principles 15 and 16. However, it is unclear what makes a CHRP substantive, that is, what separates a CHRP that is just words and a policy that can improve a business' human rights footprint? This question is salient, as is the question of what is at stake. Could a substandard or unsubstantive CHRP actually do harm? Indeed, CHRPs could act as a smoke-screen – an illusion that a business is taking human rights seriously when it is not. This chapter argues that while the UN Guiding Principles on Human Rights and Business and accompanying resources set core expectations, empirical questions remain regarding the substance and implications of CHRPs. Accordingly, a recently launched project is underway to fill the gap left by 'no global and widely accepted process for companies to demonstrate whether their policies and processes are indeed aligned with the UN Guiding Principles and therefore capable of meeting their responsibility to respect human rights'.[1]

There appears to be cautious optimism surrounding CHRPs, in part, because the question of substance is prominent. This cautious optimism is illustrated by Margaret Jungk,[2] a member of the UN Working Group on Business and Human

---

[1]   Human Rights Resource Centre, 'Developing Global Standards for the Reporting and Assurance of Company Alignment with the UN Guiding Principles on Business and Human Rights' (2013), available at: http://hrrca.org/content/developing-global-standards-reporting-and-assurance-company-alignment-un-guiding-principles-. The project is officially supported by the UN Working Group on Business and Human Rights.
[2]   M. Jungk, 'Shareholder's Press McDonald's to Report Human Rights Impacts', *Huffington Post Business*, 22 May 2013, available at: www.huffingtonpost.com/margaret-jungk/mcdonalds-shareholders-no_b_3317423.html.

Rights, in her analysis of a proposed McDonald's shareholders' resolution to require McDonald's to assess and publicly report on its human rights impact:

> In the past, shareholder resolutions have asked companies to adopt a policy or establish a committee recognizing human rights, but haven't required companies to make sure they're implementing those policies. Nothing against policy commitments, but they're just a first step. This year's resolution asks McDonald's to go further than producing CEO-signed statements saying it will avoid negative human rights impacts.

Jungk's point highlights how meaningless an empty CHRP can be. A vague promise that a business cares about human rights is not a first step – it is a dead end. Based on a review of over 150 CHRPs, including twenty in-depth CHRP analyses, this chapter argues that the substance of a CHRP cannot be subjectively assessed; a framework with defined indicators is imperative. The human rights based approach (HRBA) provides such a framework. The HRBA framework offers appropriate and applicable indicators against which to assess CHRPs. Assessing the whole of business operations against this framework would be an overstep, but the role of CHRPs is specific. CHRPs are a map to a business' human rights arrangement; a map for internal and external rights holders. Assessing these policies against a framework that is 'normatively based on international human rights standards and operationally directed to promoting and protecting human rights,' as the HRBA is, makes sense virtuously and operationally.[3] That the HRBA is a fitting framework for assessing the substance of a CHRP is a message to heed inside and outside of businesses.

2. PRINCIPLE 16 IN CONTEXT

Principle 16 of the UN Guiding Principles on Business and Human Rights: Implementing the United Nations 'Protect, Respect and Remedy' Framework (A/HRC/17/31), along with accompanying guidance tools outline the necessary elements of a CHRP. Principle 16 provides elaboration on Principle 15(a) of A/HRC/17/31:

> 15. In order to meet their responsibility to respect human rights, business enterprises should have in place policies and processes appropriate to their size and circumstances, including:
> (a) A policy commitment to meet their responsibility to respect human rights [...]

---

[3] Office of the High Commissioner for Human Rights (OHCHR), 'Frequently Asked Questions on a Human Rights Based Approach to Development Cooperation' (New York and Geneva: United Nations, 2006).

CHRPs are obligatory in Principle 15(a), and this holds true for 'all business enterprises, both transnational and others, regardless of their size, sector, location, ownership and structure,' as is noted in the General Principles section of the UN Guiding Principles. The onus is on the business to actively draft and enact a CHRP. This onus treats businesses as responsible duty bearers that are capable of taking control of their own human rights footprint. In other words, the UNGP acknowledges, indeed stresses, the capacity of businesses to self regulate. Doing nothing is unacceptable, as is impromptu action on human rights. The commentary on Principle 15 presents CHRPs as a vehicle for businesses to communicate that they 'know and show that they respect human rights'.[4] This knowing and showing communicates an understanding of the rules or expectations. If a business misunderstands what is expected, the CHRP makes corrections possible before harm occurs. In this sense, CHRPs can be preventative.

Principle 15 makes a broad call for action that is then deconstructed in Principles 16. Principle 16 falls under part B of Operation Principles in Section II: The Corporate Responsibility to Respect Human Rights. Under the title of Policy Commitment, Principle 16 states:

> 16. As the basis for embedding their responsibility to respect human rights, business enterprises should express their commitment to meet this responsibility through a statement of policy that:
> (a) Is approved at the most senior level of the business enterprise;
> (b) Is informed by relevant internal and/or external expertise;
> (c) Stipulates the enterprise's human rights expectations of personnel, business partners and other parties directly linked to its operations, products or services;
> (d) Is publicly available and communicated internally and externally to all personnel, business partners and other relevant parties;
> (e) Is reflected in operational policies and procedures necessary to embed it throughout the business enterprise.

Principle 16 captures the importance of CHRPs as mechanisms that embed business' responsibility to respect. Far from imposing a narrow definition of CHRPs, Principle 16 encompasses any kind of public publishing of its 'responsibilities, commitments, and expectations'.[5] Clearly, different businesses require different types of statements. Each business possesses unique duties, administrative procedures, and issues of concern based on their specific business operations. Accordingly, each business needs a customised CHRP. A corporation and company firm will have very different CHRPs, as will small, local businesses

---

[4]   Office of the High Commissioner for Human Rights (OHCHR), 'Guiding Principles on Business and Human Rights: Implementing the United Nations "Protect, Respect and Remedy" Framework' (New York and Geneva: United Nations, 2011), p. 16.

[5]   *Ibid.*, p. 16.

and large, transnational businesses. Principle 16 recognises and accepts the need for endless diversity.

Customised CHRPs are possible because the minimum expectations, set in paragraphs (a) through (e) of Principle 16, are basic and broad. The universal applicability of these minimum expectations allow for Principle 16 to be applied to any business, regardless of whether it is a company, corporation, firm, partnership, sole proprietorship, or otherwise. All of these businesses are to meet the same standard, as these standards can be adapted circumstantially. Take, for instance, paragraph (a), calling for the head individual(s) of the business to authorise the policy. What constitutes the head(s) of the company will vary based on the businesses structure and legal arrangement, but authorisation from the head(s) is universally possible. Paragraphs (b) and (c) leave it to each business to find experts to inform their policy and set internal regulations. There is no dictation of how this must be done, allowing each business to fit their own circumstances. Paragraph (d) suggests that CHRPs should be open access, and the commentary notes that the policy should be 'communicated actively to entities with which the enterprise has contractual relationships; others directly linked to its operations, which may include State security forces; investors; and, in the case of operations with significant human rights risks, to the potentially affected stakeholders'.[6] It is up to each business to define who is a stakeholder with who needs to be communicated to.

Paragraph (e) focuses on internal implementation. As the commentary notes, this requires internalisation of the policy to include awareness building, training, and the implementation of policies and procedures that 'should make clear what the lines and systems of accountability will be.' Businesses can set their own system and communicate this internally as they see fit, so long as they do have this system, with said moving parts, and do raise awareness. The Principle 16 commentary concludes with a reiteration of the importance of internalisation and implementation of CHRPs. The commentary states:

> Just as States should work towards policy coherence, so business enterprises need to strive for coherence between their responsibility to respect human rights and policies and procedures that govern their wider business activities and relationships [...] Through these and any other appropriate means, the policy statement should be embedded from the top of the business enterprise through all its functions, which otherwise may act without awareness or regard for human rights.[7]

The language in the commentary related to internalisation, including accountability, is advisory – 'should.' The importance of implementation is not

---

6   *Ibid.*, p. 17.
7   *Ibid.*

lost in this, but the wording is not forceful. Here one can observe a reluctance to be too assertive in telling business how to meet their UN Guiding Principle obligations. Simply put, Principle 16 sets the standard and leaves it to each business to determine how they reach these minimum expectations. This adaptability allows for universal application. Yet it also reflects a hedge that orients towards consensus, rather than imposition. Relevantly, Deva declares: 'the consensus rhetoric partly explains why the GPs have treated human rights too lightly'.[8]

3. ENSURING SUBSTANCE

A CHRP may appear to be compliant with principle 16 but still lack substance. This is not necessarily the fault of Principle 16 or the UN General Principles. Rather, this is the reality of implementing human rights principles and standards. Resistance, interpretation, ulterior motives, and other dynamics can undermine completely the purpose or spirit of the original content. Given the flexibility that is built into Principle 16, businesses may find ways to draft a human rights policy that has all of the prescribed moving parts, but has no meaningful function. Businesses may have reasons to avoid a substantive CHRP. If done correctly, a CHRP may expose businesses and require businesses to continuously adapt and invest time, attention and resources. Accordingly, businesses may be inclined to go through the motions and avoid a substantive policy. Simply put, there is real risk that businesses go through the motions and adopt a CHRP that improves a business's public image, but does nothing to improve the business's impact on human rights.

An empty CHRP may seem harmless. However, these types of policies and pledges can be significantly detrimental. They can give the impression that something is happening when nothing is. In other words, empty CHRPs can act as smoke-screens; as a cover for businesses to point to when asked about human rights. Indeed, the worst case scenario from a human rights perspective is a CHRP that acts as a barrier protecting businesses from inquiring stakeholders. Facilitating such inquiry is precisely the role of CHRPs.

Are the UN Guiding Principles minimum expectations too low to ensure substance? The UN Global Compact *Guide on How to Develop a Human Rights Policy* notes:

> A human rights policy can take many forms and has no uniform definition. At a minimum, it is a public statement adopted by the company's highest governing authority committing the company to respect international human rights

---

[8]   S. Deva, 'Treating human rights lightly: a critique of the consensus rhetoric and the language employed by the Guiding Principles' in S. Deva and D. Bilchitz (eds.), *Human Rights Obligations of Business: Beyond the Corporate Responsibility to Protect* (Cambridge: Cambridge University Press, 2012), p. 80.

standards and to do so by having policies and processes in place to identify, prevent or mitigate human rights risks, and remediate any adverse impact it has caused or contributed to. It should explicitly use the words 'human rights'.[9]

There are obvious questions regarding CHRPs that provide nothing more than a broad commitment to human rights and a mention of the policies and processes the business undertakes relative to human rights.[10] Even if adopted by the highest governing authority of the business, and even if external expertise is utilised, a broad commitment to human rights may be nothing more than words. A commitment that has no specific application has no practical meaning.[11] An apt example of this comes from Article 8 of the Democratic Republic of Korea's Socialist Constitution: 'The State respects and protects the human rights of the workers, peasants and working intellectuals who have been freed from exploitation and oppression and have become masters of the State and society.' Even the most heart-felt claim of devotion can be empty. The Global Compact expresses an alternative angle on this when noting that a statement 'signals a commitment to take respect for human rights sufficiently seriously to allocate management time and resources to developing and implementing a policy, including by consulting externally'.[12] This sentiment assumes that businesses are drafting a human rights policy to improve their human rights footprint. In many cases, this may be true. However, assuming or trusting the motivations of those holding positions of power is risky. Regardless of how sincere the language may seem, unspecific and unsubstantiated words on a page may be nothing more than just that. Deva recalls that certain verbiage may be used in the business-human rights interface to limit requisite behaviour: 'It is argued that a deliberate use of carefully chose terms (e.g. 'responsibility' rather than 'duty'; 'impact' rather than 'violation') and concepts (e.g. social expectations and due diligence) has the effect of rolling back the legal concretization of corporate human rights obligations'.[13] Even if external parties assist in developing the policy, there are always questions regarding the role and influence these experts and other stakeholders may have in the process. Hence, there is no way to guarantee that a CHRP is a 'precursor to a company's commitment to support human rights'.[14]

---

[9]   UN Global Compact, *Guide on How to Develop a Human Rights Policy*, 2011, p. 4.
[10]   There are some specifics that are expected of even the broadest CHRP: 'A good human rights policy should at a minimum refer to: the Universal Declaration of Human Rights; the International Covenant on Civil and Political Rights; the International Covenant on Economic; Social and Cultural Rights; and the International Labour Organization's (ILO) Declaration on Fundamental Principles and Rights at Work' (The Global Compact, 2011), p. 15.
[11]   U. Wynhoven, 'Commentary on the Importance of a Human Rights Policy Statement', Policy and Legal Office of the United Nations Global Compact, May 2010.
[12]   L. Amis, 'A Guide for Business: How to Develop a Human Rights Policy', United Nations Global Compact Office and Office of the High Commissioner on Human Rights, 2011, p. 4.
[13]   S. Deva, *supra* n. 8, p. 80.
[14]   L. Amis, *supra* n. 12, p. 4.

Neither broad human rights commitments nor brief mentions of internal human rights policies and processes ensure appropriate action. Such a CHRP does not require businesses to deliberately position themselves as duty bearers, nor does it specify the position of rights holders. Stakeholders are given no direction as to how to act on their questions or concerns. The statement is an end in itself. Such a CHRP may very well be used to protect a business' public image or to deflect human rights inquiries. This seems to be the worst case scenario for human rights; CHRPs become a means of self-protection and self-promotion for business.

A CHRP that moves beyond rhetoric and provides information about taking action is a step in the right direction. Kathryn Dovey observes: 'Without such practical implementation, there is a risk that business operations will not have the guidance they need and from the outside the policy may not stand up to scrutiny as a real commitment to human rights.'[15] Even when CHRPs explain to stakeholders how they may use or act on the policy, concerns regarding substance remain. A CHRP may confuse stakeholders, or may guide stakeholders to processes or procedures that fail to produce results. Many CHRPs declare the business' commitment to due diligence and remediation – as prescribed by Principle 15 of the UN Guiding Principles, but provide no specifics or channels for inquiry. Due diligence and remediation require processes and procedures. How accessible are these activities? Who are they accessible to? Do they provide substantive solutions or recourse? In fact, do these channels lead anywhere? Internal procedures or processes can certainly lead in circles or shuffle stakeholders to various dead ends. Procedures can be made deliberately complex to deter usage. Ideally, CHRPs would guide internal and external stakeholders to clear, accountability driven procedures, but this is rarely the case.

A range of other concerns regarding the substance of CHRPs remain. For instance, on the issue of public access, do policies reach the most impacted or concerned people? Is there any means of ensuring this? On the business's internal behaviour and conduct programme, does this mean changes in words and trainings, or changes in actual conditions? Has the business' level of compliance with human rights actually improved? In all, CHRPs may fulfil the criteria of Principle 16 without answering fundamental questions about how rights holders can exercise their rights relative to the operations of the business. Accordingly, a separate framework is needed to assess the substance of a CHRP; a framework that may help identify and assess the human rights impact, including violations, of corporate behaviour.

---

[15] K. Dovey, 'Commentary on Building a Strong Human Rights Policy from Within', *Global Business Initiative on Human Rights*, May 2010.

4. ASSESSING THE SUBSTANCE OF CHRPs THROUGH HRBA INDICATORS

The human rights based approach (HRBA) provides indicators that culminate to an appropriate and applicable framework against which CHRPs can be assessed. Such a framework gives the debate over what makes a CHRP substantive needed direction. Stakeholders need not relegate to the notion that substance is endlessly subjective, paralysing any chance to move beyond the minimum expectations of the UNGP. There may well be various assessment frameworks available, but the HRBA seems an ideal option. The very purpose of the HRBA is to assess the human rights orientation of policies and initiatives. The rationale behind applying the HRBA is, thus, both intrinsic and instrumental.[16] The argument here is straightforward: a CHRP can be considered legitimately substantive to the extent that it meets the indicators of the the HRBA.

This is not to imply that businesses ought to meet the HRBA in all facets of their operations. Businesses are not states, nor development agencies. The HRBA was developed to guide the behaviour of states and development organisations. The OHCHR specifies that the HRBA is a requisite framework applying to UN development agencies and states under their voluntary subscription to international human rights law: 'United Nations development agencies and other "subjects of international law" are legally bound to respect, and operate within the confines established by, the international legal obligations voluntarily entered into by States, including those relating to human rights respect, and operate within the confines established by, the international legal obligations voluntarily entered into by States, including those relating to human rights'.[17] The normative application of the HRBA is not fixed. Offenheiser and Holcombe discuss the extension of the HRBA to the private sector, to include non-profit and voluntary sectors working on development.[18] Extending this application to all business operations would be an overstep. Businesses need only comply with human rights. Human rights compliance is one of myriad tasks facing businesses. CHRPs deal with this particular task. It is, thus, appropriate to expect, indeed demand, that CHRPs are human rights based; that CHRPs meet normative human rights standards of operationalisation. In practical terms this means assessing CHRPs against a framework that is 'normatively based on international human rights standards and operationally directed to promoting and protecting human rights' as the HRBA is.[19] Indeed, a CHRP that is inspired or guided by the HRBA is bound to result in positive changes within a business and gain positive attention

---

[16]   Office of the High Commissioner for Human Rights, *supra* n. 3, p. 16.
[17]   *Ibid.*, p. 21.
[18]   R. Offenheiser and S. Holcombe, 'Challenges and Opportunities in Implementing a Rights-Based Approach to Development: An Oxfam America Perspective' (2003) 32(2) *Nonprofit and Voluntary Sector Quarterly* 268–301.
[19]   Office of the High Commissioner for Human Rights, *supra* n. 3, p. 15.

from many angles. Shifting from the why of filtering CHRPs through the HRBA indicators to the 'how', this section investigates the application of relevant HRBA indicators and presents empirical examples therein. A brief review of relevant indicators is in place.

Results based: A key feature of the HRBA is its results orientation. The focus is on the output or outcome, specifically the empirical improvement of human rights. The HRBA is searching for strong and convincing evidence of outcomes. Kathryn Dovey, director of the Global Business Initiative on Human Rights, declares: 'The most important element of a human rights policy is its effect upon company practice and what happens once it has been finalized.'[20] The improvement of human rights is very much a process, but results are the only way to empirically measure if the process is working.

An exceptional picture of what a results based CHRP could look like comes from Apple Inc. There may be pushes behind this orientation, given the unfavourable coverage that Apple received when news of the brutal conditions at Foxconn, then an Apple manufacturer, surfaced. Nonetheless, the detail and data provided is a useful reference point. This content is not part of a policy per se, rather it is simply titled 'Labour and Human Rights' on its webpage. The page states:

> In 2012, we expanded that program and tracked work hours weekly for over 1 million employees, publishing the data every month. As a result of this effort, our suppliers have achieved an average of 92 percent compliance across all work weeks, and the average hours worked per week was under 50.

The results orientation of a CHRP does not have to function on moving from non-compliance to compliance. Nor should it only occur after human rights failures have been exposed. Even if a business has a good human rights footprint, their CHRP can keep stakeholders up to date on what they have accomplished, what they hope to accomplish next, and whether they are on track to accomplish those outcomes.

Identification of rights holders and duty bearers: The HRBA requires the explicit recognition of duty bearers and rights holders. The onus would be on business, as the duty bearer, to recognise itself as the duty bearer. It must specify its obligations and recognise rights holders (and their entitlements). This is not exactly straightforward, because businesses have a responsibility to respect all human rights of everyone, everywhere. However, the HRBA calls for a focus on the most relevant rights holders and their rights. Specifically, the HRBA promotes the prioritisation of the rights of those individuals and communities that may be most impacted or marginalised as a result of business operations. These marginalised rights holders and their rights are to receive the most attention.

---

[20]   K. Dovey, *supra* n. 15.

Those rights holders whose rights are feasibly threatened by business operations should be recognised. Because this identification process can be difficult, it is useful to employ input from internal and external stakeholders.

The HRBA seeks not only commitments to human rights, but an ownership of the role of duty bearer by businesses. Moreover, the HRBA implies explicit positioning of rights holders (and their entitlements). The research did not reveal any CHRP that fulfilled this prescription. However, there are some useful examples to point to. The wording in Johnson & Johnson's policy explicitly articulates how the company understands its position as duty bearer, stating: 'As a corporation, Johnson & Johnson has a responsibility to respect these rights, and especially those of the more than one billion people we touch with our products and services each day, including our employees and the people who support our businesses.' Nestlé presents a similar articulation. Rio Tinto takes a good first step in recognising that its business operations have a significant impact on indigenous peoples. However, the policy fails to address indigenous peoples as rights holders, nor does it refer to the most pressing questions about Rio Tinto's impact on these communities. Rather, the policy reads:

> We respect the diversity of indigenous peoples, acknowledging the unique and important interests that they have in the land, waters and environment as well as their history, culture and traditional ways. Wherever we operate, we engage with communities and seek to understand the social, cultural, environmental and economic implications of our activities, so that we can respond to concerns and work to optimise benefits and reduce negative impacts, both for the local community and for the overall economy. We believe that this contribution to development, together with our community engagement programmes (which may include enterprise development, training, employment, community-based health and social and cultural heritage initiatives), can further contribute to the realisation of human rights.

CHRPs should be 'holistic.' John Ruggie countered the notion that businesses have a limited impact on human rights when stating:

> Companies can affect the entire spectrum of internationally recognized human rights, not only a limited subset [...] Therefore, the quest to construct ex ante a delimited list of business specific rights for which companied would have some responsibility is a fool's errand. Virtually all rights are relevant, though some may be more so than others in particular circumstances. This fact needs to inform the policies of states and companies alike.[21]

---

[21] J. Ruggie, 'Opening Remarks: Consultation on operationalizing the framework for business and human rights presented by the Special Representative of the Secretary General on the issue of human rights and transnational corporations and other business enterprises', 5–6 October 2009, Geneva.

CHRPs ought to address direct and periphery impacts. As John Ruggie observed above, there is little point in trying to cover everything. However, there are ramifications associated with adopting to narrow of a lens. A CHRP with a holistic view, thus, acknowledges direct and indirect human rights issues (both geographic and thematic).

Rev. David Schilling, Director of Human Rights at the Interfaith Center on Corporate Responsibility observed:

> First, many corporations have adopted policies that only cover a small range of human rights, most often human rights focused on the workplace. Policies need to be based on human rights as spelled out in the Universal Declaration of Human Rights, the International Covenants on Economic, Social and Cultural Rights and Civil and Political Rights and the International Labor Organization's core labour standards, while recognizing that a company will focus primarily on those rights most directly and indirectly impacted by corporate activities.[22]

Kinross Gold takes an interesting approach to accomplishing a holistic view. They present a table displaying eight rights topics, accompanied by one column describing the potential areas of risk and one column presenting applicable Kinross policies or standards.

The use of international standards and norms: this HRBA indicator is quite straightforward. The CHRP and any associated processes should be based on international human rights law. International human rights standards and instruments are the benchmark against which everything should be tested. The Global Compact strongly advises that businesses explicitly refer to the Universal Declaration of Human Rights: the International Covenant on Civil and Political Rights; the International Covenant on Economic; Social and Cultural Rights; and the International Labour Organization's (ILO) Declaration on Fundamental Principles and Rights at Work'.[23] ABB's CHRP, for example, refers to all of the above, as well as the OECD Guidelines for Multinational Enterprises.

One issue that does need addressing is the suggestion that local laws comes before a business's commitment to international human rights, as can be seen in the JP Morgan Chase CHRP which states: 'Where local law conflicts with the principles contained in this Human Rights Statement, JPMorgan Chase complies with local requirements while, at the same time, seeking ways to uphold the principles set forth in this Human Rights Statement.'

Participation/inclusion: A policy that is not operationally participatory or inclusive neglects the very individuals and communities it should be in place to benefit. The HRBA calls for participation/inclusion in both the drafting and

---

[22]   D. Schilling, 'Commentary on Adopting and Implementing Corporate Human Rights Policies. Interfaith Center on Corporate Responsibility', May 2010.
[23]   The Global Compact, *supra* n. 10, p. 15.

implementation of policies. This may mean different things in different contexts. This may entail the involvement of workers or worker representatives, the inclusion of different sector managers, impacted communities, consumers or even the involvement of civil society. The level and type of participation depends on the nature of the business. Here, the HRBA provides a similar framework to the UN Guiding Principles, which 'offer[s] a sliding-scale approach for corporation based on their size, and, ostensibly, their location'.[24] This makes participation perhaps the hardest indicator to define for CHRPs. It is nonetheless important as it 'reflect[s] the consensus between those whose rights are violated and those with a duty to act'.[25] Along these lines Kathryn Dovey observes: 'Also important is how the policy is formulated: within which business units, through consultation with communities and human rights experts or through dialogue with engaged investors.'[26] Hence, levels of participation or inclusion are correlative to a CHRP's probable substance.

Most CHRPs express some kind of commitment to stakeholder participation or engagement processes. The policies that are most in line with the HRBA are those that give specific details. A number of policies discuss collaboration with established human rights institutes. Eni, for instance, refers to its collaborations with the Danish Institute for Human Rights and the Business and Human Rights Project, IPIECA. Microsoft does not provide extensive details, but its CHRP explains the establishment of a Center on Technology and Human Rights, which promotes dialogue and cooperation. Nestle provides extensive information, breaking down its stakeholder engagement process pillar by pillar. While the quality of such inclusion efforts is difficult to determine through a CHRP, such descriptions are a good first step.

Transparency, to include accessibility: Transparency has an empowering effect. Transparency refers to a range of things. An important element of transparency is the accessibility of information. Accessibility is particularly important for the most impacted or concerned rights holders. If a CHRP is only available in English or requires access to the web, the most relevant stakeholders may be barred. Thus, the availability and distribution of the policy and other relevant information is crucial. If information is missing or unavailable transparency is not present. Dually important is the clarity of information. CHRPs that are too complex to follow are opaque. Thus, legal or business jargon may bar access. Policies can also be too broad or simplistic, or incomplete. The gauge of transparency is uncomplicated. Is the necessary information available, accessible, and actionable – can rights holders use it? If policies leave rights holders with questions and nowhere to turn, that policy likely lacks transparency.

---

[24]   R. Blitt, 'Beyond Ruggie's Guiding Principles on Business and Human Rights: Charting an Embracive Approach to Corporate Human Rights Compliance' (2012) 48(33) *Texas International Law Journal* 33–62, 43.

[25]   Office of the High Commissioner for Human Rights, *supra* n. 3, p. 17.

[26]   K. Dovey, *supra* n. 15.

A number of businesses adopted measures to make their CHRPs more user-friendly. For instance, Adidas' CHRP breaks out information into frequently asked questions, which is easy to navigate. Moreover, Adidas provides links for further information and additional questions. Gap Inc. provides individual contact information in their HR policy: 'Questions related to this policy should be directed to Kindley Walsh Lawlor, Vice President of Social and Environmental Responsibility, via social_responsibility@gap.com.' Such personal contact points literally give CHRPs life. As stated above, language is a significant determinant of accessibility. Numerous companies referred specifically to language and distribution. BNY Mellon states: 'We are happy to publish our human rights policy in every country in which we operate. We endeavour to make sure all our employees are aware of their rights, not matter where in the world they work with us.' Pepsico notes that its CHRP is available in 40 languages. In addition to the accessibility of the CHRP itself, full transparency requires easy access to inquiries. ABB provides a notable example of this, stating: 'Contact details are published on ABB's internal and external websites.' While short of providing names and personal emails, as above, ABB provides stakeholders with clear direction. Perhaps the most substantive display of transparency in a CHRP is when a business publishes its shortcomings. This is rare, but there was one example that surfaced during the research, AstraZeneca. Openness and honesty of this magnitude signals to rights holders and investors alike that a business is ready and willing to change.

Accountability: Without accessible accountability, CHRPs serve no purpose for rights holders. Accountability ensures compliance. This entails proactive and reactive measures, both of which should be covered in the CHRP. Businesses are obligated to create due diligence and remediation processes and procedures. The task of CHRPs is to make a business' accountability channels available. A policy need not describe the whole system. In practical terms, this would mean the CHRP would direct those who want to voice concern, make a complaint, contribute information, or otherwise contribute in due diligence in the appropriate direction. For remediation, an accountability-oriented CHRP would explain to concerned individuals or authorities what departments or individuals they ought to contact, whether that be the legal department or another capable contact person. Additional, because accountability is not merely reacting, CHRPs should describe and make accessible the process of monitoring that lends to proactive and ongoing accountability.

Lest this suggest that all businesses be expected to display equally extensive accountability strategies, Blitt reminds us: '[A]ny human rights policy commitment, due diligence process, or relevant remediation process is expected to be more rigorous where the corporation is larger, a greater risk of a more severe human rights impact appears, or additional national human rights obligations be in play. Conversely, smaller businesses that may be operating in less controversial areas are subject to a less rigorous compliance standard under the Guiding Principle'.[27] Regardless of whether the business in question is big or small, domestic or transnational, a company, a corporation firm, a limited-liability corporation, a partnership, or otherwise, stakeholders can judge whether they believe the accountability activities outlined in the CHRP are appropriate.

Many CHRPs refer to due diligence or remediation, but provide minimal information about how to access those channels. A number of favourable examples break this trend. Adidas Group provides an extensive overview about how Adidas addresses human rights complaints. The procedure is discussed in detail. Information about how to access these channels is provided, and Adidas refers to ongoing monitoring. Goodyear and Johnson and Johnson are two businesses that discuss accountability in detail. They also refer readers to the California Transparency in Supply Chain Act, to which they have to disclose information. This notice of a binding and enforceable accountability mechanism can be used by rights holders and those working on their behalf. Starbucks' CHRP is notable for its language urging employees to make complaints whenever a violation of the policy is witnessed. The guidance on how to do this is notable as Starbucks informs employees that '[s]uch a report, preferably in writing, can be made by following the company's Anti-Harassment / Anti-Retaliation Compliant Procedure or the Standards of Business Conduct.'

Sustainability: 'Transforming existing distributions of power – the cornerstone of a human rights-based approach – is not without its challenges. Historical lack of power can be socialized and concealed within, crippling people's propensity and ability to accept that they have rights and to claim them'.[28] The HRBA is fundamentally about sustainability, based on the premise that human rights are the only trajectory that is truly sustainable. CHRPs often refer to sustainability, but no CHRP reviewed during this research articulated the type of sustainability orientation sought by the HRBA. Sustainability in the context of the HRBA is not only about fixing existing problems or predicting future challenges; it asks what changes need to occur to ensure the human rights of all rights holders in the long term. This may mean addressing marginalisation that currently benefits the business' bottom line. The value added here may not be seen as such by those at the board meetings of businesses. In a CHRP, those pushing for human rights seek a long term vision of human rights that shows a willingness to address a business's role in marginalisation, whether it be pay structures, workplace conditions, the exploitation of legal gaps or the exploitation of communities. In this last indicator one can see the paradigmatic shift that CHRPs can compel around business and within them.

---

[27]   R. Blitt, *supra* n. 24, p. 48.
[28]   Office of the High Commissioner for Human Rights, *supra* n. 3, p. 18.

5. CONCLUSION: STEPPING STRATEGICALLY, BUT ASSERTIVELY

From a human rights perspective, a substantive CHRP is certainly worth the cost for businesses. Businesses may not, however, share the same opinion, as was displayed in the case of the proposed McDonald's shareholder's resolution to require McDonald's to assess and publicity report on its human rights. McDonald's presented a proxy statement dissuading shareholders to vote against the resolution. Jungk (2013) cites the proxy statement as saying '[i]n light of McDonald's unwavering commitment to human rights and ongoing reporting in this regard, we believe the additional reporting requested by the proposal is unnecessary [...] We further believe that the proposal represents the potential for a diversion of resources with no corresponding benefit to the Company, our customers or our shareholders.' Jungk summarised this position: 'In other words, respecting human rights costs money and provides no benefits'.[29] Jungk predicted that the resolution would not pass, but positioned the resolution as a positive development nonetheless, stating:

> Make no mistake: This resolution is probably going to lose [...] last week, Halliburton rejected a nearly identical shareholder resolution. And that's OK. More resolutions like these will be filed with other companies next year, and the next. These principles, now established, will be taken up by consumers, governments and employees. This pressure isn't going away. Whenever I talk to businesses, they tell me that identifying and reporting their human rights impacts is hard. It sure is. But so is serving millions of hamburgers every day. I like to think that sometime in the future, companies won't be able to do the latter without the former.[30]

The resolution was rejected at the shareholder gathering with 70% of shareholders voting against it. The chief executive of McDonald's reportedly argued 'that the reality of McDonald's adding more fruit and vegetables to its menu, complying with voluntary guidelines for marketing to children and supporting Ronald McDonald House Charities did not match the pressure group's depiction of the company as an irresponsible corporate citizen'.[31] The question for human rights practitioners and advocates is how hard to push. Expecting businesses to go too far on their CHRPs may cause resistance, if not backlash. At the same time, a substantive CHRP ultimately benefits the business.

The evolution of business and human rights seems to be moving towards real accountability. CHRPs are resilience plans that can mitigate future risks

---

29   M. Jungk, *supra* n. 2. '
30   *Ibid.*
31   M. Brandau, 'McDonald's defends practices at Shareholder meeting', *Nations Restaurant News*, 23 May 2013, available at: http://nrn.com/quick-service/mcdonalds-defends-practices-shareholder-meeting.

whether it be a damaged reputation, scandals, failed compliance, or lawsuits, all of which could lead to bankruptcy in the most severe cases. A CHRP is truly an investment in the future and an opportunity to stay ahead of whatever waves are to come. This holds true for businesses of all styles and sizes. The human rights side of a business is an angle of increasing interest. Operationalising a CHRP is no longer optional. Business must engage human rights and CHRPs are their blueprint. As Blitt reminds us: '[A]lthough SRSG Ruggie's freshly minted Guiding Principles might strike one as plainly non-binding and aspirational today, these same principles can and will find surreptitious ways of growing up and becoming enforceable international norms that may carry serious repercussions for corporations, officers, and ill-prepared shareholders'.[32] Businesses can try avoidance or forging their way through a CHRP, but this only compromises the business. When it comes to CHRPs, those pushing for human rights seem to be in a position of leverage. This is a position from which high expectations can be retained and asserted.

---

[32]   R. Blitt, *supra* n. 24, p. 41.

PART III
SITES OF REGULATION

CHAPTER 10

HUMAN RIGHTS AND BUSINESS

An Assessment of the Responsibility
of the State in Vietnam

Nguyễn Thị Thanh Hải

1.   INTRODUCTION

Human rights are universal in nature, and belong to all people without
discrimination. However, the extent to which these rights are realised differs
between countries, regions, and sectors, and indeed depends on the willingness
and capacity of duty bearers. This chapter examines the role of the state as the
key duty bearer to respect, protect, and fulfil human rights responsibilities in the
business field in Vietnam.

This chapter argues that human rights norms and standards are not fully
integrated in the Vietnamese legal system. In fact, corporate human rights
responsibility is not an area of significant interest, and has not been effectively
addressed by relevant government institutions and organisations. The main
challenges hindering full implementation relate to the gaps in the legislative,
administrative, and judicial systems, all of which will be addressed in this chapter.

In order to understand how human rights responsibilities are being
promoted and implemented in the business sector in Vietnam, it is important
to understand the role of the relevant actors, in particular the leading role of the
state. This chapter assesses how the state system in Vietnam is compatible with
the UN international standards on human rights and business.

This chapter provides an overview of CSR issues in Vietnam and briefly
examines the role of relevant state institutions in addressing corporate human
rights responsibility. The chapter than identifies the state's central role in
fulfilling human rights obligations by examining existing policies and laws on
corporate human rights responsibility. It also examines the legislative, executive,
and judicial bodies' contributions to the creation and enforcement of law and
policies related to corporate human rights responsibility. The chapter concludes

that, in the context of business in Vietnam, there is still a lack of capacity amongst all relevant state institutions that in effect constrains the respect, protection, and fulfilment of human rights.

2. CSR AND HUMAN RIGHTS IN VIETNAM: THE ROLE OF RELEVANT PUBLIC INSTITUTIONS

While corporate social responsibility (CSR) has been discussed globally for decades, it is a relatively new concept in Vietnam. CSR was first introduced to Vietnam in the mid-1990s, when TNCs invested in local factory facilities (initially in the footwear and garment industries) and implemented their own codes of conduct or labour standards.[1]

Since then, CSR has gained attention from a variety of actors, including corporations, international organisations and government and non-governments institutions. Nevertheless, Vietnamese interpretations and understanding of CSR are quite narrow. Many CSR initiatives fail to address corporate human rights responsibility or only incidentally incorporate specific human rights rather than taking a comprehensive human rights approach. Most commonly, CSR is understood as a code of conduct or a tool for social standards compliance. Both domestic and foreign corporations in Vietnam, especially those in export industries like the garment, footwear, and wood industries, boast about their CSR performance through compliance with codes of conduct (e.g. Nike, Coca-Cola, and Toyota) and social standards such as SA 8000, ISO 9000, ISO 14000, and the Global Compact. Foreign corporations drive compliance with most of these standards. Local corporations comply in order to access global markets, especially following Vietnam's accession to the WTO. These CSR standards are voluntary and small scale, as the codes of conduct only apply in specific corporations or industries. The standards are not strongly connected to the government and usually only cover particular aspects of CSR.

Vietnamese perceptions of CSR and human rights lack clarity of definition and purpose. Most CSR studies provide a general introduction to CSR or are translations from foreign documents and do not focus on CSR practice in Vietnam. For example, Nguyen Dinh Cung and Luu Minh Duc define CSR by merely translating the CSR definition of western CSR scholar Archie Carroll[2] into Vietnamese.[3] Similarly, the 2003 World Bank study on CSR, the UNDP,

---

[1] Vietnam Business Links Initiative (VBLI) and German Development Service (DED), 'The Current Status of "Corporate Social Responsibility" (CSR) in Vietnam' (2007).

[2] See: Carroll definition on CSR in A.B. Carroll, 'Corporate Social Responsibility: Evolution of a Definitional Construct' (1999) 38 *Business & Society*.

[3] N. Đình Cung and L. Minh Đức, 'Trách nhiệm, xã hội của doanh nghiệp – CSR: Một số vấn đề lý luận và yêu cầu đổi mới trong quản lý nhà nước đối với CSR ở Việt Nam' (Corporate Social

and the Vietnam Chamber of Commerce and Industry (VCCI) project on UN
Global Compact, all used the CSR definition of the World Business Council for
Sustainable Development which claims that:

> Corporate Social Responsibility is the continuing commitment by business to
> behave ethically and contribute to economic development while improving the
> quality of life of the workforce and their families as well as of the local community
> and society at large.[4]

CSR is often interpreted as business ethics, business culture, public relations,
a social activity, or simply charity, rather than a legal (or quasi-legal) concept
comprising obligations and responsibilities. Le Dang Doanh, a leading
Vietnamese economist, defines CSR as a category of business ethics.[5] Doanh
also mentions that when implementing CSR, corporations in Vietnam pursue
charity ventures by supporting natural disaster victims or donating to poverty
reduction,[6] as the concepts of charity and philanthropy are more familiar to
and easily accepted by the Vietnamese public and corporations than CSR.
This is because acts of charity are similar to traditional Vietnamese notions of
moral responsibility. Consequently, many corporations in Vietnam interpret
CSR as charity.[7] Corporations in Vietnam are commonly involved in charity
events (e.g. gala dinners, charity concerts, auctions, and fundraising for disaster
relief and scholarships), but do not focus on following human rights standards.
A 2009 study on corporate philanthropy in Ho Chi Minh City found that many
corporations listed one of their motives for participating in philanthropy as CSR
engagement.[8]

Although CSR and human rights have become an increasing issue of concern
among relevant stakeholders including international organisations, corporations,
NGOs, and states, there are challenges that need to be addressed to ensure the role
of these institutions in promoting and implementing human rights in business in
Vietnam.

One reason that human rights responsibility is unfamiliar to many
corporations is that their overriding concern in profit maximisation. While

---

Responsibility – CSR: Some Theoritical Concerns and Requirements for Governance Reform
to CSR in Vietnam) (2008) 23 *Tạp chí Quản lý kinh tế (Journal of Economic Management)*.

[4]   A. Dahlsrud, 'How Corporate Social Responsibility is Defined: an Analysis of 37 Definitions'
(2006) 15 *Corporate Social Responsibility and Environmental Management*.

[5]   L. Đăng Doanh, 'Một số vấn đề về trách nhiệm xã hội của doanh nghiệp ở Việt Nam' (Some
issues on Social Responsibility of the Vietnamese Businesses) (2009) 3(214) *Tạp chí triết học
(Journal of Philosophy)*.

[6]   *Ibid.*

[7]   Lin Center for Community Development, 'Corporate Philanthropy In Ho Chi Minh City,
An Update on the Status of Corporate Giving in Vietnam', 2009, p. 12, available at: www.
linvn.org/cms/upload/FCKFile/file/LIN%20-%20Corporate%20Philanthropy%20in%20
HCMC%20Dec2009_FINAL.pdf (accessed 13 July 2012).

[8]   *Ibid.*, p. 21.

conscious that the first Vietnamese CSR initiatives came from corporations, particularly TNCs, most local and foreign corporations in Vietnam do not have stand-alone human rights policies. Where human rights-related corporate activity is found in CSR ventures, these are generated by foreign pressures to integrate Vietnam into the world economy. Specific human rights, such as the right to work and the right to health, are increasingly supported by the corporate sector. For instance, corporations are actively involved in work on HIV/AIDS, contributing to the assurance of the right to health. In 2010, ten corporations received awards from VCCI and USAID project on HIV/AIDS prevention at the work place for their active participation in HIV/AIDS prevention and control and their support of the right to work for people living with HIV/AIDS.[9] Although no formal evaluation of corporate human rights compliance in Vietnam exists, it is clear that corporation's responses are broadly passive and their understanding of CSR and human rights is frequently weak or inaccurate. Corporations usually only comply with human rights in response to the demands of foreign buyers and customers.

International organisations such as the UN, and other development agencies have actively pursued human rights activities in Vietnam. The first attempts to introduce corporate human rights responsibility came from UN-supported projects.[10] At the same time, the US State Report on Human Rights Practices has expressed specific concern for the impact of corporate human rights violations on Vietnamese workers.[11] However, all of these measures are in their early stages – either raising human rights awareness, furthering government understanding, or focusing on particular areas of human rights, such as the rights of women and children. The human rights activities of corporations have not been a priority of international donors to Vietnam. UN human rights efforts in Vietnam, such as the visit of the UN Special Rapporteur on freedom of religion or belief (in 2013) did not address human rights concerns in the business sector.[12]

Concluding observations by UN treaty bodies have so far failed to address human rights issues of the business entities. Although international organisations and development agencies have been actively involved in protecting human rights

---

[9]   USAID Vietnam, 'Trách nhiệm xã hội của doanh nghiệp: 10 doanh nghiệp được vinh doanh vì tích cực đẩy mạnh công tác dự phòng HIV/AIDS và hỗ trợ việc làm cho người sống chung với HIV/AIDS' (Corporate Social Responsibility: the 10 Enterprises Honored for Promoting HIV/AIDS Prevention and Support), available at: http://vietnam.usaid.gov/node/236 (accessed 13 February 2012).

[10] See UNDP Vietnam, 'Project document: Catalysing Business Community's Role towards Greater Corporate Social Responsibility through Global Compact Principles in Viet Nam', and UNIDO, 'Helping Vietnamese SMEs Adapt and Adopt Corporate Social Responsibility (CSR) for Improved Linkages with Global Supply Chains in Sustainable Production, available at: http://csr-vietnam.eu/en/Home.htm (accessed 3 February 2012).

[11] Country Reports on Human Rights Practices for 2013, United States Department of State, Bureau of Democracy, Human Rights and Labor, Washington DC, 2014.

[12] See UN Special Representative Visits and Recommendation of the Human Rights Council, CEDAW, and CRC Committee.

in Vietnam, more support is needed for corporate human rights responsibility initiatives. The two primary issues with existing human rights projects are their frequent failure to consider the human rights impact of corporations, and the lack of a human rights approach in economic assistance projects.

NGOs, especially international and foreign NGOs, have watched human rights issues in Vietnam quite closely. That being said, their main concern is with civil and political rights, such as freedom of expression, repression of religious communities, stifling of freedom of the press and the internet, widespread use of the death penalty, and abuses of women's rights.[13] There are also a few local NGOs that focus on human rights advocacy. However, there is no strong voice advocating for corporate human rights responsibility, aside from minor support for labour rights through some international NGOs, including Oxfam and Action Aid.[14]

Hence, human rights and corporate responsibility are improperly characterised within the Vietnamese state system. The absence of specific policy and legal provisions that regulate corporations' accountability for human rights, and the absence of an effective mechanism to remedy corporate human rights violations, limit the improvement of human rights conditions in the business sector. Failure to consider the human rights impact of business activities has already produced negative results. While the arrival of foreign corporations increased national income and employment in the private sector, it has also led to human rights abuses – specifically, the violation of labour and environmental rights. Accordingly, measures to attract foreign investment should be accompanied by commitments to address its human rights implications. A human rights report conducted in 2010 by an NGO notes that corruption and other human rights abuses may increase as a result of the government's policy priority on foreign investment.[15]

Another challenging barrier to advancing corporate human rights responsibility in Vietnam is a lack of willingness and capacity by the government and its agencies, corporations, and international and local NGOs. Human rights and business are often seen as separate domains that do not interact. Although the Vietnamese government is a party to most core international human rights treaties and has taken steps to realise human rights, existing measures have not sufficiently ensure the protection of human rights in business activities. Corporate accountability for human rights has not become a priority on the governmental

---

agenda. In comparison with these minimal state efforts, corporations and other non-state actors in Vietnam have more actively participated in CSR initiatives.

In recent years, the Vietnamese government has officially adopted more policies and laws on protection and promotion of human rights. The government has also attempted to improve its commitment to respect, protect, and fulfil human rights by signing and ratifying more international human rights instruments and incorporating human rights standards domestically. Vietnam was applauded by several states of the UN Human Rights Council for its human rights record in poverty reduction, which the government considers a top priority.[16] It was praised for the effort to undertake judicial reform to promote civil, political, economic, social and cultural rights. The government has also given special attention to protecting vulnerable groups such as women, children, ethnic minorities, and people living with disabilities and HIV/AIDS.[17]

Despite these specific advances, however, Vietnam lacks a comprehensive human rights policy and any specialised human rights agency to monitor the work of all relevant institutions (including government, non-state actors, and other civil society organisations) in complying with domestic, let alone international, human rights standards. The recently adopted 2013 Constitution does not include provisions on the establishment of a domestic human rights monitoring body.

Therefore, there are gaps in policy, legal, and institutional frameworks that prevent tripartite obligation to respect, protect, and fulfil human rights. This gap is particularly evident in business, where human rights abuses take place, but the corporate abusers are not held accountable due to the weak rule of law and the lack of effective accountability system.

The Vietnamese government is aware of the negative impacts on business development and has indicated preliminary support for CSR in labour laws and through national sustainable development programmes.[18] Some business associations have been actively working for improved understanding and implementation of CSR,[19] and NGOs and other international organisations in Vietnam have also implemented a number of CSR promotion initiatives.

---

[16]   When considering Vietnam's periodic report to the Human Rights Council, many states praised Vietnam's effective poverty reduction strategies and effective reduction of the poverty rate. See: Human Rights Council, 'Report of the Working Group on the Universal Periodic Review: Vietnam', 2009, available at: http://daccess-dds-ny.un.org/doc/UNDOC/GEN/G09/163/82/PDF/G0916382.pdf?OpenElement (accessed 15 September 2013).

[17]   The Government of Vietnam, 'National Report of the Socialist Republic of Vietnam under the Universal Periodic Review of the United Nation Human Rights Council' 2009, available at: www.mofa.gov.vn/en/nr040807104143/nr040807105001/ns090423110049#JuIMa8L4WZGX (accessed 13 July 2012). Human Rights Council, 'Report of the Working Group on Universal Periodic Review: Vietnam', 2 April 2014, available at: http://daccess-dds-ny.un.org/doc/UNDOC/GEN/G14/129/10/PDF/G1412910.pdf?OpenElement (accessed 12 December 2015).

[18]   See for example, the 2012 Labour Code for the first time mentioned to corporate social responsibility in Article 4.

[19]   For example, Vietnam Leather, Foodwear and Handbag Association and Vietnam Textile and Apparel Association have been involved in a CSR project with UNIDO and VCCI Vietnam to promote CSR. See: UNIDO, *supra* n. 10.

In particular, CSR has recently become a topic of research, discussion, and teaching among media, research institutes, universities, foreign companies, international donors, and NGOs.[20]

Nevertheless, incorporating human rights into business activities remains in a nascent state of development. A 2007 Country Risk Assessment of Vietnam conducted by the Danish Institute for Human Rights found that of all the rights recognised in the Universal Declaration of Human Rights, ten rights[21] were categorised as being at high risk, eight rights[22] as medium risk and only two rights[23] as low risk in the corporate sector.[24] Vietnamese enterprises know little about international human rights standards and their application. Labour issues are typically considered among the few human rights concerns of business. Another study conducted by CSR ASIA and the Vietnam National Economics University on the four areas of the Global Compact in key industries (food processing, construction, oil and gas, mining, manufacturing, agriculture, fishing, forestry and tourism) found that businesses only linked human rights to certain areas such as labour, gender issues or land rights.[25] Many businesses were not aware of the broader need for corporate human rights responsibility, and considered human rights an abstract and foreign concept. These responses reflect a lack of understanding of the nature and form of business' human rights impact rather than a general lack of any concern for human rights in the Vietnamese business sector.

On the basis of what has been outlined in this section, the following sections analyse the roles of the state in the promotion and implementation of human rights. In particular, the sections examine existing legal provisions and the role of government and its relevant agencies in order to identify the key influences on corporate human rights responsibility in Vietnam.

---

[20]   See for example, L. Đăng Doanh, *supra* n. 5; UNDP Vietnam, *supra* n. 9.

[21]   These rights are: Right to Freedom from Discrimination (Art. 2); Right to Freedom from Forced Labour and Servitude (Art. 4); Right to Own Property (Art. 17); Right to Take Part in Government (Art. 21); Right to Peaceful Assembly and Freedom of Association (Arts. 20 and 23); Right to Work and Just and Favourable Conditions of Work (Arts. 23, 24 and 25); Right to an Adequate Standard of Living (Art. 22); Right to Health (Art. 25); Right to Adequate Food (Art. 25); and Right to Education (Art. 26).

[22]   These rights are: Right to Life, Liberty and Security of Person (Art. 3); Right to Privacy (Art. 12); Right to Freedom of Movement (Art. 13); Right to Family Life (Art. 16); Right to Freedom of Opinion, Expression, Thought, Conscience, and Religion (Arts. 18 and 19); Right to Adequate Housing (Art. 25); Right to Participate in Cultural Life (Art. 26); and Right to Intellectual Property (Art. 26).

[23]   These rights are: Right to Freedom from Torture, Cruel, Inhuman, or Degrading Treatment or Punishment (Art. 5); and Right to Fair Trial and Recognition as a Person before the Law (Arts. 6, 7, 10 and 11).

[24]   Human Rights & Business Project, 'Vietnam Country Risk Assessment', Danish Institute for Human Rights, 2007.

[25]   Global Compact Network Vietnam, 'A Review of the Social and Environmental Conditions of Industries in Vietnam against the Global Compact Principles', Report, 2010.

3.   THE GAP IN THE LEGAL FRAMEWORK FOR CORPORATE HUMAN RIGHTS RESPONSIBILITY

As noted, recent legal reform in Vietnam has resulted in robust legislation, especially in the fields of trade, investment, and business generally. Nevertheless, substantive legal developments have not occurred concerning corporate human rights responsibility. There is an absence of specific policy or regulation that directly governs the human rights impact of business activities.

Nonetheless, Vietnamese laws including the Constitution, the Penal Code, the Civil Code, the Labour Code and the Law on Gender Equality contain some provisions that can be applied to prevent or mitigate any adverse human rights impacts of corporate activity.[26] In many of these laws, obligations are imposed on 'organisations', which has been interpreted to include corporations.[27] Despite this, my review of business-related laws, including the Law on Investment, Law on Companies and Law on Environment found no provisions that directly regulate corporate protection of human rights.

Corporate human rights responsibility can include both voluntary and mandatory obligations. At the national level, legal regulation is particularly important because the primary responsibility for requiring corporations to respect human rights lies with the state. In the absence of an international treaty that directly imposes corporate human rights obligations, a clearer national articulation of corporate human rights responsibility is necessary. Some scholars argue that corporate human rights responsibilities are derived from national legal systems.[28] In developing countries like Vietnam, where the rule of law is weak, codifying human rights standards and responsibilities is significant.

Vietnam has a civil law system where legal documents including the Constitution, laws, resolutions, ordinances, decrees, and decisions issued by government institutions are the main source of law.[29] As mentioned, the state can fulfil its primary duty to protect human rights by using legislation to provide legal protection. To some extent, the Constitution and more than 13,000 legal documents in Vietnam help fulfil this duty, but the current legislative framework on business focuses on attracting foreign investment and economic growth rather than addressing corporate responsibility to respect, protect, and guarantee human rights. A close examination of existing legal mechanisms in Vietnam illustrates this.

---

[26]   C. Kaufmann et al. (eds.), *Business and Human Rights in Asean: A Baseline Study* (Human Rights Resource Centre, 2013), p. 434.

[27]   For example, Article 30 of the 2013 Constitution refers to the right to lodge a complaint or denunciation to a state body, an economic or social organisation, the people's armed forces unit or any individual.

[28]   J. Letnar Černič, *Human Rights Law and Business: Corporate Responsibility for Fundamental Human Rights* (Europa Law Publishing. 2010) p. 38.

[29]   C. Kaufmann et al., *supra* n. 26, p. 424.

3.1. CONSTITUTIONS

During Vietnam's recent history, human rights have been increasingly entrenched in the country's Constitution through successive amendments. The Constitution has undergone revision many times, with major changes occurring in 1946, 1959, 1980, 1992, and 2013. Adopted in November 2013, the last Constitutional amendment recognises as fundamental rights those affirmed in international human rights law. Chapter 2 of the 2013 Constitution contains 35 provisions on fundamental human rights and duties of citizens.[30]

The 2013 Constitution contains provisions that apply to business, including the prohibition of discrimination[31] and the right of every citizen to lodge a complaint or denunciation before any competent state authority regarding legal transgressions by a state body, economic or social organisation, people's armed forces unit, or individual.[32] Furthermore, victims of violations of the Constitution and laws that include human rights provisions are entitled to compensation for damage and rehabilitation of their honour, as provided by law. These provisions can be applied to corporations if they fall into the category of 'economic and social organisations.' In addition, state-owned corporations could be categorised as state agencies under the provision.

Nevertheless, it is not clear whether these constitutionally entrenched human rights may be applied or enforced against corporations, except for some general principles and indirect provisions. Neither the 1992 Constitution nor the 2013 Constitution contain specific provisions which protect human rights in the context of business. The lack of a human rights enforcement mechanism and legal measures to support enforcement of constitutional human rights provisions have made Vietnamese protection of human rights in business more difficult.

The current Constitution was amended when Vietnam's 'open door' policy favoured a supportive investment environment. The 2013 Constitution recognises the market economy and multi economic sectors.[33] It also encourages foreign organisations and individuals to invest funds and technology in Vietnam.

When discussions surrounding the 1992 Constitution amendment took place (leading to the adoption of the 2013 Constitution), much focus amongst scholars and the business community centred around the position of business persons and the private sector. Although the business sector is important to industrialisation and modernisation, it was neglected in the draft Constitution. Vu Quoc Tuan, an official member of the Prime Minister's research team, criticised the 2013 draft's

---

[30]   See Chapter 2, 2013 Constitution of Vietnam. The 2013 Constitution is available in English at: www.na.gov.vn/htx/English/C1479/#OUTRtwpHqlwR (accessed 1 November 2014).
[31]   Article 5, 2013 Constitution.
[32]   Article 30, 2013 Constitution.
[33]   Article 51, 1992 Constitution.

failure to include provisions on the rights and responsibilities of businesses.[34] The economist Pham Chi Lan and the business manager Le Duy Binh pointed out that Article 2 of the 1992 Constitution and the then 2013 draft state that '[a]ll State power belongs to the people and is based on a coalition between the working class, the farmer and the intelligentsia' and does not refer to business persons. The lack of recognition of the business community in the draft Constitution created a sense of exclusion of this community.[35] When the 2013 Constitution was adopted, it included a provision to encourage and create favourable condition for businessmen and businesses to do business. Nevertheless, the 2013 Constitution still lacks specific provisions on human rights responsibilities of businesses.

3.2. NATIONAL LAWS ON CORPORATE HUMAN RIGHTS RESPONSIBILITY

Domestic legislation does not specifically regulate corporations' human rights responsibilities. However, there are provisions that may cover the protection of human rights in a business context. In fact, Vietnam has implemented legislation designed to ensure that corporations actively protect labour rights. The government has signed and ratified 20 conventions of the ILO on labour related issues.[36] The Ministry of Labour, Social and Invalid Affairs has also discussed a roadmap for ratifying ILO Conventions, in which it planned to review two core Conventions on freedom of associations and collective bargaining (ILO Convention 87 and Convention 98).[37] In July 2011, Vietnam submitted its combined second to fourth periodic reports on the Implementation of the International Covenant on Economic, Social and Cultural Rights (ICESCR), which included its performance in fulfilling labour related rights to the United Nations Economic and Social Council.[38]

By and large, such international labour rights standards are incorporated in the national labour framework to ensure that corporations do not abuse labour

---

[34] N. Nhân, 'Doanh nhân ở đâu trong dự thảo Hiến pháp?' (Where is the Role of Businessmen in the Draft Constitution?), VNEconomy 2013, available at: http://doanhnhan.vneconomy. vn/201303191113419P0C5/doanh-nhan-o-dau-trong-du-thao-hien-phap.htm (accessed 10 May 2013).

[35] Ibid.

[36] Out of 20 Conventions ratified by Vietnam, of which 19 are in force, 1 Convention has been denounced; 1 has been ratified in the past 12 month.

[37] International Labour Organisation (ILO), Ratification for Vietnam, available at: www.ilo.org/ dyn/normlex/en/f?p=NORMLEXPUB:11200:0::NO::P11200_COUNTRY_ID:103004.

[38] This reported was submitted on 18 July 2011, published by the Economic and Social Council in 2013. At the time of writing, this report is awaiting consideration by the ICESCR Committee. Document available at: Economic and Social Council, 'Implementation of the International Covenant on Economic, Social and Cultural Rights. Consideration of the combined second to fourth periodic reports of States parties due in 2005 under Articles 16 and 17 of the Covenant: Vietnam' (United Nations, 2013).

rights and provide victims with compensation for any breaches. For example, the Forced Labour Convention (ILO Convention 29) that Vietnam ratified in 2007 was incorporated into eight different laws, decrees, and bilateral agreements.[39] The Convention on the Worst Form of Child Labour (ILO Convention 182), which Vietnam ratified in 2000, has been incorporated in 26 domestic legal documents.[40]

Examples of other labour-related laws include Law on Social Security, Law on Trade Unions (1990), Law on Vocational Training (2006) and Law on Sending Vietnamese Labourers to Work Overseas (2006), as well as hundreds of ordinances, decrees, resolutions, circulars, and decisions which were adopted by the Standing Committee of the National Assembly, the government, the Prime Minister and Ministries. These documents all recognise the state's duty to address human rights issues such as labour standards, safety and health, child labour, forced labour, and discrimination in the workplace.[41]

The most important labour law is the Labour Code[42] which regulates the interaction between employers and employees and any social relations directly related to labour rights. In 2012, the introduction of a new Labour Code significantly improved labour rights protection. Although there is still no provision obligating corporations to be responsible for human rights, the new code improved protection of specific labour rights such as the right to collective bargaining, increased minimum wage rates, improved working conditions, and extended maternity leave from four months to six months.[43] Unprecedentedly, the 2012 Labour Code mentioned the terms 'corporate social responsibility' and 'employer's social responsibility'.[44]

Although these developments increasingly recognise the rights of employees, the legislation still fails to specify how the law will be enforced and who will be responsible for its enforcement. The law does not specify corporations' responsibilities as key actors in relations between employers and employees, and conflicts between laws and CRS standards still exists. For example, some Vietnamese regulations on child labour, labour exploitation, working overtime, freedom of association, and environmental management are ambiguous when

---

[39] International Labour Organization, *Country Profile: Vietnam*, available at: www.ilo.org/dyn/normlex/en/f?p=1000:11110:0::NO:11110:P11110_COUNTRY_ID:103004 (accessed 7 December 2013).

[40] Ibid.

[41] For example, MOLISA has adopted Circulars 12 (20/5/2003) and 14 (30/5/2005), to provide guidance for implementing Decree 114 (2002) on payment for employers in state enterprises, foreign investment enterprises and foreign or international organisations in Vietnam. The Government also adopted Decree 133 (2007) to provide interpretation and guidance for provisions related to dispute settlement in the Labour Code.

[42] This law was adopted in 1994 and amended in 2002, 2006 and 2007 and changed to the new Labour code in 2012.

[43] Article 157, 2012 Labour Code.

[44] *Ibid.*, Article 4(2).

compared to international CSR codes of conduct or standards.[45] Furthermore, a law on social accounting and reporting has not yet been developed.[46]

The other recent legislation related to corporation was the Law on Enterprises, enacted in 2005. Article 9 establishes a range of obligations for all corporations. Among these, there is only one clause that mentions ensuring the rights and interests of employees in accordance with the Labour Law. Other human rights obligations, such as protecting affected communities or providing remedy for corporate human rights abuses are not included. While the 2005 Law on Enterprises provides legal grounds for establishing, managing, organising, and operating corporations,[47] it imposes no human rights obligations under the law.

The dramatic growth in foreign direct investment (FDI) provides an important source of capital and technological transfer,[48] and is a key driver for transforming Vietnam's economic and labour structure and promoting its development. Vietnam has revised and adopted laws to attract foreign investment and has signed bilateral, regional and international trade and investment treaties to attract and facilitate foreign trade and investment.

The Vietnamese government has failed to bring in a serious manner human rights issues into the negotiation of its Bilateral Investment Treaties (BITs) and Bilateral Trade Agreements (BTAs) or Free Trade Agreements (FTAs). Vietnam has entered into BITs with more than 40 countries since the early 1990s.[49] However, human rights issues are not mentioned by the government in any of these BITs. Yet some human rights, such as freedom of association, freedom of press, and labour standards, are included by foreign corporations and other governments in trade negotiations or agreements. For example, the Agreement on Textiles and Garments between Vietnam and the United States requires Vietnam to fulfil its commitments under ILO conventions and the corporate code of conduct.[50]

Vietnam recently signed the Framework Agreement on Comprehensive Partnership and Cooperation Between the European Union and its Member States, which places significant importance on the protection of human rights.[51]

---

[45] L. Thanh Hà, *Trách nhiệm xã hội của doanh nghiệp trong bối cảnh Việt Nam gia nhập WTO và hội nhập kinh tế quốc tế (Corporate Social Responsibility in the Context of Joining WTO and Economic Intergration in Vietnam)*, 2008.

[46] *Ibid.*

[47] Article 1, 2005 Law on Enterprises.

[48] FDI in Vietnam made up 25% of total investment in 2009 See: VNS, 'FDI follows national interests', *Vietnam News online*, 2010, available at: http://vietnamnews.vnagency.com.vn/Opinion/204759/FDI-follows-national-interests.html (accessed 15 November 2012).

[49] C. Devonshire, 'Vietnam's Bilateral Investment Treaties', *Vietnam Briefing Magazine*, 2013, available at: www.vietnam-briefing.com/news/vietnams-bilateral-investment-treaties.html/ (accessed 15 September 2013).

[50] See N.J. Sayres, 'The Vietnam-U.S. Textile Agreement Debate: Trade Patterns, Interests, and Labor Rights', 21 June 2002, Congressional Research Centre: The Library of Congress.

[51] Human rights provisions are regulated in Article 35 of this framework: '1. The Parties agree to cooperate in the promotion and protection of human rights, including with regard to the implementation of the international human rights instruments to which they are parties. Technical assistance will be provided to this end. 2. Such cooperation may include: (a) human

Typically, human rights are raised by foreign partners as a condition for loans, investment, and foreign aid, but the government and corporations in Vietnam remain hesitant to discuss human rights as part of their business agenda.

Human rights provisions are absent in business laws in Vietnam. The new Law on Investment was adopted in 2005 to create a more transparent and equal environment for foreign investment. The 2005 Commercial Law, apart from indirectly protecting human rights by protecting the 'legitimate interests of consumers', merely focuses on the technical issues of commercial activity without considering the influence of social factors (such as human rights) on commercial activity.

The role of corporations as human rights duty bearers is similarly ambiguous in most Vietnamese laws. Most laws only contain provisions that indirectly acknowledge corporations' duty to protect particular rights, rather than taking a comprehensive approach to all human rights. For example, the Law on Environmental Protection (2005) and Law on Minerals (2010) contain general provisions on protection of the environment in productive, trading, and service industries. These legal documents are not strong enough to obligate corporations to protect the right to environment. Likewise, the Law on Minerals (2010) only emphasises the environmental impact of the minerals industry rather than focusing on the duty of corporations to protect the right to environment. A robust human rights approach recognises the right to environment as both a procedural and substantive human right; that the right to environment must be respected, protected, and fulfilled by the government and relevant duty bearers.[52] The absence of a human rights approach in environmental laws has reduced the potential effectiveness of the response to environmental concerns in Vietnam.

The Law on HIV/AIDS Prevention and Control (2006) only includes provisions on the employers' responsibility to prevent and control HIV/AIDS in the workplace (Article 14), rather than a responsibility to the community as a whole. What is more, although Chapter VI of the Law on Domestic Violence against Women regulates the responsibilities of individuals, families, and organisations to eliminate domestic violence, no equivalent duty is imposed specifically on corporations.[53]

---

rights promotion and education; (b) strengthening of human rights-related institutions; (c) strengthening the existing human rights dialogue; (d) strengthening of cooperation within the human rights related institutions of the UN.'

[52] Human Rights Council, 'Human rights and Environment, Resolution A/HRC/RES/16/11', 12 April 2011, available at: www2.ohchr.org/english/bodies/hrcouncil/docs/16session/A. HRC.RES.16.11_en.pdf (accessed 1 November 2014).

[53] See the 2007 Law on Domestic Violence Against Women.

3.3. CORPORATE CIVIL, ADMINISTRATIVE AND CRIMINAL LIABILITY

The 2013 Constitution expressly recognises human rights, but does not contain provisions that clearly outline the duty of states to enforce those rights or to establish a national human rights commission.[54] The nature of corporate liability for human rights abuses, such as whether the liability is civil or criminal, remains unclarified. Under the Vietnamese legal system, corporations may be held accountable for their actions as non-natural legal persons.[55] However, their liability is limited to civil and administrative law. The legal system does not recognise any form of corporate criminal liability.

3.3.1. Civil Liability

Under Article 84 of the Civil Code (2005), organisations are recognised as non-natural legal persons that may be subject to civil liability. This liability can apply in the case of human rights abuses. Under Article 100, legal persons include state agencies and units of the armed forces; political and socio-political organisations; economic organisations; socio-political and professional organisations, social organisations, and socio-professional organisations; social and charity funds; and other organisations which meet all the conditions specified in Article 84 of the Code.[56] Article 103 further explains that 'economic organisations are state enterprises, cooperatives, limited liability companies, joint-stock companies, foreign-invested enterprises and other economic organisations.'

The recognition of corporations as legal persons is significant as it imposes civil liability for human rights violations, particularly for civil rights laid out in the Civil Code. The Code also includes specific provisions on the obligation of legal persons to provide compensation when their employees cause damage (Article 618). For example, Article 624 of the Civil Code imposes a responsibility on legal persons to provide compensation for damage caused by environmental pollution. This Article states that:

---

[54] Constitutions in many other countries clearly state that human rights provisions apply to both natural and legal persons and that the state is responsible for upholding them. See: Human Rights and Business Book. For example: Article 5 of the Namibian Constitution clearly indicates that: 'The fundamental rights and freedoms enshrined in this chapter shall be respected and upheld by the Executive, Legislature and Judiciary and all organs of the government and its agencies and, where applicable to them, by all natural and legal persons in Namibia, and shall be enforceable by the Courts in the manner hereinafter prescribed'; Article 8 of the South African Constitution affirms that the bill of rights binds natural or juristic persons.

[55] C. Kaufmann et al., *supra* n. 26, p. 431.

[56] See Article 84, 2005 Civil Code.

> [i]ndividuals, legal persons or other subjects who pollute the environment and thereby cause damage shall have to compensate as provided for by law, even in cases where the environment polluters are not at fault.

Thus, because corporations are legal persons, they have a civil responsibility to provide compensation for damage caused by emitting pollution. The Civil Code is one of few laws which provides a legal foundation for victims of corporate human rights violations to seek remedy. Despite provisions on corporate civil liability being provided by the law, few court cases regarding human rights abuses related to corporate civil liability exist.

3.3.2. Administrative Liability

In certain cases, the Vietnamese legal system can impose administrative sanctions on corporations if they violate administrative laws. Under the Ordinance on Handling Administrative Violations adopted by the Standing Committee of the National Assembly in 2002 (amended in 2008), administrative sanctions in the form of warnings or fines can be applied to any individual, agency, or organisation (including foreign organisations).[57] As organisations, any corporation in Vietnam may be liable to receive administrative sanction if they intentionally or unintentionally violate administrative law.[58]

Article 3 of the 2002 Ordinance specifies that administrative violations are handled in different ways depending on the nature and seriousness of the violation.[59] To clarify the provisions of this Ordinance, the government has issued decrees on handling administrative liability for specific issues. For example, it issued the Decree on Handling Administrative Sanctions in Environment Protection to sanction any individual or organisation, including corporations, when their actions cause environmental pollution.

If corporations are involved in violations of labour rights or the right to environment, they may be sanctioned under administrative law as provided in the laws related to labour or the environment. The Vietnamese government has adopted decrees under a number of these laws to detail specific administrative sanctions, many of which specifically recognise the legal liability of corporations. For example, Government Decree 47/2010/ND-CP on Administrative Sanctioning of Violations of the Labour Code, adopted on 6 May 2010, outlines different levels of administrative sanctions against illegal actions of employers.[60] According to

---

[57]   Article 2, 2002 Ordinance on Sanctioning Administrative Violations.
[58]   Article 1, 2002 Ordinance on Sanctioning Administrative Violations.
[59]   Article 12, 2002 the Ordinance on Sanctioning Administrative Violations provides that violations can be handled by: (a) stripping persons of permits and professional practice certificates; or (b) confiscating material evidence and/or means used to commit administrative violations.
[60]   See: Degree 47/2010/ND-CP of the Government dated 6 May 2010 on Administrative Sanctioning of Violation of the Labour Code.

this Decree, a fine of between VND 1,000,000 and VND 5,000,000[61] will apply to corporations that fail to ensure adequate labour safety standards; a fine between VND 300,000 and VND 10,000,000 is to be imposed on corporations that discriminate against female employees.

There are nevertheless significant shortcomings in the imposition of administrative liability for human rights violations by corporations. The severity of sanctions imposed on corporations has been criticised for often being too low to incentivise corporations to avoid repeat violations. For example, the fines for acts of discrimination against female employees under Decree 47/2010/ND-CP only range from between approximately US $15 and US $500. In many cases, corporations are happy to pay such a relatively small amount of money rather than reform their practices to avoid human rights violations. The effectiveness of corporate administrative liability in protecting human rights has also been criticised because there is an overlap between ministries and government agencies. Consequently, the state lacks clarity in its enforcement of administrative liability.

3.3.3. Corporate Criminal Liability

Imposing corporate criminal liability for business activities is made difficult because Vietnamese criminal law does not apply to corporations. Debate as to whether criminal liability should extend to legal as well as actual persons has increased in recent years.[62] The criminal liability of non-natural legal persons, which includes corporations, is one of the issues in the schedule for review and amendment of the Penal Code as part of the National Assembly's law-making programme of 2011–2016.[63]

Nevertheless, there are currently no grounds within the Vietnamese legal system to impose criminal liability on corporations if they have seriously abused human rights. According to Article 2 of the Penal Code, criminal liability only applies to individuals who commit crimes. Similarly, under the Penal Code, corporations as non-natural legal persons are not criminally liable for their involvement in human rights infringements.[64] The lack of criminal liability

---

[61]   The exchange rate as of 15 September 2013 is US $1 = VND 21,080.
[62]   Some scholars in Vietnam support the argument that Vietnam should amend the Penal Code to include criminal liability of legal persons, while others are opposed. See, for example: Vu Hoai Nam, 'Vấn đề trách nhiệm hình sự của pháp nhân – nhìn từ dấu hiệu hành vi' (Criminal Liablity of the Legal Person – Behaviour Approach) (Ministry of Justice, 2012).
[63]   See C. Kaufmann et al., *supra* n. 26, p. 433.
[64]   Corporate criminal liability is not a common feature in legal systems around the world. Many jurisdictions do not recognise the existence of corporate criminal liability in their criminal law, such as Brazil, Bulgaria, Luxembourg, and the Slovak Republic. Nevertheless, the question of how to impose criminal liability on corporations for wrongful conduct has been raised in many jurisdictions. Some jurisdictions recognise the co-existence of both individual and corporate criminal responsibility. J. Letnar Černič, for example, noted that corporate criminal responsibility is not a new phenomenon and that 'individual and corporate criminal responsibility can coexist concurrently'. The criminal law of many states such as the UK, the

for non-national legal persons effectively grants corporations impunity from punishment under criminal law for human rights violations.

In summary, the Vietnamese legal framework is quite comprehensive and advanced in its coverage of emerging problems such as international business and foreign investment. However, provisions on human rights in domestic legislation and bylaws documents are still limited, especially in laws relating to trade, companies, and investment. Even though existing laws contain some regulations relevant to human rights that are applicable to corporations, the Vietnamese legal framework is missing broad human rights provisions and fails to adequately compel corporations to protect, respect, and guarantee human rights. These legal gaps make enforcing corporate human rights obligations,[65] as well as providing remedy to victims of corporate violations of these rights, more challenging.

4. THE GOVERNANCE SYSTEM AND ITS INFLUENCE ON CORPORATE HUMAN RIGHTS RESPONSIBILITY

The Vietnamese governance system consists of the legislature, the executive, and the judiciary. Although the Communist Party of Vietnam (CPV) is considered a political organisation and not part of the state's formal governance system,[66] it plays a critical leadership role and has strong power in state decision-making. Any state action must be through the legislature, executive, or judiciary under the leadership of the CPV.

4.1. THE LEGISLATURE: THE NATIONAL ASSEMBLY

The main function of the National Assembly of Vietnam is to discuss, adopt, and amend the Constitution, laws, and resolutions. Many of these documents codify human rights. The National Assembly can also make decisions on, inter alia, fundamental foreign policies (including signing, acceding to, or ratifying international treaties), national defence and security issues, socio-economic

---

    Netherlands, France, Australia, India, and China recognise that corporations should and do bear criminal liability.

[65]   There have been discussions on the role and obligations of corporations on human rights. Within the UN system, the debate is particularly informed by the work of John Ruggie, the UN Special Representative on Human Rights and Business. See: Office of High Commissioner for Human Rights. 'Special Representative of the Secretary-General on human rights and transnational corporations and other business enterprises', available at: www.ohchr.org/EN/Issues/Business/Pages/SRSGTransCorpIndex.aspx (accessed 1 November 2014).

[66]   A. Luu, 'Vietnam Legal Rearch', Globalex, 2006, available at: www.nyulawglobal.org/globalex/Vietnam.htm (accessed 15 October 2013).

development plans, national financial and monetary policies, the state budget, as well as policies on ethnic minorities and religions.

The National Assembly can influence corporate human rights responsibility in three ways. First, the National Assembly has the power to approve key national economic and social projects in areas such as hydropower and natural resources use.[67] These projects and the corporations involved in the projects can directly impact human rights. For example, the 2002 National Assembly Resolution NQ13/2002/QH11 approved the development of the Son La Hydro Power Project, the biggest dam in Southeast Asia, with investment capital of 30,000 to 37,000 billion VN Dong[68] from 2005 to 2015.[69] This project significantly impacted the economic, social and cultural rights of approximately 100,000 people from 15 ethnic minorities in the mountainous and remote northern provinces of Son La and Lai Chau, who were subjected to a forced resettlement programme.[70]

Second, the National Assembly can influence human rights protection because it can sign, accede to, or ratify international treaties (including human rights treaties), approve economic and social development plans, and make policies on religion and ethnic minorities. As recognised in the 2005 Law on Signing, Accession and Implementation of International Treaties, the negotiation and ratification of any international treaty, including treaties on human rights, should be submitted to the National Assembly Standing Committee for final comments.[71]

Third, as the only law-making body, the National Assembly is responsible for drafting and adopting all legislation. Accordingly, legislation on corporate human rights responsibility must be supported and approved by the National Assembly.

---

[67] These decisions are based on five criteria: (1) projects/works with more than VND 20 billion of capital investment using from 30% of total state capital; (2) projects/works that seriously impact or have the potential to impact the environment, such as nuclear power plants, and projects that require more than 200 ha of forest land, more than 500 ha of preventative forest land, or more than 1,000 ha of production forest land; (3) projects/works that require resettlement of more than 20,000 people in mountainous areas and more than 50,000 people in other areas; (4) investment projects/works in areas of special importance to national security and defence or in areas of special history, and cultural heritage; and (5) projects/works that require special policy or mechanism decided by the National Assembly.

[68] US $1 = VND 15.450 as at 2002.

[69] Vietnam National Assembly, Resolution Number: NQ 13/2002/QH11 on solution to develop Son La Hydro Power. However, the investment capital of Son La project increased 60% more than the original plan and the duration of the implementation has been shortened 2012 instead of 2015.

[70] LD, '3 bước di dân, tái định cư của dự án Thuỷ điện Sơn La' (Three Steps to Migrate and Resettle in Son La Hydro Power Project), *Lao Dong News*, Chapter 2001, accessed 13 July 2011.

[71] See the 2005 Law on Signing, Ratification and Accession of International Treaties.

4.2. THE EXECUTIVE

The Vietnamese executive includes the central government (ministries and ministry-equivalent bodies) and local governments (provinces/municipalities, districts/towns and communes). Together, central and local governments are responsible for administering all political, economic, cultural, social, national defence, security, and external activity of the state. Under the Constitution, the government and its agencies are responsible for protecting the legitimate rights and interests of citizens, creating conditions for citizens to exercise their rights and fulfil their obligations, and taking measures to protect property, the interests of the state and society, and the environment.[72] Accordingly, the government must ensure that human rights are respected, protected and fulfilled, including in business activities.

The Vietnamese government has taken some actions to positively support the promotion and implementation of corporate human rights responsibility. Given that it has not developed a specific human rights and business strategy, the government's primary means of addressing corporate human rights responsibility are programmes administered by official bodies. These are usually concentrated on CSR activity. Recently, ministries and agencies including the Ministry of Labour, Invalid and Social Affairs (MOLISA), the Ministry of Health (MOH), the Ministry of Trade and Industry (MOIT), the Ministry of Planning and Investment (MPI) and the Vietnam General Confederation of Labour have worked with various partners, such as international agencies, corporations and NGOs, to develop programmes and projects on CSR-related issues. Examples of such initiatives include the participating in Global Compact network.[73] MOLISA has a mandate to enforce labour-related CSR, and employs labour inspectors to inspect all enterprises in Vietnam and ensure compliance with labour and employment standards.

CSR is integrated into some national strategies and programmes. For example, a recent government development strategy on Strategic Orientation for Sustainable Development in Vietnam expressed the intention to address CSR indirectly.[74] Although this strategy does not have an explicit provision on CSR, it attempts to include CSR as part of a sustainable development strategy by harmonising economic development, social development, and environmental protection.[75] For example, the National Strategy on Protection and Care of People's Health

---

72   See Article 112, 1992 Constitution of Vietnam for more information about the duties and powers of the state.
73   For example: UNDP and VCCI project on Global Compact, MOLISA and World Bank Project on Labour issues.
74   The Prime Minister signed Decision No. 153/2004/QD-TTg issuing the Strategic Orientation for Sustainable Development in Vietnam on 17 August 2004.
75   See Vietnam Business Links Initiative (VBLI) and German Development Service (DED), *supra* n. 573; Prime Minister of Vietnam, 'Government's Strategic Orientation for Sustainable Development (Vietnam Agenda 21)', 2004.

(2001–2010 and 2010–2020) implemented by the Ministry of Health, as well as the National Programme on Occupational Safety – Hygiene (2011–2015) implemented by MOLISA, set targets for government bodies to improve health and safety, including the improvement of workplace health and safety. The National Programme on Occupational Safety – Hygiene has worked closely with SMEs on improving working conditions, preventing occupational accidents and improving employees' health. The National Target Programme on Responding to Climate Change (2009–2015), which was approved by the Prime Minister and contains nine tasks and solutions, represents another government initiative to promote the right to environment. This programme is unique because it has integrated sustainable development, poverty reduction, and gender equality and represents a multi-sectoral response.

In addition to these policy programmes, Vietnamese ministries and agencies have also worked with international organisations and development agencies on projects to promote better awareness of CSR within government. For example, CSR awareness was raised in a 2003 World Bank project on strengthening the government's engagement with CSR, run in collaboration with MOLISA. This project aimed:

> [to] improve awareness about CSR among key government officials, to explore and identify government roles for strengthening CSR in Vietnam and to support government in stimulating broad dialogue with key stakeholders in key export sectors about proposed government roles in strengthening CSR.[76]

The programme raised labour concerns in the footwear and labour industry. CSR was also introduced into some of the activities of the Vietnam General Confederation of Labour, including those related to industrial relations, child labour, migrant workers and gender.[77]

Due to the rapid increase in business activities, demands by local communities to address corporate human rights abuses have increased.[78] The response of the government and its relevant ministries and agencies however, has remained quite limited. Most of the current initiatives on CSR have been restricted to small departments within a ministry or organisations rather than comprehensive, government-wide projects. Most programmes or projects are short-lived because they depend on foreign funding or the state's budget. Consequently, government initiatives on corporate human rights responsibility are vague and

---

[76] World Bank Vietnam, 'Vietnam: The World Bank and ILSSA Program of Technical Assistance: Corporate Social Responsibility in Vietnam', 2003, available at: http://siteresources.worldbank. org/INTPSD/Resources/Vietnam/VietnamCSRTAsummary.pdf (accessed 1 October 2012).

[77] Vietnam Business Links Initiative (VBLI) and German Development Service (DED), *supra* n. 75, p. 30.

[78] For example, the Bauxit project in the Tay Nguyen highland area has been strongly opposed by economists, scholars, and NGOs, due to the concern about the environment and the impact on the local community.

lack sustainability. Such measures are usually implemented indirectly through economic or social policy, strategy and programmes, and to date, few government human rights programmes or projects have focused on human rights and corporate responsibility.

4.3. THE JUDICIARY

The Vietnamese judicial system includes four institutions: People's Courts, People's Procuracy, Organisations for Mediation, and Economic Arbitrations. The court system and the Procuracy are the main dispute resolution bodies. Under the 2013 Constitution, the People's Court of Vietnam has a 'duty to ensure justice, human rights, citizens' rights; to protect socialist regimes, state's interest, rights and interests of individuals and organisations'.[79] Accordingly, at a central and local level, courts are responsible for enforcing the government's legislative efforts to promote human rights through their judgments.

Judicial reform was one of the most important features of the Doi Moi reforms,[80] and the Vietnamese judiciary is now more independent from the executive and legislature.[81] Nevertheless, the progress of the legal reform has not kept pace with the exponential growth in the economy. Accordingly, the judicial system of Vietnam still lacks capacity and full independence. This can make it difficult for human rights cases to proceed, especially where they involve rights violations by non-state actors. In particular, it seems that the judicial system lacks capacity to handle cases of corporate human rights abuse. To date, it is unknown whether the People's Court and its local courts have made any decisions on corporate human rights violations. This may partly be explained by the lack of publicly available records of Vietnamese court decisions.[82] However,

---

[79] Article 102, 2013 Constitution.

[80] The Party launched a strong judicial reform policy including Resolution 08-NQ/TW dated 2/1/2002 of the Politburo and the Strategy on Judicial Reform to 2020, issued by the Resolution No. 49-NQ/TW dated 2 June 2005 of the Politburo. These are milestone policy documents for the legal reform process in Vietnam. Among others, the Strategy addresses eight different issues including: (1) the improvement of policy, civil and criminal law and judicial proceedings; (2) identifying the functions, duties, competencies and perfecting the organisation and mechanism of the judicial body with a special focus on the improvement of organisation and operation of people's courts; (3) improvement of institutions on supplementary justice; (4) strengthening the capacity of staff of the judiciary system; (5) improving the supervisory mechanism of the elective body and promoting the people's rights to mastery in judicial bodies; (6) strengthening international cooperation in justice; (7) ensuring the facilities for judicial activities; and (8) improving the monitoring mechanism of the party towards judicial activities.

[81] Even the 1992 Constitution does not recognise the principle of separation of powers between the three branches of the state (legislature, executive and judiciary).

[82] I have researched all relevant Vietnamese judiciary websites, including the website of the Supreme People's Court. Except for some information about the judgments of economic disputes between corporations, no cases or court decisions involving corporate human rights abuses have been found. See: VIB online at: www.vibonline.com.vn/Banan/default.aspx and

another potentially significant factor in the absence of public decisions regarding corporate human rights violations is the lack of legal provisions under which such proceedings may be brought, and particularly the absence of any allowance for class actions.[83] The recently introduced commercial arbitration mechanism, adopted under the 2010 Law on Commercial Arbitration, represents a potentially promising starting point for greater engagement with corporate human rights abuses under the Vietnamese legal system.

Court access for corporate human rights abuse victims is also limited by absence of special courts for these proceedings, such as a Constitutional or human rights court.[84] The only forums in which human rights cases may be heard are specific tribunals, such as the Economic Court and the Administrative and Labour Courts. Nevertheless, cases involving human rights violations of corporations may not be justiciable in these courts due to the lack of clear legal provisions on the human rights responsibility of corporations and more generally, the inefficient and unreliable administrative and justice system.[85] Informal justice mechanisms such as mediation (Tổ hòa giải), which represents a traditional community approach, are ill-equipped to deal with conflict between corporations and communities because they were developed to address individual civil conflicts.[86]

5. GAPS IN THE POLITICAL, LEGISLATIVE, EXECUTIVE AND JUDICIAL INSTITUTIONS IN IMPLEMENTING CORPORATE HUMAN RIGHTS RESPONSIBILITY

Vietnamese law-making and enforcement institutions have not sufficiently considered the need to create a national mechanism holding government and non-state actors accountable for human rights. The lack of an independent national human rights mechanism has influenced the effectiveness of government responses to business-related human rights impacts.

---

the website of the Supreme Court at: http://toaan.gov.vn/portal/page/portal/tandtc (accessed 14 February 2013).

[83] As discussed, corporations are not subject to criminal liability.

[84] Many countries such as South Africa, Austria, German and Cambodia have their own constitutional court to deal with violations or conflicts with constitutional rights and freedom.

[85] United Nations Development Programme, 'Justice Index: Assessment of Distributive Justice and Equality from a Citizen-based Survey in 2012', 2013, available at: www.vn.undp.org/content/dam/vietnam/docs/Publications/Justice%20index_EN_FINAL%2029%20Sep.pdf (accessed 15 January 2014).

[86] See for example, Government Guiding Degree No. 160/1999/ND-CP on some issues of the Ordinance on Organisation and Activities of the Grassroots Mediation.

One of these barriers is the lack of independence of the legislature, executive, and judiciary. Although judges and people's assessors are formally independent under the law,[87] they are still influenced by government and Party policy in practice. As a result of the Party's recognition of human rights in the political instruments of Party Congresses since 1990s, more open discussion of these rights is possible and growing numbers of government and non-government human rights projects have been implemented.[88] However, the view of the Party on human rights and CSR is quite narrow. It continues to view human rights issues as requiring a political or diplomatic response to external 'reactionary forces'[89] rather than as a larger issue of domestic concern.[90] The connection between human rights and corporations is limited to specific issues, such as labour and social security, and are not expressed broadly. References to CSR in Party instruments are limited to corporations' moral responsibility to consumers and the environment.[91]

Another governance gap is the lack of awareness of corporate human rights responsibility amongst government officials, particularly those in local government. There are arguments that human rights are mainly a political matter and that, accordingly, are a concern of government rather than the private sector. This view is reinforced by the fact that CSR is often seen as a product of civil society in developed countries, which was introduced to Vietnam by foreign buyers and private firms, and not as a matter of national or international law.[92] Consequently, some argue that CSR or corporate human rights responsibility do not require government attention. A lack of understanding amongst government officials, lawmakers, and law enforcers has exacerbated a lack of political will, creating a barrier to integrating corporate human rights responsibility into Vietnamese law.

---

[87] Article 103, 2013 Constitution.

[88] For example, the recent Party Political Reports and the Strategy for Economic and Social Development (2011–2020) confirmed that the Party and Government have a responsibility to ensure human rights, citizens' rights and other conditions to ensure comprehensive development. These documents also made reference to the fact that economic reform should go hand in hand with the 'development and implementation of regulations on corporate social responsibility to consumers and on environments. Improving the understanding of corporations on market, Vietnamese law, international law and customary.' The Party has begun to consider the corporate social responsibilities of business and is arguably viewing it as a priority.

[89] The term 'reactionary forces' is often used to refer to Vietnamese citizens living overseas or groups and organisations that criticise the government.

[90] See the Political Report of the VII, VIII, IX, X and XI Congress of the Communist Party. For example, the Political Report of the XII Congress confirmed that Vietnam will 'actively participate in the universal struggle for human rights; ready to dialogue with other countries, related international and regional organisations on human rights; determine to failure any intention, conspiracy that take the advantage of 'democracy', 'human rights', 'ethnic', 'religious' issues in order to intervene into internal affair and interfere democracy, sovereignty, territorial integrity, security and political stability of Vietnam'.

[91] See for example, Đảng cộng sản Việt Nam (the Communist Party of Vietnam), 'Chiến lược phát triển kinh tế xã hội 2011–2020' (National Strategy for Economic and Social Development 2011–2020), 2011.

[92] IDI 26.

Despite recent legal and administrative reform, both judicial and administrative systems lack a comprehensive development strategy.[93] Because of the complicated administrative system and lack of judicial independence, governance in Vietnam is weak and corruption is an issue of concern. International experience shows that where governance is weak there are more human rights violations, because government cannot protect human rights and address high levels of corruption or conflict.[94]

As discussed above, human rights in Vietnam are more politicised. Particular agencies do have a mandate to look at human rights issues, but a multi-sectoral approach is absent. Currently, many human rights activities that include preparing human rights reports are coordinated by the Ministry of Foreign Affairs (MOFA).[95]

Government agencies that regulate business, such as the Ministry of Planning and Investment, the Ministry of Industry and Trade, and the Ministry of Finance, are often not directly involved in ensuring human rights protection. It is a common view that human rights are not mentioned in the work of these ministries except in some Official Development Aid (ODA) projects when human rights are often raised by donors or investors as a condition of aid or investment.

The absence of a human rights approach, especially in the ministries and departments that govern business activities, helps to facilitate corporate neglect of human rights responsibilities.

The lack of an institutional mechanism to coordinate the human rights activities of the legislature, executive, and judiciary has made enforcing corporate human rights responsibility more difficult. While foreign parliaments are often actively involved in human rights protection through mechanisms such as the ombudsmen, no equivalent agency dedicated to rights promotion exists in Vietnam. While there is a lack of an effective means of addressing human rights at the national level, it is consequently difficult to attract attention to human rights and business issues unless there is clear evidence of law infringement.

---

[93]   C. Goodlow Wescott, *Key Governance issues in Cambodia, Lao PDR, Thailand and Viet Nam* (Manila: Asia Development Bank, Programs Department, 2001), p. 60.

[94]   The International Organisation of Employers (IOE), the International Chamber of Commerce (ICC) and the Business and Industry Advisory Committee to the OECD (BIAC), 'Joint initial views of the International Organisation of Employers (IOE), the International Chamber of Commerce (ICC) and the Business and Industry Advisory Committee to the OECD (BIAC) to the Eighth Session of the Human Rights Council on the Third report of the Special Representative of the UN Secretary-General on Business and Human Rights', May 2008, available at: www.reports-and-materials.org/Letter-IOE-ICC-BIAC-re-Ruggie-report-May-2008.pdf (accessed 15 July 2011).

[95]   A large project on the implementation of International Human Rights Treaty by the Ministry of Foreign Affairs was supported by UNDP from 2008–2011.

6.   CONCLUSION

This chapter has provided an overview of the roles of government in addressing corporate human rights responsibility in Vietnam. It sought to establish how corporate human rights responsibilities are interpreted in the Vietnamese context, where human rights are politicised and unfamiliar to business. Although some constructive initiatives to enforce corporate responsibility have been developed, no consistent approach to human rights exists amongst state actor. The local business community is generally isolated from considering the key principles of respect, protection, and fulfilment of human rights. This lack of familiarity is directly related to a lack of awareness and support for corporate human rights responsibility in existing policy, law and programmes.

Vietnam's existing policy and legal framework indicates that little attention has been given to the duty to respect, protect, and fulfil human rights in business. This is caused by a lack of government state capacity that encourages weak sanctions of corporate human rights abusers. The Vietnamese government has a duty to ensure that all internationally recognised human rights are respected, protected, and fulfilled, even in the business sector, particularly given the binding nature of the international human rights instruments to which Vietnam is a party. To do so, the government should adopt policies, laws, and/or recommendations to encourage human rights protection by foreign and domestic corporations. Establishing a national human rights commission, expert body, or a focal point on human rights and business with participation from all government agencies (including those that are business related) could help improve existing human rights and corporate responsibility Vietnam.

CHAPTER 11

INVESTMENT TREATIES
AND HUMAN RIGHTS

Reflections from Mining in Latin America

Stéphanie GERVAIS

1.   INTRODUCTION

Mineral extraction in developing countries is a 'high risk' investment with unpredictable costs associated to policy changes such as nationalisation and increased regulations by host-governments. In Latin America, many governments have acknowledged demands by civil society organisations (CSOs) to cancel extraction contracts and change their mining codes to uphold human rights and environmental standards. Investment agreements signed between a country, where an extractive company is incorporated, and a host country, with resource endowments, provide investors with a sense of security over their mineral claims and conditions of profit partition. These agreements, which can take the form of Bilateral Investment Treaties (BITs), Foreign Investment Contracts (FICs), or investment chapters of Free Trade Agreements (FTAs), often contain clauses that mandate governments to compensate the company if policy changes result in a loss of profits. With now over 3,160 investment treaties between countries of all regions and economic stature, many governments, having signed on to treaties with such clauses, must weigh the costs of implementing human rights policies. If an arbitration tribunal finds a government's policies to breach the investment treaty, it will issue an award for the government to pay to the investor. Ranging from several millions to in some cases billions of dollars, these costly awards are thought to discourage governments from intervening when investment projects allegedly violate human rights.[1]

---

[1]   R. Suda, 'The Effect of Bilateral Investment Treaties on Human Rights Enforcement and Realization', NYU Global Law Working Paper No. 01, 2005; S. Anderson, J. Artiga-Purcell, A. Dreyfus, M. Perez-Rocha and M. Rocha, 'Mining for Profits in International Tribunals', Report by the Institute for Policy Studies, 2011.

There are many grounds for the emergence of conflicts between human rights policies and investment agreements in this sector. A common example in recent cases is the enforcement of a moratorium by a host government on specific types of extractive activities when the operations of these mines are the source of anticipated human rights violations. Large scale metal ore mining, for instance, risks causing harm to human health, contaminating water sources and farm land, as well as conflict with the self-determination rights of indigenous communities.[2] Investors, having acquired land titles (or exploration permits) to search for deposits, but who were then refused secondary extraction permits needed to begin operations, may claim that withholding these permits is a form of expropriation by the government and a breach of the investment treaty. The claims of a treaty breach may even occur in cases where this denial is based on the project's environmental and social impact assessment failing to meet domestic legal requirements of extraction permits (see the case of Costa Rica). Since many investment agreements contain clauses to protect investors against such types of indirect expropriation associated with the denial of permits, these investors launch suits to receive compensations for loss of anticipated profits from host states. When these two legal obligations conflict – the obligation to respect investment treaties and to enforce human rights treaties as required by domestic law – states have the option to either defend their right to regulate in front of arbitration tribunals, or to backtrack from these policies, as the 'regulatory chill' theory would suggest, in order to avoid the high legal costs associated with the suit.[3]

The mandate of the UN Special Representative on Business and Human Rights (SRSG) led to the creation of the Guiding Principles on Business and Human Rights (Guiding Principles or UNGPs) and the UN Working Group on Business and Human Rights to oversee their implementation. A key pillar of the Guiding Principles is the state's duty to protect against human rights violations committed by third parties such as business enterprises. To do so, it is recommended that states retain adequate policy space to enforce human rights protection mechanisms.[4] Unfortunately, this recommendation fails to provide guidance on how to implement human rights policies without breaching investment treaty clauses that are already in place and arbitration proceedings to resolve these conflicts why they are on the rise.

This chapter examines cases of Latin American states implementing human rights policies aligned with the UN Guiding Principles in the extractive sector to

---

[2] FIDH (International Federation for Human Rights), 'Large-scale Mining in Ecuador and Human Rights, Abuses: The Case of Corriente Resources Inc.', 2010, available at: www. refworld.org/docid/4d2e9ec82.html (accessed 21 August 2013).

[3] K. Tienhaara, 'Regulatory chill and the threat of arbitration: a view from political science', Regulatory Institutions Network, Australian National University, 2010.

[4] Human Rights Council, 'Guiding Principles on Business and Human Rights: Implementing the United Nations "Protect, Respect and Remedy" Framework', 2011, UN Doc. A/HRC/17/31, p. 12.

understand the impact of international investment agreements on the fulfilment of these principles. Although the study of the 'regulatory chill' theory is commonly applied to environmental policies, this research pulls together environmental and health policies under the international framework of economic, social, and cultural rights in an attempt to bridge the gap between the common conception of human rights as mainly entailing civil and political rights, and the progressive nature of a number of constitutions in Latin America which relate the protection of the environment to human rights. As a region, Latin America gives great insight into the human rights impacts of mining as a number of governments in the region, such as Colombia, Costa Rica, Bolivia and Ecuador, are linking explicitly, by way of their constitutions, the rights of nature and natural resources to the human right to health.[5] This expands the understanding of the overarching human health effects of this economic activity on which many developing countries rely on to attain a higher level of development.

2.   METHOD

By looking at countries that have ratified the International Covenant on Economic, Social, and Cultural Rights (ICESCR), policies aimed at preserving a clean environment, such as the banning of polluting forms of mining, are interpreted as an attempt to protect the human right to health, to an adequate standard of living, to water, and other rights specific to the cases at hand. These case studies will test the hypothesis that IIAs hinder the implementation of human rights policies, thus causing a 'regulatory chill'. Given the difficulties of predicting motives behind policy decisions, one cannot assume that IIAs in themselves are the basis for host governments to refrain from implementing human rights legislation. Rather, evidence of IIAs influencing policy is more compelling when arbitration cases arise to settle disputes over enacted domestic policies and investment agreements. As the threat of the government having to pay an award to the company becomes more credible, the conflicting nature of investment agreements and human rights policy becomes more apparent. Therefore, to study the impact of IIAs, this chapter looks at policies that are already in place and examines if governments refrain from implementing these policies subsequent to launching suits by investors.

This research applies a case study methodology to understand the role investment treaties play in Latin America regarding the implementation of human rights policies in the mining sector. Given the little amount of research in the field due to the very recent rise in arbitration cases (most of which have yet to be resolved), the objective of this research is to conduct a plausibility probe

---

[5]   A. Fabra, 'Enforcing the right to a healthy environment in Latin America' (1994) 3(4) *Review of European Community & International Environmental Law* 215–222, available at: http://bit. ly/1bzvGOI.

into the 'regulatory chill' theory. It remains a preliminary study on a 'relatively untested theory' and, as such, calls for further studies once these cases have been concluded.[6] Similar to a typical theory testing study, 'most-likely' cases of regulatory chill are used to assess the theory and identify elements of it that require more testing.

The hypothesis is tested by analysing the impact of the independent variable, the launch of arbitration suits by foreign investors using investment treaties, on the host government's implementation of human rights policies, the dependent variable. The variance of this dependent variable is evaluated by a host government's policy actions towards an investment project creating human rights concerns. The year in which the exploration permit was allocated to the investor is used as the baseline to study changes in government policy. Policy changes are then studied in juxtaposition to threats and the progression of investment disputes by looking strictly at cases where this threat is credible. In this sense, 'most-likely' cases of a regulatory chill in the mining sector are observed when the investor has taken steps to pursue international arbitration relying on a treaty which contains the mentioned clauses. The presence of these clauses increases the likelihood of the government having to pay an award to the company following arbitration proceedings. These conditions are thought to increase a government's likelihood of changing policy direction in favour of foreign investment instead of human rights.

The independent variable is thought to influence the dependent variable if the launch of an investment suit leads to government retraction of a mining policy targeted by the suit. That is to say, the use of an IIA to launch a legal suit appears to have triggered a retraction from human rights policy objectives thus *chilling* the related regulations and confirming the theory's hypothesis. In contrast, if such a retraction does not occur and the government pursues human rights-related policies, the hypothesis is invalidated. This variance is studied from the beginning of the launch of the legal suit and, as the cases have yet to be concluded, a future study will be required to fully assess this variance following the tribunal's ruling.

3.   REGULATORY CHILL THEORY

The leading theory documenting the impact of investment treaties on domestic policy, namely environmental policies, and by way of that, human rights policies, is the 'regulatory chill' theory (Leader, 2006).[7] In the current literature there is

---

6   A. George and A. Bennett, *Case Studies and Theory Development in The Social Sciences* (Cambridge, Mass: MIT Press, 2005), p. 75.

7   H. Mann, 'International Investment Agreements, Business and Human Rights: Key Issues and Opportunities', International Institute for Sustainable Development, February 2008, available at: www.iisd.org/pdf/2008/iia_business_human_rights.pdf; E. Neumayer, 'Do Countries Fail

evidence both supporting this theory and contradicting it. On the one hand, defenders of the regulatory chill theory consider human rights policies in foreign investment sectors to be heavily constrained by investment treaties. On the other hand, opponents of the theory maintain that investment treaties do not pose a threat to the protection of host states' regulatory powers, as they are within their sovereign right to do so.[8]

A regulatory chill is a phenomenon by which states 'forego needed environmental and social legislation that might negatively affect the value of foreign investment, to avoid potential liability'.[9] A common understanding of the theory is that states pre-emptively avoid adopting constraining laws in order to attract investment. However, it is difficult to attribute this avoidance to an investment agreement unless the threat of liability becomes more credible. In this sense, the *chill* is observed in cases where policies are already set in motion or expressed as an intention by governments as there are many empirical challenges to analysing the impacts of investment treaties on policies that have yet to be thought out. A popular case to illustrate the regulatory chill phenomena is that of anti-mining legislation in Indonesia that was repealed following threats by nearly 150 mining companies of filing suits under the country's bilateral and multilateral investment treaties.[10] It would be difficult to argue that the presence of investment treaties did not impact the government of Indonesia's decision to repeal the bill banning mining, as the financial threat was a rather credible one.

According to the regulatory chill theory, once the threat of arbitration proceedings becomes credible, governments would amend their policies to redress the alleged cause of the claim of treaty breach made by investors. The rationale for repealing policies affecting the mining sector stems from the fear of facing exorbitant costs of compensation awards and legal fees. Governments assume that they are at a disadvantage and have a higher risk of facing liability for several reasons. A straightforward cause for concern is the interpretation of treaty clauses by arbitration panels leading to a higher count of cases concluded in favour of the investor. An empirical study of the resolutions of arbitration tribunals found a systemic bias wherein arbitrators more often favour the position

---

to Raise Environmental Standards? An Evaluation of Policy Options Addressing 'Regulatory Chill' (2001) 4(3) *International Journal of Sustainable Development* 231–244 (revised version obtained from author, pp. 1–27); R. Suda, *supra* n. 1; K. Tienhaara, 'What You Don't Know Can Hurt You: Investor-State Disputes and the Protection of the Environment' (2006) 6(4) *Developing Countries Global Environmental Politics*.

[8] J. Coe and N. Rubins, 'Regulatory expropriation and the Tecmed case: context and contributions' in T. Weiler (ed.), *International Investment Law and Arbitration: Leading Cases from the ICSID, NAFTA, Bilateral Treaties and Customary International Law* (London: Cameron, 2005); J.D. Fry, 'International Human Rights Law in Investment Arbitration: Evidence of International Law's Unity' (2009) 9 *Duke Journal of Comparative International Law* 77–149.

[9] S.G. Gross, 'Inordinate Chill: BITs, Non-NAFTA MITs, and Host-State Regulatory Freedom – An Indonesian Case Study' (2002) 24(3) *Michigan Journal of International Law* 893–960, 893

[10] K. Tienhaara, *supra* n. 7.

of investors over states and are even more likely to do so if the investors are based in a major western capital-exporting country.[11] This study draws statistically significant evidence from '140 investment-treaty cases [and] shows that arbitrators consistently adopt an expansive (claimant-friendly) interpretation of various clauses, such as the concept of investment [while] arbitration lawyers have taken a restrictive approach in international law when it comes to human and social rights'.[12]

There is clearly a pattern of recurring clauses that conflict with the implementation of human rights policies by targeting the state's ability to change the regulatory conditions of an investment project.[13] Among these clauses, those most cited as increasing the risk for host-states are 'stabilisation clauses', restrictions on 'expropriation', 'non-discriminatory and reasonableness' clauses, 'fair and equitable treatment' standards, and 'national and most-favored-nation treatment' clauses.[14] Investors often accused the host-states of breaching these clauses in cases of a government cancelling contracts, increasing environmental standards, and launching criminal suits against investors in domestic courts. In some cases the language is clearly constraining for changes to domestic regulations and in others, the vague wording of these clauses gives investors a greater freedom of interpretation, making it difficult for states to calculate the risks of agreeing to arbitration.[15]

Although the language of these clauses blatantly poses barriers to regulations applying to foreign investment, states are said to freeze their policies only when claims are brought forward by investors to arbitration or when they threaten to do so.[16] To make these threats, the treaties must contain clauses that allow investors to bypass domestic courts and file claims through international arbitration tribunals. The current practices and customary interpretations of the treaties by arbitration tribunals are said to be unfavourable to host states enforcing public

---

[11]   G. Van Harten, 'Arbitrator Behaviour in Asymmetrical Adjudication: An Empirical Study of Investment Treaty Arbitration' *Osgoode Hall Law Journal*, forthcoming; Osgoode CLPE Research Paper No. 41/2012.

[12]   P. Eberhardt and C. Olivet, 'Profiting from Injustice: How Law Firms, Arbitrators and Financiers Are Fuelling an Investment Arbitration Boom', Corporate Europe Observatory and the Transnational Institute, 2012, p. 48.

[13]   S. Anderson, J. Artiga-Purcell, A. Dreyfus, M. Perez-Rocha and M. Rocha, *supra* n. 1; J.G. Brown, 'International Investment Agreements: Regulatory Chill in the Face of Litigious Heat?' (2013) 3(1) *Journal of Legal Studies*; S.G. Gross, *supra* n. 9; International Finance Corporation (IFC), 'Stabilization Clauses and Human Rights', World Bank Group, 11 March 2008; U. Kriebaum, 'Privatizing Human Rights: The interface between international investment protection and human rights' in A. Reinish and U. Kriebaum (eds.), *The Law of International Relations: Liber Amicorum Hanspeter Nauhold* (The Hague: Eleven International Publishing, 2007), pp. 165–189; H. Mann, *supra* n. 7; R. Suda, *supra* n. 1.

[14]   S. Anderson, J. Artiga-Purcell, A. Dreyfus, M. Perez-Rocha and M. Rocha, *supra* n. 1.

[15]   J.G. Brown, *supra* n. 13, p. 5.

[16]   K. Tienhaara, *supra* n. 3.

interest laws on investment projects.[17] The three most common tribunals to hold these arbitration proceedings are the Permanent Court of Arbitration (PCA), the United Nations Commission on International Trade Law (UNCITRAL), and the International Center for Settlement of Investment Disputes (ICSID). The latter has been the subject of a recent UNCTAD report which outlines the general concerns of the current dispute settlement system.

The financial resources needed for a country to defend itself in arbitration are often seen as a deterrent for public interest policies that may conflict with investment clauses. For instance, investors have made claims to be awarded up to US $100 billion by host-states and final awards have gone as high as nearly US $2 billion in the case of *Occidental Petroleum v. Ecuador*. The threat of these costly suits is thought to be the main deterrent to the implementation of human rights policies impacting investment projects, especially for small states confronting large multinational enterprises.[18] Although legal costs weigh both on investors and host states, in the case of a multinational firm launching a suit against a developing country, the advantage is on the side of the investor who often benefits from greater financial resources and legal expertise. Even in cases where countries are not fined or a case is thrown out, the costs of the proceedings still average nearly US $10 million.[19]

The risk of having to pay such awards is increased by the common practice of arbitration panels disregarding the motivations behind the policies implemented by host states being disputed by investors. This is cause for a second concern, given that it is not guaranteed that the defence made by governments to justify their policy choices will be given the same weight as the investors' claims as they can easily be dismissed by the panel for not qualifying as relevant to the investment dispute. Although most treaties require coherence between their investment policies and a country's domestic legal framework, arbitration proceedings can conclude that states have valid reasons for violating a treaty in the name of public interest and decide not to accord the award to investors. Unfortunately, studies have shown that in many cases, tribunals did not take into account the reasons behind policy choices when they involved human rights or public morals issues.[20] Critics point to the lack of expertise on the panel of arbitrators on the matter of public interest and human rights policies as evidence that they should not rule on the validity of these policies.[21]

Based on this analysis, host governments can potentially and in many cases have been penalised for enforcing human rights policies in investment-related

---

[17]   UNCTAD, 'Reform of Investor-States Dispute Settlement: In search of a roadmap', *Special Issue for the Multilateral Dialogue on Investment*, 28–29 May 2013.

[18]   *Ibid.*, p. 3.

[19]   J. Paulsson, 'Moral Hazard in International Dispute Resolution', Inaugural Lecture, Miami School of Law, 29 April 2010.

[20]   R. Suda, *supra* n. 1, p. 29.

[21]   UNCTAD, *supra* n. 17.

sectors. What impact does this then have on the willingness of governments to implement human rights policies? A general assumption is that investment treaties create a 'regulatory chill' as countries refrain from regulating in favour of human rights for fear of costs associated to claims being filed by investors. These considerations have led to the mention of the impact of investment treaties on domestic policy in the UNGPs. Specifically, the UNGPs' author, John Ruggie, recommends that: 'States should maintain adequate domestic policy space to meet their human rights obligations when pursuing business-related policy objectives with other states or business enterprises, for instance through investment treaties or contracts'.[22] Ruggie argues that 'the terms of international investment agreements may constrain states from fully implementing new human rights legislation, or put them at risk of binding international arbitration if they do so.' The mention of this in the UNGPs demonstrates increased support of the regulatory chill theory not only by a number of academics but also by important international governance organisations.

4.   CASE STUDIES

The case selection is based on the design of a 'most-likely' case established in the regulatory chill theory itself. A first condition to study this theory is the presence of an alleged or foreseen human rights violation related to the investment project that a government has vowed to resolve through a given policy. At the outset, if there is no expressed willingness on the part of the government to enforce a human rights policy related to the investment project, the *chilling* of policies cannot be correlated to the presence of an investment treaty. To understand how the regulatory chill phenomenon operates, these human rights policies must be in conflict with investment interests protected under a pre-existing investment agreement.

This second set of conditions relates to the presence of an investment treaty between the host-state of the project and the home state of the investor that includes stabilising, expropriation, most-favoured nation fair and equitable treatment, or umbrella clauses. This treaty must also contain a dispute settlement provision allowing the investor to bypass domestic courts to bring claims directly to international tribunals. The likelihood of a government retracting human rights policies is influenced by the investor's ability to claim a breach of these clauses and revert to the use of international arbitration to request compensation from the government. If the treaty does not contain a clause permitting the investor to bring disputes to international arbitration tribunals, the threat of having to pay large awards and legal fees is less credible. The presence of these

---

[22]   Human Rights Council, *supra* n. 4, p. 12.

clauses increases the likelihood of the government having to pay an award to the company following arbitration proceedings.[23]

This study looks at the two known cases fitting these criteria, despite there being a greater number of cases from which to draw. To narrow in on these particular cases, an examination of all concluded and ongoing arbitration cases drawn from ICSID, the PCA, and UNCITRAL related to mining in Latin America was conducted. Examples of cases that were dismissed despite meeting the regional and industry criteria are Venezuela and Bolivia, as the cases lacked substantive documentation of incidences of human rights violations. While Venezuela has a total of 26 cases in the broader extractive sector,[24] with awards ranging between US $3.2 and US $1.2 billion,[25] some of which have even been concluded in favour of the government's policies, the contested policies do not relate to human rights but rather to alternative strategies of economic development. Specifically, they relate to the nationalisation of industry to increase government revenue which does not imply fewer impacts on the environment and human rights. Also, despite an increase of arbitration cases related to human rights policies in other extractive sectors, such as oil, gas and other energy industries, predominantly in Ecuador, the selected cases pertain strictly to mining in order to provide industry-specific observations.

In itself, Latin America is the region with the highest number of arbitration cases related to the extractive sector, now representing 51% of cases at ICSID. In response to these suits many Latin American governments have taken very clear public stances challenging the legitimacy of suits launched by foreign mining investors. The policies that stem from these stances are part of a wider trend in Latin America to favour the protection of the environment and human rights over foreign investment in the mining sector as documented in these cases. Although the relationship between the environment and human rights lacks clarity in international law from a global perspective, many governments in the region have bound human rights to the protection of the environment through their constitutions. This makes it easier to claim that hazardous mining projects are a threat to human rights and public interest, and allowing governments to withhold or cancel extraction contract if they do not meet environmental requirements.

These case studies look at the process of regulating the mining sector to examine how arbitration proceedings impact host government policy direction. Each case study outlines the basis for selection in line with the criteria described in the methodology discussion, followed by a description of the human rights context of the investment project and an overview of the domestic policy response.

---

[23]   K. Tienhaara, *supra* n. 3.

[24]   M.D. Goldhaber, 'Arbitration Scorecard 2013: Treaty Disputes', *The American Lawyer*, 1 July 2013, available at: http://bit.ly/ISBT1h (accessed 16 July 2013).

[25]   K. Vyas, 'Venezuela PDVSA: Won Arbitration Case Against Opic Karimun', *4-Traders*, 29 May 2013, available at: http://goo.gl/WYChCV (accessed 16 July 2013).

A review of the particularities of the investment treaty used by the investor to launch the complaint and the arbitration procedure itself will then help determine how the dependent variable has been influenced by the independent variable.

4.1. PACIFIC RIM CAYMAN LLC V. EL SALVADOR

4.1.1. Basis for Case Selection

When discussing the impacts of investment treaty disputes on the implementation of human rights in the mining sector, the most commonly cited case is that of El Salvador and Pacific Rim. It has been highly mediatised over the past few years due, in part, to the high cost of the award sought by the investor (representing nearly 2% of the country's GDP) and to the public stance the President has taken, claiming the country's right to halt mining.[26] As the parties agreed to disclose information on the proceedings, it is also a well-documented case. This case has been selected as it fits the 'most-likely' criteria of the regulatory chill theory in that an investor has launched a costly investment complaint seeking compensation for expropriation when its project was halted by the government due to environmental and human rights concerns. Following the theory, the threat of this legal suit should cause the government to reinstate the company's mining contract. This case, however, contradicts the regulatory chill hypothesis.

4.1.2. Human Rights Context

El Salvador is a small Central American country with a large portion of the country sitting on the Central American gold belt. The mineral deposits overlap with the country's main watershed, the Lempa River, and dense farming communities that make up the second highest employment sector.[27] Over the past decade, these mineral deposits have been claimed by foreign investors, namely the Canadian-based mining company Pacific Rim. These land claims give the investor the right to explore for mineral deposits on the land. Although these titles were sold to the company, it had to subsequently file for an exploration permit to open a mine on the site.

In 2006, two years after the company applied for permits for their El Dorado project in Cabañas, they were rejected based on non-compliance with environmental requirements.[28] Concerns regarding these environmental impacts

---

[26]   CISPES, 'Release: Salvadoran president reiterates opposition to mining projects', 13 January 2010, available at: http://bit.ly/1c09bsw (accessed 6 October 2013).
[27]   World Bank Data 'Employment in agriculture', 2010, available at: http://data.worldbank.org/indicator/SL.AGR.EMPL.ZS.
[28]   ICSID, The Republic of El Salvador's Preliminary Objections Under Articles 10.20.4 and 10.20.5 of CAFTA, Case No. ARB/09/12, 4 January 2010, available at: http://bit.ly/18HbuO6, 5.

were brought forward by a large number of groups who organised around the country to protest against this project and similar ones.[29] Opposition to the mine stemmed from the knowledge that communities were increasingly sharing regarding the negative health impacts of this type of mine. The groups were advocating for their right to water, a healthy environment, and their right to life, which they consider to be endangered by the project. International development organisations also shared these concerns and published reports illustrating how increasing mining activity in the country would deteriorate other more sustainable sectors such as agriculture and ecotourism which have a longer lifespan than a mine.[30]

From this, conflicts arose among and within communities, between those who opposed mining and those who supported it and welcomed the additional income and employment. As some groups began to pressure the government to ban mining beginning in 2009, community leaders opposing the mine became the target of attacks, and some of them were tortured and killed. This was the case of Marcelo Rivera who led a campaign against Pacific Rim's project through the Association of Friends of San Isidro Cabañas (ASIC). Shortly after his disappearance, his body was found bearing signs of torture.[31] Two members of the Cabañas Environmental Committee opposing the mine, Ramiro Rivera and Dora Alicia Sorta Recinos, were also killed within the span of a week, both shot by an M-16 rifle. Sorta Recinos, eight months pregnant, was shot in the presence of her two year old son, who was injured.[32] The notice of these killings sparked reactions both from neighbouring communities and international CSOs calling for the government to investigate the murders.

These incidents and the anticipated impacts related to the mine are contested by the company. No legal suit has been launched against the company on its alleged involvement in the murders. In terms of the environmental impacts of the project, the company also maintains that this mine 'exceeds current Canadian and US environmental standards'.[33] However, the validity of the company's claims is not the subject of this research nor is it relevant to the examination of the regulatory chill theory. Rather, what is important is the government's perception of human rights issues which influences its policy choices to protect or prevent against violations. In this case, the government has clearly identified

---

[29] Terra Network Chile, 'Salvadoreños marchan contra la explotación minera', 27 July 2008, retrieved 6 October 2013, available at: http://bit.ly/1dasXhp.

[30] Oxfam America, 'Central American mining could undermine economic well-being', 11 March 2009, available at: www.oxfamamerica.org/press/central-american-mining-could-undermine-economic-well-being/.

[31] Human Rights Watch, 'El Salvador: Investigate Killing of Community Leader', 8 August 2009, available at: www.hrw.org/news/2009/08/07/el-salvador-investigate-killing-community-leader.

[32] Inter Press Service ,'El Salvador: Activists Link Mining Co. to Murders', 27 January 2010, available at: www.ipsnews.net/2010/01/el-salvador-activists-link-mining-co-to-murders/.

[33] 'Statement Filed in Arbitration Case Against El Salvador; PacRim Seeks Damages of US $315 Million', *Globe and Mail*, 1 April 2013, available at: http://bit.ly/18XTGkp.

this investment project as posing a threat to human rights as it does not believe that mining can be done in a way that does not endanger the environment and the health of its citizens.[34] It has thus expressed the intent to issue a moratorium on mining and continues to deny permits in public statements.[35] Although there is no way of determining if the government's discourse is purely a matter of gaining political capital, this commitment to protecting the environment, and in particular the right to clean water, over investment interests has endured over the course of the arbitration proceedings.[36]

4.1.3. Domestic Policy

In the early 2000s when Pacific Rim, among other companies, began to increase mineral exploration in the country, the successive Nationalist Republican Alliance (ARENA) governments had been supportive of foreign investment in the mining sector.[37] However, with push back from communities and the increased unpopularity of ARENA, President Antonio Saca withdrew the company's exploration permits and issued a *de facto* mining ban on future projects. This allowed the Ministry of the Environment and Natural Resources (MARN) to deny Pacific Rim's permits based on environmental and public health risks.[38]

This policy was solidified in the elections of 2009 when Mauricio Funes from the Farabundo Martí National Liberation Front (FMLN) ran on a platform opposing mining in the country and won. Since being in power, Funes has not moved on the issue of mining, continuing to deny new permits as there are no metal-mining operations currently active.[39] However, he has yet to successfully pass this moratorium into law through parliament. Groups such as the National Roundtable against Metallic Mining (Mesa Nacional) continue to call for an actual law to be passed by parliament to ensure a legal basis for the ban on mining in the country.[40]

---

34   CISPES, 'Release: Salvadoran president reiterates opposition to mining projects', 13 January 2010, available at: http://bit.ly/1c09bsw (accessed 6 October 2013).

35   CDHAL, 'Press Release: Salvadoran president: "My government will not authorize any mining extraction projects"', Committee for Human Rights in Latin America, 13 January 2010, available at: http://cdhal.org/en/newspaper/2010-01-13/salvadoran-president-my-government-will-not-authorize-any-mining-extraction.

36   'World Bank tribunal threatens El Salvador's development', *Aljazeera America*, 22 April, 2014, available at: http://goo.gl/Y42MJy (accessed 2 August 2014).

37   'El Salvador: Activists Link Mining Co. to Murders', *Inter Press Service*, 27 January 2010, available at: www.ipsnews.net/2010/01/el-salvador-activists-link-mining-co-to-murders/.

38   K. Gallagher, 'Stop private firms exploiting poor states', *The Guardian*, 5 February 2010, available at: http://bit.ly/1e91bXL (accessed 14 November 2012).

39   M. Karunananthan, 'El Salvador mining ban could establish a vital water security precedent', *The Guardian*, 10 June 2013, available at: http://bit.ly/ISCaRX (accessed 6 October 2013).

40   'ONG salvadoreña insiste ante Parlamento que apruebe una ley contra la minería', *America Economia*, 22 July 2013, available at: http://bit.ly/18HaXff (accessed 6 October 2013).

4.1.4. Arbitration Proceedings

This policy was the basis for the Canadian company Pacific Rim to seek international arbitration through the International Center for Settlement of Investment Disputes (ICSID) in 2009. The jurisdiction under which this claim is being brought is the investment chapter of the Central American Free Trade Agreement (CAFTA) between the United States and Costa Rica, El Salvador, Guatemala, Honduras, Nicaragua, and more recently the Dominican Republic. Although Canada does not have an investment agreement with El Salvador (the proposed Canada-Central American FTA has only led to the signing of a treaty between Canada and Honduras), nor is it a party to CAFTA, it has been able to launch this claim through its subsidiary in the Cayman Islands. By changing the nationality of this subsidiary to the United States, a member country of the agreement, the company was then able to seek jurisdiction under CAFTA.[41]

The company claims that the *de facto* ban on mining is extra-legal and in breach of several articles of the Investment chapter of the CAFTA to which El Salvador is part (ICSID, 2008, 3). Namely, Article 10.3 on National Treatment; Article 10.4 on Most-Favoured Nation Treatment; Article 10.5 on Minimum Standard of Treatment; and Article 10.7 on Expropriation and Compensation. For the breach of these clauses, Pacific Rim was initially seeking an award of US $75 million from the government, which has recently risen to US $315 million.[42] This amount was amended when the company presented its Memorial on the Merits and Quantum, which represents the final 'merit-based' phase of the arbitration proceedings. Following the review of the Memorial, the tribunal will rule on whether El Salvador must compensate the company for the requested amount.

For its part, the government's initial response was to present objections based on Articles 10.20.4 and 10.20.5 of CAFTA under which they have the right to question the merits of the dispute, i.e. the *facts* of the case.[43] When these objections were rejected by the Tribunal later that year,[44] the government then argued that the company did not have the jurisdictional basis for launching its claim and that the use of its subsidiary in the Cayman Islands (changed to the United States) was an abuse of process.[45] In 2012, the Tribunal also rejected this

---

[41]   ICSID, *The Republic of El Salvador's Memorial Objections to Jurisdiction*, Case No. ARB/09/12, 3 August 2010, p. 1, available at: www.italaw.com/sites/default/files/case-documents/ita0602. pdf.

[42]   'Statement Filed in Arbitration Case Against El Salvador; PacRim Seeks Damages of US $315 Million', *Globe and Mail*, 1 April 2013, available at: http://bit.ly/18XTGkp.

[43]   ICSID, *The Republic of El Salvador's Preliminary Objections Under Articles 10.20.4 and 10.20.5 of CAFTA*, Case No. ARB/09/12, 4 January 2010, available at: http://bit.ly/18HbuO6.

[44]   ICSID, *Decision on the Respondent's Preliminary Objections under CAFTA Articles 10.20.4 and 10.20.5*, Case No. ARB/09/12, 2 August 2010, available at: http://bit.ly/1cr1giS.

[45]   Dewey & LeBoeuf, *El Salvador's Objections under ICSID Rule 41(1)*, Case No. ARB/09/12, 3 August 2010, available at: www.italaw.com/sites/default/files/case-documents/ita0600.pdf.

objection and maintained that the company was within its jurisdictional rights to file the claim.[46]

4.1.5. Variance of the Dependent Variable

Despite the lack of guidance in treaty interpretation provided by the current investment dispute settlement bodies to defendant countries,[47] El Salvador seems rather confident of its right to ban mining in order to protect human rights. What is more, because other rulings do not provide guidance on how governments should balance both investment and human rights interests,[48] they are forced to choose the protection of one over the other – in this case they chose to protect human rights.

In this case, many elements lead to the belief that the regulations and policies adopted were aligned with the obligation to uphold human rights. Whether it is the company's EIA not meeting regulatory standards or community uprisings against the project over concerns of protecting their livelihoods, the government is, according to its mining code, well within its rights to cancel or refrain from allocating extraction permits. At the very least, the context in which these policies have emerged should be taken into account by arbitration tribunals.[49] Since arbitration panels within bodies such as ICSID are not obliged to consider these arguments if they consider themselves to lack expertise on the matter, the government of El Salvador is likely led to believe that this system favours investor interests over its own.[50]

El Salvador's decision to continue to deny permits to the company suggests that it is not falling victim to the regulatory chill theory as a consequence of an investment agreement in place. Beyond the investment agreement itself, what has truly been the test of the effectiveness of this legal tool has been the claim brought forward by investors and the arbitration proceedings which have also failed to deter the government from withholding permits from the company and declaring a *de facto* moratorium on mining. Despite the continuously growing costs the government faces if it were to lose in arbitration proceeding and were required to award the company US $315 million, the use of the investment chapter of CAFTA by the company to seek compensation has not served as a deterrent to implement human rights policies.

However, it remains to be seen if the ruling, if in favour of the investor, will force the country to withdraw the *de facto* moratorium. What is certain is

---

[46]　ICSID, *Decision on the Respondent's Jurisdictional Objections*, Case No. ARB/09/12, 1 June 2012, available at: www.italaw.com/sites/default/files/case-documents/ita0935.pdf, 35.

[47]　UNCTAD, 'Reform of Investor-States Dispute Settlement: In search of a roadmap', *Special Issue for the Multilateral Dialogue on Investment*, 28–29 May 2013, 10.

[48]　M. Wells Sheffer, 'Bilateral investment treaties: a friend or foe to human rights?' (2011) 39(3) *Denver Journal of International Law and Policy* 502.

[49]　R. Suda, *supra* n. 1, p. 29.

[50]　K. Tienhaara, *supra* n. 3, p. 12.

the very existence of a complaint under the investment treaty poses a form of limitation on a government seeking to enforce human rights regulation due to high costs of legal fees and, as such, is creating conflicting obligations between the rights of foreign investments and obligations to uphold human rights. Despite this, El Salvador's current policy favours human rights over foreign investment interests, showing that this 'most-likely' case does not pass the plausibility probe of the regulatory chill theory.

4.2. *INFINITO GOLD LTD V. COSTA RICA*

4.2.1. *Basis for Case Selection*

Costa Rica's economy is highly dependent on the eco-tourism industry which, in turn, relies on the protection of the country's ecosystem. Due to this, the government is increasingly cancelling extractive projects on its territory that do not fully comply with environmental impact assessment requirements and risk causing health and environmental damages. This has been the case for the Crucitas open-pit gold mining project operated by Industrias Infinito South America (IISA), a subsidiary of the Canadian company, Infinito Gold Ltd, formerly owned by Vannessa Ventures.[51] The project has been found in violation of the Central American Biodiversity Agreement by Costa Rica's highest court, as well as the country's Constitutional provision for the right to a healthy environment.[52]

This conflict between human rights and investment projects is also thought to serve as clear example of the regulatory chill theory at play[53] as the company has threatened and recently brought claims of a breach of the Canada-Costa Rica Foreign Investment Promotion and Protection Agreement (FIPA) to the International Center for Settlement of Investment Disputes (ICSID). However, contrary to the theory's logic, the government is upholding the constitutional right to a healthy environment and refuses to allow the project to continue despite risking having to pay a US $1.092 billion award in arbitration proceedings.

4.2.2. *Human Rights Context*

The Crucitas mining project is located in Northern Costa Rica, seven kilometres away from the San Juan River, one of the most extensive waterways in the Central American region. In her investigation into local opposition to the open-pit gold mine, DaSilva documents the perception of the potential negative impacts of

---

51 'Costa Rica court annuls Infinito Gold concession', *Reuters*, 24 November 2010, available at: http://reut.rs/1cr1ned (accessed 6 October 2013).
52 K. Tienhaara, *supra* n. 1, p. 23.
53 *Ibid.*

the project on nearby communities and the local biosphere.[54] Namely, it would require clearing two hundred hectares of the rainforest and risks contaminating water sources for thirty-two communities through acid drainage of tailing ponds according to international environmental groups.[55] Communities have also voiced concern over potential water scarcity since, according to the World Rainforest Movement, the mine will require in one hour what a family uses in twenty years.[56]

Documented health concerns surrounding open pit-mines using acid mining drainage are linked to exposure to arsenic, lead, and cyanide, which is thought to cause nervous system failure and respiratory illnesses, to name but a few.[57] Researchers have also put forward position papers on the anticipated negative social and cultural impacts related to the displacement of communities and disruption of the cultural relationship to the land.[58] CSOs have also raised concerns over the impacts on the available food and farming land.[59]

Community concerns regarding the protection of their right to a healthy environment – Article 50 of the Costa Rican Constitution – also stem from prior negative experiences with mining in the country. A common example cited is that of the Bellavista open-pit gold mine which shut down in 2007 after shifts in the earth caused the cyanide-leach pad to crack. The landslide destroyed the nearby forest along with a processing plant.[60] Because the Crucitas gold mine is designed in a similar fashion, communities, and environmental groups have organised widespread anti-mining campaigns to stop the project from moving forward.[61]

4.2.3. Domestic Policy

In response the government of Costa Rica has held many different positions on the subject of the Crucitas mining project. These differences have been seen between consecutive presidencies as well as between the executive and judicial arms of the government. First, the government of President Miguel Rodríguez Echeverría issued an initial exploration permit to Infinito Gold, in December

---

[54] J.M. DaSilva, 'Silence is Golden: An Exploration of Local Opposition to A Canadian Gold Mine Project in Costa Rica', Dissertation 2007, Faculty of Health Sciences, Simon Fraser University.
[55] *Ibid.*, p. 16.
[56] *Ibid.*, p. 22.
[57] International Cyanide Management Institute, 'Use of Cyanide in the Gold Industry', 2009, available at: www.cyanidecode.org/cyanide_use.php.
[58] A. Isla, 'A Struggle for Clean Water and Livelihood: Canadian Mining in Costa Rica in the Era of Globalization' (2002) 21/22(4/1) *Canadian Woman Studies*.
[59] Earthworks and Oxfam America, 'Dirty Metals: Mining, Communities and the Environment', Report 2004, available at: www.earthworksaction.org/files/publications/ NDG_DirtyMetalsReport_HR.pdf.
[60] D. Sherwood, 'Mine Disaster at Miramar: A Story Foretold', *The Tico Times News*, 18 January 2008, available at: http://bit.ly/18oQAW9 (accessed 6 October 2013).
[61] J.M. DaSilva, *supra* n. 54, p. 34.

2001. Then, after his election in 2002, President Abel Pacheco issued a Presidential ban on open-pit mines, declaring that he would rather have his country be an environmental leader than a 'petroleum or mining enclave'.[62] However, later that year the Constitutional Chambers ruled that projects like Crucitas should be exempt from the ban if permits were issued prior to the moratorium.[63] When the case was brought to the Supreme Court in December 2004, the court ruled to annul the exploitation permit as it was found to be in violation of Article 50 of the Constitution on the right to a healthy environment.[64]

This sparked a reaction by the company that in turn, filed a preliminary request in July 2005 to launch arbitration proceedings at ICSID seeking US $240 million for restitution of lost profits, plus US $36 million in expenses and compound interest. Two months later, Costa Rica's environmental agency (SETENA) approved the company's environmental impact assessment allowing the project to move forward and the company took the threat of international arbitration off the table.[65] As the project moved forward, the newly elected President Oscar Arias established the 'Peace with nature' national initiative with the intention of stopping environmental degradation. Later in 2007, the area near Crucitas was added to the UNESCO Biosphere Reserve (UN News Center, 2007).

Despite these environmental policies, on 13 October 2008 President Arias moved to lift the ban on open-pit mining through an executive decree, following the Ministry of the Environment and Energy's decision to re-confirm the exploitation concession by approving the revised Environmental Impact Study in April of that year.[66] The project was also declared a matter of 'public interest', allowing tree clearing for the first stage of the Crucitas mine.[67] A week later, on 21 October, the Constitutional Court ordered all tree cutting to be suspended.[68] Shortly after, the Attorney General of Costa Rica launched an investigation into allegations that President Arias had received a $200,000 donation to his foundation from Infinito Gold.[69]

In November 2010, under President Laura Chinchilla, the Costa Rican congress voted to restore the ban on new open-pit mines. However, in July of

---

62   S. Lovgren, 'Costa Rica Aims to Be 1st Carbon-Neutral Country', *National Geographic*, 7 March 2008, available at: http://news.nationalgeographic.com/news/2008/03/080307-costa-rica.html (accessed 6 October 2013).

63   J.M. DaSilva, *supra* n. 54, p. 19.

64   *Ibid.*, p. 25.

65   'Vannessa secures Crucitas enviro permit', *Business News Americas*, 1 September 2005, available at: http://bit.ly/1bJ7AWi (accessed 6 October 2013).

66   Infinito Gold Ltd, 'Management's Discussion and Analysis', 21 December 2009, available at: www.infinitogold.com/i/pdf/2009-Dec31-MDA.pdf.

67   B. Schmidt, 'Arias' Mine Decree Being Scrutinized in Costa Rica' (2008) 11(1) *Eco Americas*.

68   Infinito Gold Ltd, 'Management's Discussion and Analysis', 30 September 2008, available at: www.infinitogold.com/i/pdf/2008-09-30_MDA.pdf.

69   'Former President Oscar Arias Trial Pending on Canadian Documents', *The Costa Rica News*, 17 April, 2013, available at: http://thecostaricanews.com/former-president-oscar-arias-trial-pending-on-canadian-documents/15206 (accessed 2 August 2014).

that year, a government commission presented a study stating that the repeal of Infinito's mining concession in Crucitas would cost the government US $1.7 billion in international arbitration proceedings as it would be required to compensate the company for loss of future earnings. The company maintains that it did not provide figures for this study and had, itself, yet to calculate a new figure for the award as it did not anticipate that the mining concession would be revoked.[70] This study supported congress's decision to apply the moratorium only to new projects, thus allowing Infinito to retain its concession.[71] The executive branch, through a statement by the Vice President Alfio Piva, decided to leave the decision to the judicial branch's Administrative Appeals court.

On 24 November 2011, the Constitutional Court's Civil and Administrative Law Chamber (Sala I) annulled the Crucitas mining concession again.[72] The court found the government issued mining concession and the 'public interest' decree of Crucitas mine by President Arias to be illegal.[73] While the company's appeal request was being reviewed, Infinito launched a parallel lawsuit against professor Jorge Lobo of the University of Costa Rica, the maker of a documentary entitled 'Fool's Gold' pertaining to the Crucitas project. The suit, seeking US $1 million for defamation, was thrown out on 9 November 2012.[74]

On 4 April 2013, Infinito Gold made its final request for the government to reinstate the concession by 4 October 2013. That same day, the company sent its notice to commence arbitration proceedings if the concession was not granted by that date. In response, on 19 June 2013, for the third and final time, the Supreme Court's Constitutional Chamber (Sala IV) rejected the company's appeal of the concession annulment issued by the Administrative Law Chamber (Sala I) in November 2011.[75] In a press conference, the Minister of the Environment, René Castro, said that this ruling 'enhances the ecological profile of our nation' stating that 'we do not want open-pit mining in our country'.[76] President Chinchilla made similar statements earlier in April claiming that the case of Las Crucitas was resolved in favour of nearby communities opposed to the project.

---

[70]   M. McDonald, 'Costa Rica says it would have to pay $1.7 billion to annul mining concession', *The Tico Times News* 28 July 2010, available at: http://bit.ly/1jUQZCi (accessed 6 October 2013)

[71]   'Costa Rica lawmakers vote to ban open-pit mining', *Reuters*, 9 November 2010, available at: http://reut.rs/1jUTip5 (accessed 6 October 2013).

[72]   'Costa Rica court annuls Infinito Gold concession', *Reuters*, 24 November 2010, available at: http://reut.rs/1cr1ned (accessed 6 October 2013).

[73]   M. McDonald, 'C.R. court: "No" to gold mine', *The Tico Times News*, 26 November 2010, available at: http://goo.gl/7QluC0 (accessed 6 October 2013).

[74]   J. Lobo, 'Mining Company Fails to Silence Critic', *Canadian Association of University Teachers*, 9 November 2012, available at: www.cautbulletin.ca/en_article.asp?ArticleID=3552.

[75]   'Plan minero de Infinito Gold en Costa Rica no va', *El Nuevo Siglo*, 19 June 2013, available at: http://bit.ly/JcLikP (accessed 6 October 2013).

[76]   L. Arias, 'Infinito Gold to move forward with billion-dollar lawsuit against Costa Rica', *The Tico Times News*, 19 June 2013, available at: http://bit.ly/ISBaNH (accessed 6 October 2013).

4.2.4. Arbitration Proceedings

As mentioned above, Infinito Gold Ltd has filed two notices of intent to launch arbitration proceedings through ICSID on behalf of its subsidiary, Industrias Infinito S.A., against the government of Costa Rica for alleged breaches of the Agreement between Canada and Costa Rica for the Promotion and Protection of Investment. The latest was launched on 4 April 2013 in accordance with Article 12 of the dispute settlement process allowing for the recourse of international tribunals.[77] This foreign investment protection agreement (FIPA) contains the same clauses as most bilateral investment treaties pertaining to the protection of investments with regards to changes in domestic policies leading to increased costs of operations or expropriation. In force since 1999, two years before Infinito Gold's subsidiary was granted its exploration permit for Crucitas, Article 2 of the agreement ensures that Costa Rica accords Canadian investors 'fair and equitable treatment in accordance with principles of international law'.[78] Articles 7 and 8 establish requirements on compensation for losses and rules against expropriation. Article 12 allows for investors to bring claims of breaches forward to international arbitration tribunals.

In its statement of claim, the company alleges that the government has breached the 'fair and equitable' provision as policies have changed suddenly over the years and courts have issued conflicting rulings, giving the company an unfair and unpredictable investment climate.[79] Second, the FIPA's clauses on compensation of losses and expropriation state that:

> Investments of investors of either Contracting Party shall not be nationalized, expropriated or subjected to measures having an effect equivalent to nationalization or expropriation in the territory of the other Contracting Party, except for a public purpose, under due process of law, in a non-discriminatory manner and against prompt, adequate and effective compensation. Such compensation shall be based on the fair market value of the investment expropriated immediately before the expropriation or at the time the proposed expropriation became public knowledge, whichever is the earlier (Article VIII).

---

[77] Infinito Gold Ltd, 'Notice of Breach of the Agreement Between the Government of Canada and the Government of the Republic of Costa Rica for the Promotion and Protection of Investment', 4 April 2013, available at: www.italaw.com/sites/default/files/case-documents/italaw3016.pdf.

[78] Agreement between Canada and Costa Rica for the Promotion and Protection of Investment, World Intellectual Property Organization, 1998, available at: http://bit.ly/1bJ7uOu.

[79] K. Hall, 'Canadian gold company threatens Costa Rica with $1bn lawsuit', *Mining.com*, 11 April 2013, available at: http://bit.ly/1bzvMpF.

In their claim filed under this agreement, the company argues that the annulment of the mining concession equates to an expropriation[80] and seeks an award for anticipated future earnings of the project and expenses to date, amounting to approximately US $1.1 billion, according to the company's estimates.[81]

Although the government responded quickly to the company's notice to commence arbitration proceedings at ICSID in 2005 by reinstituting the mining concession for the project to move forward, the current government of Costa Rica seems to be responding differently to the Infinito Gold's latest notice. Regarding the first request made to ICSID, the company's CEO, Jesus Carvajal stated that 'this kind of pressure helped SETENA resolve the issue' and accelerated the emission of environmental permit due to the threat of facing a costly legal suit.[82] However, this time around, shortly after the notice of intent to launch arbitration proceedings was issued, both the judicial and executive branches of the government have moved to permanently annul Infinito's mining concession in Crucitas. In response, the company's spokeswomen, Yokebec Soto, stated that the company 'will continue with the law suit of $1 billion, the largest against the Costa Rican government today and I think in the history of the country,' and that the company will only leave Costa Rica 'once all its investment and money lost during delayed legal processes against their interests in gold mining is paid'.[83]

4.2.5. Variance of the Dependent Variable

Following the 'regulatory chill' hypothesis, the threat of the company taking legal action against the government through an international arbitration tribunal seeking over US $1 billion should be cause for the government to retract its human rights and environmental policies regarding the mining project. This is, however, to date, not the case as the President has supported the latest court rulings to permanently stop the project and is refusing to accord this mining permit despite the enormous legal costs of arbitration proceedings. This case thus brings into question the presence of a regulatory chill thought, in previous studies, to be felt in Costa Rica in relation to the Canada-Costa Rica investment treaty. Out of the eighteen policies relating to the Crucitas project since the issuing of the exploration permit in 2001, eleven are pro-human rights environmental policies to stop the mining project and seven are favourable to the investment project. Although the government was seemingly torn on the matter and went

---

80   Infinito Gold Ltd, 'Notice of Breach of the Agreement Between the Government of Canada and the Government of the Republic of Costa Rica for the Promotion and Protection of Investment', 4 April 2013, available at: www.italaw.com/sites/default/files/case-documents/italaw3016.pdf.

81   K. Hall, *supra* n. 79.

82   'Vannessa secures Crucitas enviro permit', *Business News Americas*, 1 September 2005, available at: http://bit.ly/1bJ7AWi (accessed 6 October 2013).

83   'Infinito Industries: The Most Important Law Suit Against Costa Rica', *The Costa Rica News*, 22 July 2013, available at: http://bit.ly/1jlo8OO (accessed 6 October 2013).

back and forth over a period of time, the final decision, which holds most weight, is decisively against the project. More importantly, policies introduced since the company's new arbitration claims have been supportive of human rights.

By taking this policy direction, the government is demonstrating behaviour consistent with the Calvo Doctrine wherein it is refusing to grant foreign investors greater privileges as required by the investment agreement in place and upholding its policing powers. The company's own breach of the BIT by launching arbitration proceedings, while still seeking legal remedy in domestic Costa Rican courts,[84] may be giving the government a greater hope of having ICSID rule in its favour if arbitration is to move forward. Nevertheless, future research following the conclusion of arbitration proceedings will be needed to corroborate the absence of a regulatory chill in the country despite the presence of an investment treaty protecting the Crucitas project.

5.   ANALYSIS

Despite the governments in these cases mostly standing their ground in upholding human rights-related policies that conflict with foreign investment interest, the question of establishing precedence between both areas of international law has been debated at length by legal experts. Even if they fall under two separate legal frameworks, human rights law and international investment both fall under the rules of the Vienna Convention on the Law of Treaties (VCLT). Article 30 of the VCLT establishes guidance regarding conflicting treaties. Although there are many schools of thought interpreting this article, it states that 'the earlier treaty applies only to the extent that its provisions are compatible with those of the later treaty'. In this case, the earlier treaty is the ICESCR and the later treaty is the investment agreement. To add complexity, this earlier treaty only applies if both parties are signatories.[85] For example, the United States has yet to ratify the ICESCR which implies that if a host state were to point to a conflict of treaty interpretation between a BIT and the ICESCR, the rules of the BIT would prevail as both countries are members, contrary to the ICESCR where only the host state is a member.

This does not, however, imply that the rules of the ICESCR are void and cannot be used by host governments defending their policies. Using the language of most IIAs, the investment must be in accordance with domestic law including international human rights law as ratified by the host state.[86] This 'legality' clause

---

[84]   'Calgary-based Infinito Gold Fails to Strong-arm Costa Rican Judiciary As Final Appeal Rejected by Supreme Court', *Mining Watch*, 4 July 2013, available at: http://bit.ly/1gtLwT5 (accessed 6 October 2013).

[85]   D.A. Desierto, 'Conflict of Treaties, Interpretation, and Decision-Making on Human Rights and Investment During Economic Crises' (2013) 10(1) *Transnational Dispute Management* 10.

[86]   *Ibid.*, p. 11.

may circumvent the application of the VCLT as the BIT itself gives precedence to the host-state's legal framework. Despite these legal arguments, the likelihood of investors being granted awards is much higher than that of host states due to asymmetrical litigation power, among other things.[87] That is to say, arbitration panels, as their own entity applying a distinct legal framework, can opt not to consider the human rights arguments brought by a host state. This is especially problematic when there not is only an anticipated human rights violation linked to a project being regulated by the state, but, even more so, when the investors have been accused of a crime in the host country.

Beyond giving precedence to human rights law over investment law, a number of Latin American countries have expressed the intent to withdraw from the Washington Convention allowing these suits to be brought in international rather than domestic tribunals and some have already gone ahead and done so. To date, Bolivia, Ecuador, and Venezuela have notified ICSID of their withdrawal and Nicaragua and Argentina have expressed their intention to follow suit.[88] More than solely implementing policies unfavourable to investors, leaving the investment system altogether is behaviour consistent with the Calvo Doctrine and is a further step taken by states to ensure that their sovereign right to regulate is not undermined by the use of international tribunals by foreign investors. For example, Ecuador's President has expressed that the Washington Convention is in contradiction with the country's new constitution. Article 422 prohibits the country from joining new international agreements which relinquish judicial powers to international bodies and in doing so, ensures that investors exhaust domestic legal bodies (Guzman, 2009: 5).

Moreover, recent constitutional amendments in Latin America present new legal challenges to the implementation of arbitration tribunals' decisions. Although the withdrawal from ICSID is not retroactive, the Bolivian Constitution for instance, prevents the enforcement of awards retroactively.[89] This legal argument could however be challenged by investors and this failure to comply with ICSID decisions could be brought to the International Court of Justice.[90] Other consequences relate to the country's trading and borrowing relations which could deteriorate due to the mistrust ensued from backing down from its engagements with investors as well as putting the country's accession to other treaties into question. Despite these risks, there remains a trend in which states make arguments against the application of arbitration panels' rulings leads us

---

[87]   G. Van Harten, 'Arbitrator Behaviour in Asymmetrical Adjudication: An Empirical Study of Investment Treaty Arbitration', *Osgoode Hall Law Journal*, forthcoming; Osgoode CLPE Research Paper No. 41/2012.

[88]   M. Blyschak, 'State Consent, Investor Interests and the Future of Investment Arbitration: Reanalyzing the Jurisdiction of Investor-State Tribunals in Hard Cases' (2009) 99 *Asper Review of International Business & Trade Law* 22.

[89]   C. Viteri Torres, 'Withdrawal of State Consent to ICSID Arbitration, Perspectives from the Bolivian and Ecuadorian cases' (2009) 6(4) *Transnational Dispute Management* 33.

[90]   D.A. Desierto, *supra* n. 85, p. 14.

to believe that the threat related to investors launching legal suits is less credible from the host government's perspective.

If states are to remain within the current framework of international investment law, several recommendations can be made to create a space within the legal framework to adapt to human rights policies and avoid added costs for states for enforcing other international legal obligations. For instance, developing countries could push for the greater integration of non-investment related provisions regarding economic development as do many developed countries, by removing provisions on capital control, which would ease claims that foreign direct investment activities under IIAs impede the development of local communities. To further this approach, investment tribunals could create human rights complaint mechanisms parallel to investor claim mechanisms to encourage host-states to use these legal bodies. In the same way that IIAs create rights for investors as third parties, they could also create third party rights for workers and communities affected by investment projects. Weiler provides a draft example of treaty content with provisions resembling the Alien Tort Claims Act used in the context of foreign investment in US courts.[91]

To increase accountability, a series of recommendations have been made to move *beyond* the current framework in order to require investors to share reciprocal obligations with states under IIAs rather than simply benefiting from the rights given under these treaties. This could be accomplished by increasing due diligence standards for investment projects following the model established by the UN Guiding Principles on Business and Human Rights.[92] Host-states could also call for the integration of anticorruption clauses and requirements for projects to meet domestic standards for social and environmental impact assessments. Making these assessment and diligence procedures mandatory for foreign companies through IIAs would help clarify expectations regarding the investment climate in order to better assess costs and risks from the outset. However, it is unlikely that investors' home states would agree to these added obligations since it is a 'radical departure' from the original intent of signing II. As which is to protect foreign investors and encourage FDI.[93]

Experts have also brought forward the idea of amending the procedure for deciding awards to apply a more balanced approach. Although the legal fees themselves are high, what weighs the most on states is the cost of the award itself, which is more often less than what is requested in the investor's claims.[94] Even if it is not enough to stop states from regulating in favour of human rights, it

---

[91] T. Weiler, 'Balancing Human Rights and Investor Protection: A New Approach for a Different Legal Order' (2004) 27 *B.C. Int'l & Comp. L. Rev.* 429, available at: http://lawdigitalcommons. bc.edu/iclr/vol27/iss2/8.

[92] M. Wells Sheffer, *supra* n. 48, p. 507.

[93] *Ibid.*

[94] D. Smith, 'Shifting Sands: Cost-and-Fee Allocation in International Investment Arbitration' (2010) 51 *Virginia Journal of International Law* 749.

has pushed Latin American governments further away from the ICSID system. The most prevalent recommendation is to use the proportionality test commonly used in human rights law to distribute awards.[95] Based on this theory, this creates a balance between investor interests and host-state obligations as it measures and compares the weight of the benefit and the harm achieved. This would also allow tribunals to evaluate the necessity of the measure implemented by the government and whether it was the most suitable measure.[96] Cases brought forward in Argentina illustrate how this measure could be implemented, as the arbitration tribunals in the case of *Total S.A. v. Argentina* and of *Suez et al. v. Argentina* based their ruling on proportionality of the government's policies given the economic crisis in relation to the rights of the investor.[97]

The Guiding Principles recommend that governments retain the policy space within investment agreements to enforce human rights. However these recommendations do not provide specific guidance in situations where conflict arises. The UNGPs are limited to advising countries not to sign on to treaties that will limit the implementation of human rights policies and no guidance is provided to companies as to the application of IIAs when human rights are at play. To provide effective guidance, the UNGPs need establish an order of precedence between human rights and investment interests. In addition to the UNGPs, the former UN Special Rapporteur on the Right to Food, Olivier de Shutter, has also prepared guiding principles on human rights impact assessment of trade and investment agreements for the Human Rights Council. Although this is a valuable tool for states before they enter into new trade and investment agreements, it also falls short of clarifying how states should balance conflicting human rights and investment treaty obligations once the treaty is signed and an arbitration proceeding is underway.

For instance, regarding the state balancing of investment and human rights policies, it should be recommended that the government clarify a policy's objectives, the documented trends supporting these objectives and strategies for realising these objectives.[98] Clarifying this with investors may reduce the number of lawsuits launched based on the alleged breached of fairness and non-discriminatory treatment. Also, for parties lacking experience dealing with human rights issues, a mechanism should be created to offer authoritative treaty interpretation to determine what types of human rights regulations are a sufficient cause for a breach of treaty.[99] This could be enabled by allowing civil society organisations to bring forward arbitration procedures, thus ensuring

---

[95] C. Reiner and C. Schreuer, *Human Rights and International Investment Arbitration* (Oxford: Oxford University Press, 2009), p. 18.

[96] D. Krishan, 'Balancing Human Rights and Investment Obligations: An Old Wives' Tale' (2013) 10(1) *Transnational Dispute Management* 13.

[97] S.B. Leinhardt, 'Some Thoughts on Foreign Investors' Responsibilities to Respect Human Rights' (2013) 10(1) *Transnational Dispute Management* 14.

[98] D.A. Desierto, *supra* n. 85, p. 84.

[99] R. Suda, *supra* n. 1.

better expertise in terms of human rights issues as they report independently on these issues – a measure already adopted under UNICTRAL's New Rules.

In sum, changes to the current legal framework for international investment must generate greater balance between investor rights and the human rights obligations of states. As the number of arbitration cases continues to rise, host governments in Latin America are being discouraged from signing on to new IIAs or, in the case of the extractive sector, backtracking on the distribution of permits. Clarifying the balance between both legal regimes will also create a safer investment climate as investors will have clear expectations regarding human rights and environmental requirements. Based on the investment treaty models already existing between developed countries, governments can push for similar non-investment related provisions with investors' home states without rebelling from the entire framework of investment law.

6. CONCLUSION

This chapter has relied on case-based evidence to examine the contradiction between human rights policies and provisions of bilateral investment treaties, leading to costly arbitration proceedings for both states and investors. Despite these costs, the results of this analysis show that these arbitration proceedings are not a strong enough legal tool to deter governments from implementing human rights and environmental policies. The selected cases were based in Latin America specifically in an attempt to discuss the hypothesis of the re-emergence of the Calvo Doctrine as a way of overcoming the regulatory chill phenomenon, which is thought to be specific to the region. As the selected case studies have shown, these Latin America states have gone ahead with pro-human rights policies in the mining sector despite the presence of IIAs. What is more, even when arbitration proceedings are launched, governments publicly contest these suits and move ahead with human rights and environmental legislation.

The current policy direction in the cases therefore calls for a more nuanced analysis of the impact of international investment agreements on human rights and related environmental regulations in the mining sector. This nuanced understanding would allow for the broadening of the regulatory chill theory and perhaps for the differentiation between a regulatory chill and a regulatory freeze. The latter holds a rather narrow interpretation and would only be verifiable when host-states fully withdraw policies contested by the investors. However, a chill could be documented simply when conflicts arise between a government's dichotomous obligations, thus forcing the government to be more cautious in its policy choices. In this sense, these cases do not demonstrate the presence of a regulatory freeze wherein governments withdraw regulations following the threat of an arbitration suit. Rather, the chilling effect is seen more through the ongoing conflict between investors and the state, at great financial and reputational cost for these low income countries. This chill also sends a message to neighbouring countries that failing accord investors the privileges they are entitled to under investment agreements has serious consequences.

Although these processes do not seem to cause a regulatory freeze in the effected policy space, these suits do create hurdles for pro-human rights governments through the immense costs entailed. The question then becomes, will IIAs have the contrary impact and dissuade host-governments from allocating exploration permits to foreign companies? Unfortunately, since the selected cases have yet to be concluded, future studies will be required to assess changes in the way states factor the presence of IIAs into policymaking. That is, the finalisation of these cases will help determine if there is a correlation between investor complaints and the implementation of human rights policies. Until these arbitration cases have been finalised, it is difficult to draw such stark conclusions and as more arbitration cases involving human rights policies are brought forward, the findings of this study should be updated following the outcomes of new cases. In effect, it is possible that a regulatory chill emerges only if tribunals award investors at great financial cost to governments, thus creating an incentive for governments to either respect the investment provision or refrain from signing investment treaties with developed countries.

In conclusion, with increased attention being drawn to human rights violations in the mining sector, both investors and host governments must come together to review the application of human rights policies that impact investment in a manner that does not create a lose-lose outcome as does the current legal framework for international investment. To overcome the hurdles presented by the current framework, the relevant bodies need to provide guidance for the balancing act that states must play between investment and human rights obligations once treaties are already singed and arbitration proceedings are set in motion, as well as guidance for investors to differentiate between discriminatory treatment and *bona fide* domestic legislation.

CHAPTER 12

BEYOND STATE DUTY AND CORPORATE RESPONSIBILITY

Human Rights in Industrial Zones in Vietnam

Nguyễn Hong Nga

1.   INTRODUCTION

Industrial and export processing zones[1] are considered magnets for direct foreign investment and attractive for foreign enterprises and subsidiaries of transnational corporations in Vietnam. Despite fuelling domestic economic growth by industrial development and job creation, industrial zones' performance has caused a series of actual and potential human rights violations within workplaces and in surrounding communities. Working conditions in industrial zones in Vietnam revealed a breadth of human rights abuses such as low wages, excessive overtime, temporary contracts, deteriorated working conditions, and environmental pollution which affected not only workers and their families but also people living in the surrounding areas.[2]

The 2011 United Nations Guiding Principles on Business and Human Rights (the Guiding Principles) provide a practical guidance to identify and address human rights impacts, emphasising the state duty to protect against human rights abuses, the corporate responsibility to respect human rights, and the need for greater access to victims to effective remedy.[3] Despite numerous endorsements,

---

[1]   An industrial zone is a zone that specialises in the production of industrial goods or provision of services for industrial production. Some of the main characteristics of industrial zones relevant to labour and human rights are: (a) demarcated areas, often restricted, fenced off or gated from the surrounding; (b) the feminisation of labour; (c) a significant amount of migrant workers; and (d) demands for low-paid, low-skilled workers concentrated in labour-intensive industries such as textile, garment, shoes, manufacturing, and electronics.

[2]   Di Gregorio (2003), p. 182.

[3]   HRC (2011), para. 6.

the Guiding Principles face some scepticism regarding their practicability, which depends on the context of specific countries, and an inherent voluntarism on part of the enterprises' adherence to the principles. Surya Deva argues that '[e]ven if the Guiding Principles are implemented by states and embraced by the business community, they might not make a significant difference in preventing and remedying corporate human rights abuses, especially in situations where there are governance gaps or companies are reluctant to be guided by the Guiding Principles'.[4]

In fact, in developing countries whose aim is to attract foreign investment for development, governments are often unwilling to intervene in companies' activities for fear of impairing their competitiveness. Weak states lacking the requisite governance capacity are also less able to control effectively the activities of foreign enterprises. Likewise, in authoritarian or undemocratic states where rampant corruption is common place, enterprises often lobby ruling elites to ignore their wrongdoings and disrupt the legal enforcement of human rights. At the same time, for enterprises, for the sake of profit maximisation and in the absence of a legally binding regulatory framework, corporate social responsibility (CSR) is often regarded as an added cost. This in turn undermines enterprises' propensity to voluntarily incorporate CSR.

Accordingly, both states and enterprises are often reluctant to deal with human rights abuses carried out by corporations. Meanwhile, enterprises are to some extent constrained by 'social contracts' with the society in which they operate, often expressed by demands from civil society to be socially and environmentally 'responsible', and hence achieve a 'licence to operate'.[5] The question arises as to how human rights should be integrated into business, given both the predicament that states and enterprises fail to undertake their duties and responsibilities, and civil society's demands for advocating for the protection of the rights of workers and communities? In order to answer this question this chapter addresses the role of civil society organisations (CSOs), and examines how and why CSOs engage in 'humanising' business in Vietnam. Section 2 points to the challenges of human rights engagement in industrial zones by analysing failure by the state and the resistance by companies to engage human rights in business. Section 3 elaborates on the emergence of CSOs in human rights engagement and experiences of specific CSOs working in this field. Section 4 summarises and draws some substantive conclusions. However, first, we start off with a discussion of human rights challenges in industrial zones in Vietnam.

---

[4]   S. Deva, *Regulating Corporate Human Rights Violations: Humanizing Business* (London: Routledge, 2012), pp. 114–115.

[5]   Bauer (2014).

2. CHALLENGES OF HUMAN RIGHTS ENGAGEMENT IN INDUSTRIAL ZONES IN VIETNAM

2.1. FAILURE OF STATE DUTIES: LIMITATIONS OF THE LEGAL SYSTEM

As a state party to a plethora of international human rights and labour rights laws,[6] Vietnam has obligations to ensure the full enjoyment of rights of workers in IZs, their families, and surrounding communities. The state duty to protect against human rights abuses by business within industrial zones is also referred to in the National Constitution (2013), the Labour Code (2013), the Trade Union Law (2012), and in various decrees and decisions on industrial zones' activities. However, the current legal framework in Vietnam to protect workers' and communities' rights to some extent remains incomplete and weak both in terms of legal procedure and enforcement.

First, regarding minimum wage, Vietnam has failed to establish a decent wage for employees. Despite eleven adjustments since 1997,[7] minimum wage has never been in step with basic living costs and staggering inflation. The large gap between real wages and living expenses undermine workers' living standards, education opportunities for their children, and is an important factor in understanding frequent occurrences of labour disputes and wildcat strikes in protest over working and health conditions. According to a survey of 1,000 workers in industrial zones by the National Institute of Nutrition, 30% suffered long-term energy shortages, 20% suffered from blood pressure, 20% skipped at least one meal per day, and workers' daily meals met only 89.7% of their required energy intake.[8] The situation was exacerbated by the fact that around 70–80% of migrant workers in industrial zones in big cities moved from rural areas and had financial responsibilities to their families back home. Most of them had therefore earned too little to look after their families and had to engage in excessive overtime work.[9]

Furthermore, since social and health insurance are pegged on the workers' income, which for most is officially minimum wage, workers suffer from both

---

[6] A set of universal human rights treaties such as Convention to Eliminate All Forms of Discrimination Against Women (female workers' rights), Convention on the Rights of the Child (child labour rights), International Covenant of Economic, Social and Cultural Rights, ILO's requirements particularly, Forced Labour Convention, Equal Remuneration Convention, Discrimination (Employment and Occupation) Convention, Minimum Age Convention and Worst Forms of Child Labour Convention; and WTO's principles.

[7] Adjusted in 1997, 2000, 2001, 2005, 2006, 2008, 2009, 2010, 2011, 2012 and 2013.

[8] T. Ha Dang, 'Struggle with minimum wages' (2013), available at: www.nhandan.com.vn/xahoi/tin-tuc/item/21888002-nguoi-lao-dong-chat-vat-voi-muc-luong-toi-thieu%20.html (accessed 13 March 2014).

[9] Oxfam (2013), p. 39.

underpayment and a lower level of social and health benefits.[10] Especially in some plants, employers apply an apprentice wage regulation for new workers to justify training fees and limited productivity. In turn, the actual payment is below minimum wage.[11]

Secondly, the right to collective bargaining, the right to strike, and the freedom of association in industrial zones are limited under certain restrictive conditions to organise a legal strike. Even though Vietnam has not ratified the two fundamental ILO Conventions on such rights,[12] the right to strike is stipulated in the newly adopted Constitution (2013), the Labour Code and the Trade Union Law.[13] Nevertheless, the requirement to have more than a six-month contract to join the trade union[14] diminishes workers' right to free association and collective bargaining, especially given the prevalence of verbal and temporary labour contracts in industrial zones.

Moreover, the government did not recognise the legitimacy of independent trade unions.[15] All trade unions at the national, provincial, district/industrial zone and factory/enterprise levels are under the umbrella of the Vietnam General Confederation of Labour which presents a social-political organisation under the leadership of the Vietnamese Communist Party (VCP).[16] In this sense, trade unions are directly or indirectly tied to the government.

While the domestic law authorises the right of workers to strike, the right is imposed under stringent conditions and complicated procedures.[17] These prerequisites have troubled significantly the exercise of this right and provoked social protests. In recent years, there has been a rise of wildcat and spontaneous strikes in industrial zones without trade unions,[18] which have contributed to

---

[10]   N.A. Tran, 'Corporate Social Responsibility in Socialist Vietnam: Challenges, and Local Solutions' in A. Chan (ed.), *Labour in Vietnam*, 1st edn. (Singapore: ISEAS Publishing, 2011), pp. 119–159, p. 122. According to the Vietnamese Social Security Law, employees are obliged to contribute 8% of gross income to the State Social Insurance Fund.

[11]   Interview IZAs representatives.

[12]   ILO Convention 87 – Freedom of Association and Protection of the Right to Organize and ILO Convention 98 – Right to Organize and Collective Bargaining Convention.

[13]   Vietnamese Constitution, Art. 25; Labour Code, Art. 5(c) and Chapter V; Trade Union Law, Art. 5.

[14]   Guidelines of the Statutes of Vietnamese Trade Union No. 703/HD-TLĐ.

[15]   After the Trans-Pacific Partnership agreement was reached in October 2015, Vietnam has since committed to allow workers to set up independent trade unions.

[16]   Trade Union Law, Art. 1.

[17]   A lawful strike must meet all the four requirements. First, a strike must exhausted procedure of mediation. The Labour Code requires workers to consult with representatives of trade union at the enterprise level, which entails mostly members of managing board. Secondly, more than 50% of workers must agree with the plan of the union executive Committee to go on strike. Thirdly, at least five working days prior to the strike's starting day, the trade union executive committee shall send the strike decision to the employer while also forwarding a copy to the provincial state management agencies on labour and one copy to the provincial trade union. Fourthly, when the strike begins, if the employer does not accept to settle the requirements of the labour collective, the trade union executive committee shall organise and lead the strike.

[18]   J.T.B. Kerkvliet, 'Workers' Protest in Contemporary Vietnam' in A. Chan, *Labour in Vietnam*, 1st edn. (Singapore: Mainland Press Pte Ltd, 2011), pp. 160–210, p. 173.

workers dismissals and insecure situations. Consequently, the implementation of the right to strike in Vietnam has not accommodated workers' rights but increasingly triggered social protests and frustration.

Thirdly, with regard to environmental issues, although industrial zones are legally required to conduct environmental impact assessment and environmental protection measures,[19] company performances falls short of meeting basic environmental standards. Despite incidences of environment abuses by enterprises, the authorities turn a blind eye on these problems.[20]

These limitations to the legal system in Vietnam are mostly attributable to weak governance.

First, institutional weaknesses due to understaffed and incompetent legislators and inspectors cause a huge gap in legal enforcement.[21] Government apparatuses barely provide adequate and timely guidance on legal implementation. For example, many new provisions and amendments on minimum wage, working hours, and labour contract matters have recently been added to the Labour Code; however, instructions to explain and interpret these new laws are insufficient. Guidelines for collective bargaining agreements procedure and social insurance are also absent.[22] Similarly, the Environmental Protection Law was adopted in 2005, but a decree on damages categorisation was not promulgated until 2010; the law therefore could not be enforced for five years. Equally noteworthy is the fact that government agencies failed to provide legal education especially for non-state actors such as businesses operating in industrial zones, and among inhabitants of villages who are highly vulnerable to possible human rights and environment harmful operations by businesses.

In addition, inconsistencies in laws and regulations lead to the obstruction of legal enforcement. For example, the Environmental Protection Law assigns the People's Committees to hold responsibility for environmental impact assessment and supervision in industrial zones. However, the Decree No. 29/2008/ND-CP appoints industrial zones authorities to bear this duty, though none of them fulfilled their obligations due to unclear and overlapping responsibilities.[23]

---

19   Decree No. 29/2008 ND-CP.
20   The case of Vedan (see more in section 3.3). The case of MeiSheng Textiles Vietnam (a Taiwanese company domiciled in Ngai Giao IZ, Ba Ria Vung Tau) discharging untreated water waste into the Da Den lake (which is the main water source for 90% of the local people) illustrates neglect and weaknesses on the part of local authorities in environmental impact assessments and monitoring the way in which the Department of Planning and Investment at the local level permitted MeiSheng company to operate the system without making available a water waste treatment system.
21   For instance, on average, it is estimated that only one environmental protection inspector is available for each 1,400 enterprises. See more T.M.H. Dao, 'Corporate Responsibility in Environmental Protection: A Critical Analysis on the Situation in Vietnam', speech at the Conference 'Business and Human Rights', Hanoi, 2013.
22   Interview with a journalist from *The Labor*.
23   T.M.H. Dao, *supra* n. 21, p. 8.

Secondly, another reason for weak governance lies in the political climate. Vietnam faces challenges of corruption and low levels of transparency and disclosure.[24] In our study, we learned that some factory managers made efforts to keep close relationships with inspectors so that they would be informed several days prior to inspection visitations.[25] In other cases, auditors intentionally missed or ignored abuses of regulations, and hence, managers could implement laws at their own discretion or even break laws with impunity. In the field of environmental protection, local authorities in some provinces issued 'licences to operate' for companies that had not installed a waste treatment system or operated in banned sectors.[26]

Moreover, the press and media in Vietnam is owned and controlled by the state, and freedom of expression and freedom of information remain hotly debated and sensitive.[27] Pointedly, hesitancy exists in the labour press to report on labour and environmental violations.[28]

Thirdly, regarding the economic factor, nurturing a competitive investment climate motivates the government and local authorities to overlook 'dirty' projects. In pursuit of development goals, the government keeps labour and environment standards low and thus implicitly awards more rights for investors than for its citizens. For example, local authorities permitted 11 industrial zones to operate in Binh Duong without the instalment of a water treatment system. Each zone released around 1,200–5,600m³ of waste water per day into Sai Gon River which heavily polluted the environment.[29] This move allowed local authorities to help companies reduce costs but harmed the lives of inhabitants in terms of both subsistence and health caused by water and air pollution. Similar occurrences also took place in industrial zones in Dong Nai and Ha Noi.

2.2. RELUCTANCE TO IMPLEMENT CSR

In spite of CSR initiatives and CSR start-up campaigns in transnational corporations, CSR in Vietnam has not yet been deeply and comprehensively

---

[24] Transparency International placed Vietnam's corruption perception index at 116 out of 177 countries with a score of 31/100.
[25] N.A. Tran, *supra* n. 10, p. 138, and interview with IZA representatives.
[26] In the case of Eclat Fabrics, a Taiwanese textiles company in My Xuan A2 IZ, Ba Ria Vung Tau, although the project included a fabric dyeing section that is banned under the environmental protection law, it was granted an investment certificate by IZA. Vietnam blacklisted five industries that may endanger the environment including cassava starch processing, rubber latex processing, the manufacturing of basic chemicals, tanning, and leather dressing and fabric dyeing (clothes colouring).
[27] A.W. Dang, *Civil Society Networks in China and Vietnam: Informal Pathbreakers in Health and the Environment*, 1st edn. (New York: Palgrave MacMillan, 2012), p. 50.
[28] Interview, a journalist of *The Labor*.
[29] *Vietnamnews* (2008).

integrated into local business.[30] There are a number of reasons for business enterprises to be reluctant to conduct CSR in Vietnam.

First, there is a lack of public awareness of CSR in Vietnam. While the term 'CSR' has increasingly been used in practice, 'human rights due diligence' is not employed by Vietnamese enterprises. For customers, officials, or factory owners or managers, CSR is mostly equated with charitable activities.[31] According to a survey carried out by Socially Responsible Investors Vietnam, consumers had no knowledge of CSR or business ethics; 90% of interviewees were confused about CSR and 40% understood CSR as social obligations of companies that largely include community-related work.[32] Neither workers nor customers recognise corporate responsibilities for labour rights and environment.

In addition, a majority of factory managers considered CSR 'philanthropy, certification-led and customer-driven'.[33] Hence, the implementation of CSR projects mainly concentrates on consumers and community projects in order to improve business images and reputation and attract clients and contracts, rather than to protect workers' rights and environment protection.[34] Many managers especially also believed that 'CSR is only for big, multinational corporations', or 'CSR is a luxury of the developed world', which did not fit in developing countries and listed CSR as an extra cost, rather than an investment for corporate sustainability.[35] Our study found attitudinal resistance to change the conventional thinking that businesses would not allow a voluntary integration of CSR into practical conduct of production and commerce.

The lack of awareness of CSR thus contributed to 'passive CSR implementation' in response to mandatory contractors' requirements, which in turn undermined the efficiency of CSR programmes.[36]

Second, enterprises are unwilling to take on CSR initiatives because they assume they will reduce profit. In fact, at the outset, compliance with CSR from an economic approach exerts some budgetary constraints and may lead to less profit. Moreover, subsidiaries are very flexible in moving their factories among territories if they explore a new fatter soil which can fertilise their profit-generating process. At the end of the day, enterprises have little incentive to conduct CSR and respect its principles and policies.

---

30 Mr Nguyen Quang Vinh, Director of the Business Office for Sustainable Development, VCCI talked with the Vietnam Business Forum.
31 N.A. Tran, *supra* n. 10, 125.
32 Q.C. Do, 'CSR Activities in Vietnam', *Eco-SCR Japan*, 2013, available at: www.env.go.jp/earth/coop/eco-csrjapan/en/vietnam.html (accessed 18 March 2014).
33 N.A. Tran, *supra* n. 10, p. 125.
34 *Ibid.*
35 Q.C. Do, *supra* n. 32.
36 N. Twose and T. Rao, 'Strengthening Developing Country Governments' Engagement with Corporate Social Responsibility: Conclusions and Recommendations from Technical Assistance in Vietnam', The World Bank Final Report, 2003, p. 15.

Third, the multinational and extra-territorial jurisdiction of companies in industrial zones erects another barrier to CSR implementation. Inevitably, most sub-contractors in Vietnam manufacture from more than one retailer,[37] and foreign retailers tend to apply their own Code of Conduct (CoCs) and draw on different international standards. This poses abundant demands both on factories to undertake CoCs and on inspectors to monitor them which requires multiple audits and takes time and resources to observe.[38] Additionally, most labour standards set forth in CoCs must be applied consistently with legislation of the country of manufacture, particularly, the Vietnamese Labour Code.[39] However, discrepancies between the national labour code and CoCs, for example on overtime work, result in difficulties to achieve CSR and CoCs policies that comply with national legislation.[40]

In this multi-level subcontracting structure of the global supply chain, even if violations were explored in factories in Vietnam, which are mostly at the bottom of the production chain, it is hard to bring such violations to light and to find out who is accountable for violations because of the inability to verify exact connections between local factories and transnational companies.[41] Managers at local factories in Vietnam have little decision-making power over labour issues such as wages, bonuses, or grievance resolutions. These are mainly controlled by transnational corporations' requirements and regulated by contracts. As a result, local managers are unable to regulate or be responsive for workers' petitions and demands.[42]

2.3. LEGAL, POLITICAL, AND SOCIAL CONSTRAINTS

A large number of studies have investigated the linkage between stakeholders' pressures and CSR attitudes.[43] Kölbel et al. and Smith (2000) perceived that the

---

[37] For example, a factory in the garment and textile industry provides products for different brands such as Mango, H&M, Forever 21, GAP, etc.

[38] N. Twose and T. Rao, *supra* n. 36, p. 16.

[39] N.A. Tran, *supra* n. 10, p. 121.

[40] Most CoCs permit a maximum of 60 working hours per week, more than 12 hours above the Labour Code's upper limitation.

[41] N.A. Tran, *supra* n. 10, p. 146.

[42] *Ibid.*

[43] N. Tokoro, 'Stakeholders and Corporate Social Responsibility: A New Perspective on the Structure of Relationships' (2007) 6 *Asian Business & Management* 143–162, B. Helmig et al., 'Under Positive Pressure: How Stakeholder Pressure Affects Corporate Social Responsibility Implementation' (2013) *Business & Society*; C. Moore, 'The Relationship Between Stakeholders, Corporations and CSR', White Paper, October 2012; B.A. Carroll, and K.M. Shabana. 'The Business Case for Corporate Social Responsibility: A Review of Concepts, Research and Practice' (2010) *International Journal of Management Reviews*; D. Jamali, 'A Stakeholder Approach to Corporate Social Responsibility: A Fresh Perspective into Theory and Practice' (2008) 82 *Journal of Business Ethics* 213–231.

public can exert an influence on pushing CSR implementation in business.[44] This section examines how political, legal, and social actors, particularly the government, consumers, mass media and trade unions in Vietnam can pose pressure on companies to adopt CSR policies.

As referred to above, confusion between CSR activities and voluntary philanthropy in Vietnam enables enterprises to distract from CSR policies.[45] Even if consumer movements and boycotts in Vietnam have begun to emerge, they certainly lag far behind trends in the Western hemisphere. In Vietnam as elsewhere, consumer campaigns are vested in mass media coverage, yet as the media is under government influence,[46] consumers react slowly and weakly by consumer ethical purchasing campaigning.[47]

Similarly, pressures from the government, especially from the Vietnam General Confederation of Labour (VGCL) and its tiers, have been missing or negligible; this is due to not only the 'captured' nature of trade unions at enterprise level but also its loose collaboration with other trade unions at the provincial and industrial zone levels.

At the top, the VGCL has not yet adopted a labour rights-based approach for its performance.[48] Although their understanding of CSR emphasises labour standards, there has yet to be a nationwide campaign to make companies adopt and practice CSR policies.[49] Instead, a few campaigns carried out to highlight labour rights issues merely referred to CSR as a component. In addition, since the VGCL operates under the Vietnam Communist Party and represents a central part of the Vietnamese political system,[50] ensuring workers' rights and interests is one of its goals. In this sense, the VGCL turned out to be an arm of the government rather than a workers' protector.

At the industrial zone level, VGCL required the formation of labour unions in industrial zones to prevent and settle conflicts, but they seem to be ineffective. In fact, the number of protests in industrial zones has been increasing and half of the strikes in recent years in Vietnam have taken place in foreign enterprises in industrial zones without the intervention of trade unions.

---

[44] F. Kölbel, J. Leonhardt Jancso and T. Busch, 'Corporate Social Responsibility, Public Pressure and Credit Risk: The US and Europe are not the same', available at: https://umsbe.wufoo.com/cabinet/276/291/53/p243_update.pdf (accessed 15 March 2014); Smith (2000).

[45] Q.C. Do, *supra* n. 32.

[46] D. Porta and M. Diani, *Social Movements: An Introduction,* 2nd edn. (Oxford: Blackwell Publishing, 2009), p. 176.

[47] H.T. Bui, 'Vietnam's Civil Society', *East Asia Forum*, September 2013, available at: www.eastasiaforum.org/2013/09/05/vietnams-civil-society-undergoing-vital-changes/ (accessed 15 March 2014).

[48] T. Pringle, 'Trade Union Renewal in China and Vietnam? 26th International Labor Process Conference Work Matters', 18–20 March 2008, Conference at University College, Dublin, p. 3.

[49] N.A. Tran, *supra* n. 10, p. 126.

[50] T.M. Hoang, 'Collective Agreements – A Comparative Study of Swedish and Vietnamese Labor Law Systems', Project 'Strengthening of Legal Education in Vietnam', 2010, p. 194.

According to the Charter of Trade Union of Vietnam, every company in industrial zones with at least ten permanent employees must form a trade union;[51] however, many factories do not comply with the law.[52] Even in factories where legal trade unions exist, they played no significant role in collective bargaining over wages, promotion of occupational safety and health issues, or support for legal strikes. In fact, the content of collective bargaining agreements[53] made by grassroots trade unions was usually of limited quality.[54] With the exception of several successful collective bargaining agreements where trade unions bargained for workers higher employee benefits than the legal minimum, some were identical or duplicated to the minimum stipulated in the Labour Code and/or using vague language that could even undermine the situation of workers' rights.[55] Notably, since strikes were triggered by employees without trade unions, company managers always made efforts to dismiss alleged leaders or instigators of labour disputes without any clear reason.[56]

The weaknesses of trade unions in IZs in Vietnam mainly stem from their dependency on management boards and the incapacity of trade union representatives. In fact, labour unions staffs primarily lack competency and experience to protect workers' rights. For example, in our study they were unable to design preferential working contracts for workers and ensure that the contracts were enforced.[57] Language barriers and lack of negotiating skills undermined the ability of union cadres to bargain with the management of foreign companies.[58] Also, since the majority of trade union representatives are working voluntarily without compensation, they have little incentive to focus on the 'extra' task of protecting workers' rights.[59] Moreover, most union officials are either close or part of management or selected by companies' leaders.[60] In effect, trade unions' performance is not seen as effectively pursuing the interest of its members and hence erodes workers' trust in the role of trade unions.

---

[51] The Charter of Trade Union of Vietnam.

[52] B.G. Nguyen, *Regional Social Impacts of Industrial Zones in Vietnam*, 1st edn. (Hanoi: Social Sciences Publishing House, 2012), p. 100. For example, in Phu Yen province with three industrial zones, only 10% of 2,000 companies have trade unions. In industrial zones in Vinh Phuc province, 74 out of 110 companies formed trade unions.

[53] Collective bargaining agreements refer to contractual agreements between employers and a group of employees, mostly an independent trade union, in order to regulate wages, hours, and working conditions for employees.

[54] N.A. Tran, *supra* n. 10, p. 144.

[55] *Ibid.*, p. 145.

[56] *Ibid.*, p. 178. This happened in Matrix Company in Bac Vinh industrial zone (Nghe An province), Endo company in Noi Bai Industrial zone (Hanoi).

[57] Interview, Trade union representatives in IZs in Hanoi, Vinh Phuc, in 2013, 2014.

[58] N.A. Tran, *supra* n. 10, p. 145.

[59] V. Bellgart, 'Empowering Trade Unions by Self-Commitments of Companies?', Working Paper: Corporate Social Responsibility and the Vietnam General Confederation of Labor, July 2012.

[60] *Ibid.* A survey in IZs in Binh Duong, Dong Nai and Ho Chi Minh City revealed that all labour union officials had been appointed by local managers. International Trade Union Confederation (2009).

3. THE EMERGENCE OF CSOs IN 'HUMANISING' BUSINESS IN VIETNAM

3.1. AN OVERVIEW OF CSOs DEVELOPMENT IN VIETNAM

According to the Civil Society Index, civil society is regarded as 'the arena outside of the family, the state and the market where people associate to advance common interests'.[61] Generally, a key characteristic of civil society is autonomy from the state.[62] The concept of civil society nevertheless differs in the context of Vietnam, where, in operating under a one-party regime, it is 'not *separated* from the state'.[63] Taylor describes civil society in Vietnam as 'quasi-governmental organisations' but sometimes behaving like independent CSOs.[64] By and large, CSOs in Vietnam consist of various organisations:[65] (a) mass organisations;[66] (b) professional associations;[67] (c) NGOs;[68] and (d) community-based organisations.[69] In 2010, Vietnam had an estimated figure of 1,700–2,000 CSOs encompassing a diversity of unions, associations, clubs, funds, institutes, centres, committees, and volunteer groups.[70]

Despite a surge in numbers and being treated more hospitably at present, CSOs in Vietnam have operated in a slightly chilling environment. The majority are subjected to state control rather than existing as independent organisations.[71] In order to acquire a legal status, every CSO must register with a relevant government entity, mostly the Vietnam Union of Science and Technology Associations, a professional umbrella organisation, a ministry, or a local authority.[72] Given this, very few CSOs serve public interests such as human rights,

---

[61]   F.V. Heinrich, 'Assessing and Strengthening Civil Society Worldwide: A Project Description of the CIVICUS Civil Society Index: A Participatory Needs Assessment & Action-Planning Tool for Civil Society', CIVICUS Civil Society Index Paper Series, Vol. 2, Issue 1, 2004 p. 13.

[62]   L. Diamond, 'Rethinking Civil Society: Towards Democratic Consolidation' (1994) 5(3) *Journal of Democracy* 228.

[63]   I. Nørlund, 'Filling the Gap: The Emerging Civil Society in Vietnam', Publication of SNV, UNDP and VUSTA, 2007 p. 71.

[64]   W. Taylor et al., 'Civil Society in Vietnam: A Comparative Study of Civil Society Organizations in Hanoi and Ho Chi Minh City', The Asia Foundation, Hanoi, 2012.

[65]   *Ibid.*

[66]   Including the Father Front, the Women's Union, the VGCL – Trade Union, the Veterans Association, Farmers Association and the Ho Chi Minh Youth Union.

[67]   For example the Vietnam Association of Certified Public Accountants, the Vietnam Union of Science and Technology Associations, Vietnam Journalists Associations, etc.

[68]   Including local and international NGOs.

[69]   Organisations at the neighbourhood emerge to address community needs, e.g. Association for Promoting Education.

[70]   W. Taylor et al., *supra* n. 64, p. 7.

[71]   CIVICUS, 'The Emerging Civil Society: An Initial Assessment of Civil Society in Vietnam', March 2006, p. 10.

[72]   W. Taylor et al., *supra* n. 64, p. 11.

labour rights, or environment issues and challenge government policies.[73] Instead, their activities mostly contribute to government objectives.[74] Moreover, there are several restrictive regulations on the establishment and operation of CSOs.[75] Particularly, CSOs must survive a complex and time-consuming registration process and limitations on their autonomy.[76]

At the same time, Vietnam has mainly focused on the development of mass organisations which play a dominate role in social life and have a substantial amount of members, even though their membership is not always voluntary.[77] Meanwhile, independent NGOs are misunderstood by many government officials as state dissidents, or the term 'non-governmental' is interpreted as free from state interference and control.[78] Even international non-governmental organisations do not always operate independently, but often maintain a close partnership with state apparatuses.[79] The number of independent CSOs on the other hand has been on the rise in recent years, bringing a new chapter to the dynamics of civil society in Vietnam. These CSOs have triggered several movements, which, nevertheless, only exist in the cyber world and their spill over effects to society have remained limited.

Regarding the field of operation, a majority of traditional CSOs in Vietnam have conducted projects on poverty alleviation and community-based development, especially in mountainous, rural and minority areas.[80] In the past decade, the scope of CSOs activities expanded to areas such as education improvement, gender equality, environment, and climate change.[81] In the context of CSR, a handful of CSOs have initially been involved in business-related issues, e.g. in areas of environment, consumer rights, and employees rights.[82] The engagement of CSOs has recently expanded in industrial zones, especially in labour-intensive industries of textile and garment, timber, and electronics.[83] However, classified as a middle-income country in 2010, Vietnam has begun to experience a withdrawal of a number of international non-governmental organisations[84] and other international donors while a vast majority of labour rights and CSR-related projects are running under their support. In addition, heavy reliance on

---

[73]   CDI and Association Batik International, 'Civil Society and Corporate Social Responsibility in Vietnam: Bridging the Gap', March 2013, p. 15.
[74]   *Ibid.*, p. 18.
[75]   J. Hannah, *Local Non-Government Organizations in Vietnam: Development, Civil Society and State-society Relations*, 1st edn. (Seattle: University of Washington: 2007), p. 141.
[76]   *Ibid.*
[77]   W. Taylor et al., *supra* n. 64, p. 6.
[78]   *Ibid.*, p. 22.
[79]   H.T. Bui, *supra* n. 47, p. 80.
[80]   *Ibid.*, p. 17.
[81]   *Ibid.*
[82]   CDI and Association Batik International. 'Civil Society and Corporate Social Responsibility in Vietnam: Bridging the Gap', March 2013, pp. 26, 40.
[83]   Campaigns of Oxfam, CDI and Association Batik International. 'Civil Society and Corporate Social Responsibility in Vietnam: Bridging the Gap', March 2013, FLA, the Asian Foundation.
[84]   H.T. Bui, *supra* n. 47.

financial support from international non-governmental organisations challenges the continuity and stability of human rights and CSR promotion in Vietnam.

3.2. EXPERIENCES OF CSOs IN THE PROMOTION OF HUMAN RIGHTS IN INDUSTRIAL ZONES IN VIETNAM

3.2.1. Centre of Development and Integration (CDI)

We have studied three CSOs, to be briefly reviewed and analysed here. The first organisation, the CDI, was founded in June 2005 as an independent NGO dedicated to good governance, labour rights, globalisation, CSR, and sustainable development. Within the parameters of labour rights and CSR, the CDI has carried out a diversity of projects in forms of research, policy advocacy, public campaigns, and knowledge exchange through international cooperation, conferences and action works. On project examined was dealing with human rights in industrial zones called 'Protecting and promoting migrant workers' rights in industrial zones in the North of Vietnam'. Particularly over the three-year period 2011–2014 it aims to empower vulnerable workers and have them attain decent working and living conditions in the Thang Long export processing zone and the Phu Nghia industrial zone (Ha Noi), the Nam Sach industrial zone (Hai Duong), the Khai Quang industrial zone (Vinh Phuc), and the Yen Phong industrial zone (Bac Ninh).

The three key objectives of this project were networking and empowerment of migrant workers; capacity building for local authorities to ensure the effectiveness of legal aid services for workers and policy advocacy regarding labour rights; and lobbying employers to protect labour rights. In order to accomplish their objectives, the CDI cooperated with Oxfam Novib and Oxfam Solidarité and received financial and technical sponsorship. It also collaborated with local partners such as the Department of Labour, Invalids and Social Affairs, trade unions, lawyers association, women's unions at the provincial level, and student legal aid centres of law universities for legal and technical assistance. The CDI conducted a variety of activities towards multi-stakeholders engagement with the use of bottom-up methods. Two types of activities may help highlight the work and achievements of the CDI.

The first project concerned migrant workers in terms of improving working conditions. The CDI collaborated with provincial labour unions to establish 'self-management workers groups' within IZs and in their residential communities. Aiming at sharing and learning knowledge, these groups' models enhanced the capacity of workers to access information on labour rights issues through regular meetings and collective initiatives. For instance, by early 2013 there were six worker groups formed with more than 450 members in Hai Duong. Twenty group meetings were held with the assistance of the CDI and Hai Duong provincial Labour Federation. In these meetings, workers discussed their companies' policies, proposed their aspirations on trade unions, shared information on the Labour Code, on the Trade Unions Law, and the Social Insurance Law. This helped nurture workers' consciousness on labour rights and related issues.[85] Also, the CDI offered training programmes for key leaders and legal counsellors so that they could instruct and disseminate knowledge on labour rights issues to group members. These training workshops were organised by local partners, with legal aid expertise and experts of Oxfam and curricula designed by the CDI.

In addition, tailored to the need of employees, the CDI provided legal assistance under the forms of legal education and counselling services. The formation of 'legal aid kiosks' within industrial zones and in workers' villages, as well as the development of mobile legal aids via hotlines and social networks such as Facebook groups and a website[86] removed previous hurdles for workers to share information and seek legal consultation. Especially, in the kiosks placed in Ha Noi, Bac Ninh, Hai Duong, and Vinh Phuc, the CDI equipped internet-connected computers, libraries with free books, and newspapers which were useful communication channels for workers to access information and to connect to advisors and practitioners. Booklets and leaflets regarding labour and social policies, e.g. the Handbook on *Labor and Social Rights for Workers, the Handbook for Legal Aid Skills* composed by the CDI, Vietnam Lawyers Association and labour unions were offered for free to workers and residents in kiosks and handed out to workers in industrial zones. Workers also had opportunities to acquire direct legal consultancy once a week by officials of provincial and district trade unions, lawyers of Vietnam Lawyers Association, and student volunteers. These activities reflected the attempts by the CDI in 'remedying' human rights, specifically increased awareness of workers on labour rights, health care, social insurance issues and in offering grievance mechanisms available and accessible to workers.

The second type of activities for authority and enterprises organised by CDI was public hearings and in-depth multi-stakeholder dialogues including representatives of migrant workers, companies, and local authorities (provincial and district labour confederations and policy makers) to discuss workers' complaints, labour violation cases, and potential solutions. At the end of 2013, CDI generated five pilot and two in-depth dialogues with the participation of representatives from 60 companies and 22 local authority bodies and employees. As a result, there were 40 enquiries by workers, and 34 and 40 recommendations about labour rights were sent to corporate employers in 2011 and 2012 respectively. Similarly, local authorities in five provinces received 20 recommendations on

---

[85]   For example, their accommodation and facilities (electricity price), health care, and their children' rights.

[86]   See www.hotrophaply.net.

housing, security issues, and policies for employees' children. At the central level, the project sent 35 recommendations to the Vietnam General Confederation of Labour for the amendment of the Labour Code and the Trade Union Law in 2012. This contributed to a revision of the law on a maternity leave provision. By doing so, the CDI dedicated its efforts to 'promote' human rights in the ways of supporting local and national bodies for legislation and policy making and putting enterprises on notice to pay more attention to labour rights.

In a nutshell, these activities of the CDI enhanced the legal literacy of migrant workers on their rights, provided remedial measures for them, and improved the relations between employees, managers, and trade unions' representatives at corporate, district, and provincial levels through multi-stakeholder meetings and dialogues. At the higher level, recommendations of the project contributed to the process of national law revisions and corporate regulations. Hence, with the support of the CDI and Oxfam, labour rights became better institutionalised in industrial zones.

3.2.2. Fair Labour Association (FLA)

The FLA is a NGO dedicated to protect and promote workers' rights and to enhance working conditions in accordance with international labour standards.[87] For over 15 years, the FLA has aimed to improve the lives of millions of workers, create sustainable solutions to labour infringements by offering tools and resources to companies; deliver training to workers and management, conduct due diligence through independent assessments; and advocate for greater accountability and transparency from Vietnamese companies and MNCs, manufacturers, and factories involved in global supply chains.[88]

In April 2012, the FLA Vietnam launched a two-year project 'Promoting Sustainable Compliance in Vietnam' (FLA 3.0). The project had a two-fold purpose: to improve workers' lives and increase the efficiency and public reporting of labour compliance programmes[89] with regard to labour management relations, overtime working hours, and fair wage. Beneficiaries of the projects were multi-stakeholders (which were mainly workers but also managers, customers, government, and CSOs) in more than 30 footwear and apparel companies located in industrial zones such as Quang Chau, My Phuoc I, Dong An, Cau Tram, Thuan Dao, Nhon Trach, Giao Long, Vietnam-Singapore, etc. The project was sponsored by the US Department of State and executed by the FLA in collaboration with the Vietnam Chamber of Commerce and Industry; Ministry of Labour, Invalids and Social Affairs; Vietnam General Confederation of Labour; and professional

---

[87]   See www.fairlabor.org/our-work/mission-charter.
[88]   *Ibid.*
[89]   Compliance with companies' code of conduct, FLA standards and Labor Code of Vietnam.

organisations such as Vietnam Leather and Footwear Association and Vietnam Textile and Apparel Association.

The project made a number of efforts and accomplishments on workers' rights and the promotion of CSR which allowed managers and employees to work together to improve working conditions. To do this, the project used 'sustainable compliance self-assessment tools' for managers (SCAT) and employees (SCOPE)[90] to identify and remedy persistent root causes of workers' non-compliance with labour regulations – in particular wages and labour relations – and the needs for capacity building. Based on results of the surveys, the project pointed out that the root causes are limited freedom of association, insufficient wages, and inefficient communication channels.[91]

The project organised five information-sharing workshops and factory visits to share information, identify possible benefits of participation, and action plans for factories' managers. Simultaneously, the FLA held eight Focus Group Training workshops titled 'Multi-stakeholder Consultation Workshops on Solutions and Initiatives of Labor Disputes in Apparel and Footwear Supply Chains'. Each workshop lasted for two days and trained managers, especially human resource managers, on how to improve labour disputes resolution regarding working time, wages, and safe and ethical occupational conditions and education. The FLA required participating factories to produce progress tracking charts, viewed as monthly reports that factories must fill out to document and illustrate the impact of capacity building measures 10–12 months after the completion of the training modules. This allowed factory management, brands, and the FLA to observe, track the implementation of new policies and procedures, and to initiate organisational changes if necessary.[92]

Moreover, the project offered tools for factories to improve the accessibility of grievance mechanisms for workers, in particular EASYFORM. This 'easy form' letter enabled workers to anonymously send complaints or suggestions to management boards and receive feedback from managers.[93] Also, the FLA held consultation on labour issues at the behest of workers or factory.

In cooperation with the Vietnam Chamber of Commerce and Industry and Ministry of Labour, Invalids and Social Affairs, the FLA also organised two national conferences titled 'Multi-stakeholder Dialogues on Sustainable Compliance in Global Supply Chain – Worker Relation, Wages and Working

---

[90] SCAT uses a range of multiple choice questions given to management to make self-assessment on factory performance on labour compliance issues. Similarly, SCOPE is given to workers to make self-assessment in their own perspectives.

[91] Only 40% of workers had already used such channels and 34% were dissatisfied with the solutions. Moreover, 53% of interviewees responded that their wages are insufficient to meet their basic needs.

[92] See http://ap.fairlabor.org/en/ptc.

[93] Three-stage process: step 1: workers fill in blue form letters what they complain or suggest to managers; step 2: managers respond in yellow form letters and stick them onto information board; step 3: workers fill in pink form letters on their (dis) satisfaction with managers' answers.

Hours in Textile and Footwear Industries in Vietnam' in 2013 and early 2014. In the meetings, representatives of the MNCs Chingluh, Columbia, and Patagonia had the opportunity to share their experiences on implementation of compliance self-assessment tools. Most importantly, not only did the conferences include representatives of Vietnam Chamber of Commerce and Industry, Ministry of Labour, Invalids and Social Affairs, 31 companies, brands (among others, Puma, Adidas, Nike, Columbia, etc.), Vietnam Leather and Footwear Association, Vietnam Textile and Apparel Association, and the mass media, but they participated in the discussion on a consensus on the joint initiative regarding corporate compliance with international and national benchmarks on labour rights in apparel and footwear industries. The self-assessment tools were also supposed to be applicable to other industries such as fishery, agriculture, timber, and electronics.

According to the chief advisor of FLA 3.0 Vietnam, the project initially contributed to reduce the number of workers' strikes in IZs given better collaboration and communication between workers and labour managers. FLA 3.0 discussions also suggested that wages should be based on the Asian Floor Wage, factory efficiency and Consumer Price Index in Vietnam. After the closing of FLA 3.0 at the end of 2014, the project will produce recommendations on labour policies and laws regarding living wage, minimum wage, and communication channels between workers and managers.

In short, FLA 3.0 Vietnam supported participating corporations to 'respect' human rights specifically, conduct human rights due diligence in a comprehensive way that includes all processes of assessment of labour rights risks, tracking, and reporting the effectiveness of their responses. FLA 3.0 Vietnam also ensured the protection and remedying of worker's rights by offering new grievance mechanisms. In the final phase of the project, it made suggestions to the labour law revision and had a nation-wide outreach to more than 30 companies through the FLA's network.

3.2.3. Domestic CSOs and the Vedan Case

Vedan Vietnam, a food additives Taiwanese-owned manufacturer, has operated a factory in the Go Dau industrial zone (Dong Nai) since 1991. In September 2008, Vedan was accused of heavily dumping untreated effluents into the Thi Vai River. The direct discharge of waste water without disposal poisoned the river and in turn drove the livelihood and health of tens of thousands of fish and shrimp farmers downstream into extreme destitution.[94] Many people have suffered skin rashes or digestive problems and cancer.[95] Surprisingly, it was not the first

---

[94]   P.H. Nguyen and T.P. Huyen, 'The Dark Side of Development in Vietnam: Lessons from the Killing of the Thi Vai River' (2011) *Journal of Macromarketing* 75.
[95]   *Ibid.*

time Vedan was caught conducting environmental contamination activities; it stood accused once before in 1994.[96] Despite the act of poisoning the river for 14 years, Vedan was granted a certificate of passing a pollution test in 2004 and the honour of being ranked in the top 100 safe products for community health in 2009.[97] In this sense, parallel to corporate responsibility deficit, central and local authorities did not prevent and prosecute Vedan for its environment violations.[98]

While thousands of farmers, including those from the three provinces Dong Nai, Ba Ria Vung Tau and Ho Chi Minh City, have claimed that Vedan caused pollution, representatives of the company at first denied any wrongdoings and refused to pay proper compensation to the affected locals. Meanwhile, the local authorities and the central government did not bring the case to court. The late response was derived from the lack of appropriate accountability of the Ministry of Natural Resources and Environment, People's Committee and Department of Natural Resources and Environment of Dong Nai province in handling the case. Neither the state duty nor corporate responsibility to prevent environmental damages to human rights were upheld.

The Vedan case showed the unprecedented role of domestic CSOs in Vietnam in dealing with environmental abuses, abuses which can also be understood as the violation of the human right to live in a healthy environment. In order to force Vedan to pay for the pollution, the farmers' unions and lawyers' associations at the provincial and central levels came together to help poor farmers lodge their complaints to the courts. In the first step, the municipal and provincial Farmers' Unions in Ho Chi Minh City, Dong Nai, and Ba Ria Vung Tau collected individual complaints against Vedan's environmental pollution and damages. These farmers' unions cooperated with the Vietnamese Farmers' Union, Department of Agriculture and Rural Development, Institute of Environment and Natural Resources (Vietnam National University, Ho Chi Minh City) and brought the case up for discussion in the government's cabinet meetings.[99] The organisations conducted research to investigate and measure the economic and environmental damages that Vedan inflicted to the local communities, and negotiations were held between locals and the representatives of Vedan. However, Vedan's chairman refused to attend, claiming to be occupied. Also, Vedan argued that the amount of compensation that Vietnam offered was inaccurate and exaggerated. It was willing to pay only 20% of the sum.[100] Faced with Vedan's reaction, a dozen lawyers' associations voluntarily provided legal assistance for farmers, preparing documents and collecting evidence to file lawsuits against Vedan.

Simultaneously, a boycott campaign was launched by the Vietnam Supermarket Associations and the Vietnam Standard and Consumer Association

---

[96] Phan (2012), p. 88.
[97] *Ibid.*
[98] *Ibid.*
[99] D.N. Pham, 'Vedan: A Year in Review', available at: http://tiasang.com.vn/Default.aspx?tabid=116&News=4456&CategoryID=42 (accessed 2 May 2014).
[100] T.M.H. Dao, *supra* n. 21, p. 3.

with considerable support of the mass media. The campaign started in October 2008 when giant supermarkets chains, namely Big C, Coopmart, Metro, and Fivimart declined selling Vedan products. This had spill-over effects on wholesalers and small retailers who took Vedan products off their shelves. Popular newspapers such as ThanhNien and TuoiTre provided a significant amount of media coverage with 213 articles and 508 articles respectively related to the case.[101] News on national television channels and radio programmes also called for a nationwide boycott campaign.

Thus, the company, under heavy pressure and suffering big market losses, admitted its accountability and agreed to an out-of-court pay-out of VND 210 billion (equivalent to US $10.7 million).[102] The Vedan case illustrates how policy and law changes are necessary to reduce the impact of industrial waste on the environment and force companies to observe their environmental responsibilities.[103]

In sum, in the Vedan case domestic CSOs were driving forces in bringing remedy to victims and indirectly encouraged the state to take on duty to protect through revising their laws and policies.

4.   CONCLUSION

These three case studies demonstrate the vibrant role of CSOs in the advancement of human rights in industrial zones in Vietnam. These CSOs adopted various strategies to achieve results, that is, cooperation, confrontation and network and alliance building. These combined strategies worked in order to improve laws and policies on labour and environment rights, foster the implementation of CSR and ensure effective remedy for victims.

In fact, while the CDI vigorously engaged itself in protecting and remedying the right of migrant workers in industrial zones, the FLA encouraged and supported corporations in apparel and footwear industries to protect and respect labour rights, especially CSR. Domestic CSOs in the Vedan case, including mass organisations such as farmers' unions and lawyers' associations, were very active in remedying human rights by rendering grievance mechanisms for vulnerable farmers and communities. Each of them produced varying combinations of strategies in attempts to address human rights issues. Similarly, these organisations implemented different strategic combinations; for example, the CDI and the FLA used strategies of cooperation and networks building, whereas

---

[101]   P.H. Nguyen and T.P. Huyen, *supra* n. 94, p. 80.
[102]   *Ibid.*, p. 79.
[103]   Australia ABC Radio, 'Multi-million Compensation for Vietnam Fish Farmers', 18 January 2012, available at: www.radioaustralia.net.au/international/radio/onairhighlights/ multimillion-compensation-for-vietnam-fish-farmers (accessed 1 May 2014).

CSOs in the Vedan case adopted all strategies of cooperation, confrontation, and alliances.

These cases confirmed the influence of organisational and political elements in the engagement of CSOs in addressing human rights issues. Clearly, CSOs did not act autonomously, but in partnership with other stakeholders consisting of national and provincial authorities, international or local CSOs, mass media, and civic actors. To deal with labour issues in industrial zones, both the CDI and FLA closely cooperated with the Vietnam General Confederation of Labour, Ministry of Labour, Invalid and Social Affairs. Apart from governmental organs, the CDI built up a relationship with independent bodies such as Oxfam, whereas the FLA partnered with the USDOS and the Vietnam Chamber of Commerce and Industry to strengthen their power and effectiveness of the project. The Vedan case is indicative of collaboration among local organisations, including the farmers unions, the Law Associations, Vietnam Supermarket Associations, Vietnam Standard and Consumer Association, Ministry of Natural Resources and Environment, and Department of Natural Resources and Environment at provincial level, and consumers. Essentially, the mass media prominently featured in the activities of CSOs and specifically in the boycott campaign against Vedan.

The fact that strategies of cooperation have been employed in all the cases illustrates that the intervention of CSOs into human rights and business cannot exclude the political element in Vietnam. It is evident that the domestic partners of CSOs consisted mostly of mass organisations which are under strong governmental control. The structural ties between CSOs and governmental institutions, the supreme power of the government over every aspect of peoples' lives, and the dependence of CSOs on the state undermine channels of cooperation and the effectiveness of strategies. Particularly, the strategy of cooperation between CSOs and independent trade unions may have been more beneficial for workers mobilisation than mass organisations activism.

The prioritisation of industrial development, especially the approval of numerous industrial zones with labour-intensive manufacturing industries in Vietnam has led to the prevalence of various forms of labour exploitation, harsh occupational conditions, and environmental pollution. Meanwhile, the government, to some extent, is unable and unwillingness to monitor corporate performance. This is reflected in the weaknesses of the legal framework in terms of transparency deficits but also corruption. At the same time, corporations tend to resist undertaking corporate responsibility to respect rights of the employees and surrounding communities. Rather, their actions result in 'impunity' as they take advantage of the shortcomings in current regulations. In addition, pressures from below by consumers and workers remains negligible given the lack of CSR consciousness and their rights. Especially trade unions at central, provincial, and operational levels fall short of their functions as workers' rights defenders. Instead, they became 'prolonged arms' of the government and companies' management boards.

The cases of the CDI, the FLA, and domestic CSOs in the Vedan case, demonstrated these organisations' attempts and achievements of addressing rights issues and seeking remedies for human rights issues and violations. They also confirmed that CSOs could implement a mixture of strategies to address these issues and achieve some forms of social and institutional change. It is important to note that CSOs in the three case studies did not act alone but all employed strategies of cooperation with mass organisations. This, on the one hand, can be understood as one form of cooperation of CSOs to increase power, open up closed spaces of power and gain support and impact. On the other hand, it is a consequence of a political climate of the one-party rule and lack of true independence for CSOs.

For a broader perspective, this chapter suggests that CSOs may serve as dynamic and promising stakeholders who are able to secure labour rights and raise critical voices for the voiceless concerning transparency, responsibility, and accountability of the state and corporations on human rights. First, strategies of cooperation may facilitate partnership between CSOs and central and grassroots governmental agencies such as the National Assembly, Ministry of Labour, Invalid and Social Affairs, Ministry of Natural Resources and Environment and related organs for legislative and policy discussion, consultation and lobbying. They could also form relationship with international organisations for technical and financial support. Secondly, strategies of confrontation could include public demonstrations against the government and corporations and social actions such as naming and shaming and boycott campaigns. However, the former nevertheless is not endorsed in Vietnam. Thirdly, the strategies of alliance building and networks bring together domestic and transnational CSOs. This may enable civic actors and the mass media to enhance their accumulated strength *vis-à-vis* the power of the government and corporations. Networks could ultimately encourage corporates and the state to embrace CSR as universally recognised norms through persuasion (workshops, dialogues) or sanction (boycotts).

To sum up, the role of CSOs is critical in dealing with human rights in industrial zones; however, they must operate in an environment where political, institutional, and economic hurdles are prevalent. Hence, this study draws some practical inferences. Overall, the transparency and governance of the Vietnamese authorities should be improved to ensure effective legal enforcement and a favourable environment for CSOs. Most importantly, regulations on freedom of associations related to the independence of CSOs, and in particular the legitimacy of independent trade unions and law on demonstration, needs to be re-examined.

Furthermore, there is a growing need for progressive human rights policies so that enterprises are unable to conduct 'business as usual' but conduct 'just' and responsible business for their workers and the society in which they operate. Further research is needed on whether voluntarism and self-reporting by enterprises on their business ethics is sufficient or whether additional – or altogether new – legal obligations should be put in place.

CHAPTER 13

THE APPLICATION OF THE UN 'PROTECT, RESPECT AND REMEDY' FRAMEWORK TO STATE-OWNED ENTERPRISES

The Case of the State Oil Company SOCAR in Azerbaijan

Ramute REMEZAITE

In recent years, the concept of corporate social responsibility has gradually developed as a tool to incorporate a social perspective, including the respect for human rights, within business operations. The UN Guiding Principles on Business and Human Rights (the UNGP), adopted in 2011, set global standards for the accountability of both corporate actors and states for their human rights impact.[1] Amidst calls for increased regulation of corporations given the risk of human rights violations through their activities, questions have arisen as to the regulation of state-owned enterprises. Presence of state ownership leads to a general conception that such enterprises entail stronger potential to achieve comprehensive human rights observance than ones of the private ownership. More importantly, it is suggested that commitment to and respect for human rights by state enterprises requires them to enact and incorporate human rights policies. Yet, in spite of the principle of state respect, the main puzzle addressed in this chapter is: what impact do the UNGPs have on state-owned enterprises in countries experiencing bad governance without basic principles of separation of powers, respect for civil and political freedoms, transparency and accountability?

This chapter examines the corporate social responsibility of the State Oil Company of the Republic of Azerbaijan (SOCAR) and its obligations regarding its human rights impact through the prism of the principle of the state duty to respect

---

[1] The Human Rights Council endorsed the Guiding Principles in its Resolution 17/4 of 16 June 2011.

and protect human rights as described in the UNGPs. Particularly, it focuses on violations of property rights occurring in the oil-rich areas of Azerbaijan, where SOCAR claims ownership for the use of oil extraction, and SOCAR's human rights due diligence. The key concern of the article is how to secure the protection of property rights in extractive industries. This is primarily addressed through the analysis of all three pillars of the UNGP framework; however most emphasis is on pillar three which obligates the Azerbaijani government to provide effective remedies to victims of property expropriation. The chapter analyses SOCAR's human rights responsibilities as a state-owned enterprise, the underlying hypothesis being that Azerbaijan enjoys and exerts full power over the company to prevent and redress any human rights violations committed by SOCAR. The chapter discusses the extent to which such responsibilities can be embedded in SOCAR given Azerbaijan's ownership of the company and the government's poor human rights record. The chapter also looks into the potential accountability of foreign oil companies operating in Azerbaijan, particularly companies from established democratic countries with strong corporate social responsibility policies on human rights.

1.　HUMAN RIGHTS DUE DILIGENCE IN EXTRACTIVE INDUSTRIES IN AZERBAIJAN

Research conducted by John Ruggie when he developed the UNGP framework led him to conclude that the highest percentage of cases of human rights allegations were associated with extractive industries – they dominated 28% of random cases studied by Ruggie.[2] Moreover, the extractive sector was complicit in violations in labour as well as non-labour related human rights, e.g. in activities affecting rights of communities, such as the right to an adequate standard of living, including a right to housing.

In Azerbaijan, the issue of *property rights* is at the heart of discussions on human rights compliance and the potential human rights impact of extractive industries stemming both from SOCAR's activities directly and its numerous investments fuelled by increasing oil and gas production growth. SOCAR is wholly owned by the government of Azerbaijan and participates in all oil and gas extraction activities, along with transnational companies such as British Petroleum, Statoil, and others. In recent years, its activities were followed by numerous property rights violations, despite its pronounced commitments to the principle of corporate social responsibility.

---

[2]　Addendum to the Report of the Special Representative of the Secretary-General on the issue of human rights and transnational corporations and other business enterprises, 23 May 2008, UN Doc. A/HRC/8/5/Add.2, p. 9.

SOCAR's vision is to become a vertically integrated international energy company and build on advanced experience in operation efficiency, social and environmental responsibility. Its Code of Business clearly establishes sustainability, social responsibility, and corporate ethics as the guiding principles for its operation.[3] It establishes 'corporate social responsibility as an important component of its business activities and maintains a high degree of social responsibility towards its employees, as well as the public in general'.[4] It outlines among its objectives contributions to the development of the regions where it is present, environmental measures, social programmes for its employees, and charity. The Code further details regulations on environmental protection; rights of employees, such as prohibitions against discrimination, violence and threats; and health care and safety at work. However, it remains silent on potential adverse human rights impacts and due diligence towards the communities where it operates. Regulations on solving issues and providing effective remedy are equally absent. Further, the Code does not provide any details SOCAR's priorities regarding overall social development in the country either.

In 2011, SOCAR published its first Sustainability Report where, among energy-related sustainability, it presented its contribution to economic and social and environmental development of its employees and the country at large, as well as to increasing its transparency. SOCAR's sustainability mission makes no clear reference to social growth, and only outlines the promotion of 'growth of scientific, technical, economic and intellectual potential of Azerbaijan'.[5] SOCAR's contribution to broader community welfare lacks a strategic and systemic approach and fails to target certain social groups or issues through financial investments. SOCAR's social support programme covers investments in building houses to IDPs and refugees, and new schools and hospitals in the regions.

SOCAR supports the Extractive Industries Transparency Initiative (EITI) which seeks to promote transparency and accountability of governments dependent on oil, gas, and mining revenues, along with transnational extractive industry companies present in Azerbaijan. Azerbaijan was among the first countries to endorse EITI and was the first country granted EITI compliant status in 2009. Once initiated, it was undoubtedly seen an important step towards creating transparency and accountability, as well as a potentially bigger space for engagement with civil society in Azerbaijan. The disclosures EITI requires, however, have limited value in Azerbaijan as its EITI membership only relates to the transparency of the government's revenues. EITI does not address the issue of spending of public funds, nor the issue of access for citizens to data on budgets and expenditure, which prevent them from monitoring corruption and assess whether revenues from extractive industries are used to benefit the public.

---

[3]   'Code of Business ethics on the State Oil Company of the Azerbaijan Republic', SOCAR, 2012, para. 1.1.1.
[4]   *Ibid.*, para. 2.5.1.
[5]   *Ibid.*

Although Azerbaijan has filed regular and frequent reports to EITI, domestic civil society representatives that joined the process in 2010 have expressed concerns that the implementation of EITI has stagnated.[6]

In the Open Budget Index 2012, Azerbaijan received 42 points out of maximum 100 for its budget transparency and placed itself at the very bottom of the group of countries which provide 'some' information about their budgets.[7] Although all 26 oil and gas companies in Azerbaijan participate in the EITI process, only a handful of them have agreed to report their payments on a disaggregated basis. There are many areas, including disclosure of production-sharing agreements between the government and foreign companies where transparency is still absent.

The EITI process focuses on promoting transparency but does not include human rights abuses that are often associated with oil and gas industries. Among others, these can include demolitions, forced evictions, and other property rights violations, deriving from operations of oil and gas industry for investments funded by oil revenues. Therefore, the promotion of transparency without a firm call for the respect for human rights undermines the goal of accountability which could otherwise have a positive effect on society. Azerbaijan undermines the civil and political rights of its citizens, including their right to access information, and exercise zero tolerance of any criticism or exposure of wrongdoings by the authorities through investigations into corruption by civil society and the media. Azerbaijan impairs public participation and debate in the distribution of public funds, largely consisting of oil revenues. Domestic human rights groups and the international community raised concerns over the unprecedented crackdown on critical voices, leading to the detention and judicial persecution of prominent human rights defenders and investigative journalists, the *de facto* closure of independent non-governmental human rights and media organisations, including those involved in the EITI process, and independent media outlets.[8] The members of the national EITI coalition were forced to leave their offices, and most of the members' bank accounts were frozen.[9] Given that free and active civil society participation is a cornerstone of the initiative as it forms a part of the EITI

---

[6]   'Statement of the Coalition of NGOs for Improving Transparency in Extracting Industries', available at: http://eiti.org/files/Statement%20of%20EITI%20NGO%20Coalition%20in%20 Azerbaijan_June%2008_2011.pdf.

[7]   Rankings, *International Budget Partnership*, available at: http://internationalbudget.org/ what-we-do/open-budget-survey/rankings-key-findings/rankings/.

[8]   'Persecution of rights activists must stop – UN experts call on the Government of Azerbaijan', statement by the UN Special rapporteurs on freedom of association and assembly, freedom of expression, and on situation of human rights defenders, 19 August 2014; 'Statement at the end of visit to Azerbaijan by the United Nations Working Group on Business and Human Rights', UN Working Group on Business and Human Rights, 27 August 2014; 'The Dangerous Work of Defending Transparency', Human Rights Watch, 21 November 2014, among others.

[9]   Statement of the Coalition for 'Increasing Transparency in Extractive Industries of the Republic of Azerbaijan' on challenges encountered in the field of EITI implementation in Azerbaijan, 15 July 2014.

governance, such a clampdown on local anti-corruption and transparency groups in Azerbaijan prevents public debates on natural resource management issues. It also seriously compromises the EITI process in the country, actions with which EITI cannot afford to be complicit. Encouraged by various human rights groups, the EITI board decided to conduct a compliance check of Azerbaijan. Such a move which may lead to downgrading the state's membership status or expelling it altogether from the initiative – an outcome that is strongly opposed by the Azerbaijani government.[10] If transparency is to unleash greater accountability, respect for human rights is an absolutely essential. For now, Azerbaijan falls short of transparency in the minimalist sense of disclosing revenues, and transparency as genuine accountability as would be reflected in improved governance.

Full respect of the right to information, including right to access information, would be the first step in filling the existing gap to full transparency on government spending, largely funded by oil revenues. In 2012, however, Azerbaijan took a step in the reverse direction when it limited access to information on disclosures by corporate entities if doing so 'contradicts the national interests of Azerbaijan in political, economic, and monetary policy, the defense of public order, the health and moral values of the people, or harms the commercial or other interests of individuals'.[11] Strongly criticised by pro-transparency activists, these changes curtail public access to information on the ownership of commercial entities, the share of their charter capital owned by the state, ownership structure, and other similar data. Preventing public access to information about commercial legal entities cannot be justified by a public-interest argument. This level of secrecy causes mistrust and decreased confidence among participants of what purports to be a free market economy.

Such developments raise serious doubts about Azerbaijan's commitments to increase its transparency, inclusiveness, and due diligence in its extractive industries and expenditure. Although SOCAR's responsibility to respect human rights remains with Azerbaijan's failure to uphold its obligations to protect human rights and blatantly violates them, it becomes all the more challenging for SOCAR to meet its obligation in practice. State ownership implies that the state duty to protect human rights is relevant to how its business is conducted.

2. THE LEGAL AND POLITICAL CONTEXT OF EXTRACTIVE INDUSTRIES IN AZERBAIJAN

Geographically positioned in between Iran and Russia, Azerbaijan is one of the fastest growing economies in the Caspian Sea region. Natural resource-based

---

[10] 'Azerbaijan: Group Orders Rights-Linked Review', Human Rights Watch, 15 October 2014.
[11] Established by amendments to the laws 'On the right to obtain information', 'On state registration and state registry of legal entities' and 'On commercial secrets' adopted by the Parliament on 12 June 2012.

revenues have risen spectacularly in the recent years and dominate the Azerbaijani economy. In 2013, oil and gas income accounted for 83 per cent of the state budget[12] compared to 74 per cent in 2011.[13] The non-oil sectors remain fragile. An economy heavily dependent on oil revenues brings with it huge responsibility of managing the oil resources efficiently and in a responsible manner. It also calls for using the wealth to invest in development programmes capable of providing lasting benefits to citizens' social development, social welfare, economic growth, democratic processes afforded them, security, and overall quality of life.

Possession of natural resources like oil and gas in and of itself does not always lead to economic success for a country. It can carry risks of inefficiency and misuse and is dependent on the country's effective commitments to democracy, including transparency and anticorruption policies. Substantial literature suggests that oil impedes democratisation and supports authoritarian regime stability.[14] Several country-analyses relate regime survival in Azerbaijan to oil, making the state even more opposed to reforms.[15] In light of the country's slow ascent to full democracy and very poor human rights record, one can expect oil revenues in Azerbaijan, which have so far failed to turn oil wealth into a higher quality of life for Azerbaijani citizens, to further feed into the country's corruption and impede social development.

Citizens above the poverty line face huge economic challenges due to high consumer prices and corruption levels in the public services sector. Although the official 2013 unemployment rate in Azerbaijan was rather low (4.9%), the statistics exclude around one million Azerbaijanis who have emigrated to Russia in search of better wages.[16] In a country with nine million inhabitants, the loss of Azerbaijanis to Russia constitutes a significant number of the labour force and its absence is noticeable. Azerbaijan's shadow economy was the third largest in the world in 2007 and represented 69.6% of the country's total gross domestic product (GDP) up from 66.2% in 2010.[17]

Despite the development advances from an increase in oil and gas production in the past decade, the country's rapid economic and social development has not

---

[12]   'Azerbaijan Partnership Program Snapshot', World Bank Group, October 2014, p. 6, available at: www.worldbank.org/content/dam/Worldbank/document/Azerbaijan-Snapshot.pdf.

[13]   'Azerbaijan', Natural Resource Governance Institute, available at: www.revenuewatch.org/countries/eurasia/azerbaijan/overview.

[14]   See inter alia M.L. Ross, 'Does Oil Hinder Democracy?' (2001) 53(3) *World Politics* 325–361; S. Aslaksen, 'Oil and Democracy: More Than a Cross-country Correlation?' (2010) 47(4) *Journal of Peace Research* 421–431.

[15]   See inter alia F. Guliyev, 'Oil and Regime Stability in Azerbaijan' (2013) 21(1) *Demokratizatsiya: The Journal of Post-Soviet Democratization* 113–147; V. Gojayev, 'Azerbaijan: from Bad to Worse', *Spotlight on Azerbaijan, Foreign Policy Centre*, 2012, pp. 27–28.

[16]   'Azerbaijan Partnership Program Snapshot', World Bank Group, October 2014, available at: www.worldbank.org/content/dam/Worldbank/document/Azerbaijan-Snapshot.pdf.

[17]   C. Prentice, 'The countries with biggest shadow economies', *Bloomberg*, available at: http://images.businessweek.com/ss/10/07/0729_worlds_biggest_shadow_economy/4.htm.

been without controversy.[18] Azerbaijani civil society cites a lack of economic diversification, sector corruption, lack of transparency, and high unemployment and underdevelopment outside the capital Baku as critical challenges which need to be addressed.[19]

According to the government's reports, the number in households living below the poverty level has dramatically decreased from 46.7% in 2002 to 15.8% in 2007.[20] In 2006, the GDP expanded by a record 34.5% in real terms and was the world's highest growth rate for the second year running. By far, the greatest engine of growth has been the oil and gas sectors. According to the State Oil Fund of the Republic of Azerbaijan (SOFAZ), which seeks to generate oil revenues for future generations, in addition to major funds allocated to the state budget, state resources are being directly allocated to projects such as settlement problems of the country's refugees and internally displaced persons (i.e. Nagorno Karabakh conflict, which resulted in more than 600,000 IDPs in Azerbaijan), infrastructure projects, reconstruction of irrigation systems, railways development, development of Azerbaijani youth exchange programmes, and further development of oil fields.[21] Much needed investments and improvement in healthcare, social security, and educational system may well be funded by annual allocations of state budget, the expenditure of which is difficult to monitor by media and civil society due to widespread abuses of a right to access information, as argued earlier.

Lack of transparency, good governance and respect for basic freedoms is yet another key factor preventing effective social and economic sustainable development in Azerbaijan. Azerbaijan's government remains politically repressive. In 2014, Freedom House assessed the Azerbaijani media as 'not free', ranking it 183rd place out of 197 countries.[22] Azerbaijan's media remains *not free* in each ranking since 2004. In 2014, Reporters Without Borders ranked Azerbaijan 160th out of 180 countries.[23] Reporters Without Borders had also previously attributed the country's sustained repressive environment on freedom of expression to the country's increasing oil and gas wealth.[24] In 2012, Transparency International Corruption Perception Index ranked the country 139th out of

---

[18]   'State Oil Fund of the Republic of Azerbaijan', Annual Report 2011, available at: www.oilfund. az/uploads/annual_2011en.pdf.

[19]   'After the BCT pipeline and EITI validation: Where are Prosperity and Transparency in Azerbaijan?', October 2012. Crude Accountability Report, p. 6, available at: http:// crudeaccountability.org/wp-content/uploads/2012/10/Azerbaijan-Lacking-Prosperity.pdf.

[20]   World Bank Report on Azerbaijan, 2008.

[21]   'State Oil Fund of the Republic of Azerbaijan', Annual Report 2013, available at: www.oilfund. az/uploads/annual_2013en.pdf.

[22]   'Freedom of the Press 2014', *Freedomhouse*, available at: www.freedomhouse.org/report/ freedom-press-2014/press-freedom-rankings#.VE_cdEtNbHg.

[23]   'World Press Freedom Index 2014: Eastern Europe and Cetral Asia', *Reporters Without Borders*, available at: http://rsf.org/index2014/en-eastern-europe.php.

[24]   'Paradoxically, the economic boom that the country has experienced since the Baku-Tbilisi-Ceyhan pipeline was inaugurated in 2006 has bolstered this trend by vastly increasing the authorities' resources and strengthening the impression that the international community cannot touch them', see: http://en.rsf.org/report-azerbaijan,91.html.

174 countries. Azerbaijan was also ranked weak in the Resource Governance Index by Revenue Watch, holding 28th place out of 58 countries in the oil, gas, and mining sector.[25]

The survey conducted by the Baku-based Center for Economic and Social Development with the aim to measure public awareness on spending of oil revenues revealed that the majority of interviewed citizens were doubtful about the effective utilisation of and transparency over oil revenues – unlike the public servants.[26] Most extractive companies that were interviewed responded that they did not cooperate with civil society organisations, stressing that there was no need for such cooperation. None of the oil-producing companies interviewed obtained complete information on the targeted use of the funds they had paid to the government. Only 25% of the interviewed companies said that they disclosed audit results to the public in a timely manner. The survey showed that public access to audit results of either foreign oil companies or government-initiated projects in terms of activities was limited. It is noteworthy to mention that the three interviewed groups – state institutions, oil companies, and citizens – had very different approaches to transparency. 70% of respondents employed by government-linked institutions claimed that citizens had adequate access to information about how their government utilised oil revenues. Yet 82% of citizens interviewed said they had no idea about revenue and spending from the state oil fund. The interviewed government entities insisted that they simply preferred to cooperate with media outlets over civil society institutions. Although all interviewed government bodies claimed that there was effective use of and transparency over oil revenues, 81% of surveyed people reported the opposite.[27]

The government displays little tolerance for independent voices that openly criticise considerable corruption and human rights abuses in the country. Amidst an overall climate of repression on dissent, in which any critic might be targeted at any moment, individuals who raise candid questions about government corruption and mismanagement are at particular risk of reprisal. Harassment and politically motivated prosecutions frequently have been used to target civil society activists and journalists, among others, who dare to challenge the government or senior figures on these topics.[28] Among the most alarming cases was the arrest of the award winning investigative journalist Khadija Ismayilova who was sentenced to seven years in prison under politically motivated charges of tax evasion, illegal

---

[25]   'The Resource Governance Index (RGI) measures the quality of governance in the oil, gas and mining sectors of 58 countries', Natural Resource Governance Institute, available at: www.resourcegovernance.org/rgi.

[26]   V. Bayramov, T. McNaught and E. Rshidov, 'Managing Resource Revenues in Oil-Rich CAREC Countries: The Case of Azerbaijan', Center for Economic and Social Development, April 2011, available at: http://cesd.az/new/wp-content/uploads/2011/05/CESD_Paper_Oil_Revenues_Management_Azerbaijan.pdf.

[27]   Ibid., p. 24.

[28]   'Extractive Industries: A New Accountability Agenda', Human Rights Watch Report, 21 May 2013.

entrepreneurship and abuse of power. Ismayilova is well known for her extensive reporting on government corruption, including exposing the business interests of the ruling family, she has previously received threats related to her investigative journalism and also faced a criminal trial for defamation.

Such examples of repression on media and civil society demonstrate an ever-increasing pattern of zero tolerance for criticism, and call for accountability and transparency and exposure of the abuses. It has become extremely difficult to implement effective control over lucrative sectors of the economy, particularly after the Azerbaijani parliament adopted legislation in June 2012 that allowed Azerbaijani companies to withhold information pertaining to their registration, ownership structure, and shareholders. As stated by the NGO Coalition for Improving Transparency in the Extractive Industries in Azerbaijan, arrests of activists 'aim at threatening Azerbaijani human right defenders, and other active NGO activists striving for increasing transparency and struggling with corruption, and making them abstain from defending human rights and freedoms, and social initiatives in spending of oil revenues.'[29]

3. SOCAR'S ADVERSE IMPACT ON PROPERTY RIGHTS

3.1. HOUSE DEMOLITIONS, ILLEGAL EXPROPRIATIONS, AND FORCED EVICTIONS AS A PRICE FOR URBANISATION AND FURTHER DEVELOPMENT OF OIL INDUSTRY

Since 2008, fuelled by the oil boom and increasing oil revenues, the Azerbaijani government has engaged in a wide-reaching programme of urban renewal and started significant infrastructure projects in the capital Baku. According to media reports in 2014, the Azerbaijani government spent half of its budget on construction projects.[30] In the course of the programme, the authorities have illegally expropriated hundreds of properties, primarily apartments and homes in middle class neighbourhoods, to be demolished for the construction of parks, roads, a shopping centre, and luxury residential buildings. According to local human rights groups, in 2009–2011 only, 3,930 houses were affected by the government's urbanisation policies.[31] The government has forcibly

---

[29]   'Statement of the Coalition of NGOs for Improving Transparency in Extracting Industries', IETI Coalition, 6 June 2011, available at: http://eiti.org/files/Statement%20of%20EITI%20 NGO%20Coalition%20in%20Azerbaijan_June%2008_2011.pdf.

[30]   'The fall in oil prices, and the 2015 budget', *BBC News Azerbaijan*, 17 November 2014, available at: www.bbc.co.uk/azeri/azerbaijan/2014/11/141117_azerbaijan_budget_analyst.

[31]   'Property Rights in Azerbaijan: Restrictions and Challenges', Public Association for Assistance to Free Economy, Policy Brief, 2014, p. 5, available at: www.freeeconomy.az/site/ assets/files/1308/property_rights_in_azerbaijan.pdf.

evicted thousands of homeowners, often without warning, and at times in clear disregard for residents' health and safety, in order to demolish their homes. It has refused to provide homeowners with fair compensation based on the market values of properties, many of which were in highly desirable locations and neighbourhoods.[32] Violations of property rights reportedly mainly occur in cases of property expropriation for state needs, expropriation of land shares, and sometimes private houses for road and water pipes constructions.

SOCAR, which was given the ownership rights to a number of areas for the purposes of oil exploitation during the period of the Soviet Union, in turn engages in similar violations of property rights, either as a result of oil exploitation or urbanisation projects. Rights groups have expressed concern over public plans to demolish 50,000 houses by the Baku City Executive Authority and 35,000 houses by SOCAR for oil extraction purposes.[33] As of the spring 2014, 22,000 lawsuits were pending before domestic courts on behalf of SOCAR for permission to evict allegedly illegal homeowners in SOCAR administered areas without compensation.[34]

With little hope for citizens to seek justice in domestic courts that are widely dependent on the executive power, the increasing number of cases pending before the European Court for Human Rights (ECtHR) related to demolitions and expropriations of property in Azerbaijan is a clear indicator that property rights are quickly becoming a serious human rights concern in the country.

3.2. CASE STUDY: FORCED EVICTIONS AND HOUSE DEMOLITIONS IN THE SULUTEPE AREA

The Binagadi district of the capital Baku is a potentially oil rich area, with several oil and gas production administrations located there. At the same time, the Binagadi district is home to 400,000 inhabitants, including 32,000 refugees and internally displaced people from the Nagorno Karabakh war with Armenia in the late 1980s to early 1990s. Since then, thousands of houses were built in the area. The local authorities administering the area have issued permissions to local residents to build houses, which SOCAR has deemed illegal as it claimed its ownership of the area due to its potential oil extraction. Beginning in November 2011, SOCAR intensified its efforts against the local residents by demolishing houses and forced evictions of local residents claiming the ownership of the area and therefore illegality of properties built there. The confrontations with local residents

---

[32] 'They took everything from me: forced evictions, illegal expropriations and house demolitions in Azerbaijan's capital', Human Rights Watch Report, 29 February 2012, available at: www.hrw.org/reports/2012/02/29/they-took-everything-me-0.

[33] Interview with the Baku-based Public Association for Assistance for Free Economy, 19 May 2013.

[34] *Ibid.*, p. 22.

escalated in April 2012 when SOCAR employees demolished at least 30 houses located in the area, despite numerous claims from the residents regarding proof of ownership issued by local authorities. SOCAR dismissed the official ownership documents as illegal, claiming the area as its own on account of the potential oil production field and therefore reportedly offered no compensation to local residents, referring them to the local authorities.[35] The attempted demolitions ingnited clashes between local residents and SOCAR security employees when heavy machinery was brought in to demolish the houses. The residents were not given the opportunity to take any of their belongings and were driven from their apartments with batons. Dozens of them were injured and one journalist severely beaten by SOCAR security guards while the police present at the scene failed to disperse the conflict and prevent violence.

Such actions demonstrate that SOCAR failed to consider and adequately address the concerns of the affected stakeholders, as it was clear that the adverse impact would grossly violate residents' rights. The company failed to carry out a human rights due diligence assessment to prevent or mitigate such an impact, and in particular, it failed to account for potential adverse impact on the rights of people, a duty established by Principle 17 of the Principles. Instead, SOCAR engaged in proactive violent actions.

The residents did not oppose SOCAR's general policy to use the area for oil production or other purposes but rather questioned the fact that SOCAR was given permission by local executive authorities to continue the constructions even though they were deemed to be illegal. The confrontation between the village residents and SOCAR has persisted ever since then without any legal solution. The burden of finding a solution obviously falls on the local authorities and SOCAR rather than residents themselves as SOCAR's claim over the lands was held up against local authorities' mandate to issue property permits on its lands.

3.3. ASSESSMENT OF SOCAR'S SOCIAL CORPORATE RESPOSIBILITY OVER THE VIOLATIONS AND ABSENCE OF EFFECTIVE LEGAL REMEDIES

International human rights treaties generally do not impose direct legal obligations on business enterprises. However, the actions of business enterprises, just like the actions of other non-state actors, can affect the enjoyment of human rights by others, including those of communities where their operations take place in the present case. The UN Framework can be considered a universal voluntary commitment towards promoting more effective protection of individuals and communities against corporate-related human rights abuses. Despite its

---

[35] 'SOCAR advises tenants of houses demolished in Sulu-Tepe to sue local authorities', *Caucasian Knot*, 12 April 2012, available at: http://eng.kavkaz-uzel.ru/articles/20719/.

voluntary nature, it lays down a basis for social corporate responsibility for human rights abuses stemming from company operations.[36] It clearly established the principle that business enterprises should respect human rights. This means that companies should avoid infringing the human rights of others and should address adverse human rights impacts with which they are involved.[37] The principle is also recognised in soft law instruments such as the Tripartite Declaration of Principles Concerning Multinational Enterprises and Social Policy and the OECD Guidelines for Multinational Enterprises – both located within organisations to which Azerbaijan is a state party.[38]

Azerbaijan is a state party to all international human rights treaties and other complementary instruments that set human rights standards for enterprises.[39] Legal liability and enforcement of international human rights standards by business are therefore largely defined in national law. In other words, companies operating in Azerbaijan legally can go about their activities so long as they do not cause harm to individuals' human rights in the process.

As a corporation operating in Azerbaijan, SOCAR holds a baseline responsibility to respect all human rights as stated in the UN Guiding Principles and under relevant national laws. Its commitment to respect human rights should further be strengthened through its state ownership. Therefore, SOCAR, being a fully state-owned company, is subject to national laws establishing companies' obligation to not violate human rights and the state's responsibility to protect human rights once such violations occur.

Neither SOCAR policy nor its operational instruments, including those related to social corporate responsibility, make any explicit reference to its commitment to establish human rights due diligence processes or provide access to remedy once such violations occur. Notably, it is equally silent on direct operations of the company, such as potential oil production in residential areas. No regulation on the assessment of actual or potential human rights impacts exists. There is no guidance regarding what to do if such situations were to occur or processes to enable the remediation of any adverse human rights impacts SOCAR contribute to or otherwise cause.[40]

Responsibility for human rights violations, however, exists beyond company's own commitment to human rights. As provided in the Guiding

---

[36] J. Ruggie, 'Protect, respect and remedy: a framework for business and human rights: report of the Special Representative of the Secretary-General on the Issue of Human Rights and Transnational Corporations and Other Business Enterprises', UN Human Rights Council, 7 April 2008, UN Doc. A/HRC/8/5, available at: www.refworld.org/docid/484d2d5f2.html.

[37] Guiding Principle 11 of the UN 'Protect, Respect and Remedy' Framework.

[38] J. Ruggie, *supra* n. 36, para. 23.

[39] Azerbaijan ratified the European Convention for Human Rights on 15 April 2002; International Covenant on Civil and Political Rights on 13 August 1992, International Covenant on Economic, Social and Cultural Rights on 16 August 1996, among others.

[40] Guiding Principle 15 provides for clear processes and policies 'to ensure human right due diligence to identify, prevent, mitigate and account for how they address their impacts on human rights'.

Principle 12, the responsibility of business enterprises to respect human rights refers to internationally recognised human rights – the bare minimum – akin to those expressed in the International Bill for Human Rights. Therefore, SOCAR, in its operational activities, has committed to respect the right to property of individuals, among other human rights, as is established by the Universal Declaration of Human Rights, and Azerbaijani national legislation.[41]

The Constitution of Azerbaijan recognises a right to property as a constitutional right of every individual in the country. It ensures ownership rights and protects owners from the arbitrary deprivation of their property in the event of a court decision and where owners are fairly compensated for their loss based on the value of the property.[42] Article 43 of the Constitution protects individuals from unlawful eviction, stating that '[n]o one shall be deprived of his/her residence', and places a positive obligation on the state to 'take measures in order to implement the right to a residence.'[43] Moreover, the Criminal Code makes 'deliberate destruction of or damage to property' an offence.[44]

The Land Code of the Republic of Azerbaijan establishes that a right of individuals to a plot of land appears on the basis of 'decisions of relevant bodies of executive authorities or municipalities'.[45] Therefore, according to the existing applicable laws, Sulutepe inhabitants whose property was demolished by SOCAR security had a lawful right to their property, as granted by the authorised local authorities. If ownership rights of Sulutepe inhabitants, which date back to the the early 1960s under the Soviet regime, were overruled by SOCAR's claims to the lands, dated back from early 1960s under the Soviet regime, SOCAR would have a right to expropriation the land for state needs, under certain conditions, as provided by the relevant national laws.

International human rights law recognises that a right to property may be subject to interference by the state in the interest of the common good, such as for purposes of development. Expropriations and evictions are envisaged in

---

[41]   Article 17 of the Universal Declaration of Human Rights: '1. Everyone has the right to own property alone as well as in association with others. 2. No one shall be arbitrarily deprived of his property'.

[42]   Article 29 of the Constitution of the Republic of Azerbaijan, 12 November 1995: 'Ownership right I. Everyone has the right to own property. II. Neither kind of property has priority. Ownership right including right for private owners is protected by law. III. Everyone might possess movable and real property. Right of ownership envisages the right of owner to possess, use and dispose of the property himself/herself or jointly with others. IV. Nobody shall be deprived of his/her property without decision of law court. Total confiscation of the property is not permitted. Alienation of the property for state or public needs is permitted only after preliminary fair reimbursement of its cost.'

[43]   Article 43 of the Constitution of Azerbaijan: 'No one shall be deprived of his/her residence. The State shall give loans for the construction of houses and blocks apartments, shall take measures in to implement the right to residence.'

[44]   Article 186 of the Criminal Code of the Republic of Azerbaijan.

[45]   Article 55 of the Land Code of the Republic of Azerbaijan, 25 June 1999, No 695-IQ, unofficial translation: http://taxes.caspel.com/2009/uploads/qanun/2011/mecelleler/torpaq_mecellesi_eng.pdf.

both Azerbaijani and international law. However, the authorities can resort to expropriations only in exceptional circumstances for purposes that are clearly in the public interest, and with appropriate due process, including the provision of fair compensation.[46] In such a case, SOCAR, as a state representative, would have a legitimate right to expropriate lands in the Sulutepe area for state needs; namely, for oil and gas production.

Law on expropriation of land for state needs establishes a limited number of purposes that justify expropriation of private property for state needs: the construction of roads or other communication lines (including oil pipelines), for purposes of defending a state border, the construction of defence facilities, or construction of industrial mining facilities.[47] Expropriation for state needs must be based on a decision of the Cabinet of Ministers and property owners must be notified in writing that their properties will be expropriated no less than one year in advance and demolitions must be sanctioned by a court decision.

SOCAR possessed no such court order at the time of demolitions, which therefore means that SOCAR's evictions and subsequent demolition campaign of the Sulutepe homes did not meet the requirements under national law, even if SOCAR possessed a right to lands in the Sulutepe area.

SOCAR was not mindful of the social corporate responsibility principles to respect human rights, particularly in terms of preventing and mitigating human rights violations and taking appropriate actions when they occur. SOCAR's headquarters acknowledged to the media that 'SOCAR does not encroach on residents' ownership rights, but takes steps to ensure oil and gas operations in its territory'.[48] This raises serious doubts on how social corporate responsibility principles are being entrenched by SOCAR in practice. In its public statement on the demolitions in Sulutepe SOCAR highlighted that 'illegal occupation of these lands makes SOCAR unable to fulfil its obligations regarding the provision of lands under the Production Sharing Agreements, which can result in arbitration or court actions against SOCAR, hence the Azerbaijani Government'. It went further to state that the municipal authorities abused their powers by carrying out the illegal sale of the Sulutepe lands to the public. SOCAR claimed these lands were contaminated with oil waste and had oil and gas reservoirs.[49]

---

[46] Article 17 of the Universal Declaration of Human Rights: '1. Everyone has the right to own property alone as well as in association with others. 2. No one shall be arbitrarily deprived of his property'; Article 1 of Protocol 1 of the European Convention on Human Rights: 'Every natural or legal person is entitled to the peaceful enjoyment of his possessions. No one shall be deprived of his possessions except in the public interest and subject to the conditions provided for by law and by the general principles of international law'.

[47] Article 3 of the Law on Expropriation of Land for State Needs of the Republic of Azerbaijan.

[48] 'SOCAR advises tenants of houses demolished in Sulu-Tepe to sue local authorities', *Caucasian Knot*, 12 April 2012, available at: http://eng.kavkaz-uzel.ru/articles/20719/.

[49] SOCAR also stated that, since 2010, it has brought legal actions on a large scale, to demolish and remove illegally built houses belonging it in various parts of Baku. Until today, SOCAR has made more than 15,000 claims, more than 4,000 of which have been ruled in its favour and some are still being processed.

Interviewed residents claimed that many of them had to pay bribes to local authorities in order to obtain permission to stay which aptly reflects the broader picture of widespread corruption in public sector. Corruption is endemic to public authorities and interactions with them. For example, a 2009 survey of the International Finance Corporation and World Bank revealed that 71% of firms operating in Azerbaijan were expected to give 'gifts' to receive construction permits, nearly three times the regional average.[50] Residents therefore expressed little hope the issue would be resolved through appeals to local authorities to obtain compensation.

One component of a fair and transparent expropriation process is the existence of a mechanism for resolving grievances. Lack of access to effective remedies to secure and protect property rights of individuals is an overarching concern due to conflicting applicable laws and policies. SOCAR pursued evictions and demolitions either without court orders or where court cases were still pending, thereby raising serious questions as to whether the courts can provide an effective means of redress.

4. AZERBAIJAN'S OBLIGATION TO SECURE ACCESS TO EFFECTIVE REMEDY FOR PROPERTY RIGHTS VIOLATIONS

Given that SOCAR is a fully state-owned company and the existence of loopholes in national regulations on real property and lands, this clearly put into question the responsibilities of the government of Azerbaijan for and to securing access to effective remedy but also in taking preventive measures in securing property rights as such. The state's role in ownership and management of SOCAR means that the state duty to protect human rights is relevant in how its business is conducted. As provided in the UN Guiding Principles, states are not per se responsible for human rights abuse of companies. However, states may be in breach of their international human rights obligations where such abuses can be attributed to them, or where they otherwise fail to take appropriate steps to prevent, investigate, punish, and redress private actors' abuses, including through effective policies, legislation, regulations, and adjudication.[51] The existing legal gap in terms of land ownership, followed by the failure to enforce existing laws, and the existence of widespread corruption among public authorities ensures direct responsibility to the government of Azerbaijan for SOCAR property

---

[50]   'Enterprise Surveys: Indicator Descriptions', 27 March 2014, available at: www.enterprise surveys.org/Data/ExploreEconomies/2009/azerbaijan/~/media/FPDKM/EnterpriseSurveys/ Documents/Misc/Indicator-Descriptions.pdf.

[51]   'Guiding Principles on Business and Human Rights', United Nations Human Rights Office of the High Commissioner, New York and Geneva, 2011, available at: www.ohchr.org/ Documents/Publications/GuidingPrinciplesBusinessHR_EN.pdf.

rights violations. The government holds a positive obligation to ensure effective enforcement of existing laws or take certain measures to reasonably correct a negative situation.[52] Currently, there is no law that would regulate oil and gas exploration, production, and development in Azerbaijan.[53] In addition, the UN Guiding Principles encourage governments to provide effective guidance to companies on how to respect human rights throughout their operations. However, to date, in the case of SOCAR, no effective solution of the state level has been achieved despite the fact that Azerbaijan enjoys and exerts full power over the company, which enables it to prevent and redress human rights violations committed by the company.

Azerbaijan should take additional steps to protect against human rights abuses by business enterprises that are owned or controlled by the state, including, where appropriate, requiring human rights due diligence.[54] A requirement for human rights due diligence is extremely relevant where the nature of business operations poses a significant risk to human rights, as in the case of SOCAR's implementation of its oil extraction operations in oil rich areas. Among its other international human rights commitments, Article 11 of the International Covenant on Economic, Social and Cultural Rights (ICESCR) to which Azerbaijan is a party, establishes the obligation to protect the right to adequate housing, which includes protection against forced eviction.[55] Its General Comment 4 on Article 11 of ICESCR states that 'all persons should possess a degree of security of tenure which guarantees legal protection against forced eviction, harassment and other threats.'[56] If evictions are to take place, in order for them not to be considered 'forced,' they must be carried out lawfully, only in exceptional circumstances, and in full accordance with relevant provisions of international human rights law.

Where a business enterprise is controlled by the state, an abuse of human rights by the business enterprise may entail a violation of the state's own international law obligations. It particularly applies to situations where companies fail to identify that they have caused an adverse human rights impact and refuse to cooperate in its remediation through legitimate processes, like it is in the case of SOCAR.

---

[52]   'Guiding Principles on Business and Human Rights', United Nations Human Rights Office of the High Commissioner, New York and Geneva, 2011, commentary on Guiding Principle 3, available at: www.ohchr.org/Documents/Publications/GuidingPrinciplesBusinessHR_EN.pdf

[53]   'Azerbaijan country report', *The Economist: Intelligence Unit*, accessed 27 May 2013.

[54]   'Guiding Principles on Business and Human Rights', United Nations Human Rights Office of the High Commissioner, New York and Geneva, 2011, commentary on Guiding Principle 4, available at: www.ohchr.org/Documents/Publications/GuidingPrinciplesBusinessHR_EN.pdf.

[55]   International Covenant on Economic, Social, and Cultural Rights, UN Doc. A/6316 (1966), entered into force 3 January 1976, acceded to by Azerbaijan on 13 August 1992.

[56]   'General Comment No. 4, The Right to Adequate Housing The Right to Adequate Housing (Art. 11(1) of the Covenant)', UN Committee on Economic, Social and Cultural Rights, UN Doc. E/1992/23 (1992), para. 8.

As a part of its duty to protect individuals from business-rela... rights violations, the government of Azerbaijan must take appropriate steps to ensure access to effective remedy to victims of such violations, primarily through judicial and other appropriate means, including the provision of proper compensation or alternative housing. Lack of judicial independence, however, is of great concern in Azerbaijan where the executive branch continues to exert its influence, particularly in cases brought against public authorities.[57] Claims in cases of violations of property rights resulting in evictions and demolitions are often the rule not exception. The judicial system is also affected by the lack of a unified and cohesive legal regime and cannot effectively constrain the executive's abuses of power. The 'hands off' approach taken by the Azerbaijani government stems from its own lack of political will for the respect and protection of the rights of its citizens. Victims of property rights abuses cannot seek effective remedy against companies in the domestic courts and are left with regional human rights mechanisms such as the European Court of Human Rights.[58]

4.1. THE NEED FOR INCREASED PROTECTION OF HUMAN RIGHTS DEFENDERS WORKING ON CORPORATE RESPONSIBILITY

The brutal attack on Idrak Abbasov, the international award-winning journalist who was severely beaten by roughly 20 SOCAR security guards when filming the demolition of dozens of houses in Sulutepe area, demonstrates the particular vulnerability of those reporting on corporate social responsibility and exposes even more abuses by companies.[59] In early 2014, the investigation into the attack was suspended by the law enforcements agencies. The perpetrators remain unpunished despite the presence of sufficient visual evidence. This is common practice in Azerbaijan. The current government severe crackdown on media freedom and the impunity of those responsible for attacks on journalists and media workers is well documented. Independent journalists, human rights defenders, and others seeking to express their opinions, investigate issues of

---

57 'Concluding Observations, Azerbaijan', Human Rights Committee, 2009, para. 12, available at: www2.ohchr.org/english/bodies/hrc/hrcs96.htm; 'Azerbaijan 2012 Human Rights Report: Executive Summary', Country Reports on Human Rights Practices for 2012 United States Department of State, *Bureau of Democracy, Human Rights and Labor*, available at: http://photos.state.gov/libraries/azerbaijan/749085/hajiyevsx/hr_report2012.pdf; 'The honoring of obligations and commitments by Azerbaijan', Council of Europe Parliamentary Assembly, Resolution 1917 (2013), para. 12, available at: http://assembly.coe.int/ASP/Doc/XrefViewPDF.asp?FileID=19451&Language=EN.

58 Report of the Baku-based Public Association for Assistance to Free Economy, submitted for the review of Azerbaijan by the Committee of Economic, Social and Cultural Rights, April 2013.

59 M. Cooper, 'Azerbaijan: Index award-winning journalist Idrak Abbasov brutally beaten', 18 April 2012, available at: www.indexoncensorship.org/2012/04/azerbaijan-idrak-abbasov-beaten/.

---

public interest, or criticise government authorities have been attacked, harassed, threatened, and imprisoned.[60]

The UN Guiding Principles establish Azerbaijan's obligation to take appropriate steps to investigate, punish, and redress business-related human rights abuses. These include the harassment of journalists and other human rights defenders.[61] The sensitivity of the work of such a group makes it necessary to take additional measures to secure their protection and ensure access to effective remedy, which is rendered weak and ineffective in Azerbaijan. The need for better protection of human rights defenders working on corporate accountability has been increasingly recognised on the international agenda. In its report to the Human Rights Council in its 23rd session, the Working Group on business and human rights noted 'that conflicts between communities and businesses had led to the harassment and persecution of human rights defenders investigating, protesting, seeking accountability and access to remedies for victims of alleged abuses linked to business activities'[62] and recognised 'the important and legitimate role of civil society organizations, trade unions and human rights defenders in raising awareness of the human rights impacts and risks of business enterprises and activities'.[63]

Azerbaijan did not only fail to foster corporate cultures in which respect for human rights should be an integral part of doing business, including in state-owned companies where the government has the most direct impact in that regard. By failing to ensure effective protection of rights of individuals in business-related human rights abuses and provide access to effective remedy, Azerbaijan violates its own human rights obligations towards securing full enjoyment of human rights in its territory.

5. THE CORPORATE SOCIAL RESPONSIBILITY THAT FOREIGN OIL COMPANIES BEAR FOR SOCAR'S BUSINESS-RELATED HUMAN RIGHTS ABUSES IN AZERBAIJAN

In 2014, 25 oil contracts with 33 foreign companies from fifteen different countries, including Statoil, British Petroleum (BP) and Exxon, were contracted by the Azerbaijani government to produce crude oil in the country. BP extracts one

---

60 Among others, see 'Azerbaijan: Journalist Viciously Attacked by Police', Human Rights Watch, 19 April 2012, available at: www.hrw.org/news/2012/04/19/azerbaijan-journalist-viciously-attacked-police.

61 Paragraph 25 of the Guiding Principles.

62 'Report of the Working Group on the issue of human rights and transnational corporations and other business enterprises', Human Rights Council, UN Doc. A/HRC/23/32, 14 March 2013, para 6.

63 *Ibid.*, para. 49.

third of its total global liquids production (oil and gas) from Azerbaijan. Statoil, for which Azerbaijan is biggest overseas operation, is the second most significant western petroleum investor in Azerbaijan. Both companies are also known for their well-established internal policies on social corporate responsibility. The Norwegian government holds 67% of shares of Statoil and is a strong supporter of human rights standards in its foreign policies, including in the field of business and human rights. The influence that such oil companies operating in Azerbaijan potentially hold in promoting corporate social responsibility and challenging business-related human rights abuses by SOCAR, given their close business affiliations, in unquestionable.

Statoil's social corporate responsibility principles form an integral part of its operations both in Norway and abroad. It follows a strong commitment to contribute to the sustainable development in the countries where it works, with human rights being one of the key priorities. Statoil declares a proactive approach towards promoting human rights, good governance, and anticorruption in countries in which it does business.[64] Statoil's commitment to transparency and anticorruption, among others, is endorsed through the disclosure of all its revenues and payments in the countries in which it operates.

In Azerbaijan, where the probability that oil revenues are more likely to feed into more corruption than poverty alleviation or further social development is high, the disclosure of tax payments to its government is insufficient. A stronger stance and assuming greater responsibility concerning the fate of these resources and their impact is needed to make a serious commitment to effective social corporate responsibility principles and contribute towards the country's sustainable development. Here, the key solution for Statoil would be to integrate social corporate principles consistently within its business strategy in the countries where it operates. In that regard, respect for human rights and transparency should be an inherent part of Statoil's business strategy and properly established alongside its economic interests. This, however, requires a proactive aptitude from Statoil, one that is not currently evidenced from its activities in Azerbaijan, despite its proactive commitments to voluntary corporate responsibility mechanisms like the UN Global Compact.[65]

On the other hand, given Norway's strong human rights commitments globally, the fact that the Norwegian government owns 67% of Statoil shares brings with it additional obligations to promote human rights in countries where it operates.[66] If Statoil's proactive approach towards social corporate

---

[64] Statoil's policy and principles on social corporate responsibility.

[65] Statoil participates in the UN Global Compact platform since 2000, see 'Participants and Stakeholders', United Nations Global Compact, available at: www.unglobalcompact.org/participant/8782-Statoil.

[66] United Nations Convention against Corruption from 2000, entered into force in 2005. Norway is state party from 2006, available at: www.unodc.org/unodc/en/treaties/CAC/signatories.html.

responsibility principles is not properly integrated within its business strategy, it is the Norwegian state's role as owner to ensure effective protection and promotion of human rights where applicable. In this regard, good incentives may include clear routines to properly process shareholder information, and clearly defined responsibilities and legal consequences. As of this writing, the Azerbaijani policy of indifference does not square well with the UN Global Compact Principles, the UN Guiding Principles on business and human rights (which are strongly backed by the Norwegian government in the UN system), or with the principles on which the Norwegian society has been built. Moreover, Norway's proactive stance in acknowledging the role of human rights defenders in protecting and promoting human rights is remarkable.[67] The Norwegian government and Statoil should not remain indifferent to the abuses of journalists and other human rights defenders covering and reporting human rights abuses of SOCAR, when Statoil has committed to social corporate responsibility principles in Azerbaijan.

6.   CONCLUSION

The UN Guiding Principles recognise and are grounded in states' existing obligations to respect and protect human rights. The Principles further recognise the role of business enterprises perform in the society and are led by the need to comply with all existing laws and human rights standards. The case study of SOCAR demonstrates that the impact of state ownership of a company is largely dependent on the extent to which state commitments to human rights are genuine. Strong democratic countries with embedded human rights policies potentially bring additional incentive to state-owned enterprises to ensure a comprehensive human rights observance. Governments that encroach on the fundamental freedoms and human rights may discourage companies from upholding corporate social responsibility principles. This raises serious concerns as to what impact the UN Guiding Principles may have on state-owned enterprises in countries with poor human rights record where their implementation is often most needed.

When states fail to meet their duty to protect human rights, the responsibility of companies to respect human rights does not change; however, it can become all the more challenging, especially for state-owned companies to meet that responsibility in practice. The scale of these challenges depends largely on the extent to which the rule of law, including the enforcement of appropriate national legislation and access to effective remedy, is secured. The abusive property

---

[67]   Norway has been the initiator and active supporter of acknowledging the role of human rights, including the adoption of the UN Declaration Right and Responsibility of Individuals, Groups and Organs of Society to Promote and Protect Universally Recognized Human Rights and Fundamental Freedoms (also called UN Declaration on Human Rights Defenders), adopted by the UN Human Rights Council resolution, UN Doc. A/RES/53/144, 8 March 1999.

rights practices of state-owned SOCAR support the hypothesis that a company's corporate accountability record is strongly dependent on the government's human rights record. In SOCAR's case, clearly established corporate social commitments do little to help this. SOCAR's abusive practices and prevailing impunity surrounding property rights violations have continued given unequivocal violations of domestic laws securing property rights of individuals, lack of an independent judiciary and access to effective remedy, suppression of the freedom of the press, and absence of a strong participatory involvement of civil society. Moreover, the 'hands off' policy of the Azerbaijani government, which itself is complicit in gross property rights violations for the sake of further urbanisation, serves as a green light for SOCAR to retaliate against those who try to expose its abuses and leaves them without any effective remedy to seek justice.

In countries like Azerbaijan with unambiguous human rights violations and absence of any civic or political pluralism, foreign oil companies from well established democratic countries should make their business presence conditional to the fact that SOCAR would uphold basic domestic laws and UN Guiding Principles. By cooperating with SOCAR, such companies like Statoil or BP undermine not only their own corporate social commitments but also compromise their governments' efforts to promote respect for human rights in business in Azerbaijan.

CHAPTER 14

THE INVISIBLE MINORITY

Status of the 'Differently Able' People in the Export Industries in India

Rituparna MAJUMDAR

1. INTRODUCTION

The great author and activist Helen Adams Keller once said that 'science may have found a cure for most evils; but it has found no remedy for the worst of them all – the apathy of human beings'. While estimates vary, according to the United Nations, around one billion people live with disabilities globally – they are the world's largest minority. The World Health Organisation estimated more than six hundred million people across the globe live with disabilities of various types due to chronic diseases, injuries, violence, infectious diseases, malnutrition, and other causes related to poverty.[1] According to the Government of India's 2001 census record, India has more than 21 million disabled persons.

India has ratified the UN Convention on the Rights of Persons with Disabilities of 2007 which prohibits 'discrimination in workplace' and ensures 'reasonable accommodation'. Therefore, India has an obligation to work for the rights of persons with disabilities (PWDs). In spite of that they are subjected to multiple deprivations with limited access to basic services, including education, employment, rehabilitation facilities, etc. Widespread social stigma plays a major role in hindering their normal social and economic life. This is the reason often given by corporation managers for not hiring PWDs in the workforce in labour intensive industries, e.g. in garment companies. Empirical data indicate that only 0.5 per cent of people working in the public sector are disabled. The numbers of

---

[1] Gerard Quinn et al., *Human Rights and Disability* (United Nations, 2002), available at: www.nhri.net/pdf/disability.pdf.

those employed within the private sector also remains miniscule, and has only a recorded 0.3 per cent, while multinationals have 0.05 per cent.[2]

Yet, with the rise of globalisation, the influence of CSR is rapidly increasing in India. Among corporations, there is a general increase in awareness to include disabled people in their workforce, especially with the government's plea to implement the Persons with Disabilities (Equal Opportunities, Protection of Rights and Full Participation) Act of 1995.[3] Chapple and Moon highlight that social initiatives of businesses in India mostly consist of involvement in community development, education, health and disability.[4] Despite the introduction of a new labour code of conduct and request for social audits, international codes like Fair Labor Association, Fair Wear Foundation, OHSAS, Business Social Compliance Initiative, and the Social Accountability Standard (SA 8000) do not refer to disability rights as such, but often include clauses of 'discrimination' and 'harassment' that may apply to persons with disabilities.

Following from the above, this chapter addresses efforts made by the corporations to include PWDs. It uses data gathered from garment companies in India.

2. INDIAN EXPORT INDUSTRY AND CORPORATE SOCIAL RESPONSIBILITY

India's import and export policies for manufactured products have been considerably liberalised since 1991 which brought in rationalisation of export incentives and led to a major transformation of the trade policy for manufacturers in India, from a highly restrictive one to an almost free one.[5]

In table 14.1 below, India's exports by major regions/countries are depicted since sixties until 2011. The table projects Asia, European Union and United States of America as the main regions of export where almost 86 per cent of the market is catered to. From the table below, we also see that since the 1960s there has been perpetual slowdown in the export market in these countries, except the period of 2005–2006 when statistics changed and the major share of the exports was now being produced for Asian countries as against EU and USA.

---

[2]   'Promoting Inclusive Development through CSR: Equal Opportunities to People with disabilities', FICCI ADITYA BRILA Group, available at: www.ficci.com/events/21040/Add_docs/Concept-Note.pdf (accessed 24 November 2014).

[3]   The act provides for not less than 3 per cent reservation in employment for persons with disabilities, of which 1 per cent vacancies each are to be reserved for persons with blindness or low vision, hearing impairment and loco-motor disability or cerebral palsy in the posts identified for each disability – although not applicable for private organisations.

[4]   W. Chapple and J. Moon, 'CSR in Asia: a seven country study of CSR website reporting' (2005) 44(4) Business and Society 415–441.

[5]   S. Hashim, C.K.S. Rao et al., Indian Industrial Development and Globalisation (New Delhi: Academic Foundation, 2009).

Table 14.1. India's exports by major regions (in per cent)

Country/ Region	1960–61	1970–71	1980–81	1990–91	2000–01	2005–06	2010–11
EU	36.2	18.4	21.6	27.5	22.7	20.09	20.02
USA	16.0	13.5	11.1	14.7	20.9	5.75	10.2
Africa	6.3	8.4	5.2	2.1	3.2	6.75	6.5
Asia	6.9	10.8	13.4	13.4	14.3	50.42	56.2

Source: Economic Survey, 2012 (www.thehindubusinessline.com, accessed 28 May 2013).

With the unrestrictive trade, it brought in the multinational attention to corporate social responsibility in the form of adoption of code of conduct and implementing compliance standards for the welfare of the employees and employees alike. In recent years, increasing attention has been given to the concept of CSR which is a pragmatic response to consumer and civil society pressures. Now the government of India has also passed legislation for all companies (under the Companies Act 1956) for mandatory CSR engagement by spending 2–4 per cent of its total annual profit on community development and other CSR initiatives.

3. DISABILITY AND INTERNATIONAL HUMAN RIGHTS

Disability right under human rights is viewed as individuals with a wide range of abilities and each one of them willing and capable to utilise his/her potential and talents. Society, on the other hand, is seen as the real cause of the misery of people with disabilities since it continues to put up numerous barriers as expressed in education, employment, architecture, transport, health and dozens of other activities. Articles 6 and 7 of the ICESCR (International Covenant on Economic, Social and Cultural Rights) guarantee the right to work. In addition, these provisions need to be read in conjunction with the guarantee of non-discrimination in the enjoyment of rights contained in Article 2(2).

The issue of disability is not specifically mentioned under the scope of the two components of the International Bill of Human Rights, the International Covenant on Civil and Political Rights (ICCPR) and the International Covenant on Economic, Social, and Cultural Rights (ICESCR). Under the other hard law treaties by UN General Assembly (namely the International Convention on the Elimination of All Forms of Racial Discrimination (ICERD); the Convention on the Elimination of All Forms of Discrimination against Women (CEDAW); the Convention on the Rights of the Child (CRC); and the International Convention on the Protection of the Rights of All Migrant Employees and Members of their Families (ICPMW)) only the CRC contains a specific disability-related article;

it requires that states parties recognise the rights of children with disabilities to enjoy 'full and decent' lives and participate in their communities.[6]

India, being a federal polity, has a National Policy for PWDs which specifically addresses the need to apply the constitutional vision to persons with disabilities and some states of the country are in the process of putting together a policy on disability. In addition, there exist four disability specific legislations which apply throughout the country. The National Policy on disability was adopted in 2006 while the four pieces of legislation came into existence in the 1980s and 1990s. The Constitution of India which inter alia has incorporated a range of Fundamental Rights, apply to citizens with disabilities in equal measure (Articles 14, 16 and 43).[7] According to a World Bank Report 2007, the employment rate of disabled people has actually fallen from 42.7 per cent in 1991 to 37.6 per cent in 2002. As per the 2001 census, 34.5 per cent of persons with disabilities were working. Implementation of national legislation and policies have however been very poor, and not much progress have been made in particular relating to social obstacles preventing persons with disabilities, or specific groups of persons with disabilities (for example young persons with disabilities, women with disabilities or persons with intellectual/psycho-social disabilities), from enjoying the right to work on an equal basis with others. Table 14.2 below summarises the employment percentages of PWDs among all men and women, in urban and rural India. According to the 2000 National Sample Survey schedule, it shows that there are 63 per cent employed as against 1.5 per cent unemployed; however more men are employed (84 per cent) as against 40 per cent of women in employment. This does show the gender discrimination and further marginalisation of women under the marginalised disabled class. It is interesting to also see that rural India employs PWDs more (67 per cent) as against urban areas (50 per cent). But what really needs to be seen from the following table is that most of the 63 per cent of employed persons are self-employed (19 per cent) or engaged as casual labour in works other than public works (21 per cent).

---

6   M.A. Stein, 'Disability Human Rights' (2007) 95(1) *California Law Review* 75–121, available at: www.jstor.org/stable/20439088.

7   The comments have been compiled based on the information received from the O/o Chief Commissioner for Persons with Disabilities and the information available with the National Human Rights Commission of India.

Table 14.2. Distribution of the all-India working age population (15 to 64 years old) by usual activity status in 1999–2000

	All	Male	Female	Rural	Urban
Employed	62.5	83.9	40.4	67.0	50.4
Self-employed, as an own account work	18.5	30.0	6.6	19.8	15.2
Self-employed, as an employer	0.6	0.9	0.2	0.5	0.6
Self-employed, as helper	13.3	11.1	15.4	16.3	5.0
Regular wage/salaried employee	9.1	15.1	3.0	4.8	20.6
Casual labour in public works	0.1	0.2	0.1	0.1	0.1
Casual labour in other types of works	20.9	26.6	15.1	25.5	8.8
Unemployed	1.5	2.2	0.7	1.0	2.6
Not in labour force	36.0	13.9	58.9	31.9	47.0
Educational institutions	8.0	9.9	6.1	6.4	12.3
Domestic duties	17.1	0.3	34.5	13.7	26.2
Domestic duties and free collection of goods	7.5	0.1	15.2	8.7	4.4
Rentiers, pensioners, remittance recipients	0.6	0.7	0.4	0.4	1.0
Not able to work owing to disability	0.6	0.8	0.4	0.6	0.6
Beggars, prostitutes	0.1	0.1	0.1	0.1	0.1
Others	2.2	2.1	2.1	2.1	2.4

Source: S. Mitra and U. Sambamoorthi, 'Employment of Persons with Disabilities: Evidence from the National Sample Survey', *Economic and Political Weekly*, Vol. 41, No. 3, 21–27 Jan. 2006, pp. 199–203, calculations based on the NSS, schedule 10 of 55th round.

According to the employment projection given in the Eleventh Plan, in the chapter 'Employment Perspective and Labour Policy', 58 million job opportunities will be created in the Eleventh Plan period leading to a reduction in the unemployment rate to below 5 per cent. Over the longer period up to 2016–2017, spanning the Eleventh and Twelfth Plan periods, the additional employment opportunities created are estimated at 116 million. The unemployment rate at the end of the Twelfth Plan period is projected to fall to a little over 1 per cent. There is thus a wide gap between the employment rate of people with and without disabilities in the country.

With the review of literature, it was observed that studies pertaining to the status of persons with disabilities in export processing units are either few and far between or not easily accessible. Most of the studies highlight the disability among women employees in industries and state that disabled women and girls almost face a double dose of discrimination, shaped by the particular culture in which they live.[8] Habib's study also enunciates the feminist perspective to the issue of disabled employees.[9] It further adds that field studies and experiences signify that compared to disabled men, disabled women tend to suffer more from poverty and isolation. They receive less support from the family and the community and have more difficulty in obtaining services (mainstream services and rehabilitation). They are likely to be more economically dependent, mainly due to a high rate of illiteracy and limited vocational training, making them less attractive to employers; and to endure more physical, sexual and psychological violence and abuse. However these studies have not been seen in the perspective of the status of such employees in any of the export industries in India.

In one of the studies by Punnett, Robins et al.,[10] the prevalence of soft tissue disorders in the garment industry has been studied. It further studies the motor problems which result from work in the garment industry. Stitching tasks, especially the setting of linings into jackets, had a much higher prevalence of persistent pain than employees performing other tasks.

Majumder analyses the impact of women's waged employment on their health.[11] The analysis in the paper shows that the female employees employed in the garment industry of Bangladesh had to pay a high price in terms of ill-health to acquire a socio-economic status in the society with their waged employment. A large number of female employees suffered from various illnesses after starting work in the garment industry in spite of the fact that due to waged employment they could afford to buy better food and better accommodation, which have a positive impact on health. This is mainly due to overwork, uncongenial working conditions and above all because of wide-ranging labour law violations.

Mitra and Sambamoorthi report on the employment of persons with disabilities in India based on recent data from the National Sample Survey.[12] The study shows that the employment rate of persons with disabilities is relatively low compared to that of the all-India working age population, with great variations across gender, the urban/rural sectors and states. A multivariate analysis suggests that employment among persons with disabilities is influenced more by individual and household characteristics than human capital.

---

[8] C. Brisson, A. Vinet et al., 'Effect of duration of employment in piecework on severe disability among female garment workers' (1989) 15(5) *Scandinavian Journal of Work, Environment & Health* 329–334. C. Brisson, A. Vinet et al., 'Disability among female garment workers: A comparison with a national sample' (1989) 15(5) *Scandinavian Journal of Work, Environment & Health* 323–328. L. Hershey, 'Disabled Women Organize Worldwide' (2003) 33(1/2) *Off Our Backs* 16–18.

[9] L.A. Habib, '"Women and Disability Don't Mix!": Double Discrimination and Disabled Women's Rights' (1995) 3(2) *Gender and Development* 49–53.

[10] L. Punnett, J. Robins et al., 'Soft tissue disorders in the upper limbs of female garment workers' (1985) 11(6) *Scandinavian Journal of Work, Environment & Health* 417–425.

[11] P. Paul-Majumder, 'Health Impact of Women's Wage Employment: A Case Study of the Garment Industry of Bangladesh' (1996) 24(1/2) *The Bangladesh Development Studies* 59–102.

[12] S. Mitra and U. Sambamoorthi, 'Employment of Persons with Disabilities: Evidence from the National Sample Survey' (2006) 41(3) *Economic and Political Weekly* 199–203.

Stein on the other hand emphasised the disability human rights approach, developing a 'disability human rights paradigm' that combines components of the social model of disability, the human right to development, and philosopher Martha Nussbaum's version of the 'capabilities approach', but filtering these frameworks through a disability rights perspective to preserve that which provides for individual flourishing and modify that which does not. The article further argues that disability-based human rights necessarily invoke both civil and political ('first-generation') rights, as well as economic, social, and cultural ('second-generation') rights to a greater degree than previous human rights paradigms. The article highlights that each of the seven core United Nations treaties theoretically applies to disabled persons in varying degrees, but that they are rarely applied in practice.[13] Compounding this problem, General Assembly soft laws explicitly referencing disability are legally unenforceable.

In an interesting approach to social disability studies like that of Mog and Swarr[14] explore the intersections between transgender and disability studies. Their study puts tremendous attention on the similarities between those who are considered 'queer' as well as 'disabled' and claims that other movements for social change will help facilitate deeper analyses of the workings of oppression as well as means for achieving socio-political change.

4.   METHODOLOGY

It was thus felt imperative to conduct such a study to see the prevalence of PWDs in the export industries in India and what changes have been made in the companies with the introduction of CSR initiatives and human rights approach. The present study was conducted in the National Capital Region (NCR) which consists of three primary cities, namely Gurgaon, Noida and Delhi. The three cities combined form a major industrial hub in northern India. In order to understand the status of the persons with disabilities in export industries in India, a sample of 75 export companies were randomly selected. These companies mainly manufacture garment products and accessories, leather goods, shoes, automobiles and parts and electronic goods.

To understand the existing recruitment policies and level of inclusion of persons with disability, the respective company owners, human resource managers and compliance staffs were interviewed. The recruitment policies and company standing orders were also looked at. The kind of disability included in the study has been of two kinds of physical disability (like motoric problems, physical impairment) and social disability (like transgender and eunuch).

---

[13]   M.A. Stein, 'Disability Human Rights' (2007) 95(1) *California Law Review* 75–121.
[14]   A. Mog and L.A. Swarr, 'Threads of Commonality in Transgender and Disability Studies' (2008) 28(4) *Disability Studies Quarterly*.

From the literature reviewed and gaps assessed, the following research questions were developed:

(a) Does the company contain a clause on PWD and its inclusion in its recruitment policies and procedures?
(b) What impact has CSR made in the inclusive growth of PWD into the work culture of the companies?
(c) Is the company self-motivated to encourage persons with disability to be included in the employment?
(d) What are the policies governing employees who are rendered disabled during their tenure in the employment?
(e) What welfare mechanisms are available in the company for the person with disabilities?

Keeping in mind the above questions, the objectives of the present study was designed based on exploratory research methodology. The aim of the study was:

(a) To understand the existing recruitment policies with regard to people with disabilities in export trading industries;
(b) To study the reach of these policies and to analyse their impact with respect to the needs of persons with disabilities.

In order to conduct statistical analysis, the data were categorised and coded in accordance with the objective of the study and presented in the form of tables and diagrams. The major findings which were observed during the study are listed below.

5. MAIN FINDINGS

The findings highlight the status of PWDs in policy inclusion of recruitment and termination; the status of employment in the industry and the prevalence of PWDs in the export industries. This section is divided primarily into two categories delineating the profile of the respondents and then the main findings.

6. PROFILE OF THE RESPONDENTS

In the following table 14.3, we see the types of export factories which have been randomly selected for the purpose of the research study. Of the total, 55 companies produced garments and accessories, seven companies produced leather items, two produced shoes, three were automobile companies and eight were electronic companies.

Table 14.3. Types of export factories selected

Types of export factory	Frequency	Per cent
Garments and accessories	55	73.3
Leather goods	7	9.3
Shoes	2	2.6
Automobile	3	4.0
Electronic goods	8	10.6
Total	75	100

7. RECRUITMENT POLICIES OF COMPANIES

In today's rapidly changing business environment, a well-defined recruitment policy is necessary for organisations to respond to its human resource requirements in time. Therefore, it is important to have a clear and concise recruitment policy in place which should be non-discriminatory and encourage people from all sections irrespective of their caste, religion, gender, race or any disability. Most of the respondents stated that since it is not mandatory for them to incorporate PWD workforce, it is not imperative for them to include employees in the general workforce. Thus, 97 per cent of the companies have a recruitment policy which states that 'no discrimination would be practiced at the time of recruitment' followed by the procedures of recruitment. Although the policies reviewed during the course of the study observed that none of them specifically mentions PWD inclusion or disability as one of the elements for non-discrimination during recruitment.

Table 14.4. Recruitment policies concerning PWDs in companies

Do you have recruitment policies concerning PWDs in your company?	Frequency	Per cent
Yes, we follow non-discriminatory approach to recruitment	73	97.3
No	2	2.6
Total	75	100

8. STATUS OF EMPLOYMENT OF PWD EMPLOYEES

During the interviews, the status or prevalence of the persons with disabilities existing in the industry was observed. Of the total respondents, there were only five such employees who were either physically challenged or challenged via society to work (like the transgender). From the field assessment, it was observed that one company employed one visually impaired woman in production work, and a person with hand motor problem in their production process, and another company employed three transgender persons in their manufacturing site. It was further observed that the first two employees were working in the garment sector while the transgender workers were working in a shoe company.

Table 14.5. Prevalence of PWD employees in companies

How many PWD employees do you have in your factory?	Frequency	Per cent
Less than 3	2	2.6
Between 3–5	3	4.0
Above 5	Nil	Nil
None	70	93.3
Total	75	100

9. ACCESSIBILITY TO WORK

Making the workplace accessible is an important criterion for the smooth functioning of human resource in a company. The respondents were asked if they provide financial support to disabled people like transportation facilities, or access to the company premises via ramps. Only some companies (13 per cent) provide transportation facility for their workers and employees. Only 3 per cent of the companies provide ramp friendly buildings; however no other extra provisions are meant to be provided for PWD employees.

Table 14.6. Provisions for accessing work

What are the provisions provided to PWDs at work?	Frequency	Per cent
Transportation	10	13.3
Ramp friendly building	2	2.6
No special provisions	63	84
Total	75	100

10. TERMINATION OF PWD EMPLOYEES

Termination of an employee is usually involuntary when they are asked to leave a job for various reasons, for example downsizing of the company, bad employee behaviour, unsatisfactory performance and so on. Thus, table 14.7 studies the termination clauses (whether in writing or in practice) which exist in these industries for the PWD employees. Although it was observed that there is no written evidence, discrimination does take place in practice. Thus we see that there were various termination clauses as against recruitment practices (as seen in table 14.4) for PWDs in the companies. Where 71 per cent of the respondents stated that no disabilities have ever occurred to employees during any employee's tenure in their company, 21 per cent stated that they would shift their employees if they are rendered disabled owing to company work on the premises; 7 per cent stated that they would provide medical help as per the insurance eligibility of the worker and would terminate, if need be, since they would be rendered less productive or unproductive. Only 1 per cent of the respondents stated that they would just terminate the employees if they were found to be disabled during work.

Table 14.7. Termination clause for PWDs

What kind of termination clause exists in your company for PWDs?	Frequency	Per cent
Terminate employees if disabled during work	1	1.3
Provide medical care and terminate if employee not fit for work	5	6.6
Shift employee to suitable job profile	16	21.3
No disabilities during work were registered	53	70.6
Total	75	100

11. IMPACT OF CORPORATE SOCIAL RESPONSIBILITY AND LABOUR RIGHTS

In the table below, we study the impact of CSR on the company's attitude towards the mainstreaming of PWDs in their workforce. The majority of respondents (53 per cent) stated that they never thought of incorporating PWD policies in the light of multiple labour standards or voluntary code of conduct which they have to endorse owing to export business, while 37 per cent said that CSR ideals had no impact on their understanding of disability rights; they rather concentrate on other areas of labour welfare and rights like providing them with social security benefits, freedom of association and better working conditions. Whereas 3 per cent stated that CSR approach partially enhanced their understanding but issues relating to PWDs are never discussed in any forum or conference, 7 per cent stated that they have incorporated the PWDs not only in their policies but also their workforce.

Table 14.8. Impact of CSR in changing employer attitude towards PWDs

Did CSR change your perspective towards PWDs	Frequency	Per cent
No, it didn't	28	37.3
Yes it did	5	6.6
Partially	2	2.6
We never thought about it before	40	53.3
Total	75	100

12. TRAINING AND DEVELOPMENT

Training programmes are directed toward maintaining and improving current job performance, while development programmes seek to develop competencies for future roles.[15] The company respondents were asked if they are provided any training and development specific to their work profile, to which 97 per cent respondents stated that no such training is provided while 1.3 per cent provide training only during the induction.

Table 14.9. Training and development imparted

Do you provide training and development (related to work) for the PWD employees?	Frequency	Per cent
Yes	1	1.3
No	73	97.3
Induction training provided only	1	1.3
Total	75	100

13. HEALTH AND SAFETY

The health and safety training of the employees in a company, especially in the export processing zones, is an important aspect in maintaining the compliance

---

[15]   S.K. Bhatia, *Training and Development: Concepts and Practices* (New Delhi: Elegant Printers, 2009).

status of most factories. With the introduction of ISO and OHSAS standards, the application of occupational safety and health (OSH) is even more imperative these days. The international media too has become very sensitive to the issues concerning OSH owing to such bad examples from Bangladesh or China.

The risk assessment should also consider the essential elements of the job; the length of time and frequency of any hazardous situations; and any reasonable adjustments that can be made to reduce the hazard. So the respondents were asked if they take PWD employees into account in such risk assessment and train them for fire safety and evacuation and first aid, to which 1 per cent of the companies responded that they have trained their PWD employees on OSH issues and 45 per cent stated that they shall do so when they have PWD employees in their company, while 55 per cent stated that they do not have any specific training modules for the PWD employees.

Table 14.10. Health and safety training imparted to PWDs

Do you provide training and development (related to OSH) for the PWD employees?	Frequency	Per cent
Yes	1	1.3
No	41	54.6
We will, when we have PWD employees	34	45.3
Total	75	100

In the following section, five case stories have been included of PWD employees working in the export processing zones and factories of companies which have employed or not employed PWDs in their workforce.

14. CASE STUDIES

14.1. WORKER A, FEMALE, AGE 30 YEARS: CHECKING DEPARTMENT, GARMENT MANUFACTURING UNIT

Worker A is originally from Gorakhpur, Uttar Pradesh in north India. Her life started with being a visually challenged girl which happened as a result of negligence on her parents' part at the time of her birth; since then she has gone from partial blindness to being fully blind. Due to a poor family background and the impairment, her parents could not send her to a special or regular school. However, it was her uncle (mother's brother) who brought her to the city at the age of 15 years and enrolled her in vocational training courses. Gradually she learnt the art of embroidery; however she could not do much with the skill since she did not have buying capacity and needed monetary support for survival. One of her acquaintances was at that time working with a garment factory in Delhi and she mentioned to her a vacancy in the checking department. There was an initial hesitation from her side and the side of the garment factory's owner; however they hired her due to her capacity to learn things fast and their inclination to incorporate people with disabilities in the factory. Thus her life started in this company and she has been working with the same for the past seven years now. She believes that the management is neither extra cautious nor absolutely negligent about her; rather they treat her like any other worker. She also believes that working in an environment like this makes the other workers sensitive to the needs of people like her who are physically challenged but not capacity challenged.

14.2. WORKER B, TRANSSEXUAL, AGE 32 YEARS: MACHINING DEPARTMENT, SHOE MANUFACTURING UNIT

Worker B, along with two more such employees (transgender), has been associated with the company for the past four years. They work in the machining section in a shoe manufacturing unit in Noida, Uttar Pradesh. The worker is from Delhi and the parents live in an urban slum in Mangolpuri. The worker has two other siblings who work as clerks in private organisations. The worker realised that he is 'different' during his early teens and was obviously the butt of all jokes in the area he lived and the bullies included his siblings. However, due to the support of his parents, he managed to get employed in this company. Before that he was associated with another company but due to high incidences of bullying, he left the company in the first six months. According to him, this company though does not have any such practices since there are two more employees like him employed in the same department who are his friends and confidantes and, secondly, the company culture has started accepting them as 'normal' and have, apart from some friendly banter, never really commented on their gender expression. The worker is one of the good employees and has been once rated as the 'employee of the month'.

14.3. COMPANY OWNER A, MALE, AGE 55 YEARS, OWNS GARMENT MANUFACTURING COMPANY IN DELHI

The factory owner has been associated with the garment manufacturing business for the past 20 years, his father having introduced him to the business and legacy. The company has around 450 employees in its unit and processes like cutting, stitching, printing, finishing and packing are conducted inside the premises. He has two employees in his factory who are physically impaired, one visually challenged and the other has motor problems in one hand. The visually impaired girl has been working in the checking department and the other male worker has been working in the printing section. He believes that the idea of incorporating PWD employees was neither intentional nor a gesture to show off the humanitarian side of the company which according to him is 'a facade under the corporate social responsibility gamut'. He further believes that, CSR or no CSR, if someone wants to be ethical, humanitarian and fair in their business, they will irrespective of what the international labour standards and local legislations tell them to. He states that:

> There are number of ways to dupe the government and legislation thinking that we live in a highly corrupt nation, but I want to have a good tension free sleep during night. Our company does engage in overtime work and we do pay single overtime but it's something I alone cannot change. The buyers and suppliers working with us too have to equally share the cost involved in labour welfare and following of national regulations.

He added that it is no different to employ PWDs in the regular workforce than employing other employees. He rather believes that they are prone to be more productive since their other senses are so sharp and owing to their disabilities they need to prove a point to society to excel in their respective assignments. Saying which, he said that in spite of the company encouraging PWD employees in the workforce, not many applications are received at the time of recruitment.

14.4. COMPANY OWNER B, MALE, AGE 40 YEARS, HEADS AUTOMOBILE COMPANY IN GURGAON

Company owner B is the Managing Director of Production and has been associated with the company for the past ten years. The company does not have any specific policy on PWD and believes that the kinds of work processes which are engaged in the industry are highly skilled and can be undertaken only by a physically and mentally fit person. He further added that owing to the rigorous working hours and demands of the work, they deliberately recruit fewer women in the production work; however they have female employees in the human resources and business development departments. He added that:

> Although it may seem discriminatory from outside to not recruit PWDs or women employees but the demand of the industry is such that no such initiatives (CSR) can bring in the change. It's all about production in the end of the day.

The company owner also added that he personally believes in the mainstreaming of PWDs but it has to be specific to industries which demand fewer skills and less rigorous work. He argued that in spite of sounding prejudiced the fact that they have certain disabilities and that it renders them less productive as against other employees cannot be ignored.

The owner was further asked about the company termination policy, as in what happens when a worker is injured and thus disabled in the process of working in the company. On this, he shared a case where one such incident happened many years ago and the worker lost one of his hands during his work in the manufacturing processes. He was thus provided the best medical treatment by the company and his family compensated handsomely; however they could not retrieve his work profile back. Giving him another suitable job would mean his salary and status going down, which was not acceptable to either the company or the worker. He therefore added that even if the company incorporates all humanitarian ideals into its CSR process it cannot practice or preach it owing to the hard targets associated with the industry.

14.5. COMPANY OWNER B, FEMALE, AGE 73 YEARS, HEADS GARMENT MANUFACTURING UNIT IN NOIDA

The company owner in this case was female, which is rarely seen in the industry. However, this lady started the business as a small merchandising firm in the 1970s and from then she took over the business of her late husband's legacy and grew it further. It is a 300 worker factory which exports to major international buyers and follows the international labour standards like that of Social Accountability International (SA8000), BSCI (Business Social Compliance Initiative) and Fair Wear Foundation (the Netherlands). They do not have any policy nor do they have any PWD workers in their factory but they still believe that if there is such a case during recruitment, they would not discriminate on the basis of his/her physical impairment. She also believes that disability is all in mind; she further added:

> Lot of people may think that I am disabled owing to my old age and inability to move and match up step as fast as other youngsters in the business do, however that doesn't deter me to do what I want. That doesn't stop me from thinking about the welfare of my employees and my company. I have well trusted employees who are associated with my company for more than 15 years, had it not been for the love, care and good working conditions why would they stay? Therefore, if you have the will, you have the way!

This company has been experiencing worker dissatisfaction for the last two years owing to lower yearly increases in wages due to which many employees have left the company in the past one year (around 40 employees). On this issue, the owner did not share much except that the company is facing a financial crunch due to the bad economy in the west as a result of which the industry is becoming hugely competitive and incompliant with worker expectations. She concluded by saying:

> Not much we can do if the buyers do not contribute in the process of worker development.

15. DISCUSSION

While the Indian constitution prohibits discrimination, it does not prohibit discrimination on the grounds of disability per se. The fundamental right to life enshrined in the Indian Constitution provides the guarantee of life with liberty and dignity to all persons resident in India. The right of persons with disabilities to respect, dignity and freedom is part of this generic right to life. The recognition of disability as part of a larger terrain of human diversity is something that has not yet entered official discourse on disability rights. However, with the introduction of various legislation and welfare schemes with special measures for PWDs, it demonstrates commitment to strengthen non-discrimination based on someone's physical and social disability through affirmative action.

Policies are the window to establishing set procedures and guidelines and delineating the ethos of a company's functioning. In this chapter we have seen that 97 per cent of the companies have a recruitment policy which states that 'no discrimination would be practiced at the time of recruitment' followed by the procedures of recruitment. Although the policies reviewed during the course of the study observed that none of them specifically mentions PWD inclusion or disability as one of the elements of non-discrimination during recruitment. The reason provided by the majority is that it is not mandatory for them to incorporate PWDs into their workforce.

To understand the prevalence of persons with disabilities in the industry, we observed only five such employees out of the total sample size. The reason for the non-inclusion of PWDs is also that no adequate accessibility to work is provided; for example, only some companies (13 per cent) provide transportation facilities for their workers and employees. Only 3 per cent of the companies provide a ramp friendly building and no other extra provisions are meant to be provided for PWD employees. Only 3 per cent of the companies have training modules related to work for PWDs and only 1 per cent provide OSH training to PWDs in their company, which is in spite of recruiting them in their workforce. And most of the respondents (45 per cent) stated that they will develop training modules for PWDs only once they start incorporating them, otherwise there is no need. It is interesting to see however that 21 per cent of the companies shift their employees to a suitable job profile when the employee is found to be disabled during work. And 7 per cent of the companies, if it is found that an employee has been rendered disabled during his/her employed years, then the employee would be provided medical benefits and would be terminated since he/she would not be capable of working henceforth. These responses primarily came from automobile companies which are mainly strenuous and need physical fitness for employees to work.

With the legitimacy now being given to CSR, it is becoming the new cornerstone for companies to showcase their contribution to society. So when asked what impact CSR ideals have had on the company's policies in creating and re-inventing principles on PWD, only 7 per cent of the companies emphasised that they would do something particular for PWDs. The contribution towards PWDs would range from community work to health camps or donations made to special educational institutions; however they would not be specific to mainstreaming to the system of employment. Further to that the case stories depicted that CSR implementation has to be inclusive and every stakeholder, including companies, employees, the government, and brands which are sourcing from India, has to participate to incorporate the principles in the company ideology.

16. RECOMMENDATIONS

A company's ability to deliver a quality product while being fair to its employees and the environment is now an essential part of being a viable entity. Based on the findings, more robust methods are required to have a more positive impact on the industry:

– There has to be a clear commitment to policy development and its implementation especially from the top management.
– Mainstreaming and inclusive employment should be the mantra of functioning of all companies. Only then can a real change be brought in with regard to including PWDs into regular employment. Because disabled persons do not have to restrict themselves to doing traditional vocational work like basket making or cot making, they are meant for and can participate in the normal workforce if provided with the right amount of support and openness from the companies employing them.
– It is also important to make reasonable adjustments at work which would make accessibility easy and PWD-friendly, like making ramps, providing training and development on OSH and so on.
– Incorporating PWDs into the workforce should be encouraged and treated as a good practice.
– Buyers sourcing through Indian companies should also incorporate clauses relating to PWDs in their company code of conduct.
– The occupational health and safety standards should be maintained and audited keeping persons with disability in mind. In addition, clear and definite mechanisms should be delineated in company codes for recruitment,

termination or leaving work which should emphasise non-discrimination and encourage inclusivity.

As Scott Hamilton (Olympic Gold Medallist) once said, the only disability in life is a bad attitude. Therefore most disability is created by societal standards. To respect human rights and uphold the principles of corporate social responsibility, we must integrate the ethos of inclusion of persons with disability in our occupations and relationships and make a social model which is truly egalitarian.